INVESTMENT BANKING

Investment Banking: Institutions, Politics, and Law

ALAN D. MORRISON AND WILLIAM J. WILHELM, JR.

OXFORD
UNIVERSITY PRESS

OXFORD

UNIVERSITY PRESS

Great Clarendon Street, Oxford ox2 6DP

Oxford University Press is a department of the University of Oxford.
It furthers the University's objective of excellence in research, scholarship,
and education by publishing worldwide in

Oxford New York

Auckland Cape Town Dar es Salaam Hong Kong Karachi
Kuala Lumpur Madrid Melbourne Mexico City Nairobi
New Delhi Shanghai Taipei Toronto

With offices in

Argentina Austria Brazil Chile Czech Republic France Greece
Guatemala Hungary Italy Japan Poland Portugal Singapore
South Korea Switzerland Thailand Turkey Ukraine Vietnam

Oxford is a registered trade mark of Oxford University Press
in the UK and in certain other countries

Published in the United States
by Oxford University Press Inc., New York

British Library Cataloguing in Publication Data

Data available

Library of Congress Cataloging in Publication Data

Data available

Typeset by SPI Publisher Services, Pondicherry, India
Printed in Great Britain
on acid-free paper by
Ashford Colour Press Ltd, Gosport, Hampshire

ISBN 978–0–19–929657–6 (Hbk.)
978–0–19–954418–9 (Pbk.)

1 3 5 7 9 10 8 6 4 2

Contents

Prologue		vii
List of Figures		xi
List of Tables		xiii

1. Introduction   1

     Market trends   7
     Industry structure   15
     Investment bank activities   21
     The growing dichotomy between specialists and
        generalists   30
     Conclusion   35

2. Institutional Theory   37

     Property rights, institutions, and the state   38
     Non-state institutions   45
     State decision-making, the law, and extra-legal
        contracting   59
     Conclusion   62

3. An Institutional Theory of Investment Banking   65

     Information, innovation, and property rights   67
     Information marketplaces and investment banking   71
     Internal organization   88
     Industrial organization   92
     Conclusion   95

4. Investment Banking Origins   97

     Information exchange   98
     Institutions and the law   101
     Mercantile networks   107
     Early capital markets   117
     Conclusion   120

5. The Rise of the Investment Bank   121

     Merchant banking   123

The legal and political environment   126
The evolution of investment banking   136
Conclusion   153

6.   Investment Banking in the Age of Laissez-Faire   155

Legal and political environment   156
Technological advances   157
The Civil War and retail investment banking   160
Investment bankers after 1873   162
Investment banking after 1873   170
Conclusion   184

7.   Leviathan and the Investment Banks   187

Changes to the legal and political environment   188
Legislation, regulation, and investment banking   196
Industry evolution   215
United States versus Morgan Stanley   220
Conclusion   223

8.   The Modern Industrial Revolution   225

Early computer advances   227
Early changes to market structure   231
Real-time computation   238
The revolution in financial economics   242
New human capital businesses   249
Conclusion   263

9.   Inside the Investment Bank   265

Investment bank partnerships   267
The joint-stock investment bank   280
Conclusion   291

10. What Next?   293

Large, complex banking organizations   294
Trading off reputation and financial capital   301
Small, focused investment banks   304
Conclusion   315

Bibliography   317

Index   339

Prologue

The Securities Act [of 1933] will be fully justified if it drives the government into the investment banking business. (William O. Douglas)[1]

Justice Harold R. Medina stated in 1954 that 'it would be difficult to exaggerate the importance of investment banking to the national economy.'[2] This remark remains true today. Investment banks lie at the heart of the capital allocation process in both America and England, and they are of increasing importance elsewhere. Their actions are sometimes controversial, and their business activities have attracted press and government scrutiny for over a century.

Although it sometimes seems that everyone has an opinion on the investment banking industry, we lack a coherent theory to explain its existence. A voluminous historical literature examines the history of investment banks, both individually and in the aggregate, a legal literature analyzes the rules under which shares are issued and traded, and a financial and economic literature describes the incentives facing investment bankers and their clients, and uses this to explain the mechanisms that they use when trading. But there is very little to explain precisely what it is that investment bankers add to economic life. This is the goal that we have set ourselves in this book.

It is not enough to answer this question in purely financial terms. Much economic power is exercised through investment banks, and to a varying extent, politicians have assumed that some of this power has been devolved to the banks. The quotation at the top of this page is an excellent illustration of this point. William Douglas was a graduate of Columbia Law School, worked briefly as a newly minted attorney for the Cravath firm, the dominant member of the Wall Street bar, and was for six years a professor at the Yale Law School. He rose to fame during the New Deal, and later would be the longest-serving Supreme Court Justice ever. His comment reflected a widely held contemporary

---

[1] In correspondence to Felix Frankfurter on February 19, 1934, quoted in Skeel (2001: 123).

[2] Medina ([1954] 1975: 15): see chapter seven for the context in which this remark was made.

opinion that Wall Street banks were over-powerful, and that they should be 'superseded' in their security market dealings by a system that allowed for more rational governmental allocation of resources. One of the defining features of the New Deal was an increased level of financial market regulation.

As we shall see in the course of the book, New Deal controls over financial markets started to erode almost as soon as they were introduced. The final stage in this erosion was the 1999 repeal of the Glass–Steagall Banking Act. At the end of the twentieth century, investment banks collectively had attained a level of power, visibility, and freedom of action which was in many respects comparable with that enjoyed by JP Morgan & Co. at the beginning of the century. But like Morgan, investment banks were soon the target of a regulatory and political backlash of the type witnessed repeatedly throughout the industry's history. Once again, investment bankers were accused of exercising excessive power in an irresponsible fashion. The consequence was further regulatory intervention in the industry.

We cannot understand investment banks without understanding what brought Douglas and people like him to their point of view. For this, we need a deep understanding of the institutional environment within which investment banks work, and we need to understand precisely what it is about their activities that attracts the attention of politicians. The activities of legislators, and the actions taken in response by the investment bankers, have shaped the contours of today's investment banking industry, and thus have affected the development of Anglo-American capitalism.

We address these issues by developing an economic rationale for investment bankers, and attempting to situate it in a broader social and legal context. We hope that this 'institutional' perspective on investment banking sheds some light on the evolution of the modern investment bank, and helps to explain the legal and political aspects of investment banking. But it comes at a price: although we are not lawyers or historians, writing this book has forced us to confront legal and historical questions. We are not attempting to create fresh scholarship in either field; we hope instead to use the legal and historical literatures to shed some light upon the operation of a central economic institution.

We are grateful to the many people who helped us while we were writing this book. We received excellent support from our research assistants, Thomas Knull, Qiao Ma, Mary Weisskopf and David Wilhelm. Special thanks are due to Brendan Abrams for doggedly tracking down a good deal of the historical data, as well as for compiling bank capitalization data. Paul Bennett, Steve Wheeler and the staff at NYSE archives were extremely helpful with the compilation of twentieth century investment bank partnership data, and we are also happy to acknowledge assistance with data from Sang Lee of Aite Research and Marc Greene of Greenwich Associates, the staff at the Mudd Library, Princeton University, for providing access to the Harold R. Medina Papers, and the Securities Industry Association.

For informative and instructive conversations about the practice of investment banking we are particularly grateful to Don Chew, Peter Engel, Jim Harris, Shaw Joseph, Mike Millette, Bill Schnoor and Vic Simone. Ed Perkins and Alexander Ljungqvist were particularly helpful in checking academic facts. Our early thoughts regarding partnerships were shaped in conversations with Bruno Biais, Zhaohui Chen, Steven Tadelis, Bharat Anand, Oren Sussman and Colin Mayer; David Smith made some very helpful comments upon early drafts of the historical material in the book.

Finally, our families suffered almost as much as we did while we worked on this book, and we are deeply appreciative of the sacrifices that they made. We hope that they think it was worth it.

Alan D. Morrison and William J. Wilhelm, Jr
Oxford and Charlottesville, 2006

List of Figures

1.1 US and global securities market activity (billions of US dollars, CPI-adjusted: 1983 dollars) 2

1.2 Equity market capitalization as a percentage of GDP for major industrialized countries 2

1.3 New York Stock Exchange average daily trading volume, 1960–2004 (millions of shares) 8

1.4 The US investment banking industry, 1955–2000 13

1.5 Investment bank employees and capitalization, 1979–2000 (top five banks by capitalization) 14

1.6 Income producer revenue and compensation (ten largest banks by capitalization) 14

1.7 Equity underwriting fees as a percentage of gross proceeds 24

1.8 Debt underwriting fees as a percentage of gross proceeds 25

1.9 Morgan Stanley daily 99 percent per one-day trading VaR 27

1.10 Investment bank revenues (percent of total revenue, ten largest banks) 31

3.1 The investment bank's information marketplace 72

3.2 Relative importance of tacit and technical skill for investment bank activities 89

5.1 Foreign trade using Bills of Exchange 125

5.2 US net capital inflows, 1790–1900 144

8.1 Advances in processing power, 1950–2001 227

8.2 Holdings of outstanding US equities, 1945–2000 232

8.3 Merrill Lynch revenue sources, 1961–70 233

8.4 Cost of computing, 1950–2001 239

8.5 Underwritten debt and equity (common and preferred) as a percentage of GNP 250

8.6 Public and private securities issuance, 1935–63 253

10.1 Origins and precursors of leading investment banks 297

List of Tables

1.1 Global derivatives market   10
1.2 Markets for derivative financial instruments: notional principal amounts outstanding, 1986–96 (billions of US dollars)   11
1.3 Notional principal value of outstanding interest rate and currency swaps of the members of the International Swaps and Derivatives Association, 1987–June 1996 (billions of US dollars)   12
1.4 Underwritten common stock (thousands of US dollars) US transactions   17
1.5 Mergers and acquisitions (thousands of US dollars) US transactions announced during year   18
1.6 Morgan Stanley business lines   32
1.7 Percentage of net revenue by functional area for Lazard Freres and Morgan Stanley   33
4.1 Ratio of stock turnover to nominal capital, 1704–55 (currency amounts in sterling)   119
5.1 Capitalization and partnership size for leading investment houses, 1815–18   143
5.2 Capitalization and partnership size for leading investment houses, 1850–5   153
6.1 Dollar increase in stocks and bonds issued by US Railroads, 1875–95   176
6.2 Consolidations per year in the US manufacturing sector   183
7.1 Corporate issues, by class of security, 1919–29 (millions)   218
8.1 Client underwriting relationships in the 1950s and 1960s   256
9.1 Average partner tenure in 17 prominent investment banks   282
10.1 Sources of net revenue for Goldman Sachs. Levels of net revenue (millions of US dollars) and percentages of the total are reported for major business lines for the three years prior to the IPO, and the year ending November 30, 2007   302

1

Introduction

Securities markets are an increasingly important source of investment funds in the developed world. Corporations and entrepreneurs use the securities markets to raise capital by selling voting rights over their actions, and also future revenue streams resulting from these actions. Their counterparties are widely dispersed investors ranging from individual (retail) investors to large collective investment vehicles such as pension funds, insurance companies, and mutual funds. While this type of finance has always been important, capital market activity exploded worldwide during the last quarter of the twentieth century. Figure 1.1 illustrates trends for both securities issuance and mergers and acquisitions activity. The dollar value of securities offerings, both in the United States and worldwide, rose sharply beginning in the early 1980s. Mergers and acquisition activity is highly cyclical but the US merger wave during the 1980s was exceptionally strong by historical standards and it in turn was dwarfed by the merger wave of the late 1990s.

Broadly speaking, two types of securities are issued in public securities markets. *Debt* securities promise a fixed schedule of payments, but their holders receive voting rights only in the event that the payment schedule is violated. The holders of *equity* securities receive voting rights, but are entitled only to whatever income remains after debt obligations have been met. These rights can be sold easily in securities markets. As a result, corporations that rely upon security markets for their finance do not in general form close relationships with their investors. Arm's-length financing such as that raised in public equity markets has long been an important source of funding in the United States, the United Kingdom, and Japan, but it is significantly less important in other major economies like France and Germany. Nevertheless, the latter are increasingly shifting toward public market finance. Figure 1.2 illustrates the recent experience of these countries by reporting their equity market capitalization as a percentage of GDP

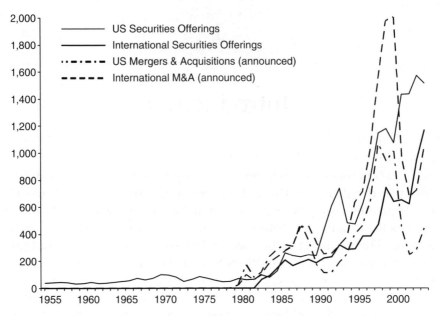

Figure 1.1. *US and global securities market activity (billions of US dollars, CPI-adjusted: 1983 dollars)*

Sources: Securities Industry Association (SIA), Securities Industry Factbook.

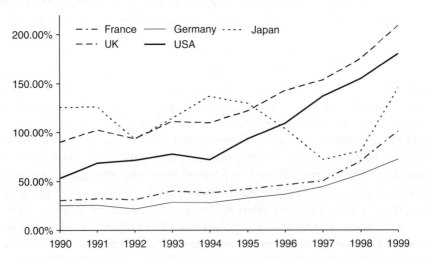

Figure 1.2. *Equity market capitalization as a percentage of GDP for major industrialized countries*

Sources: SIA, Securities Industry Factbook (2001).

during the 1990s. Germany and, especially, France are noteworthy examples of a broader shift away from a relatively modest reliance upon public equity financing. Nevertheless, bank financing remains an important source of short- and medium-term debt financing even in markets with traditionally strong public securities markets. See Allen and Gale (2000) for a comprehensive survey of the theory and evidence on this topic.

Securities markets are distinguished from other sources of finance, such as bank loans, by the importance that they place upon prices. Information relevant to a corporation's business is dispersed across many economic actors. When the corporation is publicly traded, this information is aggregated in the security's price through the competitive interplay of these self-interested actors. Relative prices provide information about resource constraints in the economy which helps corporations to plan and to evaluate their own activities.

In contrast, there is in general no market for the income from a bank loan, and hence the bank cannot rely upon prices to provide it with information about its counterparties. Instead, lenders form close relationships with their borrowers, as a result of which they acquire the information that they need to evaluate their investments. This information is not widely disseminated, and bank depositors therefore play no part in interpreting or gathering it. Bank lenders substitute for the price mechanism by intervening directly in the operations of the businesses to whom they lend money.

The intermediary role of the bank lender as a substitute for the price mechanism in generating information and reflecting it to the corporate borrower therefore distinguishes bank finance from security market finance, where investors generate information themselves and, when corporations fail to respond to price signals, intervene for themselves. Nevertheless, intermediaries play an important role in the security markets, and we call them *investment banks*.

The investment bank's most important role is in arranging the issuance of new securities by corporations and entrepreneurs in need of new capital. Their clients for this activity range from small operations raising public equity capital for the first time via an *initial public offering* (IPO), through to mature firms which return regularly to the capital markets to fund ongoing operations and new projects. Investment banks also act for governments and government agencies when they issue public debt securities. The securities markets for newly issued securities are generally referred to as *primary markets*. The term is slightly misleading in the sense that there is no separate formal market for new securities: the issuance process involves the creation of a completely new market.

The markets in which securities trade after they are issued are known as *secondary markets*. The most visible example of a secondary securities market is the New York Stock Exchange (NYSE). We have emphasized the role of securities markets in aggregating widely dispersed information into a single price. For this to happen, securities must be easily transferred between traders. The ease with which secondary market trade can occur in a given security is known as its *liquidity*. Liquidity varies across securities and across market structures, which vary enormously, despite the recent and profound shift from human intermediation to electronic trading platforms.

In liquid securities markets agents have an incentive to gather information, and to trade upon it. This incentive does not exist when an intermediary, such as a loan-making bank, sits between the corporation and its depositor-investors. Hence the importance of investment bank intermediaries in the capital-raising process may at first sight appear rather strange. The purpose of this book is to explain their economic role.

Unlike loan-making, or *commercial*, banks, investment banks have traditionally committed little of their own capital to the firms for which they have arranged financing. Nor have investment banks routinely engaged in active, ongoing monitoring of their client firms: any attempt to do so would undermine the role of the security markets in generating and aggregating relevant information.[1] Nevertheless, we argue that, like the commercial bank, the investment bank's central activity is informational.

Investors are less willing to invest in securities issued by firms about whose future performance they have little information. Conversely, such firms may gain little market feedback concerning their business decisions when the investor segment to which they appeal is quite narrow or uninformed. These problems are at their most acute when securities are first issued. Investors at this time may have little understanding of the issuer's business, and firms are most in need of market feedback when they issue new securities. Both of these problems act as a drag on security issuance: uninformed investors are unwilling to

---

[1] Although we explain in chapter eight why Michael Milken did so with such great success in the early development of secondary markets for subinvestment grade debt, or *junk bonds*.

purchase securities, and firms are unwilling to raise capital, without a good idea of the likely market reaction.

Given the right data, some investors may be able to estimate demand information for new securities, and hence the right price for the issue. They could profit from this information if they used it to trade in the security after issuance. Persuading them to reveal it instead, so that the new issue can be more accurately priced, is therefore possible only if the issuer can promise to pay them adequately for their knowledge. But it is notoriously hard to write enforceable contracts over knowledge of this type. In many cases, the contracting problem is so severe that it could prevent the issuance of the security, and hence market-based information production.

We argue in this book that the core function of the investment bank is to overcome this problem. Of course, it can never create court-enforceable contracts over the price-relevant information that is essential to new security issuance. Instead, it creates a network of investors who trust the investment bank to stand as an intermediary between them and new security issuers, rewarding them for providing their, otherwise private, information, and using this information to establish market demand conditions and thus more accurately to price the issuer's securities. This network functions as a sort of informal market in price-relevant information. Participants engage with one another via a combination of explicit and implicit, or relational, contracts. The latter are enforced by the investment bank, rather than by the courts. We therefore refer to the investment bank's network as an *information marketplace*. The bank's ability to enforce implicit contracts in this marketplace rests on its reputation for balancing many counterparties' conflicting interests.

Its core function of managing an information marketplace provides an investment bank with a comparative advantage in other security market activities. For example, we have already noted that active intervention in under-performing corporations that rely upon security market finance is performed by investors, rather than by their financial intermediary. One mechanism for intervention is the market for corporate control. Investment banks are able to use their information marketplaces to acquire information which is of value to potential bidders, and hence merger and acquisition (M&A) advisory work is an important part of their business.

Given their expertise in the primary security markets, it is natural that investment banks should be active players in the secondary markets, too. For example, their willingness to buy and sell securities in secondary markets reassures their investor client base that they will be able to exit their investments when they choose to do so. They also provide their corporate clients with market services which go beyond pure fund-raising. Investment banks actively advise corporations on their capital structure and how it might be altered better to serve the firm in its pursuit of business interests. In their modern capacity as *financial engineers*, investment bankers increasingly help to implement their advice through the design and placement of derivative contracts that lower funding costs, reduce the threat of financial distress, or sharpen performance incentives within the firm. In many instances, the bank serves as the original counterpart to derivative contracts, but it generally seeks to lay off the associated risk by making offsetting trades in liquid secondary markets for related securities.

Finally, investment banks increasingly use their security market skills in the asset management business, both directly and indirectly. Investment banks have sharply increased their direct participation by managing and marketing mutual funds and hedge funds. As recently as 1980, the ten largest NYSE member firms (measured by capitalization), all large investment banking concerns, earned less than one percent of their total revenues from asset management fees. By 1990, this figure had risen to 4.17 percent, or about two-thirds of the share of revenue generated by underwriting fees. In 2004, asset management fees accounted for 7.5 percent of revenues for the ten largest member firms, or about 60 percent of the share accounted for by underwriting fees.[2] Banks also serve this market segment indirectly through their provision of *prime brokerage* services that address the trading concerns of institutional investors, most of whom trade more frequently and in larger quantity than their retail investor counterparts.

Later in the book we develop a theoretical model of investment banking, and we bring it to bear upon the historical evolution of the industry from its early origins in the eighteenth-century Atlantic trade to the present day. This chapter sets the scene for our discussion by describing the modern investment bank. We start by examining important trends in securities markets, and exploring their implications for the operation of investment banks. We argue that for some investment banks, technological advances in the last quarter of

---

[2] Securities Industry Association, Securities Industry DataBank.

the twentieth century served to increase the importance of financial capital relative to tacit human skill. These changes have had a profound effect upon the structure of the investment banking industry: some institutions have concentrated upon activities where the human element remains paramount; others have embraced new technologies, and have created the economies of scale and scope needed to succeed in those business lines that rely increasingly upon large amounts of financial capital.

We close the chapter by examining more closely two investment banks that typify this industry division. Morgan Stanley is an exemplar of the large-scale investment bank. It has grown rapidly in the last two decades since shifting from private partnership to public ownership, combining with the retail brokerage operations of Dean Witter, and moving into a wide range of businesses from its narrowly focused origins in corporate advisory services. This transition has led to a dramatically increased emphasis on financial capital relative to human capital in Morgan Stanley's production process. Within the last year, the rising tension between human and financial capital came to a head as the firm's CEO, Phillip Purcell, whose roots lie in the financial capital-intensive side of the business, was forced out in favor of John Mack, who more nearly represents the traditional, human capital-intensive side of the business.

In contrast, until very recently Lazard Freres remained a small private partnership, focused almost exclusively on the advisory businesses in which human agency remains critical. Lazard's recent IPO marked both the culmination of the steady demise of private partnerships within the top tier of the industry, and also exemplified the ongoing experiment in public ownership of boutique advisory firms whose key assets remain people over whom shareholders have only very weak property rights. The tension between human capital and financial capital will be a recurring theme throughout the book, as we attempt to explain the industry's various idiosyncratic, and long-lived, characteristics.

MARKET TRENDS

We argue in chapter three that the core function of the investment bank is creating an environment in which information production will occur. It accomplishes this by creating an information marketplace, in which a small coterie of investors provide the bank with information. Agreements over information production cannot be enforced in court, but repeated interaction between the parties in the marketplace builds trust between them, which underpins their market relationships.

The core information-creation activity of investment banks has scarcely changed since the inception of securities markets (see chapters four to seven). However, the way in which it has been prosecuted has changed constantly in response to technological, political, legal, and demographic changes. In recent years the investment banking landscape has been transformed by the information technology revolution, and by the simultaneous explosion in financial engineering techniques and derivatives trading. These changes increased the efficient operating scale for investment banks, and hence increased the importance of financial capital; they simultaneously reduced the importance in trading rooms of human experience and judgment, as opposed to technical prowess.

The impact that these factors have had upon secondary market trading over the last forty years is illustrated in figure 1.3. The NYSE's average daily trading volume increased fourfold in the 1960s from slightly more than three million shares to a maximum in 1968 of about 13 million. At this stage problems with antiquated back-office

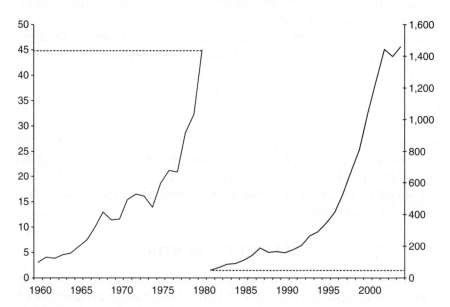

Figure 1.3. *New York Stock Exchange average daily trading volume, 1960–2004 (millions of shares)*

Source: New York Stock Exchange.

systems forced the computerization of firms like Merrill Lynch whose primary business was retail trading. They could achieve the necessary operating scale only through an injection of financial capital, and the Exchange recognized this in 1971 when it allowed member firms to operate as publicly traded corporations.

Trading volume continued to grow. By 1980, it had increased by a further factor of four from its 1970 level, forcing the Exchange to introduce (in 1976) the designated order turnaround (DOT) system for electronic routing and execution of small orders against quotes provided by floor specialists. A further fourfold expansion of trading volumes in the 1980s reached its peak at the time of the October 1987 market crash. Following a brief period of retrenchment and continued heavy investment in trading technology, average daily trading volume grew by a factor of nearly ten between 1990 and 2004.

Market developments in the 1980s were driven by both demographic and technological changes. As we have already noted, security ownership patterns changed. Moreover, cheaper computer power and developments in financial theory enabled investment banks to implement sophisticated pricing and risk-management algorithms for the first time. As a result, the computers that supported the growth in secondary market activity also to some extent substituted for human agency in matching buyers and sellers. For example, computer-managed trading books are important in the markets for foreign exchange and for financial futures. Nevertheless, while market-making operations demand significant financial capital and face narrowing margins, they remain an important source for information to the largest investment banks. As of October 31, 2004, only seven specialist firms coordinated trading in the 2,609 NYSE-listed stocks, and three of these firms were controlled by banks with significant investment banking interests.

Computerization in the 1980s also enabled the development of the derivatives markets, whose recent growth is documented in tables 1.1–1.3. Derivatives contracts allow corporations to adopt very specific risk positions, which they can use strategically to manage their total exposures. An important example is the option. An option purchaser has the right to perform a specific trade on a particular date. So a corporate wishing to reduce its exposure to the level of the Japanese yen could buy an option to purchase a specific quantity of yen at a given price, thereby protecting itself against price rises beyond this level.

Table 1.1. *Global derivatives market*

Year	Exchange traded	OTC	Total
1988	1,304	1,654	2,958
1989	1,767	2,475	4,242
1990	2,290	3,450	5,740
1991	3,519	4,449	7,968
1992	4,633	5,346	9,979
1993	7,761	8,475	16,236
1994	8,898	11,303	20,201
1995	9,283	17,713	26,996
1996	10,018	25,453	35,471
1997	12,403	29,035	41,438
1998	13,932	80,318	94,250
1999	13,522	88,202	101,724
2000	14,156	95,199	109,355

Note: Notional principal amount outstanding in billions of US dollars. OTC data after 1998 is not strictly comparable with prior years.

Sources: Bank for International Settlements (http://www.bis.org) and International Swaps and Derivatives Association, Inc. (http://www.isda.org)

Derivatives markets are an increasingly important part of the relationship between an investment bank and its clients. By trading in non-standardized, or 'over-the-counter' (OTC) derivatives, investment banks can provide tailor-made solutions to their clients' investment and risk-management problems: the growth of OTC markets is illustrated in table 1.1. They provide a particularly striking example of the trends that have shaped investment banking in recent years. As in the secondary security markets, participation in the derivatives markets requires investment banks to commit their own capital. Moreover, the skills that they need are more akin to engineering than to the judgment- and relationship-based knowledge of the traditional investment banker.

The increasing importance of financial capital for investment banking has raised the minimum operating scale for investment banks. This trend is illustrated in figure 1.4. As recently as 1980, the ten largest investment banks by capitalization averaged about $600 million in capital (CPI-adjusted to 1983 dollars). By 2000, the figure had risen

Table 1.2. *Markets for derivative financial instruments: notional principal amounts outstanding, 1986–96 (billions of US dollars)*

	1986	1987	1988	1989	1990	1991	1992	1993	1994	1995	1996
Interest rate futures	370.0	487.7	895.4	1,200.8	1,454.5	2,156.7	2,913.0	4,958.7	5,777.6	5,863.4	5,931.1
Interest rate options	146.5	122.6	2792	387.9	599.5	1,072.6	1,385.4	2,362.4	2,623.6	2,741.8	3,277.8
Currency futures	10.2	14.6	12.1	16.0	17.0	18.3	26.5	34.7	40.1	38.3	50.3
Currency options	39.2	59.5	48.0	50.2	56.5	62.9	71.1	75.6	55.6	43.2	46.5
Stock market index futures	14.5	17.8	27.1	41.3	69.1	76.0	79.8	110.0	127.3	172.2	198.6
Stock market index options	37.8	27.7	42.9	70.7	93.7	132.8	158.6	229.7	238.3	329.3	380.2
Total	618.3	729.9	1,304.8	1,766.9	2,290.4	3,519.3	4,634.4	7,771.1	8,862.5	9,188.2	9,884.6
North America	518.1	578.1	951.7	1,155.8	1,268.5	2,151.7	2,694.7	4,358.6	4,819.5	4,849.6	4,839.7
Europe	13.1	13.3	177.7	251.0	461.2	710.1	1,114.3	1,777.9	1,831.7	2,241.6	2,831.7
Asia-Pacific	87.0	138.5	175.4	360.0	560.5	657.0	823.5	1,606.0	2,171.8	1,990.1	2,154.0
Other	0.0	0.0	0.0	0.1	0.2	0.5	1.8	28.7	39.5	106.8	59.3

Source: Scholes (1998: 362, table 1).

Table 1.3. *Notional principal value of outstanding interest rate and currency swaps of the members of the International Swaps and Derivatives Association, 1987–June 1996 (billions of US dollars)*

	1987	1988	1989	1990	1991	1992	1993	1994	1995	June 1996
Interest rate swaps										
All counterparties	682.9	1,101.2	1,502.6	2,311.5	3,065.1	3,850.8	6,177.3	8,815.6	12,810.7	15,584.2
Interbank (ISDA member)	206.6	341.3	547.1	909.5	1,342.3	1,880.8	2,967.9	4,533.9	7,100.6	—
Financial institutions	300.0	421.3	579.2	817.1	985.7	1,061.1	1,715.7	2,144.4	3,435.0	—
Governments	47.6	63.2	76.2	136.9	165.5	242.8	327.1	307.6	500.9	—
Corporations	128.6	168.9	295.2	447.9	571.7	666.2	1,166.6	1,829.8	1,774.2	—
Currency swaps										
All counterparties (adjusted for reporting of both sides)	182.8	319.6	449.1	577.5	807.2	860.4	899.6	914.8	1,197.4	1,294.7
Interest rate options	0.0	327.3	537.3	561.3	577.2	634.5	1,397.6	1,572.8	3,704.5	4,190.1
Total	865.6	1,657.1	2,489.0	3,450.3	4,449.5	5,345.7	8,474.5	11,303.2	17,712.6	21,068.9

Source: Scholes (1998: 363, table 2).

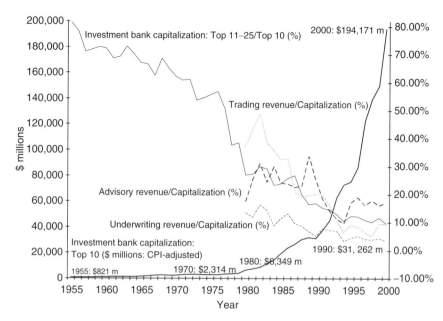

Figure 1.4. *The US investment banking industry, 1955–2000*
Note: The advisory revenue data series is the 'other' revenue category reported by the SIA. The most important component of this category is fees from OTC derivatives and M&A advisory work.
Sources: SIA, Securities Industry Databank and Factbook.

to nearly $20 billion. Over the same period, the capitalization of these banks nearly doubled relative to the 15 next largest banks. The pattern of increasing capitalization and concentration of capital is even more pronounced when traced back to 1955.

The increased requirement for capital arose alongside a sharp rise in the number of investment bank employees (see figure 1.5). In 1979, the five largest banks by capitalization employed about 56,000 people in total, with the employee rolls of individual firms ranging from about 2,000 to 27,000 people. By 2000, the top five banks employed about 205,000 people, with individual bank employees ranging from 12,000 to 72,000.

Notwithstanding the rise in employee numbers, the importance in investment banking of human capital relative to financial capital fell over the period under consideration. The quadrupling of employee numbers was swamped by the increase in capitalization. In 1979 (CPI-adjusted) capitalization per employee ranged from $27,000 to

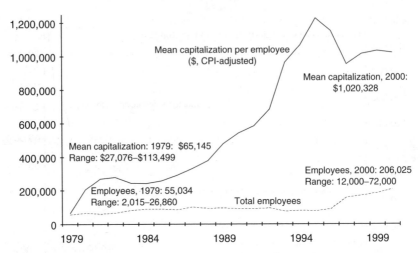

Figure 1.5. *Investment bank employees and capitalization, 1979–2000 (top five banks by capitalization)*

Sources: SIA, Securities Industry Databank and Factbook.

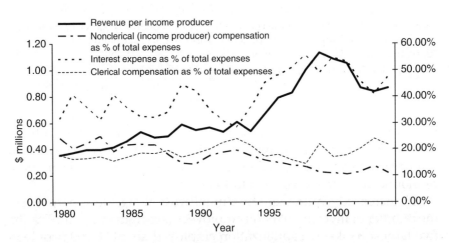

Figure 1.6. *Income producer revenue and compensation (ten largest banks by capitalization)*

Sources: SIA, Securities Industry Databank and Factbook.

$113,000, with a mean of $65,000. In 2000, per-employee capitalization ranged from $875,000 to $3,585,000, with a mean of about $1 million.

A final indication of the declining relative importance of human capital is illustrated in figure 1.6, where we report as a percentage of total expenses revenue per income producer and their (non-clerical) compensation for 1980–2004. Revenue per income producer increased fairly steadily through 1995 and then nearly doubled over the next five years, before pulling back with the stock market decline. Over the same period, nonclerical compensation declined from over 20 percent to around ten percent of total expenses. Clerical compensation (as a percentage of total expenses) remained fairly stable over the period. By contrast, interest expenses, which provide a rough approximation of payments to financial capital, fluctuated between 30 and 45 percent of total expenses until 1994, when they began tracking closely the rising path of revenue per income producer.

In sum, the ever-increasing trading volumes of the secondary securities markets, the increasing power of distributed, desktop computing, and the explosion of derivative trading in investment banks have had two consequences. First, investment banks that rely upon a security market presence to deliver their core informational services need more financial capital than ever before. Second, these investment banks are less reliant upon hard-to-find, judgment-based, tacit professional skills which can only be acquired on the job. There is a declining dependence on human capital per unit of production within the industry.

INDUSTRY STRUCTURE

We have argued that investment banks are primarily concerned with the creation of informational assets. Since these assets cannot be the subject of formal financial contracts, the investment bank creates an environment within which mutual trust underpins agreements to find, and to pay for, price-relevant information. Hence, as we demonstrate in greater detail in chapters two and three, investment banks rely upon their reputational capital. Moreover, investment banks have traditionally relied upon tacit human skills that are hard-to-acquire and hard-to-prove or to disprove. The bank's ability to sell these skills again rests upon its reputation: indeed, we argue in chapter nine that the need to maintain a reputation for highly skilled employees explains the historical use in investment banks of the partnership form of organization.

The importance of tacit human capital, the need to tie this capital to the investment bank, and the value of reputational capital can help us to explain the industrial organization of the investment banking industry. First, reputations are hard-to-acquire (and easy-to-lose). Hence new investment banks, which have no reputation, face a substantial barrier to entry. As a result, the investment banking industry has been highly concentrated throughout its history. This observation can be usefully documented using industry 'league tables', which report firm rankings by the dollar value of transactions that they complete. Tables 1.4 and 1.5 summarize investment bank rankings for the last four decades. They show the dollar value of new US-underwritten common stock issues for the banks that managed them (i.e. that acted as 'bookrunner'), and also the value of mergers and acquisitions for which the banks acted as advisers.

Several facts are immediately apparent from tables 1.4 and 1.5. First, the market for managing US common stock offerings has become increasingly concentrated during the last half century. The 1960s began shortly after the last major antitrust challenge to the investment banking industry. During this decade, the top five banks by market share accounted for 38 percent of the value of US shares brought to market during the decade, and the top ten banks accounted for 62 percent. By 2003, the top five and top ten investment banks accounted for 64 and 87 percent of market share, respectively.

It is also noteworthy that many of the names that appeared at the top of the league tables during the 1960s maintained a leading position in 2003. In fact, every bank among the top ten in the 1960s that does not appear in 2003 was absorbed by one of the 2003 top ten banks at some point in the intervening period. This observation is consistent with our statement that reputational capital presents a significant barrier to entry into the investment banking industry.[3] Investment bank reputation is a focal point of our analysis throughout the book.

We have already pointed to the technological changes that raised the minimum operating scale for retail-oriented investment banks in the 1970s. This was the basis for a wave of consolidations, which saw many of the highly ranked investment banks of the 1960s folded into those which remained in 2003. Some of the highly ranked names of 2003, such as Citigroup, UBS, JP Morgan, and BancAmerica, are

---

[3] The 'tombstone' advertisements announcing the completion of a transaction provide further evidence of the importance that investment banks place upon reputation (see Hayes, 1971, and Carter and Manaster, 1990). The banks participating in a transaction are listed in the corresponding tombstone advertisement according to their roles and, among banks serving similar functions, their perceived standing in the industry.

Table 1.4. *Underwritten common stock (thousands of US dollars) US transactions*

1960–69		1970		1980		1990		2003	
First Boston	$3,989	Merrill Lynch	$591	Merrill Lynch	$2,233	Alex. Brown	$2,975	Merrill Lynch	$20,184
Merrill Lynch	3,721	First Boston	345	Morgan Stanley	1,623	Goldman Sachs	2,634	Citigroup	19,526
Lehman Brothers	3,218	Kidder, Peabody	321	Kidder, Peabody	1,188	Salomon Brothers	1,756	Goldman Sachs	14,554
Blyth	2,732	Blyth	262	Goldman Sachs	952	Merrill Lynch	1,596	Morgan Stanley	12,116
White, Weld	2,546	Eastman Dillon	256	First Boston	818	Lehman Brothers	1,013	UBS	10,273
Morgan Stanley	2,258	Stone & Webster	239	Dean Witter	758	First Boston	929	CS FirstBoston	7,355
Goldman Sachs	2,220	Morgan Stanley	211	Blyth Eastman	639	Paine Webber	911	LehmanBrothers	6,575
Dean Witter	2,000	White, Weld	135	Lehman Brothers	629	Morgan Stanley	911	JP Morgan	6,031
Kuhn, Loeb	1,931	Lehman Brothers	134	EF Hutton	465	Smith Barney	807	Bank of America	4,069
Kidder, Peabody	1,891	Smith Barney	132	Salomon Brothers	454	Dean Witter	759	AG Edwards	2,708
Total market	$43,022		$4,224		$12,841		$20,082		$119,503
Top 5 market share	38%		42%		53%		50%		64%
Top 10 market share	62%		62%		76%		71%		87%

Note: Full credit to bookrunner, equal credit to joint book runners.
Source: Securities Data Corporation.

Table 1.5. *Mergers and acquisitions (thousands of US dollars) US transactions announced during year*

1980		1990		2003	
Morgan Stanley	$10,564	Goldman Sachs	48,223	Goldman Sachs	$60,377
Lazard Freres	6,579	Morgan Stanley	45,820	JP Morgan	30,143
Salomon Brothers	4,683	First Boston	41,009	Merrill Lynch	29,838
First Boston	4,456	Salomon Brothers	33,163	Citigroup	26,773
Merrill Lynch	2,977	Lazard Freres	25,181	Lehman Brothers	22,143
Lehman Brothers	2,657	Dillon, Read	22,239	CS First Boston Intl	20,449
Shearson Lehman	2,600	Morgan Guaranty	15,840	Morgan Stanley	15,549
Kidder, Peabody	2,169	Merrill Lynch	15,218	CS First Boston	13,832
Dean Witter	1,687	Shearson Lehman	12,430	Deutsche Bank	13,222
Goldman Sachs	1,535	Lehman Brothers	10,903	Bear Stearns	10,286
Total market	$24,371		$238,370		$176,036
Top 5 market share	120%		81%		96%
Top 10 market share	164%		113%		138%

Note: Full credit given to each eligible adviser.
Source: Securities Data Corporation.

commercial banks. They were allowed egress into the investment banking industry only when legal restrictions on their activities were removed by the 1999 repeal of the 1933 Glass-Steagall Banking Act. This resulted in a further wave of investment bank consolidation in the 1990s.[4]

The M&A advisory business relies upon human skill and judgment, and hence is at least as reputationally intensive as the new issues business. Table 1.5 reports league tables for banks engaged in this business for 1980, 1990, and 2005. Once again, this is a highly concentrated business. Many, though not all, of the top underwriters levered their reputational capital into a strong position in M&A advisory work.[5] Moreover, some firms have largely specialized in M&A advisory services: Lazard Freres is a noteworthy example. Investment banks like Lazard have been joined in recent years by a new group of specialized 'boutique' banks that focus on M&A and corporate restructuring. The boutique operations have been founded by prominent bankers who have left bulge-bracket firms to start their own businesses. We argue in chapter ten that they chose to do so because it was very hard to combine their own, highly human-capital-based and reputationally intensive, specialisms with the emphasis upon scale and financial capital of the modern bulge-bracket firm. Prominent examples of firms that were founded in this way are Greenhill & Co. and the Blackstone Group.

Until very recently, M&A advisory specialists were privately held and had relatively small balance sheets. They nevertheless exercised considerable influence, particularly in the most prominent transactions where they were engaged for their highly specialized expertise. More recently, many of these firms have been forced to rethink their competitive strategies. Both Lazard and Greenhill have elected to join the ranks of publicly traded firms.

The data from tables 1.4 and 1.5 concerning industry size and shape that we have already discussed probably understate the concentration of market power within the investment banking industry. Although investment banks compete aggressively to manage securities

---

[4] Figure 10.1 on page 297 provides a visual presentation of reorganization and consolidation among the most prominent banks from mid century forward. Corwin and Schultz (2005) provide a comprehensive listing of mergers and acquisitions involving investment banks from 1997 to mid-year 2002.

[5] Note that these market shares are difficult to interpret in the light of the industry convention of granting full credit to multiple advisers on a single deal. Hence, market shares for the top five or ten banks can exceed 100 percent of the total.

offerings, and to advise on M&A and restructuring transactions, they also routinely join forces to serve as comanagers and coadvisors. The vehicle through which this occurs for security issuance is the underwriting syndicate. Syndicates are contractual arrangements that bind several firms to collaborate for a single transaction.

We argue in chapter three that syndicates are valuable because they increase the value of an investment bank's reputation in binding itself to work for its corporate clients.[6] Like the relationships within an investment bank's own information marketplace, cooperation within syndicates is sustained by long-lived relationships: although individual syndicates are short-lived, the same banks routinely join forces for many transactions. Admitting its peers into its own syndicate gives an investment bank the opportunity to join future syndicates in which it is not the lead manager. An extreme early example of cooperative reciprocal behavior of this type is the exclusive but informal arrangement between Goldman Sachs and Lehman Brothers in the (co-)origination of deals which ran from 1906 to 1920, and which continued on a less exclusive basis at least until the early 1930s.[7] Despite periodic episodes of public criticism and regulatory interference, there is considerable evidence that reciprocal cooperation has remained an important characteristic of the industry.[8]

Investment banks have traditionally maintained relatively exclusive client relationships. This serves the interests of clients who enter the market relatively infrequently, because concentrating their deal flow with a particular institution enables them to establish an ongoing relationship based upon reputation and trust.[9] Again, a noteworthy example is provided by Goldman Sachs, who, starting from 1956, had a nearly fifty year exclusive banking relationship with Ford Motor Company. We argue in chapter eight that recent technological changes have reduced the difficulty of creating and sustaining reputations with clients. As a result, the exclusivity of client–bank relationships has diminished in recent years. This trend became pronounced during

---

[6] The lead manager in an underwriting syndicate experiences an additional reputational boost, because its position earns it a stronger placing in the tombstone advertisement.

[7] See 'Brief for Defendant Goldman, Sachs & Co. on Motion to Dismiss Under Rule 41 (b)' filed in *U.S.* v. *H.S. Morgan et al.*, United States District Court for the Southern District of New York, Civil No. 43-757, 1953.

[8] See Carosso (1970), Hayes (1971), Eccles and Crane (1988), Benveniste, Busaba, and Wilhelm (2002), Corwin and Schultz (2005), Pichler and Wilhelm (2001), and Ljungqvist et al. (2006).

[9] See Baker (1990) for a discussion.

the 1990s when commercial banks started to enter the lucrative securities underwriting business. They obtained a toehold in this market through the practice of 'tying': offering lending facilities on attractive terms to prospective security issuers, or threatening explicitly or implicitly to withdraw lending facilities from clients who engaged other banks for issuance business.

The investment bank's investor base is able to provide it with demand data and hence is an integral part of its information marketplace. As a result, the investment bank maintains close relationships with key investors, so that it can create trust and hence ensure that valuable information is created and paid for. We study investment bank relationships in greater detail in chapter nine.

INVESTMENT BANK ACTIVITIES

We now put some meat on the bones of our industry-level generalizations by examining in greater detail the operations of a modern investment bank.

The central investment banking function is the generation and the retailing of price-relevant information. Traditionally, 'investment banking' refers to advisory functions that rest upon the provision and interpretation of this type of information. This type of advice is provided to firms and governmental organizations that wish to raise funds in the securities markets; to corporations that aim to purchase another firm's securities in order to control it; and to corporations that need to renegotiate with security holders, and to restructure their liability structure, generally in order to avoid bankruptcy.

Traditional investment banking relies upon the experience, the skills, and the reputations of its practitioners. It is therefore more closely associated with human skill than with financial capital. However, as we argued above, the information-creation activities of many investment banks rely increasingly upon their secondary market presence, as traders and principal investors. Participation in these activities requires a sizable capital commitment. We have already discussed the importance of securities and derivatives market-making to many modern investment banks. Many of these banks use the information that they acquire from market-making to commit their own funds to the market, an activity which is referred to in the industry as 'proprietary trading'. And investment banks are increasingly eager to make large principal investments in firms, some of whom they advise. This type of principal investment, known collectively as 'merchant banking', ranges from venture capital investments in fledgling firms to private equity investments, which are often made to support the reorganization of mature firms.[10]

In addition to their capital-intensive trading and principal investment activities, investment banks provide advisory services to secondary-market investors through their asset management arms. Asset management does not place the bank's capital at stake: it generates fees from investment advice and portfolio management services for wealthy individual and institutional clients.

In the succeeding subsections, we describe the activities of the modern investment bank in greater detail.

Traditional Investment Banking

Traditional investment banking relates to advisory work in securities issuance, and also in the M&A market. In this section, we illustrate the general nature of these activities by describing the bank's role in an IPO.[11]

Corporations may decide to perform a securities issue, or they may be identified as a prospect and approached by an investment bank. In either case, investment banks at this stage analyze the firm's prospects and financial status, so as to determine whether the transaction makes sense for the firm, and on what terms. Banks rely when performing this analysis upon experience gleaned from similar deals, as well as upon information provided by the firm. Issuers generally promote competition among banks at this stage, and select their investment bank from a field whose members compete in a 'bake-off' presentation of their analysis.

Once the investment bank has been formally engaged by the corporation, it deepens its analysis in order to prepare the firm's prospectus. The prospectus is the legal document of record, and the bank's responsibility for 'due diligence' in its preparation exposes the bank to the risk of litigation in the event of misstatements, or omissions of relevant facts. In the United States, submission of the preliminary prospectus (the S-1 statement or 'red herring') with the Securities and Exchange Commission (SEC) constitutes registration of the offering.

---

[10] See 'Wall Street Looks for Slice of Private-Equity Pie', *Wall Street Journal*, 26 September 2005, p. C1.

[11] We describe US practice. Jenkinson, Morrison, and Wilhelm (2005) provide a detailed account of both European and US practice.

The SEC reviews the red herring prospectus over a period which usually lasts several weeks. During this time the bank coordinates a sales effort aimed at mutual and pension fund managers and other institutional investors. The bank also assembles a syndicate of other banks, which assist in the sales and distribution effort, and later share in the underwriting risk. Alongside the sales effort, the bank starts to gather the price-relevant information upon which a successful issue relies. It does so by canvassing institutional investors for indications of the price at which they would purchase shares, and the quantity that they wish to buy. The price and/or quantity bids which the banker receives are used to build a 'book' for the offering. They are not legally binding. However, as we have already discussed, repeated interaction and trust between the parties ensures that these informal promises are honored. Failure to do so would probably result in exclusion from future issues.

When the SEC has approved the issuer's prospectus, the bank and issuer agree upon an offer price that reflects both investor feedback and current market conditions. Once issued, shares are traded in the secondary market. The investment bank's responsibilities at this stage include making a market in the shares, and providing research coverage aimed at prospective investors. As we discussed on page 9, market-making is financial capital-intensive, because the bank may be required to take a substantial position in the securities.[12] In contrast, research coverage relies upon human capital, and is perceived as especially valuable when the bank employs a prominent, or 'all-star', research analyst for the issuer's industry segment.[13] Neither the market-making nor the analyst role forms the basis of an explicit contractual agreement between the issuing firm and the investment bank. However, like its counterparts in the primary market, the investment bank is unlikely to renege upon its promises, because doing so would damage its reputation and with it, its future revenue streams.

The investment bank is remunerated for its expertise by legally acquiring the shares from the firm at a discount to the offer price. The discount, or spread, for moderately priced US IPOs generally hovers around seven percent.[14] When the investment bank acquires the shares, it 'underwrites' the issuing firm's proceeds against unexpected market movements. The risk to which this exposes the banks is

---

[12] See Ellis, Michaely, and O'Hara (2000).
[13] See Ljungqvist et al. (2006) and citations therein.
[14] Chen and Ritter (2000).

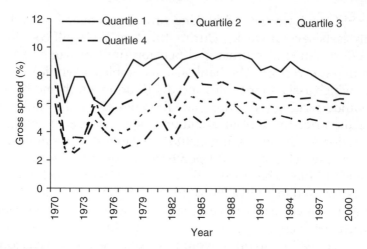

Figure 1.7. *Equity underwriting fees as a percentage of gross proceeds*
Note: The first quartile contains the smallest offerings (measured by gross proceeds).

minimal: the shares are generally sold within hours to the institutional investors who make up the investment bank's book.

The mechanics of Seasoned Equity Offerings (SEOs) and debt offerings are similar but generally less complicated than those of IPOs, if for no other reason than that pricing can be carried out relative to either perfect (in the case of the SEO), or close, substitutes already actively traded in the market. Merger and acquisition and restructuring services involve analytical methods that are similar to those used in securities offerings and may include associated securities transactions.

Over the course of the twentieth century underwriting spreads collapsed in both the debt and equity markets. In 1913, investment banks earned 5–10 percent of the value of a bond offering and 20–25 percent on a common equity offering. In 1940, bonds and common equity carried average spreads of about 2 and 16 percent, respectively.[15] Figures 1.7 and 1.8 show that both debt and equity spreads continued their decline through the early 1970s. Equity spreads rose somewhat until the late 1980s before declining further. A similar pattern obtained among the smallest nonconvertible debt offerings, but by the late 1980s spreads for both large and small debt offerings were in sharp decline. The decline in spreads corresponded with the

---

[15] Calomiris and Raff (1995).

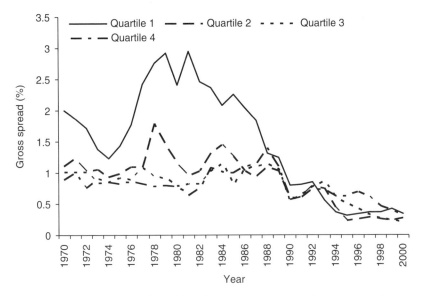

Figure 1.8. *Debt underwriting fees as a percentage of gross proceeds*
Source: Securities Data Corporation.
Note: The first quartile contains the smallest offerings (measured by gross proceeds).

entry of commercial banks into the underwriting business, as Glass–Steagall restrictions were first weakened and then abolished. Commercial banks had considerable expertise in debt funding. Moreover, debt offerings present far less serious informational frictions than do equity offerings. Thus it is natural that debt spreads responded more rapidly and in a more extreme fashion to competition from the new entrants.[16] By 2000, debt spreads for both large and small offerings had fallen below 50 basis points (i.e. 0.5 percent of gross proceeds).

In contrast, while information technology has simplified certain aspects of the equity market, it has not displaced relationships and tacit human capital from their central position in the valuation and placing of new issues. Correspondingly, equity underwriting fees, after falling to about eight percent by 1965, have remained relatively stable in the aggregate. As we explain in chapter eight, however, the aggregate figures mask some important changes in the market, and ongoing experiments with electronic auctions suggest that equity

[16] For similar reasons, the debt markets adapted more rapidly to pressures toward mechanization of issuance and trading practices. See chapter eight.

markets will follow the path of debt markets, albeit perhaps not with such force or speed.

Trading and Principal Investment

In contrast to traditional investment banking activities, trading and principal investment both require a commitment of financial capital. The skills that these activities involve are largely distinct from those of the traditional investment banker, although in areas such as venture capital and private equity investment analysis there is some overlap.

Recent advances in financial theory and in information technology have revolutionized the trading business. Many of the rule-of-thumb approaches to trading that prevailed before the 1980s have been replaced by precise and codifiable techniques that can be acquired at arm's length in professional schools. As a result, trading skill has become increasingly commoditized, and the importance of human relative to financial capital has diminished accordingly. We outline below some of the trading room activities in which financial engineering and computer science have had a particularly profound effect.

First, powerful computers have facilitated the introduction of 'program', or 'basket', trading strategies. The New York Stock Exchange (NYSE) defines a program trade as one that involves the simultaneous purchase or sale of at least fifteen stocks, with a combined value in excess of $1 million. These trades are frequently executed with the goal of matching the performance of a market index such as the S&P 500.[17] Institutional demand for these trades continues to grow as technology drives down their costs.[18]

Second, a combination of advanced computing and mathematically sophisticated financial modeling has enabled more traders to identify price discrepancies across markets. Investment banks develop strategies to profit from these discrepancies in-house, and they also outsource this work by investing in hedge funds. Many of the funds in turn purchase execution services from the bank.

Third, investment banks have in recent years earned substantial profits from the production and distribution of the over-the-counter

---

[17] Another product of the financial economics revolution is the widely shared belief that this is the most efficient way for most people to invest in the stock market.

[18] During the week ending August 12, 2005, program trading accounted for 15 percent of the daily trading volume on the NYSE. Of the five most active program traders during that week, three (UBS, Lehman, and Credit Suisse First Boston) executed most of their trades for their own account rather than on behalf of clients (*Wall Street Journal*, August 19, 2005, C7).

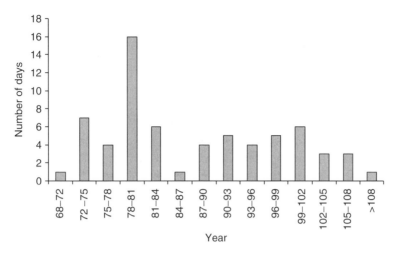

Figure 1.9. *Morgan Stanley daily 99 percent per one-day trading VaR*
Note: Quarter ending May 31, 2005: dollars in millions.

derivative contracts described on page 9. The bank generally acts as counterpart in these deals. It typically earns a fee upon entering into the contract, and must then manage its exposure so as to avoid large future losses. This type of business is naturally capital-intensive, and it exemplifies the modern emphasis upon technical skills, frequently acquired in professional schools.

Information technology has also altered management practice in these areas. Older approaches to managing trading portfolios relied upon judgment, trust, and rule-of-thumb heuristics. These have been supplanted by sophisticated techniques based upon statistical analysis and computerization. The most common of the new techniques is the Value-at-Risk (VaR) approach, which in its original incarnation was developed in the early 1990s by JP Morgan. The VaR figure for an operation indicates the probability with which it will lose more than a given amount over a specified time horizon. For example, a trading book with a one day 99 percent VaR of $1 million will experience a greater loss with one percent probability. Value-at-Risk numbers give senior management a simple handle upon riskiness, which is comparable across business lines. They can be aggregated[19] to give a firm-level VaR, which firms frequently report in their annual reports.

---

[19] But not by adding them: portfolio effects ensure that the VaR of the whole is less than the sum of the VaRs of the parts.

For example, figure 1.9, which is taken from Morgan Stanley's 05/05 10q filing, shows the firm's daily distribution of daily trading one day 99 percent VaRs for the quarter ending 31 May, 2005. There was one day in which the firm estimated that with one percent probability it could have lost more than $108 million. There were 16 days during which the corresponding figure was between $78 and $81 million. The average daily VaR during the quarter was $87 million. Similarly, in its most recent quarterly earnings report (for the quarter ending February 24, 2006), Goldman Sachs reported record earnings of $2.48 billion but with a VaR of $92 million, up nearly 50 percent from the same quarter the year before.[20]

VaR is not a perfect measure. It does not perform well when market conditions vary significantly from the assumptions underlying its estimation. Moreover, differences in the ways in which firms measure VaR, and the degree to which they apply it to nontrading functions, make comparisons across firms difficult. Notwithstanding these problems, VaR is a powerful and an increasingly ubiquitous tool. It is routinely reported to senior management at the close of day and to shareholders on a quarterly basis. It often serves as a key input to incentive-based compensation plans.

The increasing commoditization of trading knowledge has made it easy for investment banks to replicate the successful trading strategies of their peers.[21] One bank's capital is as good as another's, the basic knowledge used in trading systems or used to value companies has been widely dispersed via business-school training, and startup costs for the development of trading platforms have collapsed with the price of computing power. To the extent that staff are central to the success of a trading operation, they can take their skills to a competitor.

Only when analysis is relatively tacit, deal-specific, and is conducted within the context of a strong client relationship, can banks expect consistently to reap a fair reward for investments in R&D on a fee-for-service basis. Although these conditions obtain in traditional investment banking, they do not in the dealing room, where trading staff mobility and trading strategy replication undermine investment banks' incentives to invest in trading R&D. They have responded in two ways. First, trading and principal investment functions are extremely opaque. Firms are very secretive about their strategies, and they provide only a broad characterization of their returns to trading and principal investment. There are no league tables, and comparative

---

[20] *Wall Street Journal*, March 15, 2006, C1.   [21] See, for example, Tufano (1989).

rankings are few. In the absence of any legal protection, opacity limits competitors' access to knowledge generated within the bank, and can help to limit the mobility of people in whom it is embedded.[22] Second, investment banks have recently started to patent the methods upon which their ideas rest. Patenting of financial ideas was believed to be impossible until the 1998 appellate court decision in *State Street* v. *Signature Financial Group* changed expectations regarding the enforcement of business method patents. Since then, there has been a flurry of financial patent applications.[23]

Asset Management and Securities Services

Traditional investment banking generates fees from a corporate client base. Asset management and securities services use the information networks of traditional investment banking to generate fees from an investor client base. These are relatively new businesses, which reflect the increasing importance of institutional investors and the aging population.

Asset management generates fees from the investment advice and portfolio management services provided to retail and institutional clients. While most investment banks historically concentrated in their retail businesses upon wealthy individuals, they increasingly attract smaller individual investors by offering their own managed investment funds. Once acquired, fund management clients tend to be relatively immobile, and hence the business generates a revenue stream which is rather more stable than the rest of the bank. While banks with long-standing reputations for high-quality wholesale services have an initial advantage in this market, success requires substantial fixed investments in marketing and distribution channels, and hence is once again dependent upon scale economies.

Securities services include trade execution, clearing, settlement, reporting, and lending collateralized by securities positions. Although securities services can generate considerable revenue (Goldman Sachs earned $380 million in net revenues during the quarter ending February 25, 2005), they also demand significant capital investment.[24] Like the trading activities to which they relate, securities services have become increasingly commoditized in response to technological advances that have promoted standardization and mechanization.

[22] Morrison and Wilhelm (2004).   [23] Lerner (2002).
[24] *Wall Street Journal*, May 20, 2005.

This trend has been particularly pronounced in the retail brokerage business in which Merrill Lynch traditionally specialized. Since the NYSE's 1975 abolition of fixed commission rates this business has become more competitive and less profitable.

In contrast, the wholesale market for prime brokerage services is less standardized, but like retail broking, it has become more dependent upon financial capital. This trend is in large part attributable to an explosive growth in the number and size of hedge funds, which in turn reflects an outsourcing of activities that would once have been performed within investment banks' proprietary trading operations.[25] The most recent estimates place the number of hedge funds worldwide at over 8,000.[26] The dominant firms in the prime brokerage market, Goldman Sachs, Bear, Stearns, and Morgan Stanley, increasingly serve hedge funds by providing advice related to 'risk arbitrage', private equity and complex derivative transactions, as well as providing capital and sophisticated electronic platforms for complex trade execution. Hedge fund business is concentrated among the largest investment banks: aggressive attempts by smaller firms to capture some of the revenue it generates have resulted in lower fees, higher salaries for the key individuals, and a greater bank willingness to assume risk as hedge fund financiers.[27]

Figure 1.10 illustrates relative revenue by functional area for the top ten investment banks by capitalization, as reported to the Securities Industry Association (SIA). Commission income has declined sharply since the elimination of fixed commission requirements. Although it is a very volatile revenue source, the share of total revenues generated by trading declined over the same period. The largest revenue increases occurred in asset management and in the 'other related securities business' category, of which the two major components are fees for corporate advisory services and over-the-counter derivatives dealing.

THE GROWING DICHOTOMY BETWEEN SPECIALISTS AND GENERALISTS

Figure 1.10 suggests that relative revenue growth is strongest among businesses that rely most heavily on human capital. These businesses

[25] Jean-Michel Paul, *Wall Street Journal*, November 8, 2004. Also see chapter ten for further discussion of this point.
[26] *Wall Street Journal*, March 8, 2006.
[27] *Investment Dealers' Digest*, March 3, 2003 and *Wall Street Journal*, May 20, 2005.

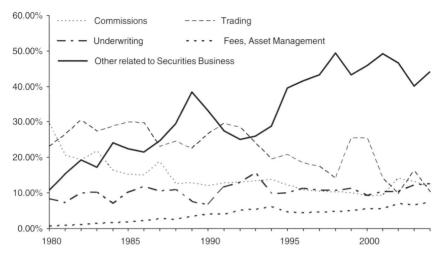

Figure 1.10. *Investment bank revenues (percent of total revenue, ten largest banks)*
Sources: SIA, Securities Industry Databank and Factbook.

include traditional investment banking functions and more sophisticated trading and asset management activities. The most prominent
banks attempt to complement efforts in these areas by strengthening
their presence in distribution functions that depend heavily on financial capital. Others have followed a path of specialization, focusing
upon the creation and maintenance of specialized human capital,
while contracting at arm's length for more commodity-like execution
and distribution capacity. Morgan Stanley and Lazard Freres are useful prototypes for illustrating this dichotomy.

Morgan Stanley was founded as the investment banking successor
to JP Morgan when the 1933 Glass–Steagall Act forced the separation
of commercial and investment banking functions. From the time it
was founded, Morgan Stanley occupied a position at or near the top
of the investment banking industry, particularly for advisory services
in corporate transactions. When the bank went public in 1986, it had
105 partners, and at year-end 1985 it had a total of 4,000 employees and $672 million in capital. The firm was closely affected by
the secondary market changes that we documented earlier, and it
expanded rapidly following its public offering. In 1997 the firm made
a major attempt to move beyond its origins in serving corporations
and institutional clients by merging with Dean Witter, Discover & Co.
The combined entity is now one of the largest full-service investment

Table 1.6. *Morgan Stanley business lines*

Institutional Services	Individual Investor Group	Investment Management	Credit Services
Investment banking	Investor advisory	Mutual funds	Credit card
Institutional sales & trading	Private wealth management	Alternative investments	Mortgage lending
Research		Retirement securities	Insurance

Source: Annual Report (2004).

banks: it closed 2004 with 53,284 employees and $110.8 billion of capital.[28]

Table 1.6 provides a condensed version of Morgan Stanley's structure and business lines, as reported in the firm's 2004 annual report. The Institutional Securities group essentially combines what we characterized above as the investment banking and the trading and principal investment functions. The Individual Investor Group and Investment Management between them account for the bulk of what we characterize as asset management and securities services. The Credit Services division separates Morgan Stanley from most of its investment banking peers.

In contrast to Morgan Stanley, Lazard Freres has recently focused upon advisory services related to corporate acquisitions and restructuring. At times it has been one of the most influential firms in this field. We have already argued that traditional investment banking is extremely reliant upon special human skills. As a result, Lazard's fortunes have rested in recent years upon one or a few key individuals such as Andre Meyer, Felix Rohatyn and, most recently, Bruce Wasserstein. The firm went public only in May 2005. Lazard entered the institutional asset management business in 1970, and it currently derives around a third of its revenue from this source (see table 1.7). Prior to its IPO, the firm's remaining businesses (around ten percent

---

[28] As a point of comparison, Merrill Lynch was for many years the standard bearer among full-service investment banks, and arguably it remains so today. In 1971, Merrill was among the first investment banks to go public when the NYSE permitted member firms to do so. At year-end 1971 the firm had 217 partners, 18,000 employees and $393 million in capital. The firm's 1971 capitalization was more than three times that of its nearest competitor (Bache & Co.) and dwarfed Morgan Stanley's 1971 capitalization of $17.6 million. At year-end 2004, Merrill Lynch had 50,600 employees and long-term capital (equity, long-term debt and deposit liabilities) of $199 billion.

Table 1.7. *Percentage of net revenue by functional area for Lazard Freres and Morgan Stanley*

	2002		2003		2004	
	Lazard	MS	Lazard	MS	Lazard	MS
Investment banking	47%	13%	60%	12%	54%	14%
Financial advisory	46%	5%	58%	3%	51%	5%
Underwriting	1%	8%	2%	9%	3%	9%
Trading, Principal investment	8%	37%	5%	45%	4%	43%
Trading	5%	18%	3%	30%	2%	23%
Investments	2%	0%	1%	0%	1%	2%
Commissions	0%	11%	0%	8%	0%	8%
Net interest and dividends	1%	8%	1%	7%	0%	9%
Asset management, Securities services	45%	30%	35%	26%	40%	26%
Fees	41%	21%	32%	19%	36%	19%
Commissions	4%	7%	4%	6%	4%	6%
Net interest and dividends	0%	1%	0%	1%	0%	1%
Net revenue ($ millions)	$1,166	$19,127	$1,183	$20,857	$1,274	$23,765

of the total) derived from securities underwriting and commissions, and trading profits associated with principal transactions.[29]

At the end of 2004, Lazard had 2,584 employees, of whom 207 were managing directors: these were about ten times the levels reported during the 1970s. The firm's 2004 year-end capitalization of $982 million was modest by industry standards, but substantially greater than the constant $17.5 million reported from 1957 until at least the late 1970s. The apparent capital growth is misleading, however, as the earlier figures vastly understated the personal resources of the firm's partners, which, when necessary, were brought to bear on the opportunities facing the firm.

Table 1.7 shows the contribution of each functional area to net revenues for both Morgan Stanley and Lazard Freres for the years

[29] The restructuring plan associated with the IPO provided for separation of these businesses from the firm's ongoing corporate advisory and asset management businesses.

2002–4.[30] The contribution from investment banking to Lazard's net revenue ranged from 47 to 60 percent, and virtually the whole of this came from advisory services, rather than underwriting. In contrast, investment banking operations accounted for only 12 to 14 percent of Morgan Stanley's net revenue, with the bulk of the contribution arising from underwriting fees. The corresponding figures for trading and principal investment are very different. Lazard generates very little revenue from these activities.[31] The largest fraction of Morgan Stanley's revenues comes from trading and principal investment, with the bulk of this figure being accounted for by the firm's proprietary trading operations. Finally, on a relative basis, asset management and securities services are far more central to Lazard's revenues than they are to Morgan Stanley although, on an absolute basis, Morgan Stanley's 2004 $6.2 billion revenue in asset management and securities services far outstripped the $514 million posted by Lazard in the same area.

The clear implication of these figures is that Morgan Stanley is now very much committed to complementing human capital-intensive businesses with a significant presence in financial capital-intensive businesses.[32] Lazard Freres remains centered upon the human capital-based advisory businesses that enabled the industry to operate with relatively small levels of financial capital prior to the 1980s. Although Lazard's recent public offering is perhaps best understood as a mechanism for transferring control from the firm's founding family and a small group of partners of long standing (led by Michel David-Weill) to a new generation of bankers led by Wasserstein, it occurred at a time when other prominent advisory boutiques have either gone public (e.g. Greenhill and Thomas Weisel) or have sold significant private equity stakes to outsiders (e.g. Houlihan, Lokey, and Zukin) in pursuit of large and permanent infusions of financial capital. The boutique firms coexist with full-service banks that combine advisory services

[30] The contributions do not always sum to 100 percent because we have excluded credit services (for Morgan Stanley) and marginal revenue sources that do not fit within our functional classification scheme. Lazard figures are reported in the firm's S-1 filing with the SEC. The comparable figures for Morgan Stanley are reported in the firm's annual report to shareholders.

[31] Although, in the past, Lazard partners routinely invested their own capital (as opposed to that assigned explicitly to the partnership) in deals for which they advised.

[32] Morgan Stanley's capital dependence is further evidenced by the substantial VaR figure reported above. The firm's most recent quarterly report indicated an average VaR of $84 million, up slightly from the previous quarter.

with the ability to make significant financial capital commitments. At the end of the book we speculate as to how this competition is likely to unfold.

CONCLUSION

Securities markets are an important source of funds for corporations and entrepreneurs. Operations in these markets are intermediated by investment banks: the purpose of this book is to provide an economic rationale for their existence. This chapter has set the scene for this discussion by outlining the main activities of a modern investment bank. We have highlighted some of the themes to which we refer repeatedly throughout the book: the importance of investment banks in stimulating information production and exchange; the central role of reputation in underpinning investment banker activities; the traditional importance to investment bankers of human capital and relationships; and the impact that computerization and codification of many investment banking practices has had in the last three decades upon the composition and the operation of the investment banking sector.

The remainder of the book is organized as follows. In the next two chapters we provide a theoretical explanation for the investment banks as a coordinator of a marketplace for information. This places investment banks squarely within the broader literature on financial intermediation, and points to the importance of the political and legal environment for the operation of investment banks.

With the theory in place we examine in the following four chapters the evolution of the investment-banking industry from its origins in the eighteenth-century North Atlantic trade. This analysis serves two purposes. First, examining the successes and failures of investment banks under a variety of legal, political, and technological regimes helps us to a deeper understanding of the investment bank's role in resolving problems in the exchange of information. Second, the historical evolution of investment banks gives us a number of examples against which we can evaluate our theory.

The final section of the book provides an analysis of the industry's current structure and performance, and offers some informed speculation regarding its future evolution.

2

Institutional Theory

The capitalist system of production derives its potency from the absence of a central planner who allocates resources to productive activities, and distributes output. Instead, individuals allocate resources as they see fit, and they bargain over the returns from their activities. The state is restricted to an enabling role.

For a number of reasons, the decentralized capitalist approach has proved more efficient than the alternatives. First, individuals understand their goals and desires better than anyone else, and hence will be better able to judge whether a particular allocation will most effectively meet their objectives. Second, when people believe that their income is directly related to their effort, they are more likely to work hard. Third, a state-controlled central planner may well be less concerned with the well-being of its citizens than with some other, purely political, motive.

A fourth reason, which proves particularly important in this book, relates to the importance of situation-specific information in economic decision-making. This includes not only information about the quality and quantity of available physical goods, but also about the abilities and motivations of the interested parties, and their willingness to participate. As Hayek (1945) famously observed, a central planner could never cope with the immense volume of information that would be required to make every decision centrally. Furthermore, much of the required information is privately held, and it may be difficult to persuade individuals to part with it. Even if parted with, it may be nuanced and impossible to record systematically.

Many of these problems can be avoided by giving individuals the ability to act upon their own initiative when allocating resources. An agent who is less able to use an asset than another will transfer it by selling it at a price that reflects its usefulness elsewhere. Agents whose local knowledge and expertise leads them to believe that they can use an asset efficiently will reflect this information by paying to use the asset. And agents who believe that their income is directly related to their efforts will tend to work harder.

Economic self-determination is therefore efficient.[1] It is not however ubiquitous. In this chapter, we discuss the social artifacts upon which economic self-determination rests. We argue that the main requirement is a system of *property rights*, which allows people to establish control over assets and to sell this control to others. The artifacts that support a system of property rights are called *institutions*. The institutions in successful capitalist economies are able to assign property rights in complex ways.

While some of these institutions may be state-supplied, many will not be. Non-state institutions often support relational contracts in settings where it would be cost-prohibitive or impossible for state-supplied institutions to adjudicate and enforce explicit contracts. Trade in informational assets is especially challenging to a system of state-enforced explicit contracts. We argue in the next chapter that investment banks evolved as non-state institutions to support this type of trade; in the ensuing four chapters, we trace this evolution in detail.

PROPERTY RIGHTS, INSTITUTIONS, AND THE STATE

Property Rights

We start by defining property rights. There are of course several definitions already. Ours focuses upon institutions that support decentralized decision-making in complex and advanced capitalist economies. We regard property rights as the central device in capitalist economies, and our definition reflects this assumption.

Property rights are concerned with access to *assets*. In general, assets are objects whose allocation is economically important. An asset could be a physical object, such as a building or a field, but it need not be: the control of patents is economically important, but they represent intellectual, rather than physical, property. A more subtle example, which is important in this book, is price-relevant information about productive processes. Since such information affects investment incentives, its allocation among financial capitalists is important.

We define two components of an agent's *property rights* over an asset. The first describes how the agent is entitled to employ the asset

---

[1] Many authors have argued that it is morally superior, too: for example, see Nozick (1974).

or its by-products. The second describes how such entitlements can be transferred to other agents.[2]

This definition is widely applicable. A crude system of property rights would bundle together all of the entitlements associated with an asset. Acquisition of any of the entitlements could then be accomplished only by purchasing the entire asset. This is the type of property right which most people have over their cars: while the right to drive a car after noon is logically distinct from the right to drive it before noon, the two are usually packaged together. Efficiency might be well served by a system that enabled separation of these property rights. Indeed, many taxicab drivers in Oxford have established such dual property rights over their vehicles in order to maximize the aggregate return to the vehicle and the associated taxi license.

More mature and subtle systems of property rights enable partitioning and assignment of the entitlements to an asset among many agents. For example, the simplest assignment of title to the income stream generated by a loan or a portfolio of loans involves a single purchaser. More advanced systems of property rights enable multiple investors to (say) establish distinct rights over the first 80 percent of coupon repayments, over the next ten percent, and over the (riskiest) final ten percent. This type of property right has recently been established through the creation of a market for collateralized loan obligations. Much of modern financial economic theory rests on the assumption that complex cash flow property right assignments are feasible. This justifies the use of arbitrage-free approaches to security valuation, which rely upon the assumption that the sum of the values of (familiar) disaggregated cash flow streams is the same as the value of their (unfamiliar and possibly very complex) sum.

We define a *contract* to be a binding agreement under which property right entitlements are transferred between two agents. An agent's ability to write contracts therefore forms a part of his property rights.

---

[2] The things that are the basis for property rights in law are defined in a more narrow (and more precise) fashion. An excellent discussion of this topic is provided by Penner (1997: ch. 5). Legal property rights are the subject of things first whose association with an owner is *contingent*: that is, they are separable from the person who holds them, who must therefore be able to prove that he does (i.e. to establish title); and second for which the asset could equally belong to anyone. We argue in this book for a broader conception of property rights that includes items to which title cannot easily be established, and which are sometimes very hard to alienate. To be sure, these things cannot be the basis of a legal contract. It is precisely this observation which leads us to our discussion of extra-legal institutions, and ultimately, to our theory of the investment bank.

Our definition of contract is wide-ranging. It covers _any_ agreement under which rights are effectively transferred. It therefore includes arrangements which cannot be enforced in a court, either because they are hard to prove before a third party, or because the court would refuse to enforce them. Indeed, many of the agreements which we refer to in this book as contractual are not recognized as such under the law.[3]

While a contract could conceivably be a binding promise to transfer an entitlement in the future without payment,[4] contracts in general involve the exchange of one property right for another. The simplest exchanges involve the exchange of rights over physical assets: for example, an exchange of a lawn mower for a chain saw, or the exchange of a chair for cash. Such exchanges are easy to identify and to enforce.

Most financial contracts are less simple. At least one of the parties is generally exchanging a nontrivial property right. For example, a financial capitalist might exchange property rights over his capital (easily defined, when it takes the form of cash) for property rights over part of the income stream that an entrepreneur generates using the capital. A more complex exchange might involve an exchange of human capital[5] for the same property rights over the income stream.

---

[3] If they are to be recognized by the law, contracts require explicit _offer_ and _acceptance_ by the counterparties, and it must be possible to demonstrate that the contracting parties intended to create legal relations. For a contract to be legally binding, it must be supported by _consideration_: in other words, a party must receive compensation for obligations assumed under the agreement. See Beatson (2002: 32–50, 69–72, 88–111).

[4] Such an agreement would not be recognized as a contract under Anglo-US law, where promises have contractual force only if the promisor receives some form of _consideration_ in exchange for his or her commitment (see n 3 above). This requirement has been criticized by liberal legal scholars such as Fried (1981), who argue that contracts should be regarded as promises between agents who are sovereign over their own property. Fried argues that such a promise is morally binding and hence should be enforceable. In arguing that allocative efficiency, and hence welfare, is raised by enabling agents to make whichever commitments they like, we arrive at the same conclusion for slightly different reasons.

[5] Again, from a purely legal perspective this is a problematic example. In law, an agent's property rights over his own time are restricted, because he is prevented by statute from selling himself into servitude (see the discussion on p. 43). This reflects a difference in approaches to property rights: from our perspective, an agent has property rights over his time, and these include a statement about their alienability. Naturally, it is harder to contract upon human capital than upon a bottle of wine. This does not prevent anyone from selling some of his labor time for a year, with a right imposed by statute on his side to withdraw it at will, and with corresponding rights (insofar as these are not restricted by labor law) on the employer side to break the contract at will.

An example of the former transaction is a share purchase: of the latter, an employment contract under which a manager is paid entirely in shares or share options.

Institutions

Property rights are not in general the result of a positive system of design. They are however a social idea and hence their enforcement mechanisms are man-made. Throughout this book, we refer to the mechanisms that enforce property rights as *institutions*.

We have argued that property rights are useful because they facilitate the devolved decision-making upon which capitalist economies rely. Such decision-making is efficient because it allows individuals to make the most of their knowledge of local conditions, and to apportion the returns from productive activity in such a way as to provide the most effective incentives to all of the involved parties. In the absence of well-functioning property right institutions, assets are likely to be allocated inefficiently, and entrepreneurial activity will be either suppressed or misdirected.[6]

In the light of this discussion, we therefore define institutions to be *strong* or *weak* according to the number of entitlements that individuals have, and their freedom to transfer those entitlements.[7] We sometimes refer to strong or weak property right systems: by this, we mean economies with strong and weak institutions, respectively.

The freedom to transfer entitlements is closely bound up with the ability to make commitments. For example, an entrepreneur might wish to attract capital by contracting to return to investors 90 percent of the returns that their capital generates under her management. After receiving investors' capital on these terms, the entrepreneur might be tempted to understate the returns generated by her project,

---

[6] De Soto (2000) presents evidence which suggests that African development has lagged that of the West in large part because an inability to establish title over assets has undermined entrepreneurial activity. A massive literature, which is too large to cite in full, documents the importance of well-functioning property rights institutions for economic development. See, for example, North (1977), North and Thomas (1973), North (1983), Acemoglu, Johnson, and Robinson (2002), Acemoglu, Johnson, and Robinson (2005), Acemoglu, Johnson, and Robinson (2001), Acemoglu and Robinson (2000), Besley (1995), Knack and Keefer (1995), Mauro (1995), Johnson, McMillan, and Woodruff (2002a, 2002b), Rodrick, Subramanian, and Trebbi (2002), Field (1991), and Davis and North (1971).

[7] This clearly relates to the quality of legal enforcement, also. We discuss the court system on page 45 below. Barzel (1997: 3) builds it into his definition of property rights, which includes the stream of benefits that an agent can expect to earn from his possession of an asset. This expected income is clearly reduced by a poor legal system.

and to keep the difference. If she cannot be prevented from doing so then her commitment is worth no more than paper on which it is written. This type of commitment problem undermines the entrepreneur's ability to transfer her property rights over the fruits of her economic activity, and hence characterizes a weak institutional environment. In contrast, strong institutions enable such contractual commitments and hence increase economic activity.[8]

The State

Since the state has monopoly access to the force required to enforce entitlements, it is a central institution. Although some authors[9] have argued that society can exist without a state, in practice, as North (1990: 14) has noted, 'we do not observe political anarchy in high-income countries'. A state that stands ready to enforce contracts strengthens the institutional environment. In so doing it enables commitments of the type discussed in the previous section, and so raises welfare.

Nevertheless, it is well understood that the state can weaken institutions, too. This can happen in two main ways. First, the state may use its legal force to confiscate assets.[10] This may happen when self-interested legislators respond to interest group pressure; it may equally reflect a selfless desire to engineer an equal wealth distribution. In either case, a rapacious state undermines institutions and diminishes the strength of property rights. The basic fear that assets will be confiscated in an unpredictable way weakens the entitlements of their nominal owners, and therefore reduces their ability and their incentives to allocate them effectively.[11]

Straightforward state theft is relatively uncommon in the developed world. Heavy redistributive taxation is not. Taxation is (mostly) predictable: its effect is to ensure that certain of the returns from an asset cannot be contractually apportioned between individuals. Hence, even when assets are deployed in a way that avoids taxation,

---

[8] North (1993) stresses the importance of institutions in facilitating credible commitment.

[9] See in particular Friedman (1974).

[10] That a despotic or authoritarian state can impede economic progress by undermining property rights is well documented: see, for example, Acemoglu, Robinson, and Thierry (2004) and Sen (1999).

[11] As Harold Demsetz (1967: 347) says, 'Property rights are an instrument of society and derive their significance from the fact that they help a man form those expectations which he can reasonably hold in his dealings with others.'

the possibility that they may be taxed undermines property rights as we have defined them.

The second way that the state can undermine institutions and so weaken property rights has received less attention from economists. Without attempting directly to tax individuals, the state can legislate to prevent certain types of entitlements from existing at all, or to prevent certain types of contract from being written. For example, many seventeenth-century migrants from the United Kingdom to America paid their way by entering into indentured servitude: they sold their labor for a period of years to an employer in the New World. Although it appears to have been a rational response to problems in the markets for labor and capital,[12] indentured servitude is now outlawed in both the United States and the United Kingdom.

In abolishing indentured servitude, the state undermined an agent's property rights over his own person. The abolition decision reflected a number of social and philosophical arguments against indenture. The state's role was therefore *purposive*: rather than simply providing a framework within which devolved decision-making could occur, it attempted to shape social outcomes. A purposive state need not engage in direct distributional manipulation: it can simply alter social structures and norms so as to prevent certain actions and contracts, and to encourage others. Michael Atiyah (1979) argues that the state has in the last two hundred years moved increasingly from a neutral facilitating role to a more purposive one. Michael Oakshott (1975) characterizes this movement, as we have done, toward a view of the state as an 'enterprise association': that is, toward a coordinating body which serves a purpose.

Our argument is that strong institutions leave individuals with as much freedom as possible to exploit their assets, to create property rights over them, and to pass those rights on. Hence, when it acts either rapaciously or purposively, the state undermines property rights. This happens because it restricts the ability to establish entitlements to assets and to their by-products, and because it restricts the transfer of those rights. Strong institutions as we have defined them facilitate individual discovery and economic progress. They may come at a social cost, and if it is excessive then the state may indeed have a role as an enterprise association. This should not however blind us to the fact that state interference has the potential to undermine

---

[12] See Galenson (1984) for a review of the historical evidence and a careful economic analysis of indentured servitude.

property rights, even when it does not involve direct taxation and wealth transfer.[13]

At this stage, we pause to examine some of the existing institutional literature in the light of our discussion. Possibly the most influential recent writing about institutions is by Douglass C. North. In his 1994 Nobel lecture, North states that 'Institutions are the humanly devised constraints that structure human interaction.' In other words, institutions are rules for social living. Some of these may be passed down from the legislature and be formally enforced; others may be embedded in language and culture. Much of North's work is concerned with the interaction between organizations and institutions, and the way that this interaction affects the development over time. North argues that institutional development is path-dependent, and that it need not be entirely rational. Since institutions have such a significant effect upon social interaction, we cannot understand the evolution of economies, and the reasons for economic success and failure, without understanding the institutional arena within which economic activity unfolds.

Like us, North is concerned with the social, technological, and economic factors that drive institutional evolution. North also emphasizes the importance of property rights and contract to economic development. But, unlike us, he does not place property rights at the center of his discussion. We define property rights to include the extent to which transfer of entitlements is possible, and we identify institutions completely with the strength of property rights. Hence North's claim (1994: 361) that 'It is the polity that defines and enforces property rights' is only partially true in our framework.[14] *Any* agent who has an entitlement to an asset, and who can freely transfer that entitlement, has property rights over it. This is true even when his rights cannot be established and enforced in a court: in this case, his rights are established not by the polity, but by a private mechanism. Indeed, we argue below that private property rights institutions are

---

[13] Mnookin and Kornhauser (1979: 980–4) highlight a particular example of this in the context of divorce. If the law assigns all decisions over child access to one party in a divorce, it prevents the parties to the divorce from coming to equitable arrangements themselves. This will result in outcomes which are inferior from the perspective of both the parents and the child.

[14] One context in which the state must define property rights is when it apportions public goods (such as wild animals or publicly owned land) to private individuals (such as hunters or farmers). The mechanisms that it uses to do so have a significant effect upon social outcomes: see Alchian and Demsetz (1973), Anderson and Hill (1975), and Anderson and Hill (1990).

frequently a response to attempts by a purposive state to restrict property rights.

In more recent work, Acemoglu and Johnson (2005) distinguish between 'property rights institutions', which constrain asset expropriation by governmental elites, and 'contracting institutions', which support private contracts, by which they mean written transfer agreements that can be legally enforced. As defined in their work, Acemoglu and Johnson find that property rights institutions have a strong effect upon economic success or failure, while contracting institutions have no significant additional effect.

Acemoglu and Johnson start from a view of institutions as 'the social, economic, legal, and political organization of a society', while we start from the primacy of a broad conception of property rights. In the context of our definition, widespread asset appropriation is necessarily evidence of weak institutions. In contrast, a lack of formal contracting mechanisms need not be, because the private sector institutions may evolve to take their place. Acemoglu and Johnson confirm that this occurs. In fact, we argue that to the extent that a formal legal code in a purposive state rules out certain types of contract, it may evidence weaker institutions than a minimal system for formal contracting which leaves room for private sector innovation.

We turn now to the operation of non-state property rights institutions.

NON-STATE INSTITUTIONS

The Courts

The state is an important institution. However, when it is a monopoly institution, it will be a weak one. This of course does not imply that the state itself is weak: on the contrary, it is the strength that the state derives from a monopoly right to define property rights that undermines them. This is partly because politicians have such strong incentives to prey upon some sections of the population in order to attract the support of others, but even in the absence of predatory behavior property rights are weakened when the state has a monopoly over property-right specification. The (rather implausible) state which aims selflessly to maximize welfare by acting as an enterprise association will of necessity interfere with the free transfer of assets, and the exercise of economic initiative. This weakens property rights, and we have argued that in so doing, it will undermine economic efficiency.

It follows that a strong institutional framework must incorporate a non-state-intermediated means of establishing and transferring property rights. Provided it serves to undermine state predation, the exact form of the alternative institution is not necessarily important. Indeed, Acemoglu and Johnson's work (2005) is supportive of the thesis that, provided the state cannot simply steal assets, the precise mechanism by which they are transferred is not particularly important.

Notwithstanding these observations, the most important mechanism for establishing entitlements and transferring them is the court system. In the contractual context we divide the courts' functions into two categories, although there is some overlap between the two. The first function is *enforcement*. The courts enforce statutory contractual legislation (for example, prohibiting certain types of contract), and they enforce private bilateral contracts. Within the boundaries established by legislation, the courts act independently of the state, although they rely upon the support of the state to enforce their decisions.

The relationship between the state and the courts is central. A strong court system upon which individuals can rely for enforcement enhances their ability to commit to economic contracts, and hence strengthens property rights and increases economic efficiency.[15] However, the state has a natural tendency arbitrarily to interfere in the operations of the courts in response to political exigencies. However noble its motives, in doing so it will weaken property rights and ultimately, welfare.[16] In a strong institutional environment, the state's rapaciousness is ultimately checked by the law, which places limits upon the legislature's actions.[17]

If the only role of the courts was enforcement, it would be hard to understand why contracting parties ever went to court. If the outcome of a case was predictable, then they would avoid the costs of litigation by simply agreeing to settle outside the court.[18] Indeed, most technical

---

[15] We argue in n. 23 below that the effectiveness of the court in enforcing contracts depends upon the damages standard which it adopts. From a purely institutional perspective, expectation damages appear to be most efficient.

[16] This is hardly a fresh insight. Hume (1777: 375) famously argued that 'Public utility requires that property should be regulated by general inflexible rules', and that an inevitable consequence of this is that laws 'deprive, without scruple, a beneficent man of all of his possessions, if acquired by mistake, without a good title; in order to bestow them on a selfish miser who has already heaped up immense stores of superfluous riches'.

[17] See the discussion on page 59.

[18] This is not to say that courts would be irrelevant. The anticipated costs of litigation have an effect upon incentives to break contracts: as MacLeod (2006) notes,

economics assumes, either implicitly or explicitly, that legal actions will not occur: this is one of the important distinctions between legal and economic contract scholarship.[19]

So when parties know in advance how the courts will behave in every state of the world, bargaining in the shadow of the courts should prevent court actions from ever occurring. In practice though, contracts do not cover every possible contingency: in the real world, the parties to a contract cannot enumerate every possible state of the world and specify precisely the actions that they will take in each state.[20] In other words, contracts are inevitably incomplete.[21]

Incomplete contracts are the subject of an important microeconomic literature.[22] In most of this literature, the parties to a contract are unable for technological reasons to record their response to an event, although they appreciate that it is likely to be important. At a later stage agreement on the uncontracted contingency becomes

the standards required by a contract have to be high enough to ensure that it is worth going to court for enforcement. Djankov, la Porta et al. (2003) show that court costs vary greatly across jurisdictions, and argue that they are inefficiently high in developing countries. A theoretical literature examines the effects of court verification costs upon the behavior of contracting parties: see, for example, Townsend (1978) and Gale and Hellwig (1985).

[19] The costs of litigation can be used to explain 'nuisance suits', brought by one party in the hope that the other will settle (see, for example, Bebchuk, 1988). Court litigation may then be an attempt to establish a reputation which will protect against such suits. This still leaves the majority of court actions unexplained.

[20] Indeed, in cases where they expect to rely upon non-court intermediated contracts, they may choose not to do so. See the discussion of reputational contracting on page 52.

[21] According to Schwartz (1992), even a contract which provides clear rules governing the interaction between the parties can be incomplete if its terms do not vary with the state of the world. Hence, a fixed price supply contract could be deemed incomplete if it fails to specify price variations in states of the world where one party makes or loses an unusually large amount of money. Schwartz shows that the courts will often complete these contracts, provided they can do so through the application of a general rule which can be used in future cases. This is a subtle point. A contract which the courts can complete in this sense could have been completed *ex ante* by the contacting parties. That they did not is probably evidence of intent: as we noted on page 58, and Schwartz acknowledges on page 317, even when it is motivated by efficiency concerns *ex post* legal activism can be *ex ante* inefficient. As Schwartz states, in some cases such activism reflects a wider social goal. From our perspective, whether it is motivated by *ex post* efficiency or by social concerns, court alteration of contracts with unambiguous consequences undermines property rights and hence reflects weaker institutions. See the discussion of the purposive State on page 43.

[22] See, for example, Bolton and Scharfstein (1990), Grossman and Hart (1986), Hart and Moore (1995), Hart and Moore (1989), Hart and Moore (1988), Hart and Moore (1990), and Hart and Moore (1994). Hart (1995) provides a clear survey of the major ideas.

possible, and the parties bargain over their actions. The bargaining is anticipated up front and, to the extent that agents will be forced in bargaining to share the fruits of their labors, they are less willing to work hard.

The economic literature on incomplete contracts has advanced our understanding of the dynamics of contracting relationships, of the efficiency consequences of incomplete contracts, and of the consequences of contractual incompleteness for industry structure. But, in common with the economic literature on complete contracts, it assigns no active role to the courts: agents always anticipate in these models the results of court enforcement, and they bargain in the shadow of the court to obtain agreement, without ever entering into litigation.

In reality, bargaining of this type is stymied by genuine disagreement over the meaning of a contract, and hence over the likely actions of the courts. In these situations, litigation may be the best way to resolve a dispute. The second role of the courts is therefore to *interpret* ambiguous or incomplete contracts, and it is this which explains costly court actions.

How should a court interpret an ambiguous contract? Strong institutions facilitate the free exchange of property rights, and in particular, they allow agents to assume binding commitments.[23] Hence, their decisions should not overrule the freely expressed will of the contracting parties at the time of contracting. When it is not clear from contract documentation what this was, the courts should attempt as far as possible to divine it.[24] This might be accomplished through the

---

[23] This discussion is related to a debate in the legal contracting literature: namely, what level of compensation should the courts require when a contract is broken? The law distinguishes between *expectation* damages, under which the promisee receives compensation for what would have been received under the promise; *reliance* damages, in line with harm or costs caused by the broken promise; and *benefit* damages, where the promisor pays the benefits received from breaking the promise. Scholars who interpret contracts in the liberal tradition as promises tend to argue morally for expectation damages (Fried, 1981); others, who argue that contracts reflect socially sanctioned modes of behavior, make a case for reliance and benefit damages (Atiyah, 1979). Of course, it is cheaper to break a promise when one faces only reliance or benefit damages. Since we argue that strong property rights require agents to be able to make credible long-term commitments, we suggest that expectation damages are a feature of strong institutions, and that benefit and reliance damages are in general associated with weak institutions.

[24] Schwartz (1992: 271 n. 8) discusses this process. In a strong property rights environment, the courts base their decisions on what the parties probably expect of each other. As Schwartz notes, this is distinct from a decision based upon 'reasonable expectations', which is normative phrase, reflecting a view of how people *ought* to behave, rather than how they *do*. See also the discussion on page 191 of contract interpretation.

interpretation of a legal code to which the parties had access; or it might simply reflect the assessment that a reasonable and neutral third party would make. The latter approach is the essence of the common law approach to contracting which prevails in the United States and the United Kingdom. The common law uses social mores to adjudicate over uncontracted outcomes for which legislation does not exist. At least in theory,[25] the court's role in the common law is therefore to discover the law, rather than to create it.[26]

So the courts have two roles: enforcement and interpretation. The court's enforcement role relies upon the cooperation of the state. In strong systems that are governed by the rule of law, the mere existence of the courts will be sufficient to preclude their use for enforcement when contractual meaning is clear. The courts therefore act, and their design therefore only matters, when an incomplete contract requires interpretation. In short, the structure of the courts matters because contracts are incomplete.

The enforcement activity of the courts is logically prior to their interpretation role. To see why, imagine that the courts were unable effectively to enforce agreements, or that in doing so they made completely arbitrary and unpredictable decisions. In this case, the parties to a contested contract would not use the courts to intermediate over incomplete or contested contracts: if neither believed that the courts were reasonable, neither could expect the court to uphold his interpretation. In this case the courts would never be used for enforcement, or for interpretation. The irrelevance of weak courts would not reflect contractual completeness: either a private sector alternative to the courts would arise or, more likely, economic activity would be greatly curtailed. The interpretative role of the courts therefore rests upon their legitimacy and effectiveness as an enforcement mechanism.

Our attempts to explain the importance of court structure are related to seminal work performed by Coase (1960), who discussed the role of institutions as devices for allocating property rights and costs. Coase argues that when property rights are clearly assigned

[25] Legal positivists dismiss this as a fiction, claiming that laws are commands which reflect conscious decisions made by judges, sovereigns or legislatures. Two important works in this vein are Austin ([1832] 1995) and Hart ([1961] 1997). Oliver Wendell Holmes' contribution to this school of thought is discussed on page 191.

[26] Hayek (1973) argues that property right institutions under the common law reflect tried and tested social mores and customs and that they are valuable because they codify existing practices, whose successes we can seldom adequately explain. His work suggests a possible bridge between North's emphasis (1990) upon social and cultural rules, and our concentration upon property rights.

and bargaining is costless, economic actors will always agree upon the welfare-maximizing course of action. He concludes that the assignment of property rights is important only when bargaining is impeded. This observation was captured in Stigler's famous (1966) formulation of the 'Coase Theorem': in the absence of transactions costs, institutions are not important.[27]

Demsetz (2003) criticizes the Coasian emphasis upon transactions costs, arguing that they should not be distinguished from other types of economic costs: property right assignments are an endogenous response to *all* relevant economic effects, and singling out transactions costs for special attention is appropriate only insofar as state actors have an advantage in resolving them. Hence, like us, Demsetz is concerned with the property rights institutions that support a particular allocation of economic resources, rather than with the costs of agreeing to performing a transfer between agents.

The courts affect economic outcomes either when they are ineffective or in some way circumscribed, or when contracts are incomplete. In either case, agents can be expected to search for extra-legal mechanisms to establish and to trade property rights. This is the primary function that we identify with the modern investment bank and, at a more general level, it is the subject of the next subsection.

Extra-Legal Institutions

Many forms of property rights are secured if the courts operate in a predictable fashion and without the interference of the state. Sometimes, however, the courts may be politically undermined: they may have little ability to make nuanced judgments, or they may be prevented from enforcing some contracts. Equally, the courts may be undermined by technological limitations. For example, it may be impossible to establish rights to some assets, such as the price-relevant information in which investment banks deal, because they lose their value as soon as they are publicly revealed. Entrepreneurs whose ability to contract is reduced for political or technical reasons will naturally attempt to create alternative, private sector, property rights

---

[27] It seems that Coase regrets the ubiquity of his eponymous theorem. He argues (Coase, 1988: ch. 6) that mainstream economists have been misled by a poor understanding of the Coase theorem into assuming that institutional structure does not affect economic outcomes.

institutions for themselves. It is to these 'private law' institutions that we now turn.

We illustrate the importance of extra-legal institutions with an example which is a response to extreme contractual incompleteness. When several people decide to combine their skills in a productive activity, they may be unsure before they begin precisely what proportion of their time will be devoted to their various tasks. Similarly, it will be hard for them to predict which customers they will attract, to whom they will sell their product, and which of them will be responsible for the relationships. They will be aware that at some stage an unforeseen opportunity may arise, but they clearly will not know what it will be, and they will not anticipate its effects upon their working relationship.

In this situation, it is clearly unreasonable to expect the productive relationship to be governed by a formal contract. The people concerned will make minimal legal commitments, and they will commit to respect some non-contractual mechanism for making decisions. This type of arrangement is common: we usually refer to it as a *firm*. Coase (1937) first recognized that the firm is a natural response to contracting problems.[28] Although firms have a legal existence, and their actions are to some extent circumscribed by statute,[29] within the boundaries set by the law agents are free when they create a firm to adopt whichever authority structures they choose. In this sense, every corporation is a web of extra-legal contracts, and the corporation is therefore an extra-legal institution.

How does the corporation perform its enforcement role? We have already noted the demise of indentured servitude contracts: in their absence, the firm cannot compel an employee to act against her wishes. Similarly, it cannot imprison an employee. In fact, the employer's only sanction is to deny the employee something. The simplest way to do this is to fire her; a more subtle one is to deny her promotion. These sanctions impose a cost upon the employee whose severity varies depending upon circumstance. Firing an employee

---

[28] Coase was ahead of his time. His work spawned a related literature from the late 1960s: see Alchian and Demsetz (1972), Williamson (1985), Jensen and Meckling (1976), and Cheung (1983).

[29] By sinking costs to create standardized and predictable corporate law, the State probably facilitates the creation of the private property structures. Of course, there is a countervailing tendency to interfere for the usual reasons in corporate laws, as in others. This topic is important, but it is beyond the scope of this book.

is costly when she will struggle to find an equally attractive job;[30] denying her promotion is costly when she cannot get it elsewhere.[31]

When an employee subjects herself to the extra-legal authority of the firm she relies upon the firm to keep promises to which it is not legally bound. Why does she trust the firm to reward her for keeping her side of the bargain, and to punish her only when she does not? The answer is at the heart of extra-legal contracting: the parties to extra-legal contracts rely upon their *reputations*. The employee will only trust a firm which has in the past kept its promises. Firms that renege upon their promises cannot expect in the future to be trusted, and so will lose their ability to contract without the courts. To the extent that extra-legal contracts are necessary in its business, this harms the firm.

Hence extra-legal contracts are credible to the extent that it is costly to break them.[32] The costs of reneging upon an agreement are often reputational. They therefore rely upon a future stream of reputation-intensive business: if technological or legal advances lower the importance of reputation, reputationally enforced extra-legal contracts are more difficult to enforce.[33]

Reputations are created and maintained in the context of a repeated trading relationship. Such relationships are usually characterized by a mixture of formal legal contracting, and informal extra-legal relational contracts. Stewart Macaulay (1963) interviewed key business personnel and legal counsel for a number of (mostly Wisconsin) companies to document this type of relationship. He found that in the context of long-term continuing relationships, businessmen frequently committed themselves to significant exchanges quite casually.[34] Since it

---

[30] So the firm might optimally choose to pay the employee more than her outside option so as to add potency to the threat of dismissal. See Shapiro and Stiglitz (1984) and Stiglitz (1987).

[31] This is a central idea in informationally opaque businesses such as investment banks. See Morrison and Wilhelm (2004), Morrison and Wilhelm (2005*b*), and chapter nine.

[32] The classic economic exposition of extra-legal contracting underwritten by repeated trade is due to Klein and Leffler (1981). They show that contractual performance in a purely bilateral trading relationship requires prices to be far enough above cost.

[33] See the discussion on page 58, and also the discussion of Bankers Trust on page 246 in chapter eight.

[34] 'For example, in Wisconsin requirements contracts—contracts to supply a firm's requirements of an item rather than a definite quantity—probably are not legally enforceable. [Of the people quizzed about this] none thought that the lack of legal sanction made any difference. Three of these people were house counsel who knew the Wisconsin law before being interviewed' (Macaulay, 1963: 60).

is costly and difficult to write formal contracts, this was probably a cheaper and more precise way to deal. For example, the counterparts to these deals appear to have benefitted from a high degree of flexibility.[35]

It seems clear from Macaulay's work that the contracts he studied were reputational.[36] The agreements concerned were part of a long-term relationship. If either party had lost its reputation for abiding by the spirit of the relationship, both would have had to fall back upon the law. This would have reduced the precision of the agreements between them, and would have imposed substantial costs upon both parties. In contrast, Macaulay found that carefully planned legal contracts were in practice used only for large one-off transactions (such as the sale of the Empire State Building), and for those in which bargaining power was extremely skewed. In both cases the costs of reneging on informal contracts might, for at least one party, have outweighed the reputational benefits of complying with them. The parties thus fell back upon formal legal processes.

Interestingly, Macaulay's findings suggest that parties *prefer* where possible to use extra-legal contracts, rather than to rely upon the courts. Litigation is a last resort, and it is evidence of a breakdown in relational contracting. This point is developed by Macneil (1974, 1978), who points to the inevitable incompleteness of long-term contracts. As he argues, reputationally enforced norms of behavior are a far more effective basis for an economic relationship than a series of discrete contracts based upon classical contract law.

Given the importance of repeat business to reputationally enforced contracts, it appears at first blush that their effectiveness must be limited to bilateral economic relations with frequent and extended interactions. If a large firm expects to deal with a customer only once, it will face an overwhelming temptation to break the implicit agreements between them. But this is true only if the reputation that it has with one counterpart is not transferable to others; if in ripping off one customer it damages its chances of dealing with others, the

[35] Macaulay's subjects were happy to break contracts, and did so frequently: 'all ten of the purchasing agents asked about cancellation of orders once placed indicated that they expected to be able to cancel orders freely subject to only an obligation to pay for the seller's major expenses such as scrapped steel' (Macaulay, 1963: 61).

[36] He expands upon this point in a later article (Macaulay, 1985: 468): 'People in business often find that they do not need contract planning and contract law because of relational sanctions. There are effective private governments and social fields, affected by but seldom controlled by the formal legal system.'

firm will be more circumspect in its dealings with small and relatively insignificant customers.

Complex exchanges that rely upon implicit agreements are possible only if the counterparties can rely upon the reputational mechanisms which enforce them. It is therefore in the firm's interests (and society's) to find some way of extending the reach of its reputation as far as possible. This will be accomplished automatically if the firm's poor dealings with one counterpart are observable to others. For example, because the firm's employees form a close-knit group who observe one another's dealings with the firm, the firm's reputation as an honest employer is at risk whenever it deals with any of them. However, it may be harder for the firm's customers to see each other's dealings. This could reflect technological problems, such as geographic dispersion or an inability to document convincingly the details of their dealings with the firm; or it could be because proving malfeasance would require the release of commercially confidential information. In either case, the firm will struggle to build a single reputation with a sufficiently broad base of customers to sustain relational contracting.

The natural response to this problem is the professional body. A professional body that simply gathers information from customers and publicizes it automatically extends the reach of its members' reputations. In doing so, it enhances their ability to contract. A broad range of professional bodies may fill this role. For example, when information is commercially confidential, it may be necessary to gather it in secrecy and then simply formally to reprimand any miscreants. This is one of the functions of a self-regulatory organization. We relate it to the operation of the syndicate in chapter three.

Bernstein (1992, 2001) discusses the operation of professional bodies as noncourt contract enforcers in the diamond and the cotton industries, respectively. Her evidence is consistent with a role for the professional bodies as clearing houses for information. For example, she notes that failure to comply with a ruling of a cotton industry professional body results in expulsion from the body. This harms local and international business, not least because a firm expelled from a professional body is patently no longer bound by its rules. The associated costs are a sufficient threat to ensure compliance. Like Macaulay, Bernstein stresses the value of flexibility.[37] She stresses the importance of both social links between industry participants, and also of what

---

[37] For example, she states that 'although cotton industry trade rules and contracts provide clearly specified delivery times, it is understood that when making an adjustment is not too costly to the merchant, the adjustment will be made' (Bernstein, 2001: 23).

she refers to as 'information-intermediary based trust', which concerns formal methods for transmitting reputation information, such as circulars reporting the names of transactors who refused to arbitrate or to comply with an award against them. We identify a similar role for investment bank syndicates in chapter three.

Bernstein's evidence is contemporary. Milgrom, North, and Weingast (1990) argue that similar methods were employed in medieval Europe. They are concerned with the enforcement of contracts between agents who cannot call upon the law, who are very geographically dispersed, and for whom communication is very hard. They present a formal model which suggests that in this circumstance, a third party 'law merchant' can serve as a store of trader reputation. The law merchant maintains a database of information about traders, which they can access before transacting in exchange for a fee. The merchant fines agents who deal with counterparts against whom a judgment is outstanding, and records a failure to pay. Agents who paid up front for information revelation can take their disputes to the merchant for binding arbitration; failure to settle is recorded by the merchant. Milgrom, North, and Weingast show that with these rules, merchants will prefer to pay for access to the database, and will settle any judgments in order to avoid the costs of future lost business. They argue that this was effectively the system that governed the operation of the European Champagne fairs of the thirteenth century which dominated commercial activity in the entire Western world before the advent of the geographically dispersed nation-state.

The law merchant in Milgrom, North, and Weingast's work is the analog to the professional body which we analyzed above. By maintaining records about its counterparts, and providing access to them for a fee, it provides its members with a way of exposing their reputations in trade. Without this exposure, they would be unable to transact at all.

Greif, Milgrom, and Weingast (1994) examine another medieval example of a professional body. Between the tenth and fourteenth centuries, traveling European merchants found it hard to enforce the contracts that they wrote with the rulers of the cities and states in which they operated. Greif, Milgrom, and Weingast give several examples of merchants who were cheated, or even attacked. Trade in the absence of formal international law would therefore have been impossible without a system of private enforcement:[38] Greif et al. show that the

---

[38] Benson (1989) discusses the evolution of the Law Merchant, which governed commercial contracts in this period. He states (p. 647) that 'This body of law was

merchant guild evolved as a professional body that provided the requisite enforcement. It maintained information about the treatment of its members, and enforced sanctions against a counterpart who cheated one of them. A trader who cheated with one member of the guild therefore lost his reputation with every member. The cost of losing trade links with every member of a guild was too great to bear and, as a result, guild members knew that they could trust their counterparties. Conversely, agents who were not members of a guild could not rely upon their counterparty's reputational concerns to ensure that enforcement occurred. Naturally, this gave guild members something of a competitive advantage.

The effectiveness of the professional body is only as good as its ability to communicate with its members. As a result, there is a technological upper bound to the size of a reputational network. This point is illustrated by Greif (1989, 1993, 1994), who studies another medieval example of collective enforcement. Greif examines the Maghribi, Jewish Mediterranean traders operating in the Muslim world at a time when the law courts were poorly developed, operated very slowly, and had very limited enforcement powers. Since individual traders sold very valuable cargos and operated on an infrequent basis, trade could occur only if the reputational costs of stealing from one trader extended to many others. The Maghribi formed a social grouping within which information sharing was feasible: they achieved reputational reach by refusing as a group to trade with a transgressor. Greif provides evidence that this was a sufficiently potent threat to enforce contracts.[39]

Greif analyzes the problems of sustaining a coalition of this type. Members of the coalition must invest the time and effort required to disseminate trading experiences, and also to learn about transgressions against other members of the group. Furthermore, the costs of sanctions busting must be sufficiently high to discourage it. As a result, Greif notes that the size of the Maghribi trading network was constrained by the information technology available to its members, and he argues that its members had to be sufficiently wealthy to suffer

voluntarily produced, voluntarily adjudicated and voluntarily enforced. In fact, it had to be. There was no other potential source of such law, including state coercion.'

[39] A large literature shows that societies without formal law fall back upon repeated interaction between individuals who can rely upon bonds of ethnicity or kinsmanship to underscore their dealings, and who can expect through repeat dealings to overcome informational problems. See Landa (1981), Geertz (1978), and Posner (1980).

from the withdrawal of its distribution network. In this context, Greif contrasts the Maghribi with the Genoese traders, who were more atomistic and did not maintain the collective enforcement systems of the Maghribi.

Each of the examples we have provided concerns trade across borders when traders cannot rely upon international law to enforce contracts. In these circumstances, trade relies upon reputational enforcement. Trades will therefore occur only if the counterparts can find some way of placing their reputations at risk; at the same time, traders without reputations will be unable to trade. It follows that traders who have a reputational network have a competitive advantage: if they can, they will attempt to prevent their competitors from building such a network. Professional bodies that are monopoly preservers of corporate trading reputations therefore have a substantial amount of power, which they may attempt to use in order to introduce restrictive trading practices.[40] We argue later in the book that these observations can help to explain the nineteenth-century emergence of the American investment bank.

Relationship Between Legal and Extra-Legal Property Rights Institutions

In practice, of course, extra-legal contracting occurs today in a world with well-developed legal institutions. Indeed, the formal law affects informal quasi-legal structures like the ones that we examine in this subsection. One important application of the formal law in informal extra-legal contracting concerns the creation of threat points.[41] If the counterparties to a trade anticipate that their interaction will be governed through an informal extra-legal contract, they may nevertheless write a formal contract which incorporates some clearly specified costs of deviation from a standard pro forma trade agreement. In practice, trade will be governed by the extra-legal contract and the formal legal contract will not be invoked: its purpose is not to govern

---

[40] For example, Banner (1998: 266–7) shows that the NYSE Board (the precursor to today's NYSE) started in 1817 to organize brokers into a cartel with respect to their commission levels. See page 135 of chapter five for a more extensive discussion of the NYSE as a reputation-enhancing professional body.

[41] A very thoughtful early exposition of a related point is due to Mnookin and Kornhauser (1979: 968–9), who argue that divorce cases are usually negotiated before they reach court. They argue that the role of the formal law is to provide the parties with fallback negotiating positions. However, in their discussion the formal law is not determined, as it is in our discussion, via *ex ante* contracting between the parties concerned, but reflects external social norms.

the day-to-day terms of trade, but to increase the costs of breaking a relational contract.

For example, a supplier who is unable to deliver goods on time may expect some flexibility from his purchaser in day-to-day trading. However, when the purchaser regards the delay as too much, or as occurring too frequently, she may deem that the terms of the extra-legal trade have been broken. In this case the supplier will lose a valuable future stream of business. He will in addition be sued, and will be forced to pay out under the terms of the formal legal agreement. It is important to note that the purchaser will have several opportunities to sue under the terms of this contract: she chooses not to do so in order to sustain the relationship upon which the extra-legal contract rests. The formal contract is intended to strengthen the informal contract, and not in general to govern the terms of trade.

A similar point is made by Bernstein (1996a), who criticizes the United States Uniform Commercial Code's fundamental principle that courts should seek to discover 'immanent business norms', and use them to decide cases. The consequence of this is that a formal contract could be overruled in court because it does not reflect past business practices between the litigants. But this is because past business practices reflected the terms of an informal, and undocumented, contract: the formal contract is intended to provide a basis for court action in the event that the informal contract is breached. The reliance upon informal contracts is evidence that the relationship cannot adequately be governed by formal legal contracts. Anything that undermines the formal contract's effectiveness as an enforcement tool reduces the applicability of relational contracts, and hence undermines trade. Hence, if the court extrapolates from past behavior into a specific interpretation of a contract, it prevents this valuable behavior from emerging in the first place.

Formal legal contracts also serve as an alternative to informal extra-legal contracts. If an agent reneges upon a reputational deal, he can always fall back upon a relationship that is intermediated by formal contracts. These contracts rely upon the strength of legal institutions, and not upon reputation. If the contracts are sufficiently close to the relational ones, and the legal institutions are sufficiently strong, reputation therefore ceases to be important. As a result a substantial barrier to entry is removed.[42] This has consequences for the structure of an

---

[42] Johnson, McMillan, and Woodruff (2002a, 2002b) note this effect in post-Soviet countries: because they reduce the need for reputational capital in transactions, courts lower switching costs, and hence lower barriers to entry.

industry that previously relied upon traders with access to a large reputational network: see chapters eight and nine for a discussion in the context of investment banking.

When detailed contracting is sufficiently powerful, strong legal institutions thus obviate the need for reputation. To the extent that this leads to heightened competition, it is likely to be a good thing. However, legally enforceable contracts are unlikely to be as nuanced as reputationally intermediated agreements. A shift from the latter to the former may therefore be damaging. This point is highlighted by Baker, Gibbons, and Murphy (1994, 2002), who argue that technological advances that improve formal contracts sufficiently raise the value of relationships which rest upon them. This lowers the cost of reneging upon a reputational contract, and so renders the latter impossible to enforce, even though it generates superior outcomes.[43]

STATE DECISION-MAKING, THE LAW, AND EXTRA-LEGAL CONTRACTING

Our central argument is that knowledge is dispersed, and that it is most effectively used when decisions are made by individuals, rather than by a central agency. When production is organized along capitalist lines, good laws should therefore support devolved decision-making, and they should not attempt to prejudge its outcome by expressing a central preference for particular economic methods or outcomes. A society in which this is the case is subject to the *rule of law*. While liberal writers make a moral case for the rule of law (see, for example, Hayek, 1973), our justification rests upon economic efficiency: the rule of law strengthens property rights.

In practice, the state has a role beyond contractual enforcement that involves raising and distributing revenues. There are of course strong arguments for some state expenditure on items like defense and social security. This type of expenditure presents problems for a system of property rights, however. It involves the transfer of property rights not by contract between the agents concerned, but by a state bureaucrat who does not have property rights over the assets.

State expenditure is therefore characterized by noncontractual asset transfers. There is no a priori reason why this should be efficient. But when the rule of law obtains, it should at least occur in a way that does not attempt to prejudge economic and social outcomes. In practice, this is hard to achieve: like every other social actor, the

---

[43] See Dixit (2004: ch. 2) for a related model.

state bureaucrats responsible for the spending respond to economic incentives. Those who stand to gain or lose from state spending decisions will naturally attempt to influence the bureaucrats' decisions. Their competitive lobbying is usually referred to as *rent-seeking*. If the noncontractual transfer of assets by the state is inefficient, rent-seeking which influences its outcome is likely to be even more so.[44]

Rent-seeking is a response to the state's power to impose noncontractual property rights transfers. In its simplest form, it involves lobbying by individuals to receive property rights benefits from the state such as monopoly licenses,[45] or preferential regulatory treatment.[46] It might equally involve an attempt by state functionaries to use their distributional powers to extract benefits from the people they regulate.[47]

Rent-seeking naturally affects the evolution of private sector institutions. When people and corporations expect to be the focus of bureaucratic rent-seeking, they will naturally attempt to design mechanisms that shield their activities from the state. One way to do this is to restrict the amount of formal documentation that surrounds their dealings. Increased state power therefore acts as a catalyst for the formation of extra-legal property rights institutions. Hence, extra-legal contracting is a response not just to technological limitations to contracting technologies, but also to features of the polity.

The development of private contracting institutions creates centers of economic power that lie outside the formal legal system. This happens precisely because it is difficult for the state to transfer property rights that have no formal legal existence: private property rights institutions are less subject to bureaucratic rent-seeking. It is therefore to be expected that bureaucrats in search of votes and political influence will attempt to bring private institutions into the public arena by giving them legal existence. This introduces some path-dependency into institutional evolution: private institutions developed in order to avoid state rent-seeking will become the subject of litigation or legislation, as the state attempts to bring them into its sphere of influence. The state's actions will be resisted by the private institutions that it faces, and will also give rise to new institutional developments.

---

[44] Tollison (1982) makes a similar point, arguing that competition over State decisions is via votes rather than prices, and that we have no reason to believe that allocation via votes is economically efficient.

[45] See Tullock (1967) and Krueger (1974).   [46] Stigler (1971).

[47] McChesney (1987).

In summary, the state's power to compel property rights transfers undermines efficiency for three reasons. First, it weakens property rights institutions. When the state takes its cut, some of the returns from assets cannot be contracted upon, and this lowers productivity. Second, the state is not usually concerned primarily with allocative efficiency; even when it is, its decisions are usually inferior to those of the people on the ground.

If we want the state to provide goods such as a social safety net then we probably have to live with the first two costs. But in creating a state which has the powers needed to enforce contractual agreements, and giving that state the power to transfer property rights extra-contractually, we potentially create a third cost. When transfers occur at the discretion of the state, this discretion becomes a focus of economic activity. Producers devote efforts to securing favorable bureaucratic decisions, and bureaucrats work to extract rent from producers.[48] Extra-legal institutions spring up to avoid the attentions of the state.

The natural response to this third problem is to limit the powers of the state.[49] This is one of the purposes of a constitution that separates the judiciary from the legislature, which we mentioned on page 46. When the courts scrutinize the legislature's actions, and can rule them illegal, the legislator's discretion is curtailed, and with it the potential for rent-seeking.[50]

Notwithstanding the remarks in the previous paragraph, the courts tend to reflect social mores. Hence, when the social climate favors a purposive state, so will the courts. And discretion is an inevitable artifact of a state that favors certain economic and social outcomes over others. So, even in countries that subject legislation to judicial

[48] In addition, unproductive bureaucratic work will become more attractive in societies where rent-seeking is profitable. This will cause distortions in the direction of *human* capital. See, for example, Murphy, Shleifer, and Vishny (1991).

[49] This is a standard observation in discussions of constitutional design. See, for example, Hayek (1978), Weingast (1995), Weingast (1997), and Gordon (1999). In the more specific context of regulation, it is made by Martimort (1999), who argues in a formal model that regulatory rent-seeking can be prevented only by dramatically circumscribing the regulator's freedom of action. Olson (1993) and Barzel (2000) both argue that in some circumstances, the sovereign will itself design constitutional limitations over its freedom of action, because the incentive effects of the resultant commitment not to expropriate its subjects may raise the sovereign's income.

[50] We examine two examples of relevance to the investment banking industry in chapter seven: the US Supreme Court's ruling that the New Deal's National Industrial Recovery Act (NIRA) was unconstitutional (p. 206), and the government's defeat in its antitrust action against the investment banking industry (p. 220).

review, moves toward the purposive state will increase bureaucratic discretion, and will generate the rent-seeking and private institution building which accompanies such discretion. As we discussed earlier in the chapter, the state became increasingly goal-oriented throughout the twentieth century. In line with our argument, McChesney (1987: 109) states that 'The level of constitutional scrutiny of legislative expropriations involving private contract and property rights has declined throughout the twentieth century.' We argue later in the book that the early-twentieth-century development of the investment bank can be explained by the interaction of this political shift with cotemporaneous technological shifts.

CONCLUSION

We conclude this chapter by summarizing our argument and highlighting some of the conclusions upon which we rely later in the book.

We argue that, because information is dispersed and hard to communicate, economic decision-making should be devolved to the most local level possible. For this to occur, agents must be able to establish entitlements to use an asset, and to transfer those assets freely. We refer to the combination of an agent's entitlements to use and to transfer an asset as his *property rights* over the asset. We define an *institution* to be any mechanism that enforces property rights. Strong institutions are a precondition for efficient devolved economic decision-making. However, strong institutions could operate in the private sector, and hence property rights need not be established in formal law.

Our discussion of institutions and property rights leads us to several conclusions.

A strong and unchecked state is associated with weak property rights institutions. Property rights cannot exist in a meaningful sense unless the state's power is restricted. This is frequently achieved by the judiciary. For this reason, we regard the courts as separate from the state.

At the same time, economic life is impossible unless the state is strong enough to enforce the laws, and in particular to enforce contracts. Contracts are interpreted in the courts. Strong property rights institutions allow for complex contracting over complex assets, such as labor time or the future returns to a productive process.

In practice, the state's enforcement activities are undermined by two problems: first, there are technological limitations to the contracts that can be written and adjudicated in court; and second, any discretion afforded to state employees will become the focus of rent-seeking activities which undermine the enforcement and the writing of formal legal contracts. Both of these problems give rise to private institutions.

Private institutions facilitate the creation and exchange of property rights that, for either of the reasons in the preceding paragraph, cannot be underwritten by the courts. Contracts written under private institutional arrangements generally have no legal force: contract breach is discouraged by the attendant reputational costs. Since trade is frequently impossible under the formal law, it is in the interests of traders to establish private institutional mechanisms which allow them to risk their reputations. The most obvious example of such a mechanism is a professional body that publicizes malfeasance.

The state, the courts, and the private institutions affect one another's operations, and all are affected by technological change. When technological change facilitates formal contracting, it reduces the value of private reputations and so undermines the institutions which maintain them. Similarly, when technological change improves communications it will widen the applicability of private reputations and so will enhance the role of private institutions.

Changes in the relationship between the state and the courts affect the extent of rent-seeking activities. For example, more discretion will accrue to state bureaucrats if the courts become more willing to accept a purposive, as opposed to a merely enabling, state. This will result in greater rent-seeking activities, both by private sector bodies and by the state. Such activities undermine the value of formal legally defined property rights. In response, individuals and corporations turn increasingly to private-sector institutions whose activities are harder to prove, and hence to control.

Highly successful private institutions will serve as a focus for state rent-seeking, particularly when the state functionaries have discretion. Hence we should expect them to become the basis of both litigation and legislation.

3

An Institutional Theory of
Investment Banking

If there were no investment banks, would we be materially less well off? And if so, why?

Surprisingly little has been written to address these questions directly. Although a large literature explains the operations of the investment bank, and explains how investment banks lever their connections and their reputations to perform their tasks, little has been done to explain why, if investment banks did not exist, we would need to invent them. In other words, there is no *theory of the investment bank*. A theory of investment banking would be of far more than purely academic interest. A good theory should cast light upon the evolution of the investment bank, and may guide future strategic decisions within the industry. Moreover, investment banks are increasingly mired in controversy, and there are growing pressures for their increased regulation. Without a clear understanding of the economic benefits of investment banking, regulators are operating in the dark. A theory of investment banking is required to illuminate the policy discussions. In this chapter we attempt to provide such a theory.

In contrast to the investment bank, academic economists have been writing about the theory of loan-making institutions, or *commercial banks*, for years. Commercial banks have a number of economic roles, but all relate to the central market activity of devolving economic tasks to the most appropriate agent. The monetary system which separates production from consumption decisions is operated by banks: they provide their investors with liquidity insurance through first-come, first-served deposit contracts, and because they channel their funds into illiquid assets, they also perform maturity transformation. Maturity transformation leaves banks exposed to economically destructive runs, and a good deal of ink has been spilled in the analysis of this problem, and of the appropriate response.[1]

Running the payments system and providing liquidity insurance are two complex and essential tasks which are most efficiently managed by a specialist institution. There is however no a priori reason why this institution need be a bank. The most important role of commercial banks is enabling entrepreneurs, and more established corporate actors, to respond to economic opportunities. They accomplish this by breaking down some of the informational barriers that exist between entrepreneurs and investors: without this service, capital-constrained innovators could not attract funds. Only those with sufficient capital could then develop new ideas, and the distinction between investors on the one hand, and entrepreneurs and corporations on the other, would not exist.

Commercial banks are concerned with asymmetries of information between borrower and lender, as a result of which lenders are unsure that they can trust their borrowers not to abscond with funds. This type of agency problem can be resolved through monitoring, but the associated costs are too high for small investors to bear. Diamond (1984) shows that a diversified bank can efficiently resolve these problems by aggregating investments and monitoring them on behalf of a widely dispersed investor base. Monitoring of this type sends a positive signal to the wider marketplace: the value of bank certification and the consequences of superior banker knowledge have been widely investigated.[2]

We argue in this chapter that, like commercial banks, investment banks break down informational barriers between investors and entrepreneurs that would otherwise prevent investment from occurring. It follows immediately that their activities raise economic activity, and hence that they are welfare-enhancing. Although they certainly gather some information for themselves, we do not think that this is the primary role of investment banks. Instead, we argue that the investment banks are concerned with the dissemination of *price-relevant information*. When financial markets are working effectively, such information naturally finds its way into financial security prices.

---

[1] Diamond and Dybvig (1983) provide the classic treatment of the liquidity insurance justification for deposit contracts, and discuss in detail the concomitant problem of bank runs.

[2] James (1987) and a number of succeeding authors show that bank certification reduces the cost of other sources of funds. The relationship between bank certification and capital structure is studied by Holmström and Tirole (1997).

We argue however that price-relevant information is particularly valuable *before* securities have been sold, or even created. There is no reason to assume that either a capitalist or an entrepreneur would know at this stage what the securities will be worth. Without this information they will be unable to decide whether a new project is worthwhile, and some valuable opportunities will not be developed. It is therefore important that people and firms with special abilities to generate price-relevant information find it worthwhile to do so, and to reveal it so that entrepreneurs and capitalists can make well-informed asset allocation decisions. The most efficient way to do this is to establish property rights over the information. We argue that this cannot be achieved by the courts: instead, investment banks function as informal extra-legal institutions that create the property rights needed to make the primary security markets function effectively.

INFORMATION, INNOVATION, AND PROPERTY RIGHTS

Our material well-being rests upon complex production processes which take raw inputs and transform them in several stages into consumer products. For example, the final stages of car tyre manufacture are far removed from the rubber plantation. Similarly, the process that turns a sheep into a restaurant meal is a lengthy one.

In capitalist economies, the people working in the supply chain for a complex consumer good need not understand the entire process by which it is manufactured. In fact, no one *need* have a complete picture of the production process and arguably, no one *could* have. At each stage in the process, a person or a firm acquires property rights over the key assets involved in production and combines them in a way that increases their value, before selling their rights over the completed asset.

When it is performed in this way, production is unplanned. The people working with intermediate goods need not even know how the product of their labor will finally enter the consumer economy. Because they are willing to sell to the highest bidder, allocative decisions in production respond flexibly to changes in the economy.

This is an efficient way to organize economic activity. It is feasible only if the various parties in the production line are able to establish property rights over the inputs which they use, and to sell property rights over their outputs. Effort expended to create important inputs or intermediate goods over which property rights cannot be established will not be profitable and hence will not occur. So complex production requires that property rights can be established over the key assets as they move along the supply chain.

Hence, the property rights institutions of the previous chapter are essential if complex production is to occur. In much production, the key assets are physical (for example rubber or sheep). Property rights over these assets can be established by way of formal court-enforceable contracts, or, as in chapter two, using extra-legal contracting institutions for which the main function of the formal law is to provide threat points to the parties concerned.

In advanced economies, many supply chains rest upon *intellectual*, as opposed to physical, assets. The most important examples concern innovations. Consider, for example, an entrepreneur designing a new production process. Precisely because the process is new, he may have insufficient knowledge of demand conditions to decide whether it is worth developing. Thus demand information is central to efficient investment: without it, some good ideas will not be pursued and some bad ideas will be. In the language of chapter two, demand information is an intellectual or informational *asset* which is an essential input into the production process.

Informational assets have been extensively studied by economists. Much of the existing literature concerns the development of innovations which are themselves intellectual assets, such as a method for synthesizing a new drug. When information about these innovations leaks, they can be copied. A weak property rights regime for intellectual property therefore reduces the profitability of this type of innovation and thus the likelihood that it will be pursued in the first place.

It is important to stress that most of the innovations with which we are concerned in this chapter are not themselves intellectual assets. Even when the innovator has a natural monopoly over a physical innovation, implementation will occur only if he can attract capital. The information that we are concerned with is needed by capitalists to evaluate potential innovations. Even innovators with deep pockets need this information: without it, neither an entrepreneur nor a well-governed corporation will invest. But unlike the information content of intellectual assets, publicizing value-related information on which decisions to innovate rest need not reduce the innovation's intrinsic value. Indeed, the information will become common knowledge as soon as the innovation is given a chance to prove itself in the marketplace.

Information about *any* type of innovation is essential if it is to attract sufficient capital to bring it to market. This type of information affects the capital allocation decision, but it does not affect the intrinsic value of the innovation: we can accurately refer to it as 'price-relevant information'. Price-relevant information is clearly distinct from the assets which it concerns, even when those assets are themselves informational.

Price-relevant information serves two economic roles. The first, which we have already highlighted, concerns the allocation of resources to economic innovations: without accurate price-relevant information, capital may be allocated to the wrong projects, or it may not be invested at all. The second role concerns the incentives of people and corporations to innovate. When price-relevant information is hard to find, so that innovations are less likely to attract capital, the incentive to innovate is impaired. Hence economies in which price-relevant information production is discouraged will suffer from resource misallocation, and also, because innovation is discouraged, from lower-growth rates.

In short, price-relevant information plays an essential role in every economy. In more developed economies, innovations are complex, and hence price-relevant information is harder to generate and to interpret. Its production is therefore a specialized activity: throughout this chapter, we refer to a person or a firm that fulfills this role as an *information producer*. While it is true that both institutional and individual traders invest in and share value-related information, for reasons that we discuss shortly institutional investors have a stronger incentive to make such investments. Hence we envision information producers as being largely institutional, rather than individual, investors.

Information producers must be incentivized to gather and to reveal information. This is relatively easy to accomplish in liquid secondary markets for securities, where it is possible to profit by trading on private information.[3] But we have argued that price-relevant information is most valuable before a new idea has been tested in the market. Information revealed in this situation is valuable for secondary market trading only if the secondary market price is sufficiently inaccurate

---

[3] This is an obvious argument for the legalization of insider trading. The classic exposition of this perspective is due to Henry Manne (1966). For analysis which is at least partially sympathetic to his perspective, see, for example, Carlton and Fischel (1983), Leland (1992), Bernhardt, Hollifield, and Hughson (1995), and Easterbrook (1981).

to guarantee a profit to the information producer.[4] The information producer guarantees this most effectively by withholding his information, but doing so deprives the innovator of an important asset and hence undermines investment efficiency.

In the light of our discussion in chapter two and above, the most efficient way to incentivize information production would be to create property rights over it. A strong system of property rights would ensure that the information producer alienated her information only when she wished to do so, and then to a counterpart whom she chose. This would ensure that investment in information gathering occurred only to the extent that it was valuable, and that it was sold to the agent who could put it to the most productive use.[5]

For three reasons, it is however virtually impossible to establish formal property rights over information. First, it is very hard to convince a potential purchaser of information that it is accurate, and hence to extract a fair price. Second, it is hard to prove that an agent acquired information from its producer, and hence enforcing payment for information is difficult. Third, an agent who sells information does not at the same time alienate it: she is still able to pass it on to third parties. Hence she could sell it to multiple parties and thus diminish or destroy its commercial value to any one of them.

These problems cannot be overcome with legal contracts. The quality of information cannot, in general, be proved in court, and hence could not form the basis of a contingent legal contract. Even when it is obvious to the parties concerned, proving satisfactorily that an agent has received or used information is probably impossible in court. Finally, any attempt to identify an informational asset in court will immediately cause its dissemination. This has precisely the same effect as a multiple sale. In addition, it precludes competitive tendering for information.

In summary, the innovations that drive economic progress may rest upon informational as well as physical assets. This is as true of innovations that are not themselves intellectual as it is of those that are: price-relevant information about innovations is essential if they are to be developed. The informational assets, or the ability to create

---

[4] This observation lies at the heart of the microstructure literature. See Grossman and Stiglitz (1980), Kyle (1985), and succeeding work.

[5] Credit rating agencies, which create a somewhat different type of information, manage to exist solely by selling this information. Like investment banks, the value of their product depends upon their reputation. See Cantor and Packer (1994) and Sufi (2006).

them, may reside apart from the agents who use them. When this is the case the incentive to create or to communicate the information rests upon the creation of property rights over it. But any attempt to do this using the courts will cause the information to leak, and hence will destroy its value. In other words, the courts are not able to carve up property rights over the innovation so as to separate critical information about it from the control rights over, and the income stream from, it. When critical price-relevant information cannot be generated by the agent with property rights over the development of the innovation, the innovation will not be developed, and economic development will be retarded.

We argued in chapter two that in circumstances where economic progress is impeded by technological limitations to formal legal institutions, substitute property rights institutions are likely to evolve in the private sector. Our argument in this chapter is that the investment bank is such an institution, designed to establish informal property rights over price-relevant information.

INFORMATION MARKETPLACES AND INVESTMENT BANKING

Under a system of legally enforceable property rights to price-relevant information, information producers could auction exclusive rights to their knowledge in a competitive market. We have already argued that such a system is a technological impossibility. Investment banks evolved as extra-legal institutions, in the sense of chapter two, that created marketplaces in which informal property rights over price-relevant information can be traded. In this section we describe the operation and the management of these marketplaces.

Price-relevant information is valuable to the information producers who create it, to the investors who use it to determine their demand for new securities, and to the innovators who bring new securities to market. A market for informal property rights over information should therefore include all three classes of trader, although of course one agent will frequently assume two of these roles. We have already seen that the special properties of information preclude the creation of a price for it which varies in the traditional way, in response to fluctuations in supply and demand. The investment bank substitutes for the price mechanism: it acts as an intermediary between the producers and the users of price information.

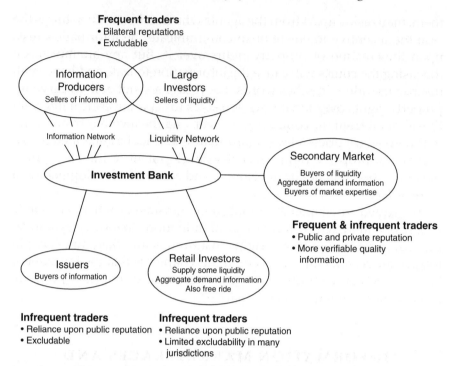

Figure 3.1. *The investment bank's information marketplace*

The investment bank therefore sits at the nexus of an informal *information marketplace* for price-relevant information. The information marketplace is illustrated in figure 3.1. It consists of a number of networks of traders, which we discuss below.

We argued in chapter one that the central investment banking activity is security issuance. Information producers are the key to this activity. They could be large-scale investors, such as pension funds, or they might be smaller investors who specialize in information production, such as private equity firms wishing to exit their investments. The investment bank maintains relationships with several information producers: collectively, we refer to them as the bank's *information network*. The investment bank contracts informally with the members of its information network, promising to compensate them for price-relevant demand information about new issues.

It is important that an investment bank be able to place a fairly priced issue. To the extent that its information network is unable to absorb the securities which it prices, the investment bank therefore needs access to substantial capitalists who can take as much of the issue as necessary. These agents constitute the investment bank's *liquidity network*. As indicated in figure 3.1, some members of the liquidity network may also be information producers. However, the liquidity network need play no part in pricing an issue: its main role is to provide guaranteed liquidity. In return, its members are promised some degree of compensation by the investment bank, and are promised that the issues they buy will be fairly priced.

The members of the investment bank's two networks are frequent traders. Together, they provide the pricing and the liquidity that the investment bank sells to its clients, and the investment bank compensates them for doing so. The networks rely upon informal contractual undertakings between their members and the investment bank. As a result, the investment bank's reputation is essential in sustaining its network, and hence in performing its core activity. Many investment bank decisions involve trading off the future value of enhanced reputational capital against the value of liquidating some of that capital immediately. An important decision of this type concerns the composition of the investment bank's networks: crucially, the investment bank can elect to *exclude* agents so as to provide the most cost-effective incentives to the network members.

Alternatively, the bank might influence the behavior of network members by investing directly in information production or liquidity provision. With respect to the former, most large investment banks operate significant research departments whose research efforts overlap with those of the information producers within their networks. Such investments provide banks with bargaining power in negotiations with information producers but are difficult to justify on a stand-alone basis. Just as information producers are unable to sell their information at arm's length, so are investment bank research departments. Thus it was common until quite recently for banks to subsidize 'independent' research through investment banking and proprietary trading functions. Both sources of subsidy create potential conflicts of interest with respect to issuers and other bank clients. These conflicts appear to have been especially severe during the late 1990s, a point to which we will return in chapter ten.

Banks invest in liquidity provision along two dimensions. First, some banks maintain unusually large and well-coordinated retail investor networks. Retail investors are distinguished from other users of the information marketplace in that they frequently have legal rights to participate in the marketplace on the same terms as institutional investors. In practice, this means that they are able to deal on the same terms as information producers whose terms of trade reflect the active efforts that they make to price a deal. Retail investors are more likely to enter and leave the information marketplace at will, and more likely to trade infrequently. Although individual retail investors are unlikely to have any special knowledge of the demand for a new issue, aggregate demand information from a large pool of retail investors can be valuable to an investment bank. Perhaps more importantly, when such networks are sufficiently large and well coordinated, they can provide a credible fallback position in negotiations with institutional liquidity networks and thus complement the threat of exclusion mentioned above.

As figure 3.1 illustrates, investment banks also invest in liquidity provision via their presence in secondary markets. As we noted in chapter one, a presence in the secondary market is valuable for several reasons. First, it reassures primary market investors that they will be able to exit their investments in the future, and hence lowers the cost of the primary market liquidity network. Second, investment banks learn information about market sentiment from secondary market trading which is useful to them in their primary market activities. Third, investment banks are able by committing their own capital in the secondary market to earn a return from market knowledge gleaned from their customer contacts. Fourth, it is increasingly necessary for investment banks to bundle derivative trading with the other services that they offer their clients. Secondary market trading relies to some extent upon implicit contracting: for example, investment banks frequently demand reciprocation from other banks to whom they quote prices. On the whole, though, secondary market trading involves promises which are observable, and which can be documented. Hence, at least in mature markets, reputation is less important for secondary market contracts than it is for other investment bank activities.[6]

---

[6] Chen and Wilhelm (2005b) show that common practice in the liquidity provision function can be interpreted as an *informal*, reputationally sustained, arrangement between banks and the informed members of their liquidity networks. From this perspective, initial allocations that favor institutional investors do not reflect an attempt to place shares in the hands of the ultimate investors but rather are one step in a distribution process that is complicated by extraordinary incremental information production triggered by a securities offering. Effectively, large investors provide liquidity alongside the bank and thus ease the transition to normal secondary market trading. Their willingness to provide liquidity reveals information and the cost of gaining their cooperation is diminished by their repeated dealing with the bank.

The investment bank coordinates the information network illustrated in figure 3.1 on behalf of issuers. Issuers require price information, and demand liquidity from their investment bank. Issuers are relatively infrequent participants in the information marketplace. As we argue below, this has significant implications for the informal contract between them and the investment bank, which promises to issue their stock at a fair price. Nevertheless, their contract is reputational. And, like the frequent players of the information and liquidity networks, issuers may be turned away by an investment bank that values its future reputation more than any immediate benefits to be derived from accepting their business.

In the next subsection, we examine the way in which an investment bank maintains the reputation upon which its business rests. In the following subsection, we analyze in detail the informal reputational contracts between the investment bank and the members of the information marketplace.

Investment Bank Reputation

Like all extra-legal property rights institutions, investment banks rely upon their reputation. While much of the academic literature on investment banks includes a casual acknowledgment of the role of reputation in underpinning the investment banker's promises, the central importance of reputation to everything the bank does is seldom acknowledged. In this subsection we describe investment bank reputation, and we show how the investment bank manages its networks so as to maximize the yield derived from its reputational capital.

The investment bank can fulfill its economic role of creating property rights over price-relevant information only if the informal contracts it writes with the members of its information network are credible. When its counterparts believe its promises, we say that it has a good reputation. In general, failure to perform on a contract impairs an investment bank's reputation with some of its counterparties. When they stop believing the investment bank's promises, they leave the network. Clearly, this departure undermines the investment bank's future business. When the banker breaks an informal contract, it is therefore electing to liquidate some of its reputational capital. The investment bank will work to maintain its reputational capital for as long as its value in future business exceeds the immediate returns from liquidation.[7]

---

[7] See page 246 for an example of this trade-off at work.

This mechanism is understood by the participants in the investment bank's information marketplace. Not only will they cease to believe the investment bank's promises when it breaks them: they will do so as soon as they believe that the ongoing value of reputational capital is exceeded by its liquidation value. Hence the investment bank will manage its reputational capital and its information network so as to maximize the cost of immediate liquidation. As we argued on page 54 of chapter two, this is most effectively done by extending the reach of the investment bank's reputation. It is relatively less attractive for an investment bank to break a promise with one agent when doing so damages its reputation with many other agents. Hence, when an agent can rely upon the same reputational capital as many other agents upon whom the investment bank depends, he will be more willing to participate in the information marketplace. Conversely, if the members of a network do not communicate with one another, the network must be small if its members are to trust the investment bank.

Investment banks use their reputations to support two types of contractual commitment: those with the frequent traders who comprise its information and liquidity networks; and those with the issuers and retail traders who trade in the information marketplace on an intermittent basis. We consider the two types of contract in the light of our preceding observations.

If investment banks are to maintain their information network, they must sustain a reputation for paying for information. We show in the following subsection that payment is made in two ways. First, the investment bank discounts new issues, so that the information producers who purchase them earn an income from their price information. Second, the investment bank allocates securities to the most effective information producers. Underpricing is easy to observe, and it is generally hard to vary its terms between IPO participants. Hence if the investment bank wishes to maintain its network of investors, it will continue to underprice new issues. Security allocation is rather more complex. While allocations of new securities are verifiable (share ownership is demonstrable), the quality of information revealed by a particular network member is not. An investment bank could therefore claim falsely that it had received poor information from an information producer, and provide him with a low share allocation. Any attempt by the information producer to reveal his information, and hence to expose investment banker cheating, would occur either before price discovery had occurred in the secondary market, and hence would reduce the value of his information to zero, or after price discovery had occurred in the secondary market, in which case it would be incredible.

In short, there is no way for the investment banker to create a widely observed public reputation for rewarding information producers for their efforts. As a result, it has to create a bilateral reputation for doing so with each member of the network. Breaking a promise with one member of the network need not damage the investment bank's reputation with the other members. The only cost to the investment bank of breaking an informal contract with one of its information producers is therefore a reduction in the size of its information network. The cost of this is a reduction in the quality of its price estimates. This places an upper bound upon the size of the information network at the point where further expansion would lower the cost of breaking a contract below the (fixed) costs of honoring it.

The reputational foundations of the investment bank's contracting relationship with its information network have been widely studied. In contrast, less attention has been paid to the bank's ability to contract informally with the security issuers who use its marketplace.[8] Potential issuers are concerned with the investment bank's reputation for price discovery. For example, Nanda and Yun (1997) present evidence that investment banks experience a significant decline in market value when they take an overpriced issue to market, as well as when they take a dramatically underpriced issue to market. Both are evidence of poor price-discovery skills. Issuers will pay more to deal with an investment bank that has access to skilled information producers.[9]

---

[8] Although a large literature examines the agency problem between the issuer and the investment bank which renders relational contracting important: see, for example, Baron and Holmström (1980), Baron (1982), Loughran and Ritter (2004), Bias, Bossaerts, and Rochet (2002), Ljungqvist and Wilhelm (2003), and Muscarella and Vetsuypens (1989).

[9] An exceptionally skilled information producer could conceivably gain an undesirable level of market power relative to the bank. To avoid this happening, the bank could produce some information itself. To the extent that banks are able to do so, they force external information producers to trade more aggressively on their private information: in turn, this lowers the cost of learning such information. The challenge to the bank, however, is reaping a fair return on its information production costs, given that direct trading on such information might conflict with the interests of issuing firms. In this light, we can understand the historical tendency to bundle research for sale with other investment banking services: see Chen and Wilhelm (2005a). Cliff and Denis (2004) report that underpricing of new issues is correlated with the presence of a star research analyst, which suggests a mechanism by which firms might indirectly compensate banks for internal information production.

The importance of price-discovery skills in attracting issuers points to an important scale effect in information production. Since many of the costs of information production are fixed, the per-deal cost to the investment bank of incentivizing it is falling in the size of the investment bank's deal flow. Recall that the maximum network size is attained when the cost of honoring a contracted incentive payment equals the benefits from breaking it. Since the incentive payment is falling in deal flow, it follows immediately that the maximum network size is larger when deal flows are stronger. Furthermore, a large network can price deals more accurately. As a result, it will attract more deals, and hence will grow still further. Investment banks therefore have enormous reputational economies of scale in information production.

Interestingly, the recommendations that investment bankers make when they take a new security to market have no significant effect upon the likelihood that they will win underwriting mandates (Ljungqvist, Marston, and Wilhelm, 2006), even though these recommendations are systematically biased (Michaely and Womack, 1999). In the light of our theory of investment banking, this is hardly surprising: when an issuer contracts with a lead underwriter, he is purchasing access to the investment bank's information network, not to its analysts.[10]

The dynamics of the investment bank's relationship with its issuer base are very different to those with its information and liquidity networks. Unlike the members of the investment bank's information network, innovators enter the information marketplace to issue securities only infrequently. Except in exceptional circumstances,[11] they cannot rely upon the value to the investment bank of their own ongoing business to provide the requisite reputational incentives to the investment bank. The investment bank's promise to market an issuer's securities at a fair price is therefore meaningful only to the extent that it

---

[10] However, Ljungqvist, Marston, and Wilhelm (2005) present evidence that recommendations serve a competitive purpose: in certain circumstances, they can increase a firm's chances of becoming a comanager. This in turn gives it a chance of being selected to manage future deals.

[11] There is considerable variation in the frequency with which issuers enter the capital markets. Some, possibly not exceptional issuers, by virtue of frequent issuance and exclusive relationships, can rely upon bilaterally formed reputations to underscore their relationship with the bank. Note though that the exclusivity of client relationships has been dropping since the 1970s. This suggests either that public reputations have become more important or that technological advances have reduced the importance of bank reputation in its dealings with investors.

affects a reputation upon which a significant proportion of its future issuers will rely.[12] The mechanisms by which issuers communicate their experiences to one another are therefore very important. It is in the investment bank's best interests to create or cooperate with effective communication systems, since without them it cannot create the public reputation that it needs to attract customers.

The information that an investment bank acquires from its client base may help it to stimulate information production within its information network.[13] As gatekeeper to its networks, the investment bank is therefore in a position to generate positive network effects among its counterparties. As Benveniste, Busaba, and Wilhelm (2002) and Benveniste et al. (2003) show, this allows for welfare-enhancing cross subsidization between network members (see p. 91). However, this comes at a price: Asker and Ljungqvist (2005) present evidence that issuers may attempt to avoid membership of investment banker networks of which their competitors are members, for fear of giving away commercially sensitive information.[14]

The importance of a public investment bank reputation has been acknowledged in the literature. Beatty and Ritter (1986) argue that investment banks need reputations for underpricing to attract uninformed investors who are subject to Rock's (1986) winner's curse problem (see p. 85). While we argue that IPO underpricing reflects the costs of information acquisition and not of attracting uninformed investors, it is nevertheless true that investors will not join the investment bank's network unless they expect to be adequately rewarded

---

[12] See n. 8 above for the literature concerning the agency problem between issuers and investment banks.

[13] This ability is the greatest for investment banks that also have lending relationships with their issuers. See, for example, Drucker and Puri (2005) and Schenone (2004).

[14] A recent survey conducted by Greenwich Associates (Investment Bank Practices, 2005) reports that for each of the years 2003–5 no more than eight percent of respondents identified whether a bank worked for a key competitor as a factor determining its selection to lead a transaction. However, there is considerable variation among respondents across industries and firms of different sizes. Large firms were more likely to identify this as a factor in their decision and, for example, 18 and 25 percent of respondents from technology and telecommunications firms respectively identified it as being of key importance. By contrast, respondents from numerous industries, including metals and mining, oil and gas, chemicals, paper and forest products, insurance and health care, were unconcerned whether or not their investment banker worked with a competitor. One could plausibly argue that the former were examples of industries in which an underwriting bank would more likely gain access to strategic information not readily available to its client's competitors and that the latter were not.

for the liquidity that they bring. Chemmanur and Fulghieri (1994) acknowledge the importance of investment bank reputation in attracting customers. In their model, investment banks generate information which investors use for pricing, and a reputation for accurate information production attracts customers, and results in higher fees.

The papers in the previous paragraph abstract from the central role that we assign to the investment bank's ability to contract informally within its information network. Hence they do not describe the means by which issuers communicate their experiences to one another, and so create a public reputation.

Issuers encounter two problems in communicating their experiences of the investment bank to one another. First, security pricing and issuance are complex activities. Issuers may not know whether their securities were fairly priced, and properly marketed. Second, it may be hard for issuers to find a forum within which they can communicate their experiences, particularly if doing so would require them to reveal some commercially sensitive information.

Syndication helps investment banks to counter the first of these problems. Syndication occurs when more than one investment bank works to price and to distribute a new issue. One investment bank manages the syndication process, and is referred to as the 'lead manager'. The lead manager earns the bulk of the fees from the syndication, and there is considerable competition to occupy this position. One way that an investment bank can increase its chances of becoming lead manager in a future issue is by communicating directly with the issuer in a current syndicate, and showing him the price evidence gathered by the syndicate. He will be rewarded for whistle-blowing on a dishonest lead manager with an increased chance of managing the next issue. This behind-the-scenes whispering within the syndicate is documented by Corwin and Schultz (2005); it is consistent with the evidence documented in footnote 10 above that comanagement opportunities yield an advantage in subsequent competition for lead-management opportunities. It goes some way towards ensuring that the issuer has well-documented evidence of malfeasance which he can publicize in the wake of a poor issue.[15]

---

[15] A complementary theory is provided by Pichler and Wilhelm (2001), who note that most of the opprobrium emanating from a mis-priced deal attaches to the lead manager, who therefore experiences the majority of the reputational hit. Notwithstanding the importance of peer-group reputation, this observation appears to undermine comanagerial incentives. Pichler and Wilhelm note that this is not the case, because much of the important work is done before the issue. Since there is

The auditing of the syndicate is of little use if firms are unable to communicate evidence of malfeasance to their peers, since otherwise the reputational cost to an investment bank of cheating is negligible. We argued in chapter two that an important means of communication between customers aiming to create a public reputation for their counterpart is the professional body. A professional body can gather information about rule infringements, and can then publicly rebuke one of its members, without revealing any commercially sensitive information. The rebuke dissuades potential customers from dealing with the rebuked party, and hence facilitates the creation of a public reputation.

There are numerous self-regulatory bodies in the investment banking industry: for example, we discuss the foundation of the NYSE on page 135, of the Investment Bankers Association (now superseded by the SIA) on page 203 and of the National Association of Securities Dealers (NASD) on page 206. In its early days, the NYSE had an institutional role in facilitating certain contracts (e.g. short-selling and long-dated transactions) which at the time were legally unenforceable. It achieved this by rebuking or expelling members who were reported by their peers to be in breach of its rules. New York Stock Exchange membership therefore provided early stock traders with a public reputation which made it easier for them to attract business.

Self-Regulatory Organizations (SROs) designed specifically to support the consumer are a more recent innovation. Before they emerged it was harder for customers to publicize information about investment banker dishonesty. Personal contacts were therefore of particular importance: entrepreneurs in industries like railroads were socially connected, and could share information without the assistance of SROs. It is of course in the best interests of investment banks that effective communication should occur between infrequent users of their information networks (issuers and investors), since without it, their clientele is greatly restricted. Investment banks use SROs as informal contracting devices in the sense of chapter two, which allow them to commit up front to behavior from which they might prefer later on to deviate.

---

such fierce competition for the lead-manager job, it is essentially awarded randomly. As a result, at the point when effort is made, every investment banker assigns a positive probability to the event that he will lead-manage the issue and so suffer the public reputational consequences of mis-pricing arising from low effort. From this perspective, the syndicate enables small work teams within which monitoring is more effective temporarily to combine forces to carry out a large-scale offering.

Finally, banks also share information with each other and with their consumers by cooperating with annual surveys of investors and analysts performed by industry journals such as the *Investment Dealers' Digest* and *Institutional Investor*, as well as by specialist firms such as Greenwich Associates. The value of these activities is clear from the above discussion: they allow the investment banker to place his reputation at stake, and hence increase his ability to commit himself.[16]

Investment banker commitment need not be created solely by private mechanisms like SROs and industry surveys. The State may also have a role to play. This is particularly true in the retail investment banking industry, where investors are small, and naturally find it hard to communicate among themselves. The 1933 formation of the SEC enabled retail investors to pursue investment bankers through the courts. Without it, firms like Merrill Lynch would have found it very much harder to build a reputation for probity with their dispersed and generally uninformed investor base.[17]

State legislation to support the extra-legal contracting that investment bankers and their counterparts would have attempted absent legal assistance has the potential to increase welfare. However, as we argued on page 60 of chapter two, legislation might also be designed to create formal property rights over things which previously only existed within extra-legal institutions. Once such property rights have been created, it becomes possible for the State to transfer them extra-contractually, and they can become the focus of rent-seeking activity. One could view some consumer-protection legislation in this light. When investment bankers and their consumers are both happy *ex ante* to commit themselves via an extra-legal contract, *ex post* legislation that breaks this commitment in favor of the consumer weakens the informal property rights regime under which the extra-legal contract was written. As we argued in chapter two, this is welfare-reductive. Much of the legal controversy around investment banks in the twentieth century centered upon attempts to move property rights from the extra-legal to the legal arena, where they could be reassigned by rent-seeking politicians.

Finally, just as they manage the composition of their information and liquidity networks, investment banks will control client access to their information marketplace so as to maximize their reputation for

[16] See Eccles and Crane (1988: 152–3) for a detailed discussion of industry surveys.

[17] Charles Merrill was an early adopter of many of the rules later made compulsory by the SEC (Perkins, 1999: 164–5). This is not to say that the SEC was regarded by the industry as an unalloyed success: see chapter seven for an extensive discussion.

accurate price discovery. In particular, they will exclude from their network agents who have the potential to undermine this reputation. For this reason, if there is a danger that it will misprice their issues to such an extent as to undermine its reputation, an investment bank may turn away some issuers. The cost of mispricing is greater for firms that have high reputations, and hence have a lot to lose. Hence, although new issuers would prefer to deal with the highest possible reputation investment bank,[18] we would expect them to be forced to use lower-quality banks until the better banks feel more comfortable that they can price them accurately. Consistent with this hypothesis, Krigman, Shaw, and Womack (2001) demonstrate that firms switch underwriters after their IPOs not because they are dissatisfied with the service of their banker, but because they want to secure the services of a more prestigious underwriter.[19] Fang (2005) shows that, although the more reputable banks can charge higher fees, issuer proceeds net of these fees are still higher than they would have been with a lower-rated bank. Moreover, Carter, Dark, and Singh (1998) show that issues underwritten by the most prestigious investment banks are of the highest quality, in the sense that they perform relatively well in the years after issue.

Extra-Legal Contracts

The investment bank manages a marketplace in which extra-legal property rights over information can be traded. The investment bank's information and liquidity networks are crucial to the functioning of the marketplace. In this section, we assume that the investment banker has the reputational capital required to run his networks, and we analyze the extra-legal contracts upon which they rest. We cite literature that is supportive of our theory, and we critique some alternative explanations of investment banking.

We start by examining the informal contracts that information producers write with the investment bank. Information producers rely upon human and physical capital, which they will acquire and maintain only if they receive an adequate return. Much of the capital investment that information producers make is sunk, and the returns that they make on their information are therefore pure profits: formally,

---

[18] See Carter and Manaster (1990), Booth and Smith (1986), and Michaely and Shaw (1994).

[19] However, IPO firms are less likely to switch underwriters for SEOs when they are satisfied with the service that they received in their IPO: see Ljungqvist and Wilhelm (2005).

they are *quasi-rents*. Investment bankers incentivize information generation and revelation by promising quasi-rents to their information
producers. The first paper suggesting that investment bankers have
to supply quasi-rents to incentivize information *revelation* in IPOs is
due to Benveniste and Spindt (1989). Van Bommel (2002) and Sherman
and Titman (2002) extend this work, arguing as we do that investment
bankers have also to incentivize information *production*.

As we highlighted above, it is impossible to prove whether or not
the information producer expended any effort, or whether it communicated the results of its efforts in full to the investment bank. The
investment bank must therefore provide the right incentives for effort
and honest disclosure. It rewards the information producer by selling
him shares below the fair price as announced by the information
producer: on average, share IPOs are discounted by an average of
about 15 percent.[20] This exposes the information producer to the risk
of an adverse price movement and hence provides some incentive to
learn about the fair price.

Of course, information producers who receive discounted shares
have an incentive to underreport their true value. Because information
producers cannot establish formal property rights over their information, they rely upon participation in an information network to
generate their quasi-rents. The investment banker, as gatekeeper to
the network, can exclude information producers who are discovered
to have misrepresented their information. The threat of exclusion is
sufficiently potent to incentivize information production and truthful
revelation to the bank, and hence is a powerful contracting tool. In
fact, Sherman (2005) argues that bookbuilding is the most effective
means of issuing new securities precisely *because* it enables the investment banker to control access to the issue.[21]

The information producer's incentives can be sharpened by making
his compensation contingent not only upon his own performance

---

[20] For surveys of the evidence, see Ljungqvist (2007) and Jenkinson and Ljungqvist
(2001).
[21] Although the majority of new issues in the United States and the United
Kingdom are allocated using a bookbuilding process (Ljungqvist, Jenkinson, and Wilhelm, 2003), this is not the only option available to the issuer. Sherman (1992) argues
that when the issuer requires market feedback to evaluate an investment opportunity, a best-efforts approach may be more effective. Using a similar mechanism to
Chemmanur (1993), she shows that pricing shares at a discount to expected value
will induce information gathering in the market place. When the project is of low
quality, a best-efforts offering will fail. When the issuer wishes to invest only in a
high-quality project this is a desirable outcome.

but also that of his peers. This 'yardstick' approach to compensation is familiar from the principal-agent literature.[22] Investment bankers can use it to improve the quality of the price signal that they sell in their network: both Benveniste and Spindt (1989) and Sherman and Titman (2002) show that incentives are sharpened when only the richest reported price is rewarded with a high allocation. Of course, increasing the size of the network has a countervailing effect in that the aggregate cost of information production increases proportionately, and with it the average level of underpricing (Sherman, 2005). The optimal number of information producers in the network is obtained by trading off these two effects.

The investment banker's ability to exclude agents from IPOs is also relevant when it deals with its liquidity network. The investment banker provides the members of its liquidity network with rents from underpriced issues against the threat of future exclusion if they refuse to participate when needed. This threat ensures that they invest even when the investment opportunity does not appear particularly attractive (Benveniste and Spindt, 1989). Indeed, Weiss Hanley and Wilhelm (1995) demonstrate that institutional investors take similar allocations in unattractive overpriced issues to those they accept in the more attractive underpriced ones.

New issue underpricing is used by investment banks as a form of compensation. It will be most effective when it is targeted toward the most valuable members of the investment bank's networks. An early theory of IPO underpricing suggests that these are the uninformed investors who absorb the bulk of the issue, and who need to be compensated for the danger that they will receive relatively high allocations in low-quality issues that are undersubscribed by informed agents (the 'winner's curse': see Rock, 1986). However, Weiss Hanley and Wilhelm's evidence that institutional participation is similar for overpriced and underpriced issues suggests that this danger is minimal. Moreover, many jurisdictions traditionally impose 'fair pricing' rules, requiring uniform pricing of all of the shares in a new issue. Such legislation is intended to benefit uninformed investors: once again, this mitigates against a story that suggests that new issue underpricing was designed to compensate them in the first place.

If investment banks run information networks, then they should target rewards to information providers in new issues. Uniform-pricing legislation undermines their ability to do this: as a result,

---

[22] See, for example, Lazear and Rosen (1981) and Green and Stokey (1983).

it increases the average level of new deal underpricing, and hence raises the effective cost of information about the deal (Benveniste and Wilhelm, 1990). We argued in chapter two that institutions will innovate around this type of inefficiency. Consistent with our argument, Benveniste, Busaba, and Wilhelm (1996) show that, even when offer prices are standardized, investment banks can target rewards to information providers by using stabilizing bids.[23, 24] These provide buyers with insurance against losses,[25] and can be restricted to information providers through the use of institutional arrangements such as 'penalty bids'. In line with this hypothesis, Benveniste, Erdal, and Wilhelm (1998) show that retail sales are attenuated in stabilized offerings, while large quantity wholesale traders are more aggressive sellers.[26]

The extra-legal contracts within investment bank information networks have been affected by other legislation. US security issuance is largely governed by the 1933 Securities Act (see p. 207), which replaced a laissez-faire system with a more rules-based approach based upon seller liability.[27] Tinic (1988) shows that underpricing increased in the United States when the Act was passed, and suggests that underpricing is entirely a form of investment banker insurance against law suits.[28] This explanation is consistent with a theory of investment bankers as uniquely informed institutions, but it is

---

[23] Moreover, institutional investors receive the majority of allocations in IPOs, and hence receive the largest share of the profits deriving from underpricing: see Aggarwal, Prabhala, and Puri (2002).

[24] See Smith (1986) for early argument along the same lines. In contrast, Chowdhry and Nanda (1996) argue that price support benefits retail investors, by reducing the winner's curse.

[25] A substantial literature examines price support in the wake of IPOs. See, for example, Ruud (1990), who argues that underpricing appears to occur solely because of price support, Asquith and Jones (1998), who dispute Ruud's findings, and Schultz and Zaman (1994), Weiss Hanley, Kumar, and Seguin (1993), and Ellis, Michaely, and O'Hara (2000), all of whom find widespread evidence of price support.

[26] 'Fair'-pricing legislation affects the composition of the liquidity network as well as the rules of the offering. Sherman (2000) shows that when the investment bank relies upon liquidity provided by uninformed investors, average underpricing can be reduced by restricting the universe of uninformed traders and forcing them to accept higher allocations in cold issues to pay for the high returns that they earn from hot issues.

[27] Lowry and Shu (2002) show that about six percent of the companies that floated a US IPO between 1988 and 1995 were sued, with average damages of 13.3 percent of the proceeds being awarded against the company.

[28] See also Hughes and Thakor (1992) and Hensler (1995).

applicable only within the United States,[29] and has been undermined by subsequent empirical work.[30]

The 1933 Act also established clear rules for communication with investors: it discourages such communication prior to the filing of the registration statement. As a result, investment banks frequently revise their initial estimate of the price range before issuance occurs. In contrast, no such restrictions on information transmission exist in European markets. Jenkinson, Morrison, and Wilhelm (2005) argue that this allows European investment bankers to use the initial price range as a commitment device, and hence to design more efficient allocation mechanisms.

We close this section by noting that some authors have argued that the investment bank's information marketplace might allow it to exercise sophisticated rights over the control structure of the issuing corporation, as well as over the information used to value it. These theories argue that investment banks underprice issues to generate oversubscription which they can then use to manage initial stock allocations in a way that either weakens external governance (Brennan and Franks, 1997), or strengthens it (Stoughton and Zechner, 1998). Since stock underpricing is readily observable in these models, the investment banker is reduced to a bureaucratic cipher. Governance-centric explanations for IPO underpricing therefore have the economically unsatisfying feature of failing to explain the existence of the investment banker intermediary. Recent empirical work appears to mitigate against these stories, and in favor of informational explanations of investment banking.[31]

---

[29] There is little risk of begin sued in Australia, Finland, Germany, Japan, Sweden, Switzerland, or the United Kingdom, but all of these countries experience underpricing. See Ljungqvist (2007: 40).

[30] Underpricing is very variable (e.g. Ibbotson and Jaffe, 1975), so the post-1933 change in underpricing observed by Tinic could be due to any of a number of factors. Drake and Vetsuypens (1993) show that sued firms are no less underpriced than firms that are not sued. Tinic's work suggests that the best investment banks should underprice less than the others, because they are less likely to be sued: this was true when he wrote his paper, but, according to Beatty and Welch (1996) ceased to be in the 1990s. However, this result is the subject of some debate: Habib and Ljungqvist (2001) argue that the apparent change may reflect a selection bias: if only firms that *need* a high degree of certification go to the highest-ranking underwriters, then their higher underpricing will be an endogenous response to the composition of their portfolio.

[31] See, for example, Aruğaslan, Cook, and Kieschnick (2004), Cornelli and Goldreich (2003), Casares Field and Sheehan (2004), Smart and Zutter (2003), and Casares Field and Karapoff (2002).

We now turn to a discussion of the organizational structure that investment banks adopt in order to build and to use reputational capital.

INTERNAL ORGANIZATION

Traditional investment banking is a human capital business. The relationships upon which an investment bank's information market-place rests are managed by its employees. Information producers are incentivized using informal contracts which are designed and imple-mented by skilled investment bank staff. Much of the investment bank's expertise is not written down anywhere. In fact, it would be impossible to distill the activities of a skilled investment banker into an instruction book.

Skills that, like those of the traditional investment banker, are hard or impossible to codify are said to be *tacit* (see Polanyi, 1966). If invest-ment banking skills could be reduced to a recipe that putative bankers could learn then they could be certified by professional schools. This would undermine the value of the bank's reputation in maintaining and nurturing these skills. Hence investment bank profits are to some extent derived from the tacit nature of investment banking skills. But tacit skills represent a problem, as well as an opportunity. It is impossible to separate tacit skills from the people in whom they are embedded. As a result, an investment bank's reputation suffers from the departure of key individuals. Moreover, investment banking skills are typically general: they could be employed equally effectively in any sufficiently reputable institution.

The relationship between the investment bank and its employees is shaped by the danger that key workers will migrate to competitor firms, and take their skills with them. As a result, investment bankers are in a position to extract in negotiation with their employers a high proportion of the returns from their human capital. Naturally, this undermines the investment bank's incentives to invest either in the infrastructure which is required to maintain its network, or in the on-the-job training which is needed to run it.

We have repeatedly argued that incentive problems of the type identified in the previous paragraph are most effectively countered by creating property rights over the disputed asset: in this case, over the human capital of the employee. However, this human capital is not codifiable and it is not possible for employees legally to pledge it to an employer. Nevertheless, it is economically desirable that human capital should be pledged within investment banks. According to the theory developed in chapter two, we therefore expect informal institutions to arise which allow for the extra-legal contracting of human capital by putative investment bankers. Investment banks attempt to achieve this by adopting organizational structures that bind investment banker skills to their employers.

Investment banks were once organized as partnerships. We argue in chapter nine that this allowed associate bankers to commit not to sell any skills that they acquired during the training process to the highest bidder. Only by joining the partnership could they achieve any return on their new human capital, and membership of the partnership bound them to the investment bank for long enough to provide them with the requisite incentives to train the next generation of bankers.

The partnership form remained valuable for as long as it could support an adequate financial capitalization for investment banks, and for as long as on-the-job training to acquire tacit skills was essential. However, as we argued in chapter one, many of the activities of today's investment banks rely upon technical skills that can be acquired at arm's length. Moreover, these activities frequently rest upon expensive information technology, and are useful only when combined with a substantial level of financial capital.

Figure 3.2 illustrates this trend. It indicates the relative importance of tacit human capital and technical knowledge for each of the most important business activities of the modern investment bank. For

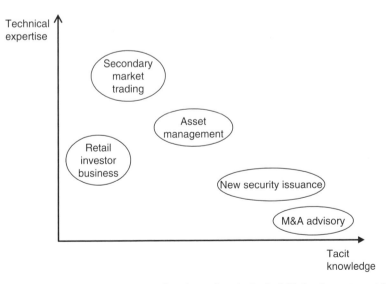

Figure 3.2. *Relative importance of tacit and technical skill for investment bank activities*

example, mergers and acquisitions work is still an advisory business, where success rests almost exclusively upon relationships and market information. Hence, while tacit human capital is very important for M&A work, technical wizardry is less so. Similarly, the traditional investment bank activity of security issuance is heavily relationship dependent. Although computers are increasingly used in the primary security markets, the key skills in these markets remain largely tacit, and business rests upon relational contracts. In contrast, secondary market trading rests upon technical skills that are closer to those of the engineer than the traditional investment banker. Trading houses do form relationships around the mutual supply of liquidity in secondary markets, but most of what they do is documented and can be enforced in court.

The other investment banking activities of asset management and retail investor broking lie between these polar extremes. We have argued that retail businesses cannot rest upon bilateral reputational contracting, and as a result tacit skill plays a small role in this business. Possibly the most important aspect of a successful retail trading operation is the back office operation, where deals are settled and documented. Since the advent of the mainframe computer, this has become a technical activity in which computer and workflow design skills outweigh human agency. Like retail broking, asset management requires expertise in documentation and settlement, both of which are technical skills. It also requires a technical understanding of the secondary market products being created elsewhere in the investment bank. While the repeated dealing relationships of the asset manager are more important than those of the retail broker, they are still of less importance than the relationships which the traditional investment banker calls upon within his information marketplace.

Figure 3.2 suggests that technical and tacit skills are substitutes within investment banks. In addition, technical skills are generally associated with greater scale and an increased need for financial capital. Since partnerships are important for fostering tacit human skill and can raise only limited capital, changes that emphasize the activities toward the top left of the figure will tend to undermine the case for the partnership. This is precisely what happened in the late twentieth century, when investment banks focused increasingly upon technical trading skills, while a greater use of computers served to increase the efficient scale of the investment bank. These effects ushered in the demise of the investment banking partnership (Morrison and Wilhelm, 2005). This left the investment banking industry with a dilemma: without the ability to tie an employee's financial capital to his human capital, how could an investment bank establish the extra-legal property rights over his skills without which the human capital-intensive aspects of investment banking were not viable?

Investment banks responded to these problems in a number of ways. First, the rise of computerization increased the codifiability of certain types of skill, and of some deal structures. These developments made it somewhat easier to establish property rights over research and development activities: it is easier to sue an innovator who takes a documented innovation to a competitor firm.[32]

Second, investment banks have attempted to take advantages of changes in US patent laws to intellectual property rights over their innovations (Lerner, 2002). Nevertheless, it is in general very hard for them to establish property rights over innovative deal structures, where their monopoly rights evaporate as soon as an issue occurs and reverse engineering is possible (Tufano, 1989, 2003; Carow, 1999). Persons and Warther (1997) argue that late movers benefit because they can observe the success or failure of early adopters. Because they do not pay for this information, there may be socially insufficient adoption of new innovations. This type of price-relevant information is of course the preserve of the investment bank: Benveniste, Busaba, and Wilhelm (2002) show that in concentrated industries, an investment banker could use its gatekeeper role to compel the later issuers to subsidize the first movers.[33]

The formal legal mechanisms of the previous two paragraphs have limited effectiveness, however. The dissolution of the partnerships made it much easier for investment bankers to switch employers. In addition, we argue in chapter nine that technological changes standardized many aspects of the workplace and hence made it easier for investment bankers to adapt to the cultural and environmental changes that previously had acted as an impediment to labor mobility. Naturally, investment banks attempted when they went public to adopt contractual provisions that reduced employee movement. They accomplished this in two ways. When they could, they created some of the aspects of a partnership contract with their senior employees, for example by giving them late-vesting shares. When a human

---

[32] See Aghion and Tirole (1994) and Anand and Galetovic (2000*b*).

[33] For further evidence of information spillovers at IPO, see Benveniste, Ljungqvist, and Wilhelm (2003), Booth and Chua (1996), Mauer and Senbet (1992), and Stoughton, Wong, and Zechner (2001).

capital-intensive business did not rely upon a complementary financial capital-intensive business this was unnecessary: the investment banks could instead spin the human capital business off.

INDUSTRIAL ORGANIZATION

Our argument so far is that investment banks manage information marketplaces within which the investment banker's reputation acts as a basis for extra-legal contracting over price-relevant information. The bank therefore devotes much of its efforts to reputation management. It accomplishes this by varying the composition of its networks in response to reputational considerations, which are in turn affected by business conditions and the technological backdrop against which self-regulatory bodies operate. The network management activities of the various investment banks clearly have implications for the industrial organization of the industry. It is to these implications that we now turn.

We start by noting that an investment bank's reputation gives it a great deal of market power. Informal informational contracts within an information marketplace are meaningful only to the extent that they are underwritten by an investment banker's reputation. Hence the investment bank is a local monopolist within its information market: at least in dealing with its smaller customers, it occupies a strong bargaining position. There appears to be little price competition among smaller corporations: Chen and Ritter (2000) show that 91 percent of deals in the $20–$80 million range are priced at seven percent. Indeed, as Baker (1990) argues, it is in the best interests of smaller corporations to maintain a close relationship with their investment banker so as to diminish the latter's incentives for opportunism. Consonant with this statement, Nanda and Warther (1998) find that the smallest corporations are the most loyal to their investment bankers, and that they are rewarded for their loyalty with lower fees.

Hansen (2001) finds that the investment banking market is neither extremely concentrated nor hard to enter. Nevertheless, the discussion in the previous paragraph suggests that there may be substantial reputational barriers to entry. This point is made by De Long (1991), who argues that the impossibility of matching JP Morgan's nineteenth-century reputation gave the firm a strong competitive position. Reputations are hard to build, and they are the source of all of the investment bank's profits. They are also extremely fragile: this observation lay behind our statement on page 83 that investment bankers would tend to turn away issuers who had the potential to undermine their reputation for price discovery. For example, the 1990 failure of the junk bond house Drexel Burnham Lambert was attributable entirely to the reputational hit that it sustained in the wake of the SEC's insistence that it fire Michael Milken and pay a $650 million fine. No other investment bank had anything like Drexel's reputational capital in the junk market. As a result, Drexel's commercial bank competitors were the main beneficiary of their failure (Benveniste, Singh, and Wilhelm, 1993).

We have already noted that investment banks manage their issuer network so as to protect their reputations. This observation indicates that the investment banking market must consist of a number of reputationally differentiated firms, each of which trades off the value of attracting more business against the expected reputational costs of accepting it. When information is hard to come by, and reputations are more valuable, we expect the most reputable banks to be most protective of their reputations, and hence we expect the market to be more segmented. Changes in information and communications technologies that improve the quality of the bank's information network will therefore tend to increase the size of the best investment bank networks, and hence will result in industry consolidation.

The value of an investment bank's information marketplace is undermined when information could leak from it. A related point is made by Anand and Galetovic (2000*a*), in a model where financial intermediaries (who could be investment bankers) gather information for themselves. Information leakage, either through staff poaching or the price mechanism, destroys information-gathering incentives in their model. They show that a system of tacit collusion can sustain a market structure in which every intermediary has a sufficiently strong local monopoly to provide information-gathering incentives. Any attempt to interfere with a competitor's business results in their model in a free-for-all which destroys the value of the market.

Unlike Anand and Galetovic, we do not regard the investment bank primarily as an information producer: we argue that it runs an information marketplace within which information producers have incentives to produce price-relevant data. The marketplace is sustained not by tacit collusion with the other investment banks, but by the investment bank's reputational capital. However, our conclusion that information leakage would undermine these incentives, and with them the investment bank's reputation, is in line with Anand and Galetovic. The danger of information leakage is heightened when an investor is a member of several investment bank networks. As a result, we expect investment banks to attempt to ensure whenever possible that they have exclusive access to their investors, and to their information producers. Doing so will protect their reputations, and so differentiate themselves from their competitors. Only the largest investors, whose spending power can significantly affect the success or failure of a new issue, will have the bargaining power necessary to obtain egress into several networks.

In summary, our arguments suggest that the investment banking market consists of a number of distinct information marketplaces, differentiated according to the reputations of the investment banks that run them. As the availability of information technology increases, the value of investment banker reputation reduces, so that the networks can grow larger, and the number of investment banks can fall. Information producers and investors will tend to have one major investment bank relationship, so as to minimize the danger of information leakage.

Investment banker networks will not be completely distinct: we argue above that powerful investors will be able to join several of them. Moreover, restrictions on network size intended to protect the investment banker's reputation lower the maximum deal size which a network can absorb. Both of these effects have deleterious efficiency consequences. The obvious way for investment banks to overcome this is to combine their networks in deals where network overlap is likely to be a problem, or when they need to raise very large quantities of capital. This type of combination is called a *syndicate*. Syndicate members account for the effects of information leakage within their combined networks, and hence raise welfare. Within a single syndicate, one member may benefit at the expense of another, but the members of a long-term repeated syndicate relationship will gain in aggregate more than they would have made from a series of non-syndicated deals where information leakage would have occurred.

We argued on page 80 that syndicates perform a valuable cross-monitoring role. This explanation dovetails nicely with our alternative story of the syndicates as a way of resolving network overlap problems. Investment banks may wish to find a (noncontractual) way to commit to form syndicates when they issue securities. Such a commitment ensures that they form a public reputation, and hence makes them more attractive to potential issuers. It can be provided by admitting to an information network an investor who is already a member of another network. Issuance performed without syndication would then result in information leakage: information producers who anticipated this would refuse to gather information, and so would undermine their investment bank's reputation. Network overlap therefore provides the right incentives to ensure that cross-monitoring occurs through a syndicate.

CONCLUSION

We conclude by summarizing our argument.

Innovations should be brought to market only if the opportunity costs of the capital needed to develop them are outweighed by their potential economic gains. Economic development therefore rests not only upon the development of new productive ideas but also upon the creation and dissemination to capitalists of information about the likely demand for these ideas. It is therefore extremely important that the right incentives exist for the production and sharing of price-relevant information about new products. The best way to create these incentives would be to assign property-rights over price-relevant information. Unfortunately, this is a technological impossibility. Investment banks are informal property-rights institutions that are designed to substitute for formal legal property rights over price-relevant information.

Investment banks create and manage information marketplaces, within which innovators in search of capital, information producers able to generate price-relevant information, large-scale investors who can provide liquidity, and also smaller investors, meet to trade informal property rights over the price-relevant information needed to float a new issue. The investment bank acts as an intermediary in this marketplace: it collects information from information producers, and disseminates it to innovators and to investors. Since the information is not contractible, the investment bank's reputation is central to its role. It therefore manages its network so as to maximize the value that it derives from its reputation.

Since it is impossible to observe every relevant parameter of the relationship between a bank and its information producers, the bank has to maintain a separate bilateral relationship with each of them. This places an upper bound on the size of the information network. The investment bank is unable to maintain bilateral reputations with the majority of its issuers, because they are infrequent entrants into its marketplace and hence the immediate benefits of cheating one of them are likely to outweigh the long-term profits from not doing so.

As a result, the bank will search for ways in which its customers can share information about its behavior: this facilitates the maintenance of a public reputation, which provides a credible commitment to play fair with issuers.

Issuers will pay more to deal with a high-reputation investment bank. Banks that issue securities from an issuer with highly uncertain quality therefore risk their reputation, and they will refuse to issue securities above some uncertainty threshold. This leads to a stratification of the investment banking market by bank reputation. Any bank's uncertainty threshold must be decreasing in the value of reputation, so technological changes that ease the acquisition of reputation must therefore result in consolidation of the investment banking business.

Reputation management involves the restriction of entry into the information network by information producers and large investors, as well as by issuers. Membership of multiple networks is likely to result in information leakage, and hence to reduce the value of the information marketplace. Investment banks will therefore discourage their information producers from maintaining active relationships with other banks. When there is overlap between their networks, investment banks are likely to attempt to internalize the associated information externalities by combining forces to form syndicates. Syndicates are relatively more likely to arise when information is widely dispersed, and when deal sizes are large.

Since investment banks rely upon the highly portable general human capital of their workforce, they have evolved methods of establishing weak extra-legal property rights over this capital, so as to avoid giving up all of the rents which it generates. In the past, investment banking partnerships served to tie human capital to the firm. More recently, sophisticated compensation arrangements have attempted to achieve the same outcome. When these have not created sufficiently strong property rights over employee human capital, investment banks have responded by spinning off divisions where human capital is particularly important.

4

Investment Banking Origins

Investment banking is a response to complex problems of informational asymmetries, conflicting objectives, and ill-defined or unassignable property rights. In a market order complex institutions like investment banks do not appear overnight, and nor are they designed. Rather, they are an evolved response to prevailing technological and economic forces; these forces are themselves shaped in turn by the institutions to which they give rise. Understanding the evolution of the investment bank can help us to understand its current role, and may help us to make sensible statements about its likely future development. Hence we take up an examination of the origins and evolution of the investment bank, beginning in this chapter with the long eighteenth century running from 1688 to 1815.

Investment banks could emerge only when certain conditions were satisfied. First, investment banks create and trade complex bundles of promises and property rights. This type of activity is possible only in a world where freely made contracts are enforceable and where property rights are respected. Hence, investment banks require appropriate legal institutions.

As we have already argued, investment banks are valuable in the presence of informational problems that undermine arm's-length price-intermediated contracts. Problems of this type can be solved on a small scale by social institutions such as the family.[1] So the second precondition for investment banking is the existence of informational frictions which cannot be solved through small-scale community-based interactions.

Maturing legal systems, which guaranteed security of property, and growth in long-distance trade, which highlighted information-based contractual problems, were both features of the long eighteenth

---

[1] Indeed, the evidence from developing economies is that, in the absence of well-protected property rights, economic activity never moves beyond the family-intermediated level. See Ch. 2 n 6.

century. In this chapter we examine these prerequisites for the emergence of the investment bank. We show how they interacted to influence the structure and performance of the mercantile networks and organizations that laid the foundation for the modern investment bank. An institution recognizable as the modern investment bank did not appear until the second half of the nineteenth century. In chapter five we argue that this required the satisfaction of a final precondition for sustaining the investment bank: commercial conditions and technologies capable respectively of generating and coping with the large volume of informational exchange necessary to support the complex reputation-intensive network described in chapter three.

We begin our discussion by providing the context for our discussion of communications and informational frictions. For most of the long eighteenth century, Amsterdam was the preeminent center of trade and finance and its preeminence was rooted in its capacity for information exchange, so we start there.

INFORMATION EXCHANGE

Seventeenth-century Netherlands was unusual in its devotion to commerce, its religious pluralism, and its limited government. Hence it is perhaps natural that Amsterdam was then the world's dominant center of commerce. Situated as it was at the nexus of international trade, Amsterdam became the center of commercial information exchange and its ability to process this information generated local skills and economies of scale that made its position as a financial center unassailable throughout much of the century.

Personal correspondence between individual merchants accounted for a large fraction of the commercial information flowing through Amsterdam. It was customary in the seventeenth century to include in such correspondence information about exchange rates and prices. Information of a more tacit nature was presumably conveyed in explicit face-to-face dealings between businessmen.[2] But it is noteworthy that the information that circulated in Amsterdam in the seventeenth century, and which bolstered its position as a center of trade, was in the main hard facts concerning market conditions and prices, and political news.

Some information was harder to quantify. For example, even if they were willing to share it, merchants might have struggled to pass on their knowledge of their counterparts' creditworthiness. To the extent

[2] Smith (1984: 992–3).

that such information depended upon the history of the counterparts' dealings with their creditors, it was of limited transferability anyway. Hence, less codifiable information resided on the whole in the agents who used it.[3]

Amsterdam also helped to develop important institutions for the widespread dissemination of commercial information. Newspapers had existed previously, but in seventeenth-century Amsterdam they were printed regularly and gave a wide circulation to information culled from the local exchanges. At the same time, merchant handbooks containing information about business conditions in major markets gained a mass market.[4] Even the Dutch East India Company's (the VOC's) Amsterdam chamber and the Exchange Bank promoted the formal dissemination of information, and the VOC eventually devoted some of its resources to the capture and analysis of such information.[5]

Finally, the presence of the Amsterdam Bourse, which had been established in 1530, resulted in information dissemination. As Baskin and Miranti (1997: 98) observe, opportunities to profit from private information encouraged speculative activity that promoted information transmission through financial market prices. The Exchange created the liquidity that underpinned this type of trading by supporting margin trading and option trading.[6]

Ironically, Amsterdam's success in promoting the exchange and widespread dissemination of information may have undermined its hegemony as a center of trade. The technological change that facilitated the rapid dissemination of hard facts reduced the value of a physical presence at the nexus of exchange. One important technological advance of this sort involved the seventeenth-century European postal system. By the middle of the century postal delivery was about

[3] However, it seems that the Dutch attempted to create a central repository for some types of credit information. When the Bank of Amsterdam was founded in 1609, 'the City of Amsterdam decreed that all bills of exchange of 600 florins or more be paid at the Bank of Amsterdam in bank money rather than elsewhere in current coin [...] The fact that exporters and importers were required to transact sizable bills of exchange meant that they had to keep accounts there' (Kindleberger, 1993: 50).

[4] See Smith (1984: 999). Both newspapers and merchant handbooks were published in several languages for sale throughout Europe; the latter provided facts about 'business procedures, taxes, laws, banking facilities, and major products available in various trading centers'.

[5] Smith (1984: 996–7).

[6] The market microstructure literature emphasizes the importance of liquidity trading in sustaining informed trade. See Ch. 3 n. 4.

as fast, especially at short distances, if not as cheap, as the modern system.[7]

The improvements in roads and sailing ships that speeded the postal service also increased the scope of information dissemination. For example, by the 1720s, there were at least 40 tax-paying newspapers in London, three of which were dailies. By the early 1770s both the number of newspapers and the number of dailies had doubled. Merchants were avid consumers of, and contributors to, the commercial information reported in these papers. Books began to circulate more widely during the eighteenth century, and they contributed to the increased volume of easily accessed commercial information.[8]

Although the dissemination of hard information was improving, Amsterdam's status as the center of the commercial world remained secure for as long as the less easily transferred tacit knowledge upon which merchants relied remained in Amsterdam. The center of gravity for this type of information began to shift from the Netherlands in the early eighteenth century as Dutch traders sent sons or other family members to serve as local agents in London.[9] The extended family networks thus created used the rapid mail service between Amsterdam and London. In time the British industrial revolution increased the relative importance of the London arm of the networks, and the pursuit of safe haven from the Napoleonic Wars sealed Amsterdam's fate.[10]

In spite of the expansion of long-distance trade, merchant operations looked much the same at the end of the eighteenth century as they had in fourteenth-century Italy.[11] The movement of raw materials and finished goods over long distances was slow and subject to the vagaries of the weather.[12] Information moved at the same pace. The 1817 opening of the 'Black Ball Line' was considered an important

[7] Smith (1984: 991): '[...] mail could be passed between Amsterdam and Paris in six days by the "ordinary" post, and in two days by more expensive express service [...] Most correspondence with London depended on twice-weekly packets, but express communication could also be bought.'

[8] See Hancock (1995: 32–6) and the citations therein for detailed accounts of the information available to merchants and the contents of one merchant's (Richard Oswald's) library.

[9] Chapman (1984: 56).

[10] See Baskin and Miranti (1997: ch. 3) for a brief account of the emergence of financial markets in Amsterdam and London.

[11] Chandler (1977: 37).

[12] Although Bruchey (1958: 284) suggests that uncertainty was less than it appears, because records indicate that arrival dates for shipments from England to America did not vary greatly from year to year.

innovation in transatlantic trade because its ships sailed monthly between New York and Liverpool whether they were full or not.[13] As the scale and geographic scope of trade grew, so too did the demand for intermediaries who could mobilize the larger sums required over the longer periods necessary for long-distance trade.[14] The general merchants who served this demand were simultaneously engaged in importing and exporting, wholesaling, retailing, banking, and insurance: they later became known as 'merchant banks'.[15]

Because communications still took weeks or months, it was necessary for merchants to delegate decision-making authority to local agents. But the forces that argued for delegated decision-making also amplified agency problems. Merchants were therefore more concerned when selecting their partners with their character than with their business skill.[16] For some time into the nineteenth century, and certainly as late as the 1830s (before the establishment of the telegraph), credit was generally limited to a narrow group with whom the lender had personal contact 'and the few attempts that were made to go beyond this (notably in the mid-1830s) ended in disaster'.[17] Before we examine how the merchant community dealt with such problems, we describe the evolving institutional and legal environment in which they worked.

INSTITUTIONS AND THE LAW

Institutional Change in the United Kingdom

The modern literature on institutional economics provides ample evidence that economic development is greatly impeded by absolutist and despotic rule.[18] Hence, as we argued on pages 45–50, an important prerequisite for growth is the creation of political and legal institutions that can act as a brake on any tendency of the sovereign to usurp property rights. Without these institutions, capital markets will not develop. The legal system within which capital markets, and later

---

[13] See Chapman (1992: 85). The voyage averaged 28 days.
[14] Neal (1990: 4).
[15] See p. 123 for a detailed discussion of the switch from merchanting to merchant banking.
[16] 'Loyalty and honesty were still more important than business acumen' (Chandler, 1977: 8).
[17] Chapman (1984: 108). Myers (1931: 52) also argues that the extension of commercial credit in America during the pre-Civil War period remained very much a personal matter.
[18] For some representative references on this, see Ch. 2 nn. 6 and 10.

investment banks, flourished, emerged in seventeenth- and early eighteenth-century England. We trace this process in this section, and we show that, once appropriate institutions had emerged, English capital markets developed rapidly.[19]

While Amsterdam was dominating the seventeenth-century commercial scene, the English[20] legal system and constitution struggled to attain the maturity that would later underpin its mercantile empire. The system by which the Crown governed parliament was largely inherited by the Stuarts from the Tudors. Parliament met at the monarch's pleasure, and its main source of influence was its power to provide the Crown with tax revenues. During the seventeenth century, the Crown's revenues typically fell short of its expenditures. The shortfall was increasingly made up through the appropriation by the Crown of private property.

The Crown's ability to govern without parliament rested upon its ability under the royal prerogative to make proclamations and royal ordinances. While the prerogative was not unlimited in scope, it conferred widespread powers, including the dissolution of parliament and the calling of elections, the declaration of war, and the granting of Charters of Incorporation. The laws generated by the prerogative were enforced through the prerogative courts rather than the common law courts. In matters relating to the prerogative, the final court was the Star Chamber, which could reverse decisions against the Crown. The King was therefore able by issuing proclamations to alter the jurisdiction of a dispute in his favor. James I and Charles I both used the Star Chamber to examine cases of sedition: in practice again, this meant that the court could be used to suppress opposition to the Crown. Finally, judges in England were paid by the Crown, which could dispense with their services if it wished.

The Stuarts' increasingly arbitrary use in the seventeenth century of their powers of prerogative in response to their financially straightened circumstances was sustainable so long as they did not need to call upon parliament for tax revenues and, of course, abuse of the prerogative reduced the need for tax revenues. North and Weingast (1989) show that the Crown used its powers to impose new customs tariffs, to extract forced loans and to change unilaterally their terms, and in selling monopolies. The constant threat of

---

[19] The historical discussion in this section draws upon Trevelyan ([1938] 1950).

[20] The Act of Union with Scotland was not passed until 1707. Wales had been subsumed 400 years previously.

state interference in freely made contracts thus undermined English commercial life.

The English civil wars of 1642–51 were the consequence of a number of complex reasons, many of which were religious. Animosity between the propertied classes in England and the Crown arising from the abuse by Charles I of the royal prerogative was however a significant contributing factor. The Long Parliament abolished the Star Chamber in 1641 by the passage of a law which required all cases concerning property to be tried according to common law (North and Weingast, 1989). At the same time, some restrictions on the movement of workers were lifted and modifications to land tenure laws in favor of the freeholder were passed. Hence, some movement toward freedom of contract and the recognition of property rights occurred.

However, England was not ready for republicanism and the monarchy was restored in 1660 with the coronation of Charles II. The restoration settlement did not prove robust to the continued demands of the later Stuarts and to their perceived absolutist tendencies. A particularly significant example in the context of financial market development was Charles II's 'stop of the exchequer', which provides a vivid illustration of the weakness of contemporary English property rights. In 1672, Charles, already financially stretched by the plague and the fire of London, and in need of funds to fight a war with the Dutch, unilaterally suspended payment of about £1.2 million-worth of his debt.[21] The stop lasted two years, after which some provision was made for the payment of arrears. However, only about six years' worth of interest payments on arrears was made between 1677 and 1689. It was extremely hard for the creditors to appeal against the monarch in his own courts, and it was thirty years before they were able to secure a House of Lords ruling in their favor.[22]

Fear in the country that the Catholic James II would impose his religious views upon the Protestant majority, coupled with his use of the royal prerogative without parliamentary approval, led in 1688 to the so-called Glorious Revolution.[23] The constitutional settlement in the wake of the Glorious Revolution restructured England's political

---

[21] The debt concerned took the form of Treasury Orders, a (largely unsuccessful) attempt to bypass financial intermediaries, and instead to borrow directly from the public.

[22] See Carruthers (1996: 60–9 and 122–7) for a detailed discussion of the stop of the exchequer.

[23] This term refers to the decision by prominent parliamentarians to offer the crown to James' son-in-law, the Dutchman William of Orange. William, a Protestant, was effectively granted the throne in exchange for his assent to a Declaration of Rights

institutions so as to curb absolutist rule by the Crown. In particular (North and Weingast, 1989: 815) '... the Glorious Revolution ushered in a fiscal revolution'. English government finances were placed on a secure footing, which served to disincentivize the Crown from attempting appropriations of the type that characterized the early Stuarts. In practice, this meant that after the Revolution, parliament acquired the central role in managing the state's debts, and that these debts were no longer the Crown's. Parliament's exclusive right to impose taxes was reasserted, and the supremacy of common law to the Royal prerogative was assured. As North and Weingast note, the supremacy of the common law served still further to guarantee property rights in England.[24]

One month after William's coronation, he entered a conflict between France and the Low Countries by declaring war on France. This act was costly and resulted in the annual recall of parliament to approve the army budget and the associated borrowings. This annual recall served to reinforce the constitutional arrangements in the Bill of Rights, and it also resulted in the 1694 foundation of a national bank, when the government invited subscribers to a new war loan to incorporate as the Bank of England.[25] It was prevented from advancing money to the government without the approval of Parliament and, as North and Weingast observe, the Bank's independence was a powerful incentive to repay loans, since a failure to do so would result in a cessation of disbursements by the Bank.

In summary, the Glorious Revolution ushered in a century in which the power of government was constrained by parliament, and when property rights and contracts were respected under the common law. 'Government was no longer seen as an instrument of radical change; rather, its functions were felt to be the handling of domestic order, the handling of public finance, the protection of commercial interests,

---

(later passed as the Bill of Rights), which placed limitations upon his ability to act without parliamentary sanction; James was allowed to escape to France.

[24] North and Weingast's work has not received universal plaudits. Clark (1996: 588) categorizes their argument as 'Whig history of the most egregious sort', arguing that England had in fact enjoyed secure capital markets since 1540. Sussman and Yafeh (2004) argue that the constitutional changes of the Glorious Revolution had little effect upon the terms upon which the British government borrowed money in the following century. Carruthers (1996: 134–6) criticizes their failure to discuss the assignability of public debt, and the importance in this context of the incorporation of the law merchant into the common law, and in particular is critical of their failure to acknowledge the importance of party politics in shaping English capital markets.

[25] The Bank's charter was the basis in 1790 of Alexander Hamilton's American banking legislation. See Hammond ([1957] 1967: 3).

the conduct of diplomacy and war'.[26] In this environment British merchants prospered, carrying out three-quarters of British overseas trade in the eighteenth century.[27] In particular, freed as they were from concerns over contract and property right enforcement, they were free to experiment with the types of contracting and relationship-based trade that later came to characterize the investment bank.

The growth in stature through the eighteenth century of the Bank of England was of equal importance in the development of the invest-ment banking institution. During the long eighteenth century, Eng-land or Britain was involved in seven extended wars and the national debt multiplied throughout this period. The institutional apparatus of the Bank of England was essential in financing these wars, and the resources that this borrowing mobilized were in large part responsible for Britain's military success against larger and wealthier countries such as France.[28] The Bank's importance in raising and managing the national debt resulted, notwithstanding some early problems regard-ing its charter renewal, in its emergence 'not only as an ordinary bank, but as a great engine of state'.[29] Indeed, during the House of Commons debate over the 1781 charter renewal, Lord North stated that the Bank 'from long habit and the usage of many years, was part of the constitution'.[30]

North and Weingast provide evidence consistent with the hypothe-sis that political and financial institutional changes after the Glorious Revolution improved contracting conditions. Better contracts generate more credible commitments and thus should reduce the cost of finance and raise the level of productive economic activity. Government debt on the eve of the Revolution was £1 million. The war and the increased government ability to tap the markets resulted in a sharp rise in debt: to £8.4 million in 1695, £16.7 million in 1697, and £78 million by 1750.[31] Over this period there was no sustained inflation: the price level in 1750 was below that of 1688. At the same time, the interest rate charged on government borrowing dropped, from 14 percent in the 1690s to 6.3 percent in 1697, and three percent in 1739.[32]

Arguably, the rise of public borrowing in the years after the Glorious Revolution served to advance Britain's commercial, as well as her military, aims. Experimentation with the placement of government

[26] Baker (1973: 203).   [27] Price (1973: 153).   [28] Dickson (1967: 9).
[29] Smith (1776).   [30] Bowen (1995: 3, 6).
[31] North and Weingast (1989: 822, table 3).
[32] North and Weingast (1989: 824, table 4).

debt led the Bank of England and the institutions with which it dealt to create a range of new securities and services. These innovations promoted innovation in both the law and the trading venues that mutated into the modern security markets. More generally, it is conceivable that eighteenth-century economic development would have followed a very different path were it not for the innovations triggered by war borrowing. Hartwell (1971: 245–50) goes so far as to suggest that the judge-made common law of England was the 'unique national characteristic that distinguished England from Continental countries' and that it triggered its lead in the first industrial revolution toward the end of the long eighteenth century.[33]

Commercial Law

Commercial law emerged from dealings within relatively small and close-knit groups of merchants. The merchants of the early eighteenth century had relatively homogeneous interests, dealt mostly with one another, and were well acquainted with commercial documents and customs. As a class, they were skeptical of the state's ability to resolve differences among them and thus relied heavily on extra-legal enforcement of agreements. This skepticism was reflected in the first part of the century by a reliance among merchants upon private arbitration.[34]

During the second half of the century, English common law recognized the complexity of mercantile disputes. 'Struck' juries, consisting entirely of merchants who were in a better position to weigh the complexities that arose in commercial disputes, were made a staple of English judicial settlement of commercial disputes by Lord Mansfield.[35] In 1741, the state of New York adopted a 1730 English statute regulating the selection of struck juries and by 1764 New York merchants refrained from appealing arbitration decisions if doing so would only place them before a jury of their professional peers.[36]

As the old law merchant was absorbed into the common law and the courts became more willing to accommodate the special needs of merchants, they began in the postrevolutionary period

---

[33] See also Levi (1988), who argues in a comparison of early modern France and England that the relatively weak position of the English sovereign with respect to its parliament gave England a greater capacity to generate state revenue.

[34] Before Lord Mansfield became Chief Justice of the King's Bench in 1756, Lord Campbell maintained that 'mercantile questions were so ignorantly treated when they came into Westminster Hall, that they were usually settled by private arbitration among the merchants themselves'. See Horwitz (1977: 147).

[35] Horwitz (1977: 155).   [36] Horwitz (1977: 155).

actively to undermine extrajudicial dispute resolution.[37] In 1803, the Pennsylvania Supreme Court announced that it would set aside arbitration decisions that evidenced mistakes in law or fact.[38] As similar positions were taken elsewhere, merchants were forced for the first time to recognize the dominant legal role of the Bar.[39] By 1807 merchant juries were no longer deciding commercial cases in New York.[40]

Both the suppression of extrajudicial enforcement mechanisms and struck juries reflected, in part, a decline in the homogeneity of mercantile interests. But, as we outline in chapter five, this occurred at the same time that the courts, especially the US federal courts, became more accommodating to commercial interests.

To the extent that courts displaced traditional extrajudicial enforcement mechanisms, it might appear that the function we ascribe to the investment bank was diminished. We contend, however, that it was precisely the codification of dispute resolution in a wide range of commercial activity that enabled institutions like investment banks to specialize in managing the far more subtle and complex incentive conflicts arising in pure information exchange. In particular, the standardization of the law of negotiable instruments (see pp. 129–132) was particularly important in enabling merchants to become merchant bankers and then investment bankers in the nineteenth century.

Before we turn in the next chapter to a discussion of the emergence of the investment bank, we examine the management by eighteenth-century merchants of information flows within their trading networks against the evolving technological and legal backdrop described above.

MERCANTILE NETWORKS

Trust as a Technological Requirement

We stress in our theory of the investment bank the importance of the network at whose center it sits. At the network's extremities lie the institutions about and from whom the bank gathers information.

---

[37] 'In 1788, the Pennsylvania Supreme Court observed that since the Revolution it had intervened more often to correct findings of fact and conclusions of law in referees' reports'. Horwitz (1977: 152).

[38] Horwitz (1977: 152). By 1833, a Pennsylvania legal writer could maintain that 'a cause decided by arbitrators, and taken into court by appeal, comes up for trial under circumstances not in the slightest degree favorable to him whom the arbitrators have thought right, than if the matter had never been investigated [before]'. (Horwitz, 1977: 152).

[39] Horwitz (1977: 144).   [40] See Horwitz (1977: 155–9).

Since information ownership in an otherwise uninformed world gives the bank the opportunity to profit either at the expense of its clients, or at that of ill-informed investor counterparts, trust is central to the investment bank's operations. Trust makes institutions comfortable revealing privileged information, and trust makes the investment bank's capitalist clients comfortable when they risk their resources at the investment bank's recommendation, and when they pay fees to do so. Hence trust is a valuable commodity for the investment bank, and the future (quasi-)rents that accrue to it ensure that the trust is not broken in the present.

Trust is unnecessary in a market where actions are contractible. Entry into such a market would be easy and, arguably, efficiency would be enhanced by greater competition and the lower transactions costs that obtain when responsibilities are clearly delineated. Investment bankers work in a market for non-contractible information. Any attempt to contract away the need for trust would of necessity reveal to an enforcement agency the information whose confidentiality was the basis for trust. At the same time, investors would learn valuable information costlessly and the investment bank could not hope to profit from its information discovery role. If investment banks were forced to operate in this way they could not exist.

Hence the centrality of reputation and trust to the investment bank's activities is more than an institutional curiosity or coincidence: it is a technological necessity. No one has found a way to obviate the need in the modern investment bank for trust. When they do, investment banks will become obsolete. The technological need to maintain information at a tacit rather than at a codified level has wider repercussions for the internal organization of the investment bank. Investment bankers rely less upon qualifications acquired in school than they do upon those acquired on-the-job and as a result, in-house training is important. Moreover, because essential personnel information is non-codifiable, the size of an investment bank is restricted by a free-rider problem in cross-monitoring by its senior members. The tacit nature of investment banking activities renders monitoring doubly difficult. As a result, investment bankers place a high premium upon personal relationships and upon trust when hiring their peers. Furthermore, until recent technological changes, investment banks were for this reason financed via inside capital as partnerships.

We return to these ideas in chapter nine.[41] Our goal in this chapter is to demonstrate that the technological requirement for trust was a

---

[41] See also Morrison and Wilhelm (2004) for a more technical presentation.

feature of eighteenth- and early nineteenth-century mercantilism. As a result, many of the features of the investment bank's network were developed in merchant networks. We focus largely upon the Atlantic trade between Britain and America. Many of the wars Britain waged in the first half of the eighteenth century were waged to protect exclusive access to the American markets[42] and some of the most important of the Anglo-American trading houses became over the course of the following two centuries the first merchant and investment banks.

The Scale of the Merchant Network

As Price (1973: 153) remarks, there is relatively little information about the London merchant houses upon which the pre-1776 Atlantic trade largely rested. Their detailed records were preserved until 1800, when they were surrendered to government commissioners paying compensation for debt uncollected as a result of the war. After this they appear to have been lost. Nevertheless, some scholarly work has been performed using the few records that remain. Price provides a detailed account of the operations of one merchant, Joshua Johnson, who represented his Chesapeake trading partners as a buying agent in London. More recently, Hancock (1995) provides a detailed account of the lives of, and the networks that surrounded, four London merchants in the eighteenth century, who sat at the heart of global (for the eighteenth century) trading networks, and coordinated the movement of people and goods through them. Much of the discussion in this section draws upon these works.

The population of Britain increased in the eighteenth century from 5 to 8.6 million, while that of the North American colonies grew from 250 thousand to about 2.15 million in 1770.[43] While the British economy grew relatively slowly in this period, foreign trade expanded rapidly. Through the course of the century, the share of trade accounted for by Europe dropped from 80 to 40 percent,[44] and by the end of the century, America was the most valuable of Britain's export markets. To some extent, England's military advances went hand-in-glove with her commercial expansion: some wars were fought to protect or to create monopoly access to new markets.

Britain's imperial expansion generated trading opportunities for her mercantile classes on a global scale. As Hancock notes, the associated coordination problems were extremely complex. For example,

---

[42] See, for example, Dickson (1967: 8).   [43] Hancock (1995: 27).
[44] Hancock (1995: 37).

the exchange of East Indian cloth for West Indian slaves required years of preparation and coordination in many markets.[45] The organizational problems that these merchants faced were for the most part new ones. They could not draw upon an existing infrastructure, and nor could they trade in an international marketplace in the modern sense, since no such marketplace existed. Communications were rudimentary and, although the English legal system was starting to assume its current form, there were significant uncertainties in international contract enforcement.

In this environment, the mercantile classes had to create an infrastructure within which they could operate, they had to find ways to circumvent the massive informational asymmetries that existed across the Atlantic, and they had to find ways of operating within an evolving common law system founded in agricultural rather than mercantile disputes. Throughout the eighteenth century, merchants on both sides of the Atlantic actively sought to avoid common law decisions involving commercial disputes.[46] Private arbitration was the common means of settling disputes, but the arbitrator's decision carried force only insofar as parties risked loss of reputation within the broader merchant community for failing to abide by the decision. Their experimentation gave rise to new organizational forms and, in the face of the technological limitations that they faced, to contractual devices that frequently relied upon trust, rather than upon legal redress.

The great thinkers of the eighteenth-century Scottish Enlightenment understood the benefits of specialization coupled with trade.[47] Yet the merchants of the eighteenth century did not in general specialize. They traded raw materials and manufactured goods, they acted as financiers for their customers, and they managed sales and purchasing networks on both sides of the Atlantic. Since there were no legal impediments to the formation of separate enterprises to manage each of these activities separately, we must look elsewhere for an explanation. It comes in the shape of transactions costs.

A transaction cost is incurred when an economic exchange incurs a real cost. For example, this could be the cost of finding a counterpart, of checking a counterpart's honesty, of drawing up satisfactory contracts, or of subjecting the counterparts to a legal obligation (such as a guaranteed severance payment). Much of modern economics

---

[45] See Hancock (1995: 37) for details of this trade.   [46] See page 106.
[47] The cannonical example of this is the pin factory that appears at the start of Adam Smith's book (1776).

ignores the existence of transactions costs, but they are central to an understanding of economic organizations and economic institutions. The choice between two organizational forms is frequently dictated by the relative levels of the costs that each will incur in the institutional context (laws, enforcement mechanisms, social norms, and technological environment) within which it will operate.[48]

As we noted on page 51, Coase (1937) used the above observations to explain the boundaries of the firm. Coase noted that economic activity within the firm is directed in response to a central plan, while activity in the marketplace occurs through arm's-length price-intermediated exchange. While there are efficiency gains from specialization and from the operation of a price system, separating activities from the firm in order to reap these gains may be costly. For example, it may be hard when transactions volumes are low to discover an appropriate price for an intermediate stage production good; when goods are of insufficient quality, it may be more costly to use the courts to chase an external supplier than to generate punishments in-house; it may be more costly to write an adequate contract for an arm's-length supplier who cannot easily be monitored than it is to provide the right incentives to an in-house agent; and so on. When the potential efficiency gains from specialization are swamped by the transactions costs that it entails, economic activities will be better directed than left to the price system.

We have already argued that eighteenth-century merchants faced enormous transactions costs. A London merchant purchasing goods in the United States was unable to see the goods, easily to visit his suppliers, or with ease to chase them through the courts. From his London counting-house, he generally had only a sketchy knowledge of market conditions in the United States and hence was placed at a significant bargaining disadvantage when dealing with local experts. Hence, his US operations would be managed by a local representative. Finding such a representative was a major challenge for a putative merchant. Hancock (1995: 83) states that:

In all of their endeavors, the associates had to find, place, and keep competent, honest, and loyal managers at the places where the goods were produced and the trades were negotiated. Since the associates managed their businesses over long distances and with rudimentary, though gradually improving, transoceanic communications, they had to rely upon individuals who could act in their stead.

---

[48] See North (1990) for a discussion of the relationship between institutional environment and choice of organizational form.

Hancock (1995: 85) notes that the merchants for whom he has data found their managers from their families and from acquaintances from their original social circles. Some of the managers worked directly for their merchants, while others were part of a worldwide network of correspondents, agents, clients, and suppliers. In every case, though, the manager's loyalty was maintained through a regular throughput of business, rather than through recourse to the law. Hence, the relationship between the merchant and his overseas correspondents was far closer than would be found in an impersonal and competitive price-intermediated market. Arguably, the Atlantic merchants started to develop managerial skills over a century before the 'managerial revolution' which Alfred Chandler (1990) traces back to the spread of the railroad. Without managerial skills, the merchant could not succeed:

Because of the key role they played in eighteenth-century commerce, ability to manage one's agents with skill often affected the outcome of investments.[49]

Informational Frictions

Informational problems generated significant transaction costs for the eighteenth-century Atlantic merchant. In this regard, Hancock (1995: 89) discusses the location of his London counting-house, from where he managed his global operations. Location was important because information was communicated for the most part orally. A good situation ensured easy communication with those 'in the know' and facilitated shopping around and also information acquisition.

Many of the coordination functions fulfilled by the merchants concerned the management of information flows. The merchant relied upon his overseas correspondents for information about day-to-day needs and opportunities in foreign markets and had to ensure that incentive structures generated this information. Merchants developed managerial skills to facilitate the processing and interpretation of the informational flows that they received. Orderly and systematic record-keeping was regarded as central:

In orderly surroundings, partners could best synthesize and analyze the ins and outs of their international shipping and trading operations and indulge their omnivorous appetite for information...[50]

---

[49] Bruchey (1958: 286).   [50] Hancock (1995: 103).

Given that information was a valuable good, it is not surprising that it was directly traded. Merchants shared data with one another. As their relationships were long-term, their incentive to provide poor information was presumably low:

...all merchants depended considerably upon other members of a wide mercantile community, upon ship captains and supercargoes, and upon other merchants resident in foreign ports [...] The interdependence of resident merchants throughout the commercial world rested upon a mutual need for services almost indispensable to the conduct of trade. Resident merchants not only supplied each other with the information upon which investment decisions often rested, but performed other services, such as advancing part of the value of goods prior to their sale and holding them for better times.[51]

On a related, but perhaps more subtle, note, merchants needed to know about their partners and correspondents. This was accomplished in several ways. As we have seen, one approach was to employ family members of long acquaintance. Another was to train new recruits in-house. This ensured that they had appropriate technical abilities (geography, arithmetic, grammar, and languages were regarded as important),[52] that they acquired tacit skills which could only be learned on-the-job and, perhaps most importantly, that the merchants could learn about them over the lengthy period of an apprenticeship. Indeed, the close knowledge that partners had of an apprentice's qualities made him a natural candidate for eventual promotion to partner:

These early counting-house experiences often led to [the associates] accumulating the financial resources of their former masters and partners.[53]

This was anticipated at the start of the apprenticeship. Established merchants charged a fee for employing teenage apprentice clerks.

The problems of the early Atlantic traders remained of central importance to their successor firms, which, as we see in chapter five, evolved into the first investment banks. Toward the end of the eighteenth century, the House of Brown emerged as a major Atlantic cotton trader. Perkin's history of the House (1975) points to advances in management practices, and their importance in mitigating informational frictions throughout the firm's history. He emphasizes the importance

---

[51] Bruchey (1958: 279).
[52] Hancock (1995: 110). Languages were important for promotion to partner, if not for less-exhaulted jobs.
[53] Hancock (1995: 244).

that the Browns placed upon communication within the firm, and with their agents, and stresses the thought and energy devoted to sustaining communication. For example:

Perhaps of greater importance than the actual contents of the firm's internal reports was the broad commitment to cooperate fully in the exchange of information and opinion. The partners placed a high premium on forth-rightness in intrafirm communications. Subordinates who failed to keep senior partners well informed about developments affecting the financial standing of customers were open to sharp criticism for their inadequacies. As a rule, the partners exhibited fairly thick skin in the give-and-take of delicate decision making, yet the slightest implication of negligence or worse the willful concealment of pertinent information invariably caused great offense and often led to bitterness and retribution. That an implied 'lack of trust' or 'want of confidence' was considered such a serious violation of the spirit of the firm indicates how devoted the partners were to the practice of keeping their associates well informed on routine matters as well as on more vital administrative affairs.[54]

The firm maintained 'remarkably harmonious relations' with (southern) US cotton agents over an extended period.[55] In part, this reflected the exclusivity of their agency relations. In turn, agents were attracted by the wide latitude the Browns granted their representatives.[56] By the middle of the nineteenth century the firm was able to charge importers comparatively high fees because they valued the services and information, especially credit information, yielded by the firm's effective management of its network.[57]

Organization

All merchants were organized as partnerships. Through most of the eighteenth century, the use of limited liability was severely restricted by the Bubble Act of 1720, but in a business like merchanting where so little was contractible, the partnership form may well have been optimal anyway: it certainly continues to be the most important organizational form in tacit informationally intense businesses to the present day. Partnerships, by forcing merchants to take a long-term capital position in the business that they were running, served to incentivize investment in activities, such as training apprentices and

[54] Perkins (1975: 127–8).
[55] Perkins (1975: 112). The firm's compensation structure for these agents is also noteworthy for an implied risk-sharing arrangement that accords nicely with the risks each party might reasonably have expected to control. See Perkins (1975: 109–10).
[56] Perkins (1975: 95).   [57] Perkins (1975: 143).

building overseas networks, that would not yield benefits easily acquired through arm's-length interaction. They provided hard incentives to the senior employees of the firm, which served to reinforce the tacit incentives provided by close association and repeat dealing. Since partners pooled their resources, they were incentivized by the partnership form to monitor one another's activities. For this reason, partnerships were in general of a sufficiently small size to allow for such monitoring: according to Hancock (1995: 105), the typical partnership among those he studied had three members.[58]

The merchant partnerships varied in their structure and in their willingness or ability to delegate authority. Of the investment banks whose genesis was in merchanting, the Browns quickly extended partnership beyond the family and, perhaps not coincidentally, delegated considerable authority throughout their network. From its origins in mid-eighteenth-century Amsterdam, the House of Barings followed a similar path to a similar end, ultimately turning control of the firm over to the first non-family member in 1828.[59] In contrast, the House of Rothschilds did not admit a non-family member to the partnership until the 1960s.[60]

Financing

Overseas trade was capital-intensive: an Atlantic merchant needed between £3,000 and £4,000 of capital, as opposed to £1,000 for a linen-draper, or £100 for an upholsterer.[61] Without developed capital markets, start-up finance was difficult to come by. Notwithstanding the legal revolution at the end of the seventeenth century, the collection of principal on loans was difficult: 26 percent of the lawsuits entered into by the associates studied by Hancock concerned loans that they had made.[62] Differences across jurisdictions impeded collection, the debtor's money and stock were exempted from actions, and one could not proceed against the body and the property of the debtor simultaneously. As a result, most start-up finance came from relatives, who could be confident that they knew what they were buying, and from inheritances.

---

[58] For a discussion of the use of partnerships for incentive management in modern investment banking and the relationship between partner free-riding and partnership size, see Morrison and Wilhelm (2005*b*).

[59] Hidy (1949).

[60] See pages 143 and 151 of chapter five for a more detailed discussion of the Rothschilds partnership structure, and of their management of their agents.

[61] Hancock (1995: 242).   [62] Hancock (1995: 249, n. 19).

Notwithstanding the collection problems alluded to in the previous paragraph, successful merchants typically had an important role as financiers. Hancock (1995: 258) states that merchants typically invested in their own businesses, other people's ventures, privately owned companies with illiquid shares, publicly monied companies' annuity and stock, government debt, and land:

As their careers advanced, their own businesses and partnerships shifted from being absorbers of funds to being generators of funds that they could invest in other people's businesses, shares, annuities, stocks, government debt, and land. The largest part of an associate's portfolio was his own business [...] But the associates did not stop with their own concerns; they consistently invested in other people's businesses, relatively small private companies and corporations whose stock was not publicly floated or quoted.

Of course, merchants had a natural advantage as financiers, in that they were typically intimately acquainted as a result of their main business activities with the institutions in which they invested. Hence, financing business partners, for example by advancing goods to them on credit, was a natural way of profiting from information that they collected in the course of their day-to-day activities. Moreover, their knowledge of local events meant that they could profitably bring their management expertise to bear as active shareholders:

In addition to using the Funds as a store of value, the associates used some investments—Grant's in the East India Company, Sargent's in the Bank of England—to increase the merchant's power in company affairs.[63]

By the end of the long eighteenth century, a few firms had amassed considerable capital. Table 5.1 reports 1810–18 capitalization for the Rothschilds, Brown Shipley, and Barings Brothers. The figures range from £0.12 million for Brown Shipley & Co. to £1.77 million for the combined Rothschilds operations. Considering that £100,000 was considered a large capitalization for a mid-nineteenth-century British merchant, even the capitalization of Brown Shipley was enormous.[64] We see in chapter five how these houses levered their connections, their expertise, and their capital into a leading position in the nascent investment banking market. They did so in the context of burgeoning stock exchanges. The leading stock exchange in 1800 was in London; we examine its development in the next section.

---

[63] Hancock (1995: 269).   [64] Chapman (1984: 40).

EARLY CAPITAL MARKETS

An active market in securities existed in London before the financial revolution.[65] In its early form, it was mostly concerned with bills drawn on or discounted in London,[66] and with the stocks and bonds of the East India Company. Trade in Exchequer orders, Navy bills, and the stock of the Royal African and Hudson's Bay Companies also started in restoration England. Given the relatively small size of the government debt, the market consisted mostly of private and corporate, rather than government, securities. This situation did not last into the eighteenth century. As Dickson (1967: 488) states, 'The age of reason was also an age of war, and the English government's voracious demands for capital to finance it easily outpaced the requirements of private companies during the whole of the eighteenth century'. Dickson disputes the commonly held belief that the Bubble Act prevented company flotation.[67] Rather, he argues (p. 489) that the private capital markets were still insufficiently developed to provide securities that individuals wished to hold, and hence that they placed their money instead into land or government securities.

The market in the 1690s centered on Exchange Alley, where in the 1690s much of the trading occurred in Jonathan's and Garraway's coffee houses. The range of securities was relatively wide: trading was for immediate or deferred delivery, although at that stage there were no standardized delivery dates. There was some trade in options, and also some trade for differences rather than in the physical security.[68]

The state made frequent attempts until the 1770s to restrict the operation of the capital markets, not least because stockjobbers were believed to have a pernicious effect upon stock prices and hence, by pushing down the price of the funds, to raise the cost of government borrowing. Several attempts to prevent stockjobbing altogether floundered in the House of Lords and were in any case probably unenforceable.[69]

Legislation was passed in 1697 to restrict the number of brokers operating in the City to 100, of whom 12 could be Jewish. Brokers were admitted by the City, had to display a badge of office, refrain from trading as principal, and could not charge more than half a

[65] Dickson (1967: 486).
[66] See page 124 for an explanation of the market for Bills of Exchange.
[67] He cites Du Bois (1971) for an argument that the Act was less of an obstacle to company flotation than previously thought.
[68] Dickson (1967: 491).   [69] Dickson (1967: 519).

percent in brokerage. The law was extended in 1708 to make unlicensed brokerage punishable by a £25 fine. There is however no evidence that this law was ever enforced.[70] On the contrary, unlicensed brokers proliferated. They combined their activities with stockjobbing.

By the middle of the century, the market had some of the sophistication of Amsterdam's market. In particular, the early 1740s saw the introduction of quarterly settlement dates, known as 'Rescounter Days' or 'Rescounters'. Dickson quotes a contemporary author[71] to explain the working of the rescounter. Brokers netted trades off as far as possible, tracing a position if necessary through several offsetting deals. Dickson argues that this process was probably the direct antecedent of the clearing operations later established by London bankers.[72]

Trading volumes mounted steadily throughout the century. This was notwithstanding the complications of transferring government stock: in contrast to those of the monied companies, the government's procedures for stock transfer were cumbersome and defective, resulting in some fraud and hence in a lower turnover. Some summary turnover statistics appear in table 4.1. Note (Dickson, 1967: 467) that no records exist for turnover managed at South Sea House.

Although absolute trading volumes rose steadily, proportionate volumes did not. Although Dickson does not highlight this point, it is possible that the decline in proportionate volumes was a consequence of an increasing concentration of jobbing activity with a few major traders accounting for the majority of the turnover of stock.[73] This would of course tend to reduce the amount of book-balancing activity between jobbers.

The specialization of the jobber is in contrast to the experience of the merchant. In the light of the earlier remarks about eighteenth-century information it is not however particularly surprising. Jobbers needed information about trades that occurred in a geographically small region between a collection of individuals who were fairly close-knit. Trades were recordable and verifiable in court, where enforcement was relatively easy. In these circumstances some specialization

---

[70] Dickson (1967: 517–18).

[71] Thomas Mortimer, *Every Man His Own Broker*, nine editions, 1761 to 1782.

[72] Dickson (1967: 510).

[73] Dickson (1967: 511–12) gives examples of major jobbers and their turnover. For example, William Cotsford in 1754 handled 36 percent of transfers and 34 percent of total revenues traded in the three percent consols.

Table 4.1. *Ratio of stock turnover to nominal capital, 1704–55 (currency amounts in sterling)*

1 Stock	2 Period of transfers	3 Approximate total transferred in year	4 Nominal capital	3 as % of 4
Bank stock	1704 July–Dec.	531,042	2,201,172	24.1
	1718 Oct.–Dec.	2,463,812	5,559,996	44.3
	1727 Oct.–Dec.	2,181,824	8,959,996	24.4
	1755 Jan.–Mar.	1,519,664	11,686,800	13.0
East India stock	1704 July–Dec.	1,611,769	1,574,609	102.4
	1718 Oct.–Dec.	1,643,072	3,194,080	51.4
	1755 Jan.–Mar.	856,033	3,194,080	26.8
5% (1717)	1718 Oct.–Dec.	4,868,628	9,534,358	51.1
3% (1726)	1731 July–Dec.	507,953	1,000,000	50.8
3% Consols	1755 Jan.–Mar.	1,684,736	9,137,821	18.4

Source: Dickson (1967: 466, table 84).

was possible and desirable. This contrasts significantly with the situation of the merchant, who dealt with informationally opaque and geographically disperse markets, and for whom third-party contract enforcement was frequently impossible.

Given the importance of trade flow knowledge for jobbers in the eighteenth (and the twenty-first) century, it was natural that trading activities should become concentrated in a single location. By 1750 this was Jonathan's Coffee House. By the 1770s it was too small to accommodate all of the trading that then occurred. The members of Jonathan's subscribed to build a new house in which they could trade: early plans to christen it New Jonathan's were shelved and it was named instead the Stock Exchange. By 1800 a boom in war finance caused it again to outgrow its premises and it moved to new premises off Capel Court, where it remained until the 1985 Big Bang.

Cope (1942: 181) estimates the size of the entire London money market *c*.1800 at several hundred individuals and firms and 700 licensed brokers, with the Bank of England at the center of activity. The brokers acted as intermediaries between the banks (about 70) and merchants, but by this time it was common for the parties to carry out multiple functions. Speaking of the firm of Benjamin and Abraham

Goldsmid, among the most prominent firms at the time, Cope notes that

They were referred to at various times as bill brokers, money dealers, loan contractors, dealers in the funds, monied men, merchants and so on. They were in fact all of these. Had they lived fifty years later they would have been described as merchant bankers.[74]

Consistent with our earlier discussion, the firm's origins were in Amsterdam, from where Aaron Goldsmid, the father of Benjamin and Abraham, moved to London around 1750. Goldsmid continued to maintain close family ties in Amsterdam and dealt in Amsterdam credits.[75] By 1792, the brothers were wealthy, and were well connected within the London market and with key government officials including William Pitt and the chief cashier of the Bank of England. They were well positioned to participate in the placement of government loans: we examine this market in chapter five, and discuss the Goldsmids' involvement in it on page 141.

CONCLUSION

The foundations of the modern capital markets were laid in the long eighteenth century. The English revolution of 1688 strengthened individual property rights, and restricted the state's freedom of action. This enabled the British Crown to borrow unprecedented quantities to prosecute the numerous wars in which it was engaged over the ensuing century. The London Stock Exchange was one of the institutions that sprang up to support trade in the resultant government debt, and it was increasingly used to transfer ownership stakes in corporations.

At the same time, merchants working in the new Atlantic trade acquired skills in managing relationships and information flows that were critical in a world with underdeveloped international laws. Their skills, and the networks they created, were to be of critical importance to the American economy in the nineteenth century, as America imported the capital it needed to support its own industrial revolution. The next two chapters trace the process by which some of the Atlantic merchants came increasingly to concentrate on finance, and ultimately mutated into investment banks.

---

[74] Cope (1942: 181).   [75] Cope (1942: 182).

5

The Rise of the Investment Bank

Economic and social life was transformed in the nineteenth century. The development of the railroads heralded an era of big business: it was possible for the first time to reap the economies of scale that come from very large-scale capitalization. Social elites became increasingly convinced of the benefits that industrialization could bring, and they fostered a legal and political environment that supported it. To an increasing extent throughout the century, the ideas of Smith and Ricardo held sway. The free market was regarded as the cornerstone of progress. Its legal expression was increasingly dominant: this was the 'golden age of the contract'.[1] Property rights, and the institutions that protected property rights, occupied an increasingly sacred position in the minds of political theorists and jurists throughout the century.

The capital required by the railroads, and later by the industrials, was largely raised through bond issues. Capital accumulation in America was insufficient to cover her industrialization, and as a result, America was a substantial importer of capital throughout the nineteenth century. American bond issues were therefore marketed in England and Continental Europe, as well as at home.

The legal and technological infrastructure needed to support these developments did not exist at the start of the century, and most of it was created by entrepreneurs, who experimented with different methods and structures as they learned about the needs of industrialists and their investors, and as the legal system developed. In the absence of a developed legal infrastructure, the entrepreneurial capital-raisers fell back upon networks and extra-legal contracting of the type that we associated in chapter four with the Atlantic traders of the eighteenth century.

This chapter traces the path that the general Atlantic traders followed via merchant banking to investment banking. The story is a

---

[1] Friedman (2005: 203).

complex one. As we will see, some of the methods used by modern investment bankers were also used to market securities in the eighteenth century. At the same time, the Atlantic traders who later evolved into investment bankers were already financing some mercantile activity. But modern investment banking could not develop until technological, legal, and political factors favored it.

The securities that investment banks distribute are valuable only insofar as they are supported by the courts. For this to occur, the corporation's right to commit itself must be recognized, and contractual commitments must be respected. At the start of the century neither of these conditions obtained. Corporations were chartered to serve a specific purpose, and it was illegal for them to pursue entrepreneurial activities that did not fall under the scope of the charter. At the same time, the courts habitually struck down contracts on the grounds that they were unfair. In the specific case of debt contracts, American states had a confusing variety of laws, which in some cases prevented interstate trade. The creation of a uniform set of laws that left economic agents free to trade as they saw fit took much of the first half of the century, and required a sea change in attitudes towards property and contract.

As corporate law and contract law evolved, so too did the investment bank. The Atlantic traders of the previous chapter became increasingly involved in commercial credit and, as the law recognized the negotiability of this debt, they started to trade it. America's rapid growth relied upon capital which had throughout the nineteenth century to be imported. The Atlantic traders were strongly positioned to distribute within Europe the bond issues through which American capital needs were met. They had developed trading networks and a reputation for fair dealing through their mercantile activities; they now leaned upon these assets to market bonds.

The financial markets were at this time just starting to develop, and a great deal of experimentation occurred within the embryonic investment banking market. Some of the structures developed failed along with their progenitors; others succeeded and went on to capture the market. The most successful structures in the nineteenth century were transatlantic networks of bond wholesalers and, in general, the firms with the closest relationships were the most important.

The main financial business of the Atlantic traders was in commercial bills and letters of credit. We begin the chapter by describing how these instruments worked, and how they were traded by the emerging 'merchant bank' financial specialists.[2] Further development required the creation of an institutional framework for corporations and for credit instruments, and we continue the chapter by tracing the evolution of the relevant laws in the first half of the century. We also provide a brief discussion of the American stock market, in which we point to its nineteenth-century reliance upon the types of private laws discussed in chapter two.

We then discuss the early nineteenth-century evolution of investment banking. We start by examining the eighteenth-century approach to bond sales: we note its reliance upon reputation and networks, and its similarity to modern distribution methods. We then discuss the major players in the pre-1837 investment banking market. The year 1837 was a watershed year for investment bankers, and we trace its consequences. The panic of that year carried off many of the early market players, and left the survivors positioned for market dominance. It also saw the creation of the investment banking house that would come to dominate the investment banking industry, and the birth of Pierpont Morgan, who by the end of the century would control it, and who would be the most powerful financial capitalist in the world.

MERCHANT BANKING

The mercantile trade between England and America remained important to both countries during the nineteenth century. Throughout the first half of the nineteenth century, approximately 40 percent of all imports into the United States came from the United Kingdom, while the percentage of exports going to the United Kingdom increased steadily from 33 to 51 percent.[3] Much of this trend was attributable to the trade in cotton. In 1785, only five bags of American cotton were imported to England; American cotton accounted for only 0.16 percent of English imports in the period 1786–90. In 1806, American imports amounted to 124,939 bags, and American imports accounted for 24.08 percent of all cotton imports into England in the period 1806–10. By the middle of the century, America provided 81 percent of England's cotton imports.[4]

---

[2] In fact, the phrase 'merchant banker' was regarded in the nineteenth-century as somewhat down-market. Most merchant bankers continued to call themselves 'merchants' until after the Second World War (Burk, 1989: 28).

[3] Buck (1969 [1925]: 2).   [4] The figures come from Buck (1969 [1925]: 34–6).

The participants in the trade formed a large and complex network stretching from the cotton growers in the South of America to their factors and agents, the shipping firms, the cotton brokers and dealers, and the manufacturers in the North of England. The wheels of trade in this market were oiled by the extension of long-term credit. Market players needed expertise to find appropriate counterparties, to check the quality of goods sold, to insure and ship the goods, and to investigate the creditworthiness of their counterparties. In other words, the skills required were analogous to those deployed by the Atlantic traders examined in chapter four.[5] As they acquired knowledge of their counterparts, the players in this market naturally started to use their skill and their reputation to finance trade by others. By the nineteenth century the main mode of trade finance was the Bill of Exchange.

The Bill of Exchange was developed in thirteenth-century Italy in response to the problems of dealing over long distances, as well as to the inconvenience of barter and of coins.[6] A Bill of Exchange is essentially an IOU with some legal status. A seller of goods (typically an exporter) draws up the Bill, which is an acknowledgement that the buyer (typically an importer) will pay for the goods at a future date. Both parties sign the Bill, and the buyer then has until the due date of the Bill to sell the goods and so to make good on the obligation that it represents.

Bills of Exchange simplified foreign trade in the following way. A London merchant who sold goods to an Amsterdam buyer would accept a Bill of Exchange in payment. The Bill, promising payment from a Dutch trader, would be valuable to another Dutch trader, who was able more easily to collect payment upon it. The London merchant could therefore sell his Bill to a second London merchant, who needed to buy Dutch goods. The second merchant could then use the Bill to pay for goods from a Dutch seller. The Dutch seller of goods would present the Bill to the original Amsterdam buyer, who would pay him for them. In the event of default on the Bill, the claims would unravel along the line of trades. In other words, the Dutch seller would claim from the London buyer who gave him the Bill; he in turn would claim from the London seller who gave it to him, and the seller would pursue the defaulting Dutch buyer through the courts.

[5] See Buck (1969 [1925]) for an exhaustive study of the operation and financing of the Anglo-American cotton trade in the first half of the nineteenth century.
[6] Kindleberger (1993: 41) provides a detailed description of the Bill of Exchange. See Carosso (1987: 8) for a more concise explanation.

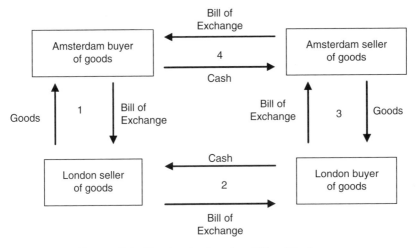

Figure 5.1. *Foreign trade using Bills of Exchange*

In the first trade, a Bill of Exchange is tendered as payment for goods sold. In the second, the Bill is sold for cash. In the third, the Bill is again tendered for goods sold: after this trade, the Bill is owned by another Amsterdam merchant. In the fourth and final trade, the Amsterdam seller of goods presents the buyer with his original Bill, and receives cash in exchange. If the Bill defaults, the Amsterdam seller falls back on the London buyer, who in turn falls back on the London seller, who then pursues the Bill drawer in Amsterdam.

This trade is illustrated in figure 5.1. In practice, a specialist trader would often intermediate the trade between the London seller and buyer of goods. Paying cash for a Bill that promised future payment was known as 'discounting' it; Bill traders were therefore known as 'Discount Houses'. Discounting Bills of Exchange was an important early function of the Bank of England.

Trade in Bills of Exchange was reputationally intensive: a London buyer would accept a Dutch Bill only if it was drawn on an Amsterdam merchant of whose creditworthiness he was confident. This presented a problem for smaller purchasers of goods: if their Bills could not be sold in overseas markets then they would find it very hard to obtain trade credit. It also presented an opportunity for internationally active merchants who had sufficient local presence to evaluate the financial standing of local traders. For a fee, they could guarantee Bills drawn on these traders. The reputation attaching to the merchant who guaranteed the Bill would then ensure its negotiability in overseas markets, and hence would facilitate trade.

It was as guarantors of Bills of Exchange that the Atlantic merchants entered trade finance, and hence became merchant bankers. The act of guaranteeing a Bill was referred to as 'accepting' it, and the merchant bankers were therefore commonly known as 'Accepting Houses'.

In addition to their business in Bills of Exchange, merchant bankers earned significant profits from letters of credit. A letter of credit was a formal guarantee of its holder's creditworthiness: they were of particular importance to traveling merchants, enabling them to lean upon the signatory bank's network of overseas merchants and bankers to make purchases in ports where they had no contacts or reputation of their own. Naturally, the letter of credit business rested not only upon the guarantor's network, but also upon its reputation. Reputations were hard to build, so the business had natural barriers to entry: Perkins (1975: 11) characterizes its structure as 'decidedly oligopolistic'.

THE LEGAL AND POLITICAL ENVIRONMENT

Corporations

The first half of the nineteenth century saw a sea change in prevailing legal and political attitudes toward corporations and contract. Legal philosophy at the start of the century stressed the role of the state in granting corporate rights, and in assessing the equity of contracts. We argued in chapter two that these attitudes reflect weak property rights, and that they are likely to undermine economic progress. They are certainly inconsistent with the common perception of the nineteenth century as an era of unbridled laissez-faire. In fact, the legal and social changes that facilitated the movement towards liberal conceptions of property and contract occurred over the course of the first half of the century, until by 1850 sanctity of property and freedom of contract had started to acquire the totemic status accorded to them by later nineteenth-century thinkers.

The state at the start of the nineteenth century was widely perceived as fulfilling a somewhat corporate role: that is to say, both jurists and the public ascribed an active role to the state in achieving specific goals. In fact, throughout the nineteenth century the public believed that government had an obligation to better the condition of the people.[7] The first half of the century saw a practical shift in the way that the state attempted to accomplish this goal.

---

[7] Friedman (2005: 120).

The intellectual climate that obtained at the end of the eighteenth century is exemplified in attitudes toward corporations. Corporations acquire their legal existence through their corporate charters, which give them the right to enter into contracts, and which expose them to the danger of being sued. The early nineteenth-century approach to the corporation is summarized in the notion of *franchise*. A franchise was a grant 'out of the inexhaustible reservoir of state power'.[8] In other words, for contemporary observers, corporate power was delegated by the state, and any freedoms that corporates held were on sufferance from the polity.

Corporate charters were granted infrequently in the eighteenth century, with a total of 335 issued to businesses.[9] As grants of state power, they conferred property rights on their owners, who generally received monopoly power within the domain covered by the charter. Since the powers of the corporation were received by grant, they were strictly limited to the activities delimited by the charter. Actions outside the scope of the charter were *ultra vires*: literally, 'beyond the powers', and if a corporation exceeded its powers, its actions were not legal. This attitude persisted as late as 1856,[10] when Jeremiah Sullivan Black, chief justice of Pennsylvania argued that any corporate action not explicitly sanctioned by the charter was excluded from it, and hence could not be enforced.

The belief that corporate powers stemmed from the munificence of the state was steadily chipped away. The landmark case of *Dartmouth College* v. *Woodward* (1819)[11] stated categorically that the state could not arbitrarily control the actions of a corporation, in this case Dartmouth College. The ruling started to establish the boundaries between public and private life that would be so central to late nineteenth-century legal thinking. However, the Supreme Court's reasoning in this case continued to reflect the idea that the corporation's powers existed at the pleasure of the state: the Court held that the corporate charter represented a contract between the state and the company, and its ruling flowed from the constitutional prohibition on state impairment of contracts. Corporate charters therefore remained property rights granted by the state, and hence retained a flavor of exclusivity and monopoly. The death knell for this perspective was sounded by the *Charles River Bridge Case* (1837).[12] The proprietors of the bridge

---

[8] Friedman (2005: 121).   [9] Friedman (2005: 129).
[10] Friedman (2005: 395).   [11] 4 Wheat 518 (1819).
[12] *Proprietors of the Charles River Bridge* v. *Proprietors of the Warren Bridge*, 11 Pet. 420 (1837).

sued the state of Massachusetts, claiming that in granting a charter to a neighboring bridge, the state had impaired the monopoly inherent in the grant of the Charles River Bridge, and they lost, on the grounds that the *only* entitlement of the original charter was to build a toll bridge. The role of the state of Massachusetts was therefore the neutral one of simply facilitating bilateral contracts between the Charles River Bridge Company and those who used the bridge: it was not of granting rights to a monopoly.

The belief that all corporate powers flowed from the state clearly undermined the ability of individuals to combine to conduct business activities, and hence undermined their property rights over their ideas. And, because the power to write charters was vested in the legislature, it resulted in extracontractual assignment of property rights. As we argued in chapter two, when legislatures (and regulators) acquire the arbitrary right to assign property rights, it becomes the focus of rent-seeking. The arguments of chapter two therefore imply that the ability to assign charters on a case-by-case basis is inimical to economic progress.

The rapid expansion of American commerce in the early nineteenth century went some way to resolve this problem. As Friedman (2005: 120) notes, the country was extremely local in 1800, and the federal government was very small. Tax revenues were tiny: in 1794 the state of Massachusetts spent $215,000. Moreover, the state operated without a trained civil service.[13] As the demand for corporate charters increased through the early years of the century, the state was therefore increasingly unable to cope with the demand for special charters. As a result, except for projects of special importance, corporate charters became standardized (Friedman, 2005, 130). At the same time, the specificity of special charters also smacked of partiality, and hence ran counter to the egalitarian ethos of the new country.[14] Rather than a device for restraining corporate interests, the special charter was increasingly seen as a way of enabling crooked legislatures to collude with them. For example, the 1845 Louisiana Constitution included a specific provision against the use of special corporate charters, except for political and municipal purposes.[15] Finally, the states started to pass general incorporation acts.

---

[13] Friedman (2005: 217) expands upon these points.
[14] See Friedman's discussion (2005: 133) of the *Mott* v. *Pennsylvania Railroad*, in which Pennsylvania's chief justice ruled that there were limits to the State's ability to award special powers to a corporation.
[15] Friedman (2005: 135).

Commercial Law

The tensions inherent in commercial law at the turn of the nineteenth century are exemplified in the differences between marine law and the laws concerning land-based transactions. The laws relating to shopping, commercial paper, and the sale of goods were treated as part of an international body of law.[16] As a result, the relevant English case law governed the Atlantic trade in Bills of Exchange. By the end of the eighteenth century, Bills had been recognized by the merchant courts for over 150 years, and problems relating to their use in English common law had largely been ironed out.[17]

This set the stage for the established merchant houses such as the Barings and the Rothschilds to start shifting their business toward the acceptance and discounting of other people's Bills. As a contemporary observer noted, their reputations would underpin their activities, and would naturally determine its extent:

When, therefore, a merchant or any person possessed of capital, has, by his punctuality, integrity, and honest dealing, so far gained the confidence of the public, that his notes pass currently as money, he ought not to be restrained in reaping the advantage of his credit. It is the fruit of his virtues; a natural right, the exercise of which does him honour; and to limit its circulation, either in quantity, denomination, or territorial extent, is the grossest injustice. The credit of a private banker will fix its own boundaries, beyond which it will seldom wander.[18]

However, as this quotation implies, many merchants in the first part of the nineteenth century faced artificial impediments to their credit business. The problems concerned land-based commerce within America, which was subject to a great deal of risk, arising because of uncertainties regarding the role of juries in commercial cases, because the states had different commercial law, and, crucially, because the laws regarding interstate commerce were unclear, and in some cases acted as a positive brake to the extension of credit.

Mercantile litigation at the start of the nineteenth century was plagued by uncertainty. At a basic level, merchants could not be sure that judges would understand the complexities of their

[16] Friedman (2005: 189) cites in support of this statement Chancellor Kent's 1832 statement that 'The marine law of the United States is the same as the marine law of Europe. It is not the law of a particular country, but the general law of nations'.

[17] Horwitz (1977: 213).

[18] Laommi Brown, *Thoughts on the Study of Political Economy, as Connected with the Population Industry and Paper Currency of the United States* (Cambridge, MA, 1809), cited by Sylla (1976).

case.[19] Moreover, late eighteenth-century jurists believed that 'the jury [are] the proper judges not only of the fact but of the law that [is] necessarily involved'.[20] In other words, juries were permitted to allow their prejudices with respect to the specifics of a case to override the common law. It is hardly surprising that, according to one contemporary commentator, 'merchants were not fond of juries'.[21] Where possible, merchants preferred to avoid the cost and uncertainty surrounding litigation by taking their disputes to arbitration.[22]

Procedural court-based problems were compounded by state-specific legal idiosyncrasies. Although the American states recognized parts of the English common law at the time of independence, there were significant variations between states. As a result, a good deal of uncertainty surrounded the laws that governed in interstate commerce.

Jurists began early in the nineteenth century to acknowledge the problems presented by unpredictable commercial courts. A number of approaches were taken to restrict the scope of juries,[23] of which the most important was drawing an increasingly clear line between law and fact: judges were increasingly required by their states to give the jury their opinion on every point of law involved in a case. Juries were required only to decide points of fact.

This procedural change had a significant impact upon mercantile activity. It enabled judges to develop a predictable commercial law, which increasingly reflected the *mores* of the merchant classes. At the same time, the courts started refusing to enforce the results of arbitration: naturally, this curtailed the extent of extra-legal dispute settlement, and forced the merchants into the courts.[24]

As state courts developed bodies of commercial law, they opened the door to larger-scale standardization. Marine law provided a precedent for federal commercial law and without it, interstate commerce was being impeded. For our story, the most important area in which this occurred was the market for Bills of Exchange. Interstate variations in commercial law generated a great deal of uncertainty amongst the holders of credit instruments as to their precise legal standing.

---

[19] Friedman (2005: 405).　　　[20] Horwitz (1977: 142).

[21] The quotation refers to an 1822 letter from Daniel Webster to Justice Story discussing a recent commercial case: see Horwitz (1977: 141).

[22] See page 106 of chapter four for a discussion of eighteenth-century commercial law.

[23] Horwitz (1977: 141–143).

[24] Horwitz (1977: 145). See also page 107 of chapter four.

Bodenhorn (2000: 199–209) provides a succinct summary of the issues that arose. The most significant of these concerned the recourse which the buyer of a Bill had to its drawer in the event of default. As we saw in Chapter 2, note 3, the common law requires a valid contract to involve offer, acceptance, and consideration. So 'how could Adams, who had given a promissory note to Belcher, be sued by Connors, to whom Belcher had transferred the note, when no consideration or explicit agreement had passed between Adams and Connors?'[25] In three important commercial states (Massachusetts, Pennsylvania, and Virginia), laws concerning negotiability were not enacted, and so the common law judgments of the courts prevailed. In general, these tended to favor debtors over creditors, and to argue against negotiability on the grounds already outlined.

At the start of the century the courts were not sympathetic to the problems caused by this lack of clarity. An early (1803) Supreme Court decision held that federal courts should apply the specific laws of the states. Chief Justice Marshall argued that courts were not entitled to establish a nationally uniform commercial law simply because it would serve economic interests: the states' rights were supreme. Indeed, this ruling prevented Virginian holders of a defaulted Bill from suing earlier endorsers, because Virginian law did not recognize a full negotiability doctrine.

The laws regarding commerce across state boundaries were even more difficult to negotiate. For example, an 1839 decision by Alabama Supreme Court found that an out-of-state purchaser of a Bill of Exchange had violated Alabama's constitutional prohibition of any bank operating within the state that had not been explicitly chartered by the Alabama legislature. As a result, the debtor in this case was able with impunity to default on his obligations.

Like the turn-of-the-century unpredictability of the jury system in commercial law, problems of negotiability generated a great deal of resentment among merchants. Restricted recourse to arbitration, coupled with a court system that seemed actively to undermine trade in Bills, weakened the value of a merchant's reputation, and seriously undermined commerce. As the judiciary became increasingly friendly toward commercial interests this situation became untenable. The major step toward resolving the confusion surrounding negotiability also established that commercial law was a federal concern. The 1842 Supreme Court case *Swift* v. *Tyson*[26] concerned the

---

[25] Bodenhorn (2000: 200).   [26] 16 Pet. I (1842).

validity of a defaulted Bill which Tyson endorsed and transferred. Its real significance arose because the Court ruled that federal courts had the right to apply the 'general' law of commerce, even if this was distinct from state law, and even if no 'federal question' was presented. Speaking for the Court, Justice Joseph Story argued that commercial law was international: not 'the law of one country, but of the commercial world'.[27] The judgment therefore cleared the way for uniform federal commerce laws, for the extension of credit across state borders, and ultimately, for the creation of investment banks.

Contracts

Friedman (2005: 203) states that 'the nineteenth century was the golden age of the law of contract'. However, although the American Constitution prevents state impairment of contracts, the domain within which contract law was applied changed through the century, and hence so did the power of the contract.

In chapter two we argued that the purpose of a contract is to transfer (broadly defined) property rights between two agents. Moreover, we argue that ability to contract is closely bound up with the strength of property rights: an agent's ability to alienate his control over an asset is a part of his property rights. If his ability to commit to transfer control is circumscribed by the courts, then his property rights are undermined.

Property rights in this broad sense were undermined by eighteenth-century attitudes toward the role of a contract. For contemporary jurists, contract law was concerned only with transferring evidence of ownership: that is, with transfer of title. The law of property was concerned with establishing title, and hence eighteenth-century contract law was entirely subordinated to the law of property.[28] When the parties to a contract had not executed its precise terms, the primary concern of the courts was therefore to ensure that title changed hands under the terms originally agreed: the courts would therefore enforce *specific performance* of the contract.

This approach to contract enforcement had profound effects. If a party had experienced losses because he relied upon the performance of a contract, he could not expect the courts to award *expectation damages* to compensate him over and above specific performance. Clearly, this weakened the power of contractual commitments. Moreover,

---

[27] Friedman (2005: 192).   [28] Horwitz (1977: 162).

parties to a contract could not always rely upon the courts to enforce specific performance. To eighteenth-century eyes a contractual obligation was unreasonable, and hence could be modified or overturned by the courts, if it was unfair. This perspective reflected a contemporary belief that one could place an objective value upon an exchange, and that it was morally right to place equitable limitations upon the extent of a contractual obligation.[29] In the language of chapter two, its effect was to attenuate property rights and hence, as we discussed in chapter two, to undermine economic incentives and to restrict commerce.

Modern contract law emerged when the courts started to recognize expectation damages. The spread of stock market trading probably made this inevitable.[30] When the only purpose of a share trade was to profit from price movements, it was hard to argue that expectation damages were an inappropriate response to a failure to deliver stock in a rising market. Similarly, the emergence of extensive internal commodity forward markets resulted in the recognition of expectation damages for commodity contracts.

Forward contracts existed in the early Amsterdam and London markets as a vehicle for hedging risks, and they remain a common derivative contract.[31] They represent an obligation to trade in the future at a price established today. No money changes hands when the forward deal is struck,[32] and at the expiry of the contract, one party will gain the difference between the contract price and the prevailing market price, and the other will lose it. Contracts of this type are clearly intended to hedge their counterparties against the adverse effects of price movements, rather than to transfer the title to a particular property. It is natural that they should be subject to

[29] Horwitz (1977: 164).

[30] Horwitz (1977: 173) notes that as early as 1793, Lord Mansfield identified speculation in stocks as creating 'a new species of property, arisen within the compass of a few years'.

[31] Baskin and Miranti (1997: 98).

[32] The advent of this type of trade therefore presented a problem to the doctrine that contracts did not exist without consideration (see Chapter 2, note 3). This is designed to ensure that 'gratuitous promises' do not have the backing of the courts. When both parties recognize value in a contract which is transacted at a market rate so that no money changes hands, both must perceive value in it. Preventing the contract from binding for lack of consideration therefore presumes that one or both parties is incapable of reasoned judgment. We argued on page 43 of chapter two that this type of prevention is welfare-reductive. Modern contract law emerged in the nineteenth-century from this conflict between a paternalistic notion of law and the need for free contracting in an impersonal marketplace.

nonperformance rather than restitution remedies, and in the early years of the nineteenth century the courts recognized this.[33]

Expanding markets also made it increasingly hard to justify objective theories of value. When traders contracted over prices several weeks hence, they clearly did so because they disagreed as to the likely future price. It was impossible in this case to argue that the trade was objectively unfair. Contemporary thinking became increasingly dominated by the political economists of the Scottish enlightenment, who argued that freely made trades were beneficial to all parties. The inevitable corollary of this line of reasoning is that value is subjective, and not objective. Hence any trade that reflects the will of its counterparties is fair, and should be enforced.

The displacement of equitable theories of contract by the will theory was complete by the 1844 publication of William W. Story's *Treatise on the Law of Contracts*.[34] By this time it was generally agreed that freely made bargains should be honored and enforced. The price agreed by the parties was sufficient proof of value, and contract courts did not investigate the price or the terms of the bargain.[35] Enforcement norms rested upon expectation damages, and hence ensured that contracting parties could rely upon the promise inherent in the contract.

Securities Trading

While commercial disputes were increasingly settled by the courts in the first half of the twentieth century, the same cannot be said of the securities markets. American attitudes toward stock trading were colored by the experience in 1792 of a speculative stock bubble and the subsequent market crash, and by folk memories of the South Sea Bubble at the start of the eighteenth century. Among Americans there was a widely held perception that securities trading led to political corruption, to inegalitarianism, and to economically disastrous panics. These attitudes were very slow to change, notwithstanding the percolation within the United States through the first half of the century of

[33] The first ruling in favor of expectations damages for failure to deliver stock in a rising market occurred in Pennsylvania and was published in 1791. Expectations damages were applied in a number of English cases between 1799 and 1810. Expectations damages had been extended to American commodities markets by 1815. In *Shepherd* v. *Hampton* (1818), the Supreme Court held that damages for nondelivery in cotton contracts should be equal to the difference between the contract price and the market price at the time of delivery; several courts adopted expectation damage standards for commodity contracts over the next decade (Horwitz, 1977: 176).

[34] Horwitz (1977: 185).   [35] Friedman (2005: 204).

the views of British political economists who extolled the virtues of untrammeled free markets.[36]

In the wake of the 1792 crash several states passed laws designed to curb speculative activities. In particular, New York passed a regulatory bill, which restricted the auctioning of stock and rendered void contracts to sell stock short; Massachusetts passed a similar bill in 1836. New York's provisions were repealed in 1858, although the Massachusetts legislation lasted until 1901. Similarly, statutes were passed in Pennsylvania (1841) and Maryland (1842) declaring void contracts for future sale of securities after more than five days.

These laws rendered certain securities transactions unenforceable in state courts, but they did not have the intended effect upon security market traders. As Banner (1998: 175) notes, 'the effect of the American stockjobbing statutes was to drive a large class of transactions out of the official legal system'. The most important mechanism by which this was done was the formation of a stock exchange. New York stockjobbers made a number of attempts to organize until in 1817 twenty-seven brokers constituted themselves as the New York Stock and Exchange Board (the Board did not become known as the New York Stock Exchange until 1863).[37] The Board was a club to which existing members could propose new members for election. It traded in closed meetings in a large room, and the prices that it established were reported in the newspapers. Between 1820 and 1840, average daily trading volume increased from 156 shares to 4,266.[38]

Although the Stock and Exchange Board did not achieve control of New York trading, its prices were the standard reference point for deals elsewhere, and it therefore exerted considerable influence. Access to the Board's price information was therefore a source of considerable competitive advantage, and exclusion from the Board was a potent threat. As we noted in chapter three, these observations are sufficient to explain the Board's ability to sustain a private legal regime that contradicted the antispeculation statutes. A Board member who attempted to use state legislation to escape from a trade would be excluded. Moreover, the Board enforced a rule that members should not trade with nonmembers who broke a contract with a member: as the Board came increasingly to dominate security trading, this sanction was sufficient to extend its reach throughout the market.[39]

---

[36] The discussion in this subsection draws upon Banner (1998).
[37] Banner (1998: 252–3).   [38] Banner (1998: 255).   [39] Banner (1998: 260–4).

In short, the Stock and Exchange Board provided an information network, which enabled it to enforce private laws that strengthened the property rights of its members:

The Stock Exchange Board was thus in part a compiler and seller of information about the creditworthiness of prospective trading partners. This information would have been more costly to obtain in the disorganized market outside the Board. (Banner, 1998: 260)

The Stock Exchange therefore fulfilled a similar role to the investment bank. The two institutions would be natural collaborators in the years that followed.

THE EVOLUTION OF INVESTMENT BANKING

The political-legal changes discussed in the previous section made investment banking possible. They created a private sphere in which contracting could occur independently of the state, but subject to its powers of enforcement. The corporate form was separated from the state and anchored in the private sphere, and the rules governing its use were increasingly standardized across America. The negotiability of corporate credit was established, and the legal impediments to geographically distant arm's-length financing were dismantled.

Once the state had assumed a passive enabling role, the stage was set for the emergence of large-scale corporations, and for the investment banks that supported their growth. We have already examined the functioning of the stock exchange in antebellum America: in this section, we trace the development of the investment banks. We start by discussing their eighteenth-century antecedents.

Early Securities Issuance

The primary function of modern investment banks is the coordination of securities offerings. Today's investment banks ordinarily purchase an entire issue from the issuing firm and then sell it in pieces at a markup agreed with the issuer. The bank therefore bears the risk that market prices will fall after the consummation of the deal, and before it unloads its securities. In view of the risk that the banks bear, this function is known as security underwriting.

We can trace the origins of modern underwriting in the eighteenth-century market for government bonds. Early eighteenth-century sales of government 'stocks' (loans) were conducted for the most part using open public subscriptions. However, by the 1740s, the use of sub-scriber 'lists' had become commonplace.[40]

The list system worked as follows. When the English Treasury wished to place government stock, it would negotiate in advance with a group of important monied men in the City, each of whom under-took to take a proportion of the loan. He did this by canvassing the support of people upon whose probity he could rely. This collection of people constituted his 'list'. To the lists of subscribers was added the 'Treasury List', which included peers, MPs, and government offi-cials.[41] Payment for stock was due in installments. The members of a list guaranteed only the first payment, after which the stock became tradable, known before all installments were covered as 'Light Horse' (as opposed to 'Heavy Horse', which was fully paid stock).

Loan subscriptions were commonly performed via lists of investors by the end of the eighteenth century. The middlemen who maintained these lists served a very similar purpose to the modern investment banker. In this section, we adopt Redlich's terminology (1968) and refer to them as 'contractors'.[42]

The Treasury and the Chancellor of the Exchequer had to consider the solidity of the undertakers presenting lists. Cope (1942: 192) dis-cusses the basis upon which this judgment was made:

Some had a reputation which was sufficient evidence of their ability to meet their obligations; others were required to make a cash deposit of anything up to £500,000, while at least one house was excluded on the grounds that its resources were inadequate. In practice the bidding was restricted to a relatively small number of leading houses.

We see here the forerunner of the modern emphasis upon repu-tational capital in investment banking. Institutions with strong rep-utations were at a significant advantage, because their reputational capital substituted for a cash commitment. Reputation had a self-enforcing effect: inclusion in a well-known contractor's list was

---

[40] There does not appear to be a definitive statement regarding the first use of the list. However, Dickson (1967: 222) argues that, judging by the level of adverse criticism which the method attracted in the 1740s, their systematic use must date from that decade.

[41] Dickson (1967: 220–221).

[42] Redlich states that the essential difference between a contractor and an invest-ment banker was that the former competed for new issues with end investors, while the latter purchased the entire issue and *then* sold it to investors. We do not stress this distinction, and we adopt the term 'contractor' merely for convenience.

tantamount to receiving a favor.[43] Subscribers relied upon their lists for receiving a stock allocation from the government, and they therefore worked hard to maximize the value of this asset. In general, they did not share the identities of list members with the public, government, or parliament. Moreover, they used their power to allocate valuable list memberships to discourage investors from joining multiple lists. Some even attempted to prohibit it: James Morgan, a 1790s loan contractor, required subscribers to his lists to sign an affidavit that they were on no other list.[44]

The contractor undertook all of the negotiations and his list members had to accept the terms which he obtained. In modern corporate finance, the benefits which small investors experience from the presence of a large investor who can act as a monitor for the borrowing company are well-understood. The situation for lenders to eighteenth-century governments was not dissimilar. The French monarchs frequently made unilateral modifications to the terms of their loans, as the English monarchs of the previous century had done. The constitutional changes wrought by the Revolution Settlement were still in their infancy and there may have been a perceived need in Britain to check any tendency of the state to appropriate investors, particularly as parliament was for the most part peopled by the landed interest, who were in general suspicious, and sometimes antipathetic, toward the monied classes. At the very least, negotiation with the state was a crucial activity for bidders. It was performed in a meeting between Treasury officials and bidders, usually in Downing Street, when the contractors bid for stock.[45]

A contractor with a large list was in a strong bargaining position with the government. This position was strengthened if the contractor had exclusive relationships with the members of his list. The concomitant danger that the contractor would abuse his negotiating position

[43] Redlich (1968: 307) states that list members did not view their subscriptions as investments, but rather a reward or 'remuneration for services rendered or as leading to advantages other than drawing interest'.

[44] Redlich (1968: 309).

[45] The need for delegated monitoring was met earlier in the eighteenth century by the monied companies (the East India Company, the Bank of England, and the South Sea Company). Sutherland (1946: 19) reports a 1781 statement to the House of Commons describing bargaining over the terms of the loan between these companies and the Treasury. She argues that as a result, a closely knit financial system arose in which the three monied companies served as a focus for the interests of individual creditors. This is suggestive of the activist position adopted by investment banks in the late nineteenth century.

to appropriate investors was attenuated by the contractor's concern for his good reputation, and the quasi-rents that it generated.

The Treasury was cognizant of the advantages to be derived from a system with endogenously generated incentive structures. In particular, it could if it wished exclude from the sale a contractor who had not in the past cooperated sufficiently. In other words, the contractor had to maintain a reputation with its investors (i.e. its list) as well as with its clients (i.e. the exchequer).[46] The need for undertakers to maintain good reputations with the Treasury ensured that they would bid for stock even when it was not particularly attractive. Dickson (1967: 222) argues that:

From the Treasury's standpoint the system had great merits. It used the mercantile community's knowledge of its own members' probity and business capacity, and in so doing enlisted in advance the support of interests in the City whose hostility would have impaired the success of any financial measure. This made it possible to raise the supplies in years of great credit stringency like 1746, when an 'open' loan would probably have failed.

Hence the rudimentary eighteenth-century list system of government stock placement had many of the features associated with modern securities underwriting. Contractors managed lists of regular investors upon whose probity their own reputation for reliability rested. The larger their list, the more valuable their participation in an offering and hence the larger their allocation. This in turn served to bolster their list. Large contractors used list membership to reward counterparties. Sellers (in the eighteenth century, the government) relied upon contractors to provide fair bids for their offerings. They set prices at a level that guaranteed oversubscription and hence were able, through manipulation of allocations, to provide incentives to reputable contractors with whom they had long-term relationships. In this environment, a contractor with limited reputation, or skills already offered by the dominant contractors, would face substantial barriers to entry. Thus loan contracting had the oligopolistic character of the modern securities issuance function described in chapter one. It

---

[46] The incentive provided by client reputations was particularly simple, as the exchequer was the only client: failure to satisfy it led to exclusion from future offerings. In contrast, most of today's investment bank clients are corporations that trade infrequently. As we discussed in chapter three, the cost of losing a client is lower, and reputational incentives are likely to be effective only if clients can communicate with each other.

is hardly surprising that loan contractors also faced similar criticism for the favored position they held.

Some contemporary observers, most notably Sir John Barnard, the independent MP for the City, argued on the grounds of fairness that issues should not be placed via negotiation with contractors, but through open offerings or public subscriptions. This enabled anyone to place a bid in the Treasury's book, with shares being allocated on a pro rata basis in the event of oversubscription. The contemporary perception that intermediating stockjobbers made superior returns by manipulating the price of new issues at the expense of the state strengthened calls for open offerings.

The argument that competition would resolve the problem of market manipulation by insiders flounders because it is impossible to identify and hence to exclude the jobbers, who therefore cannot be excluded from new issues. Modern financial economics teaches us that well-informed jobbers will then subscribe only to attractive issuers, leaving the uninformed mass of investors facing a 'winner's curse' in that their bids for stock will be most successful when the stock is perceived by informed investors as least attractive. When, as in an open offering, informed investors do not establish a tacit contract with sellers under which stock allocations provide rewards for participation and punishments for nonparticipation, there is no way to circumvent this problem.

Although he does not identify the winner's curse problem, Dickson (1967: 227–8) provides some contemporary evidence which is consistent with its presence. In response to Sir John Barnard's campaign, government stock issues in 1747 and 1748 were sold using open subscriptions, which was a return to the *status quo ante*. While the two loans in 1747 were heavily oversubscribed, the great £6.3 million loan of 1748, which occurred when uncertainty over the war in Austria was undermining the market, experienced difficulties and later installments had to be postponed. Moreover, the largest bidders for the first installment of this loan, which predated the market problems, were the major insiders. Of the 139 subscribers who took up 45 percent of the first installment, 103 drastically reduced their balances or sold out. For example, Samson Gideon, the leading stock undertaker of the 1740s, subscribed £590,000 and had sold all of it before the stock ledgers opened; Jeremia Joye, a merchant, reduced his stock from £155,000 to £1,000. In other words, public subscription did not prevent major speculators from participating in the market and, unlike list-based subscription, nor did it prevent them from using their insider knowledge at the expense of uninformed investors when market conditions turned sour.

Notwithstanding the problems identified above with public subscriptions to new loans, in 1784 Pitt took the unprecedented step of floating new debt by competitive tendering.[47] This move had two unintended consequences. First, loan contractors, who found cooperation more agreeable than competition, started increasingly to collaborate on new bids. Second, the amounts of capital needed to compete in the new auctions led increasingly to the exclusion of the ultimate investors. Both Cope and Redlich comment upon this, noting that by the end of the eighteenth century it had become unusual for one house to bid single-handedly for loans: instead, they formed lists of contractors, one of whose number would negotiate terms for all with the Chancellor of the Exchequer.[48] Moreover, like modern investment bankers, by 1795 contractors were, or allied contractors jointly and severally were, liable for the payments promised by their list members.

Market Structure up to 1837

Loan contracting was a risky activity, and its early practitioners operated in an immature legal environment, and without the organizational expertise that has developed today. As a result, there was a very high failure rate among the early loan contractors. Because they were responsible for the payments of their subscribers, they were exposed to market downturns. They also suffered at the hands of professional stockjobbers on the exchange, who conspired to depress the prices of some new issues so as to acquire them at low prices.

The most important of the loan contractors in the 1780s London market for government debt were bankers, with professional loan contractors entering the market in the 1790s: until his 1800 bankruptcy, the most important of these was Walter Boyd.[49]

From Boyd's 1799 downfall to 1810, the leading British contractors were Goldsmid and Company, owned by the brothers Benjamin and Abraham. Their rise to prominence, and their subsequent downfall, is documented by Cope (1942: 192). The Goldsmids were the first specialist Bill traders in London, and they were also the first stockbrokers to enter the loan-contracting business. It is worth noting that the Goldsmids appear to have been the first loan contractors to engage in

---

[47] Redlich (1968: 307).   [48] See Cope (1942: 192–3) and Redlich (1968: 308).
[49] Redlich (1968: 311–12).

the modern practice of primary market price stabilization: they were prepared to lend on consols at five percent. Naturally, this invasion of stock broking territory made them a number of enemies. By 1810 their business had failed, and both brothers were suicides.

The departure from the scene of the Goldsmids handed domination of the loan contracting business to the first of the merchant banks. John and Francis Baring & Co. was founded in 1763 as import and export merchants for a range of commodities: the firm was renamed Baring Brothers & Co. in 1806. The firm expanded its range of operations to include acceptances (see p. 126) and letters of credit, and in about 1800 they became significant loan contractors. They started to dominate the business in 1810, and they maintained their leading position in this business for the rest of the century.

Baring Brothers & Co. was one of two Atlantic merchants that dominated the market for transatlantic finance in the early part of the nineteenth century. The second, Alexander Brown and Sons, was American. The Browns started business as Baltimore linen merchants in the late 1790s. They were well-placed to profit from the turn-of-the-century surge in the Anglo-American cotton trade, and they opened a Liverpool office in 1810. At this time, the Browns became active as financiers of Anglo-American trade: the firm in Baltimore would authorize exporters to draw a Bill of Exchange on the Liverpool branch, and would simultaneously purchase the sterling Bill for onward sale to an American importer. Thus from an early stage, the House combined the extension of credit with trade in foreign exchange. Starting in 1811, the firm became shipowners.[50]

Both the Browns and the Barings were highly influential nineteenth century financiers. But at the start of the century, the preeminent force in international finance was probably the network of Rothschilds firms. They too were established as linen traders, but they diversified rapidly into finance. An 1818 Prussian government loan saw them enter the investment banking business,[51] although it was only in the 1830s that they began seriously to compete with the Barings in America: an opportunity to arrange the payment of a million pounds

---

[50] See Perkins (1975: ch. 2) for a detailed discussion of the rise of the House of Brown.

[51] See Ferguson (1998: 131–4). Interestingly, the loan was secured by a mortgage on the Prussian royal domains. Ferguson argues that the loan represented a watershed in the history of the European capital market: it was denominated in sterling, was issued in London, Frankfurt, Berlin, Hamburg, Amsterdam, and Vienna, and interest could be collected at any Rothschild house.

Table 5.1. *Capitalization and partnership size for leading investment houses, 1815–18*

	Year	Partners	Capital (£ m)
NM Rothschilds & Sons (London)	1818	1	0.74
Rothschilds (Total)	1818	5	1.77
Baring Brothers & Co.	1810	3	1.00
Brown, Shipley & Co.	1815		0.12

Brown, Shipley & Co. was the English arm of the House of Brown.

Sources: Ferguson (1998: appendix 3), Hidy (1949: 40), and Perkins (1975: appendix A).

owing to the Treasury in Washington from France led to the Rothschilds replacing the Barings as the federal government's London agents.[52]

Like the Browns, the Rothschilds derived much of their strength from cooperation across a reliable family network. In the case of the Rothschilds this was formed when Mayer Rothschild sent sons from Frankfurt to establish operations in Paris, Vienna, and Naples.[53] Until the 1860s the houses operated almost as a single entity.[54] Family ties alone were not sufficient fully to resolve conflicts of interest between the houses, and the family members renegotiated their complicated partnership agreements on a regular basis.[55] The Rothschilds combined their family network with a reputation for absolute discretion, a careful cultivation of leading political figures, [56] and, unlike either the Browns or the Barings, a position as stock exchange insiders. As Redlich (1968: 323) notes, their recognition of the potential of stock exchanges for floating new securities marked the Rothschilds out from the start.

The profits earned from their networks by the early merchant bankers were substantial: the margin earned by the Browns on Bill sales in normal market times was between one half and one percent;[57] their fee for guaranteeing the credit of the English buyers in the cotton market was two and a half percent;[58] for letters of credit in the first

---

[52] Ferguson (1998: 391).

[53] The Rothschilds never opened an American office, although they employed American agents. Their unwillingness to commit to America may be partially responsible for their late 19th cent. eclipse as investment bankers.

[54] Ferguson (1998: 3) states that they 'worked together so closely that it is impossible to discuss the history of one without discussing this history of all five'.

[55] Ferguson (1998: 283–7).   [56] Ferguson (1998: 5).

[57] Perkins (1975: ch. 3).   [58] Myers (1931: 70).

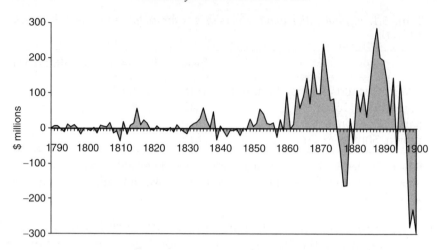

Figure 5.2. *US net capital inflows, 1790–1900*

Source: Davis and Cull (2000: 737).

half of the century they charged one to one and a half percent.[59] At the same time, the business had relatively low financial capital requirements, and relied on the contacts and the skills of a small number of partners. Table 5.1 provides summary partnership and capitalization data for the Barings, the English arm of the Browns, and the Rothschilds at the start of the century.

Like European loan contracting, American investment banking was initially concerned with the placement of public debt, which in America meant loans issued by the states and the federal government. Increasingly, though, the enormous capital needs of the railroads would come to dominate the markets. Capital accumulation at home was insufficient to meet the needs of the developing American economy, and the country was a net importer of capital throughout the nineteenth century: figure 5.2 illustrates net inflows on a year-by-year basis.

As a condition of their charter, many American chartered banks in the early part of the nineteenth century were required to subscribe to railroad, navigation, and turnpike companies.[60] As America began in the 1830s to build an infrastructure, it was therefore natural that the chartered banks should buy loans for onward sale, as well as for purely investment purposes. The largest of the institutions to do so

---

[59] Perkins (1975: 135).   [60] Redlich (1968: 325).

was the Second Bank of the United States, which became an embryonic investment bank when it acquired parts of federal government loans in 1820 and 1821. Other chartered banks entered the market later on, as the states began to float substantial bond issues.[61]

Although he has no direct evidence of this, Redlich (1968: 330) argues that in assuming a loan contracting role, American banks were influenced by English experiences. For sure, representatives of American banks came into contact with the Barings, the Rothschilds, and other European contractors. By the late 1830s, almost all New York City banks were ready to act as loan contractors. Often, funding of these trades would be simplified, as the banks would hold the purchase price of the securities on deposit until the issuer needed to use it: Redlich (1968: 311) provides numerous examples.

Unlike the incorporated chartered banks, private banks could not issue their own notes. They were smaller than the chartered banks, and they were typically constituted as partnerships. By the end of the century, the investment banking world would be dominated by two private banks. However, the private banks did not enter investment banking until 1821, when Prime, Ward, and King of New York started to participate in federal, state, and canal bond flotations.[62]

Many of the most important nineteenth-century investment banking innovations were associated with railroad financing. The 1830s was the first decade of railroad financing. In this decade, East-West railroad finance came from public bond issuance, while North-South railroads were financed mostly using private bonds.[63] In line with the need for imported capital, railroad bonds were designed to appeal to English investors.[64] Those of the 1830s set the standard for the rest of the century, being long-term (25–30 years), and convertible to stock.[65] A substantial proportion of them were sterling-denominated, with interest and principal payable in London.

The prime movers in the 1830s market for railroad bonds were Thomas Biddle & Co., a private bank, and the chartered Bank of the United States of Pennsylvania, which was run by Thomas' brother, Nicholas. Nicholas Biddle's bank established British contacts, and it was very profitable throughout the 1830s, but Biddle was a risk-taker. His strategy of lending on securities that he was to sell left him highly

---

[61] Redlich (1968: 327–30).   [62] Redlich (1968: 333–4).
[63] Chandler (1954: 249).   [64] Redlich (1968: 354).
[65] Chandler (1954: 251).

exposed to market downturns, and this led to the 1841 failure of his bank.

The Panic of 1837

The 1837 panic changed the composition of the nascent investment banking industry. The United States had witnessed rapid speculative expansion in land and in transport. Easy credit and an overextension of the domestic banking market in England and America left the system exposed to a contraction of credit. This occurred when in August 1836 the Bank of England refused to discount bills drawn on houses active in American trading. Matters came to a head when cotton prices dropped by 25 percent in early 1837.

In the ensuing crisis a number of US banks went to the wall. However, English lending to America continued between 1837 and 1839. In 1839, when a fresh panic occurred, the English held $200 million of American securities. By the time of the 1841 failure of Biddle's Bank, $120 million were in danger of suspension.

The 1837 panic had consequences which illustrate both the importance of reputation in security markets and also the political reach of the European merchant banks. Henrietta Larson (1936: 67) characterizes the response of the states to the panic and its consequences as follows:

A succession of unfortunate events, that is, the panic of 1837, the bursting of Biddle's bubble, and the repudiation of their debts by a number of States, even by rich Pennsylvania, practically destroyed foreign interest in American investments.

In fact, by 1842 eight American states and one territory had either missed interest payments or repudiated their debt altogether.[66] Public opinion in England was scandalized by the defaults. The Reverend Sydney Smith, Canon of St Paul's Cathedral and former editor of the *Edinburgh Review*, stated that he never dined with a citizen of Pennsylvania

without feeling a disposition to seize and divide him—to allot his beaver to one sufferer and his coat to another—to appropriate his pocket handkerchief to the orphan, and to comfort the widow with his silver watch, Broadway rings, and the London Guide which he always carries in his pockets. How

---

[66] They were Arkansas, Illinois, Indiana, Louisiana, Maryland, Michigan, Mississippi, Pennsylvania, and Florida (which became a state in 1845). See Sexton (2005: 27).

such a man can set himself down at an English table without feeling that he owes two or three pounds to every man in the company, I am at a loss to conceive. He has no more right to eat with honest men than a leper has to eat with clean.[67]

Nondefaulting states, and the federal government, were tarred with the same brush as the defaulters. George Peabody, who was black-balled by the Reform Club at this time because 'he was a citizen of a nation that did not pay its debts',[68] informed a correspondent that 'As long as there is one state in the Union in default, no U.S. Government bonds can be negotiated [in Britain]'. Similarly, the Barings informed a New York correspondent that 'no new loan shall be introduced here while there is any one of the states in default'.[69] The reaction of the Rothschilds was even stronger. When attempting in 1842 to issue a loan in Europe, the federal government was informed by James de Rothschild that 'You may tell your government that you have seen the man who is at the head of the finances of Europe, and that he has told you that they cannot borrow a dollar, not a dollar'.[70]

The withdrawal of overseas investors from the American bond markets had the immediate effect of shifting the center of American railroad finance from the Pennsylvania headquarters of Biddle's Bank to Boston.[71] Railroad promoters were forced to look internally for capital and, uniquely in contemporary America, New England had avoided indebtedness. Profits from international trade, shipping, whaling, and manufacturing had accumulated, and for much of the decade provided the capital for railroad developments. However, Chandler (1954) notes that at this time, little of the finance came from bonds.

The recovery of America's financial reputation was masterminded by European financiers. Early in 1841 a group of European banks led by Baring Brothers, the Rothschilds, and the Dutch house of Hope and Co. attempted unsuccessfully to persuade President John Tyler and his Secretary of State Daniel Webster to pressure delinquent states to resume payments on their debts.[72] After a similar rebuttal from the English government, the Barings began in 1843 to orchestrate a 'restoration campaign' in America against the defaulting states. Through their American agent Thomas Wren Ward and with five other

---

[67] McGrane (1935), cited by Burk (1989: 6).   [68] Burk (1989: 6).
[69] Both quotations come from Sexton (2005: 39).
[70] Jenks (1927), cited by Burk (1989: 6).   [71] Chandler (1954).
[72] Sexton (2005: 28).

European banks they organized public bondholder meetings, press articles, and lobbying. They also used members of the clergy to make their moral point. The post-1837 depression began to lift in the middle of the 1840s, and the Barings' campaign began to bear fruit, as many of the defaulting states recommenced interest payments on their debt.

Sexton (2005: 40–45) discusses the restoration campaign. He argues that the power and influence of British banks, and in particular of Barings, stemmed from their unique ability to tap the European capital markets upon which American development would rely for some years to come. Failure to meet their liabilities would lock the defaulting states out of the major investment banking networks and, by extension, out of the capital markets. As in chapters two and three, Barings and its collaborators were therefore using extra-legal means to enforce bondholder property rights. Their ability to do so signaled to investors that a bond's creditworthiness depended to some extent upon its sponsoring investment banks, and hence reinforced their market position, and the networks upon which they relied.

Industry Structure After 1837

The contours of the twentieth-century investment banking industry were sketched in 1837. The panic of that year sent a number of American banks to the wall, and it drove the chartered banks from the market. The private banks that survived the panic emerged in the 1840s with greatly enhanced reputations. Moreover, reputations were more highly valued by investors who experienced losses as a result of the panic. As a result, the surviving institutions were well placed to expand their activities in the investment banking market, and they filled the void left by the departing chartered banks.

The House of Brown escaped the crisis with the aid of some assistance from the Bank of England, and in the end lost less than five percent of its capital.[73] Its survival led to massive profit opportunities, as it covered earlier Bill sales in a very depressed market: exchange profits in the 1837–8 season offset the losses sustained in the panic.[74]

The Browns' survival signaled their skill and financial rectitude. As a result, they attained a position of preeminence in the letter of credit market. Starting in the 1840s, the Browns were the close competitors

---

[73] Perkins (1975: ch. 8).   [74] Perkins (1975: ch. 3).

of the Barings both in financing American trade and in marketing American securities.

The year 1837 was a very important year in the history of the house of Morgan, which would by the end of the century be the most important of the investment banks. In that year Pierpont Morgan was born, George Peabody moved to London, where he would found the London house that Pierpont would one day control, and Francis Drexel established the American house within which Pierpont would achieve prominence.

George Peabody had founded a dry goods business with the merchant Elisha Riggs in 1814, and in 1837 Peabody was in the same business with Riggs' nephew Samuel as his junior partner. Peabody had anticipated the panic and had realized most of his assets in advance; the firm therefore survived with its credit intact, and Peabody's reputation greatly enhanced.[75]

Peabody moved to London in 1837 in order to direct purchasing activities for himself. By the time his partnership agreement with Riggs expired in 1841 he had decided to withdraw his capital from the dry goods business in order to concentrate upon financial business. Throughout the 1840s he was a heavy dealer in American securities, and he was increasingly involved in merchant banking on his own account. The European market for American securities began to recover in the middle of the 1840s as the defaulting states began to resume payments on their securities. Now that he was established in London, this presented Peabody with a major opportunity. In July 1848, he and the Barings agreed to 'act in perfect unison in making sales' of American securities.[76]

In 1851, Peabody formally created a London house, George Peabody & Co., with £250,000 of capital. Two years later he met a young member of the New York commercial elite, Junius Spencer Morgan, and in 1854 the two became partners. At this stage, while the premier houses in Anglo-American trade remained Baring Brothers & Co. and Brown, Shipley & Co. (the English branch of Alexander Brown & Sons), Peabody & Co. was certainly the premier American house in London.[77]

---

[75] Burk (1989: 4). As evidence of the importance that Peabody placed upon his reputation, Hidy (1949: 89) cites his insistance to his partner that their credit be 'kept unsullied and all obligations met promptly at any price'.

[76] Interestingly, neither Peabody nor the Barings liked working with the London Rothschilds as they tended to undercut the market. See Burk (1989: 12).

[77] Burk (1989: 19).

Peabody & Co. survived the panic of 1857 with the aid of a Bank of England loan.[78] The end of the crisis saw George Peabody withdrawing from active involvement in the firm's affairs: he was 63 and wanted to concentrate upon philanthropy while his (poor) health lasted. From the spring of 1858, J. S. Morgan was the effective head of Peabody & Co., and in February 1859, Peabody made Morgan the formal head.[79]

As George Peabody was arriving in London in 1837, an event was occurring on the other side of the Atlantic that would have important consequences for Peabody's future partner J. S. Morgan, and for his newly born son, J. P. Morgan. In this year an Austrian immigrant named Francis Drexel established a currency brokerage in Louisville, Kentucky, before moving his business to Philadelphia the following year. In contrast to the other financiers considered in this chapter, Drexel entered the United States as an artist; he discovered currency broking while traveling around Mexico and Central America in the mid-1850s.[80] By the middle of the 1840s, he had begun trading in Bills of Exchange and railroad bonds. By the middle of 1847, Drexel was participating in the Mexican War Loan. Also in this year, Francis took his sons into partnership, and changed his firm's name to Drexel & Co. From this time, the 21 year-old Anthony Drexel occupied an increasingly dominant position in the business: he was effectively running it long before Francis' death in 1862.

Although they became extremely important private bankers, the Drexels are of most interest to the twentieth-century observer because of the important role that they played in launching Pierpont Morgan's career. The preceding chain of events can be traced back to the Drexels' first forays into government finance, which they made through Van Vleck, Read, Drexel & Co., the Wall Street office that they established in 1855 by purchasing an interest in the established firm of J. T. Van Vleck, Read & Co.

Nineteenth-century government finance, like large-scale railroad finance, relied on continental contacts who could provide the capital

[78] The crisis and its effect upon Peabody & Co. is described by Carosso (1987: 63–70). Several of Peabody's London competitors intimated that they would lend to his firm on the condition that the firm withdrew from business within a year. Without the £800,000 credit line that the Bank of England extended to Peabody, the attempt to force him out the market would probably have succeeded.

[79] Burk (1989: 23).

[80] The discussion of the Drexels relies upon Dan Rottenberg's history (2001) of the firm.

that America needed. The Drexels therefore needed to establish a relationship with an English or a European bank. Their overtures to the Barings were rejected in 1851, and three years later Francis Drexel visited George Peabody in London to discuss the possibility of a relationship. Later that year, J.S. Morgan visited the Drexels in Philadelphia before he departed for London and his partnership with Peabody. As a result of this meeting, the Drexels were named a correspondent of Peabody & Co.

The year 1837 was also the year in which the Rothschilds' American agent, August Belmont, entered the United States. The Rothschilds' failure to establish an American house reflected both their distrust of the federal system of government, and also the unwillingness of the younger generation of the family to emigrate to the New World. According to Ferguson (1998: 394), it was probably their greatest strategic mistake. The absence of a family member in America deprived the Rothschilds of American market intelligence, and restricted their ability to participate in American security markets.

Where the Rothschilds had no family representative, they relied upon salaried agents, whom they cultivated through frequent correspondence and preferential dealing.[81] Prior to the 1837 panic, this role was filled in the United States by a number of American banks, of which J. L. and S. I. Joseph was the most notable. All of their American correspondents failed in the panic, and Belmont was sent to America from Frankfurt to take stock of the financial situation, before traveling to Havana. Instead, he stopped in New York and established the private bank August Belmont & Co. Although they went along with his suggestion that he act as their agent, Belmont's initiative was a source of extreme irritation to the Rothschilds.[82] The Rothschilds never fully trusted nonfamily members, and they repeatedly considered replacing Belmont with a family member, but he proved his worth during the 1848 crisis by remitting silver to London, and by 1858, his wide-ranging network of contacts, and in particular his high social standing in America, appear to have secured his position.[83]

---

[81] Ferguson (1998: 283–7).

[82] They 'never ceased to regard him as unreliable (a feeling not alleviated by his involvement in a duel in 1841 and his conversion, evidently for the sake of social advancement, to Christianity)' (Ferguson, 1998: 394).

[83] Ferguson (1998: 576).

American Capital Market Rehabilitation

America's reputation in the international capital markets was finally restored at the end of the 1840s. The 1846–8 Mexican War generated massive government expenditure: by 1847, the deficit had reached the unprecedented level of $30 million. The Treasury responded by issuing an $18 million bond, of which the Washington, DC firm of Corcoran and Riggs took $14.7 million.[84] The firm struggled to sell its allotment, and had a brush with bankruptcy. It was therefore rather more circumspect with the $16 million 1848 loan, of which it acquired $14 million, demanding the right to market it abroad in exchange for an advance on the proceeds. The result was an early selling syndicate: the loan was placed with Barings Brothers, George Peabody, Overend, Gurney & Co., and with the Rothschilds. The latter firm took the largest part of the loan, and it initiated their large-scale involvement in American finance.[85]

The loan sale came at a good time: 1848, the publication date of the *Communist Manifesto*, saw massive social and political unrest on Continental Europe. Fears of revolution, and of government default, caused European government bonds to plummet in value. Against this backdrop, and notwithstanding its preoccupation with democracy, America looked like a safe investment haven.

The European rehabilitation of American financial securities came at an opportune time. The 1847 depression triggered a money shortage in Boston, and American entrepreneurs were forced to look to the Old World for capital. As Chandler (1954: 263) notes, this placed New York in a strong position since 'as the centre of American-European trade, New York merchants had many more contacts with the bankers and merchants of Paris, Geneva, Frankfurt and Bremen than did the businessmen of other sea ports'.

By the 1850s, then, the epicenter of American finance had finally shifted to New York. The European interest in American securities that had been reestablished by the Mexican War Loan was sustained for much of the ensuing decade: only the gathering clouds of the Civil War slowed and, at the very end of the decade, reversed the trend. Of the $444 million of American securities held abroad in

[84] The firm was founded in 1840 by W. W. Corcoran and George Washington Riggs, who was the son of George Peabody's first partner in the dry goods business. The firm was wound up when Corcoran retired in 1854. For an examination of Corcoran's career, see Cohen (1971).

[85] The loan sales are described by Sexton (2005: 54–7).

Table 5.2. *Capitalization and partnership size for leading investment houses, 1850–5*

	Year	Partners	Capital (£ m)
George Peabody & Co.	1854	3	0.45
NM Rothschilds & Sons (London)	1852		2.50
Rothschilds (Total)	1852	8	9.50
Baring Brothers & Co.		7	
Brown, Shipley & Co.	1854	9	1.42

Sources: Ferguson (1998: 516), Burk (1989: 19), and Perkins (1975: appendices A and B).

1860, about $200 million were sold back to Americans between 1860 and 1863.[86]

Table 5.2 reports partnership and capitalization data for the most important of the middle-of-the-century financiers.

CONCLUSION

By the 1861 outbreak of the Civil War, investment banking had emerged as a significant financial activity. The investment banking market was dominated by a number of private banks who leaned upon international trading networks to import the capital needed by the American states, federal government, and industrial concerns, in particular the railroads. Investment banking networks at this time were largely created through international commodity trading, and the early international investment bankers came to the business via trade finance and the market for Bills of Exchange.

A number of legal–political factors pushed the Atlantic merchants on their way toward fully fledged investment banking. Recall from chapter four that in the eighteenth century, these merchants derived much of their competitive advantage from the power that their trading networks and their reputations gave them to enforce extra-legal contracts in a world with weak formal property rights. The emergence in the first half of the nineteenth century of a will theory of contract based upon subjective notions of value and backed by an expectations standard of damages represented a significant leap forward in property rights institutions.

The stronger property rights of the nineteenth century facilitated the development of large-scale commercial enterprise. The capital

---

[86] Sexton (2005: 79–80).

demands of these enterprises created a need for investment banks, but at the same time, it also obviated the earlier need for private mercantile property rights law. Moreover, developments in commercial law were forcing disputing merchants into the courts, and away from older forms of arbitration.

These developments further reduced the (relative) value of reputations and information networks in the Atlantic trade in goods. But reputation and local knowledge remained paramount in assessing the creditworthiness of a trade creditor, or of a corporate borrower. Merchants with strong reputations and wide trading networks naturally chose to shift into the primary security markets, where their informational assets gave them an advantage in creating the quasi-legal structures upon which these markets rely. Similarly, the emergence of a stock market can be seen as a response to poor laws and restricted property rights in the secondary securities market.

The next half of the century would see the final transition from merchanting to banking. It would also witness the emergence of most of the investment banks that would dominate the twentieth-century securities markets. During this period, investment bankers would start to experiment with the retail distribution of securities, and they would adopt the advisory role that remains central to modern investment bankers. The modern syndicate would emerge, and the investment banker would assume a position at the center of American economic life. These events are the subject of chapter six.

6

Investment Banking in the Age of Laissez-Faire

If America ever saw a golden age of laissez-faire capitalism, it was in the second half of the nineteenth century. Contemporary statesmen saw a system of contracting within a minimal state as the best way of encouraging economic growth. Their intuitions were supported by prepolitical theories of property, which formed the basis for a legal orthodoxy that distinguished between public and private life. Within the private sphere, individuals were free to order their own affairs via contract.

This climate may have reflected the needs of the new industrial elite. Certainly, large-scale industrial enterprise flourished at this time. As a consequence of railroad construction, manufacturers were able to access far larger markets. The emergence of big business created fresh challenges: it required unprecedented levels of capital investment, and it resulted in the creation of a new class of professional managers, removed from the capitalists who financed their activities.

The period after the Civil War saw great strides in communications technologies. As a result, the commodity markets in which the Atlantic traders of the previous two chapters operated became increasingly standardized. Many of the legal impediments to trade that in the eighteenth century had generated their competitive advantage were by now swept away. By the end of the third quarter of the century, most of them had decided that they could maximize the returns which they earned from their valuable reputations and their networks by jettisoning their mercantile activities, and specializing in finance.

Rising capital needs and increasing specialization among financiers resulted in the creation of something like the modern investment bank. Investment bankers responded to the challenges of industrialization by experimenting with a variety of modes of capital raising. They recognized their role as the representatives of end investors, and they became increasingly concerned with corporate governance.

This chapter describes the emergence of financial capitalism in the United States up to the point where, at the close of the century, a small number of key investment bankers occupied the commanding heights of the American economy. We begin by discussing the legal and political environment within which these changes occurred.

LEGAL AND POLITICAL ENVIRONMENT

As we saw in chapter five, the development in the first half of the nineteenth century of extensive markets altered perceptions of contract. Jurists came to recognize contracts as expressions of will, which reflected the subjective value judgments of their counterparts. Hence enforcement became a way of tying people to the commitments expressed in their contracts: expectation damages prevailed, and the State made no attempt to judge *ex post* the validity or the desirability of the decisions made by the contracting parties.

Legal and political thinkers in late nineteenth-century America therefore recognized a private sphere, within which individuals were free to order their own lives. The private sphere was delineated by bright line legal categories, which separated, for instance, public law from private law. Lawyers perceived the remit of private sphere law as extending only as far as was needed to underpin private contractual arrangements. The law was therefore regarded as an apolitical sphere: according to Horwitz (1992: 16–17), it

... aspired to create a system of processes and principles that could be shared even in the absence of agreed-upon ends. [...] Thus, well before the late nineteenth century, the idea of the rule of law had emerged to oppose 'result-oriented' or consequentialist modes of legal thought.

Hence, at this stage in its development, the state had not adopted the role of enterprise association which we discussed on page 43 of chapter two. The state had an enabling role, but it did not have a purpose. This attitude went hand-in-glove with an increasingly sophisticated conception of property. Property in antebellum America was largely landed, and property law was concerned with things. As a result of increasing industrialization, the idea of chapter two that property was a bundle of rights increasingly acquired currency.[1]

---

[1] Horwitz (1992: 147) cites John Lewis's 1888 *Treatise on the Law of Eminent Domain in the United States* in support of this statement.

The expanding state came into conflict with this legal orthodoxy. If legislative changes altered the market value of a bundle of rights then the courts were liable in the last part of the century to interpret this as a taking, and to require that damages be paid accordingly. In other words (Horwitz, 1992: 161–3), Americans appeared under this interpretation of property rights to have a constitutional right to no change.

New modes of legal thinking emerged in the twentieth century in response to the problems highlighted in the previous paragraph. During the nineteenth century, however, the courts recognized most property rights as sacrosanct, and they supported a wide range of contracts. Hence, in the language of chapter two, legal property rights at this time were as strong as they had ever been. Moreover, the unwillingness of the state to interfere in private arrangements hugely strengthened the extra-legal property rights upon which we focused in chapter two.[2]

Investment banks flourished in this setting. Although, as we discuss below, their informational networks were of diminishing value in the market for physical goods, these networks were of paramount importance in sustaining their trade in securities. The agreements that they made with their security market counterparties were unconstrained by legislative interference—a state of affairs that would cease to obtain early in the twentieth century. One of the most dramatic results of this freedom of action was the emergence in the late twentieth century of the equity receivership, a body of common law relating to the reorganization of large financially distressed corporations, which was largely designed by leading investment bankers. We discuss equity receiverships later in this chapter.

TECHNOLOGICAL ADVANCES

At the start of the nineteenth century, merchants operating on opposite sides of the Atlantic were separated both in distance and, because communications were so slow, in time. Negotiations over terms of trade were therefore very protracted and were sometimes completely impractical. It was impossible for a cotton mill in the North of England to check the quality of the goods exported by a Southern American

---

[2] This is true notwithstanding the unwillingness noted in chapter five of the courts to enforce private commerical arbitration that ran contrary to commercial law. This unwillingness did not preclude extra-legal contracting within commercial bodies of the type identified in chapter two, enforced by the threat of exclusion.

farmer, and it was equally hard for the farmer to be sure of the creditworthiness of the mill. As we saw in chapters four and five, this created an opportunity for the Atlantic trader. Atlantic traders served as intermediaries between sellers on one side of the Atlantic, and buyers on the other.

The Atlantic traders had four main functions. First, they investigated the creditworthiness of buyers, maintained records of payments, and guaranteed the debts of some traders. Second, they investigated the quality of goods sold: for example, they would check cotton before it left America, and they would stake their reputation when they certified it. Third, they knew the market: they maintained substantial warehouse stocks, and were able to match buyers against sellers. Fourth, they shipped goods, and insured them while they were in transit.

For as long as information was slow in crossing the Atlantic, all of the above activities generated significant profits for the Atlantic traders. Tasks were delegated at a distance to trusted emissaries, who placed their firm's reputation on the line every time they certified creditworthiness, quality of goods, or market depth.

Improved transatlantic communications had a profound effect upon the Atlantic merchants' business. As information traveled across the Atlantic increasingly quickly, the second and the third tasks above were greatly simplified. When a buyer and a seller could rapidly share information and samples of merchandise, they had little, if any, need for an intermediary to lean upon a trustworthy member of his network. Similarly, as the costs of transatlantic shipping dropped, the margins from the fourth of the above business activities fell. Not only was shipping less profitable, but the information that it generated was widely available, and hence was no longer a source of competitive advantage.

In contrast, even instantaneous communications would not make it easy to assess an agent's creditworthiness: this required an intimate knowledge of his business, and of his financial affairs. Hence improved communications did not diminish the value of the merchant's reputation and network in finance; it was inevitable that, as communications improved, the first of the Atlantic merchant's activities should be unbundled from the other three. Technological changes in the second half of the nineteenth century therefore caused merchant bankers finally to concentrate exclusively upon their financial businesses, both as accepting houses and as investment bankers.

This shift started in the first half of the nineteenth century, as steamships started to make regular Atlantic crossings, and as the crossings became quicker.[3] The House of Brown were shipowners from 1811.[4] By the early 1830s, however, ships were less profitable than in the past. The Browns' consequential decision to limit their exposure to cotton shipping was one of the reasons that they weathered the 1837 crisis so well.[5] Through the 1840s and 1850s faster and more regular steamship crossings between the UK and the United States increased competition levels in the cotton consignment business until margins dropped so low that it was only by offering generous bundled credit deals that one could profit.[6] Notwithstanding their increasing disillusionment with the business, the Browns invested heavily in a line of steamers in the late 1840s. The investment was a disaster.

From the perspective of the Atlantic merchants, the most significant technological development of the nineteenth century was probably the opening in 1866 of the transatlantic cable. Instantaneous (albeit costly) communication transformed mercantile activities. Manufacturers in Britain and on the Continent now bought their cotton by cable on samples previously sent to them from New Orleans, Mobile, Charleston, and other exporting ports.[7] When buyers and sellers could communicate directly, uncertainty over the arrival of goods dissipated, and there was a greatly reduced need for merchants to hold warehouse inventory while they searched for counterparties.

At a stroke, then, the cable rendered obsolete the old system, whereby Liverpool merchants had received cotton on consignment and then distributed it to brokers. In the two decades following the opening of the transatlantic cable, merchant commissions in the cotton trade declined from three to one percent. By 1880, inventories stored in port declined to about ten weeks' supply. As Chapman (1984: 137) states, 'the old mercantile families were compelled to change their character radically, or to retire from business.' We have already noted that they did so by moving entirely into finance. In the years after the cable opened, the House of Brown never again earned more than five percent of its revenue from mercantile activities and the Liverpool

---

[3] Regular steamship sailings began with the 1817 opening of the Black Ball Line, the first transatlantic steamship to sail (monthly) whether or not it was full: see p 100.
[4] Perkins (1975: 21).   [5] See Perkins (1975: ch. 3) for a discussion.
[6] Perkins (1975: ch. 4) for a detailed discussion.
[7] Perkins (1975: p. 86, n. 7) provides details of direct purchases by cotton mills.

office was finally closed altogether in 1888.[8] The Barings responded to the same pressures in the same way, giving up mercantile activities in the 1880s.[9] JS Morgan & Co., the successor partnership to Peabody & Co., finally withdrew from commodities trading in 1873, at which time the firm, with the New York and Philadelphia members of its network,[10] decided that their future lay in the development of an international securities business to serve the needs of governments and large businesses.[11]

THE CIVIL WAR AND RETAIL INVESTMENT BANKING

The American Civil War of 1861–5 was costly in terms of dollars, as well as lives. The federal government was forced to issue bonds at an unprecedented level. Abraham Lincoln's First Secretary to the Treasury, Salmon P. Chase, was distrustful of banks and struggled to raise funds, partly because he would issue bonds only at par, and partly because he refused to deposit the receipts from his bonds with the banks, insisting instead upon payment in specie. One consequence of Chase's attitudes to the capital markets was the emergence for the first time of aggressive marketing of new issues to retail customers. The driving figure behind this move was Jay Cooke.[12]

Cooke had received his training in investment banking with EW Clark & Co. of Philadelphia, where he was firstly a clerk, and later on a partner. He and Anthony Drexel, who was by this time running Drexel & Co., knew one another, although there was a significant financial disparity between them: in 1861, the Drexels had a capital base of between $1 and $2 million, while Cooke had $150,000.[13] So when in 1861 Cooke established his own Philadelphia house, Jay Cooke & Co., he would have valued a relationship with the Drexels from a financial perspective as well as from a reputational one.

Such a relationship was established later in 1861, when Jay Cooke & Co. and Drexel & Co. made a joint bid for the contract to sell a $3 million Commonwealth of Pennsylvania loan. Cooke brought a flair for selling to the table, as well as political connections: his brother,

---

[8] Perkins (1975: ch. 4).   [9] Chapman (1984: 32–3).
[10] These were respectively Drexel, Morgan & Co., and Drexel & Co.: see page 167.
[11] Burk (1989: 38).
[12] For a detailed life of Cooke, see Larson (1936). Extensive discussion of his activities in the Civil War and thereafter also appear in Redlich (1968: 356–60), Rottenberg (2001: 61–72), and Carosso (1970: 14–16 and 23–5).
[13] Rottenberg (2001: 60–1).

Harry D. Cooke, was a friend of the Treasury Secretary, Salmon P. Chase. Pennsylvania had low creditworthiness, and the best market bids for the six percent bonds were likely to be of the order of 75. The Cooke–Drexel syndicate won the selling job on the basis of Cooke's proposal to sell the bonds at par through an appeal to patriotism.

Drexel's contribution to the sales effort was its reputation, and it was largely silent through the campaign. Cooke used revolutionary sales techniques to reach small investors: he placed advertisements in newspapers, he distributed flyers throughout the state, and he sent agents throughout the state to see bankers and other potential investors. Attempting to reach retail investors in this way was a completely novel idea, and most of Cooke's investment banking peers viewed it with extreme suspicion. It was nevertheless a success: the issue was oversubscribed at par.

In the wake of this success, and leaning upon his connection to the respected house of Drexel, Cooke made a successful bid to act as the federal government's agent. His sales effort for $500 million of federal loans used many of the methods of the Philadelphia loan sale: he publicized the loan using brass bands, newspaper advertising, and he coordinated by telegraph from his Philadelphia office a national sales force of 2,500. In this way, he eventually sold at par $360 million of the Union's six percent bond issues, or 75 percent of the total.[14]

By the end of the Civil War, Cooke was one of the best-known investment bankers in America. For selling over $1 billion of Treasury War bonds, he had made slightly in excess of $1 million. He had less need of the Drexels, and his relationship with them slowly died. He now set to work building a private banking network, with New York and Washington affiliates and, from 1870, a London house Jay Cooke, McCulloch & Co. His London partner, Hugh McCulloch, established strong European ties with the Rothschilds, who instructed Belmont to support Cooke's future bond operations.

However, Cooke's experience of peddling war bonds to patriotic investors had not furnished him with the skills or the contacts needed to raise tens of millions of dollars for corporate issuers. Although he continued to peddle government debt, it was his move into corporate finance which was to prove his undoing. He gained control of the Northern Pacific Railroad, and set out to raise $100 million to finance its construction of a line from Dulath through the Rockies to the West

---

[14] Rottenberg (2001: 67).

Coast. The railroad built faster than Cooke could raise funds,[15] and by 1872 had run out of cash. Rottenberg (2001: 107) states that, by the end of 1872, the Northern Pacific was 'paying its workers in scrip, bridges were collapsing, roadbeds were washing out, and George Child's *Public Ledger* was comparing them to eighteenth century Britain's South Sea Bubble'.

Cooke's final throw of the dice was his lead position in the marketing of a new $300 million issue to finance the government's war debt. Although his fees from the sale would be low, he would have the funds for a year before the government needed them, and this could have tided him over. However, slow bond sales and tight money prevented this from happening, and in 1873 Cooke's bank failed. The resultant panic brought down many established Philadelphia and New York banks.[16]

INVESTMENT BANKERS AFTER 1873

The investment banking landscape as it appeared after the smoke cleared in the wake of the 1873 panic looked much as it would do forty years later. Many of the houses that dominated the industry at this time continued to do so for the succeeding century. In line with our previous analysis of the industry, these firms relied upon trading networks populated by people they trusted: in the nineteenth century, this trust was still founded upon national and family connection. Redlich (1968) and Carosso (1970) identify the two most important sources of investment banking networks to be German-Jewish immigrants and New England Yankees.

German-Jewish Investment Banking Networks

By the end of the Civil War, August Belmont, the Rothschilds' American agent, occupied a prominent position in American society. He was named chairman of the Democratic National Committee in 1860, and retained this position until his death in 1872. Consequentially, he devoted less and less of his energy to finance. The war had in any case left the Rothschilds disillusioned with America: they were skeptical of

[15] Cooke's failure to market the bonds is discussed by Carosso (1970: 24–5). His problems were twofold. First, he failed to interest European bankers in the bonds. This difficulty was compounded by the 1870 outbreak of war between France and Prussia, which made European investors unwilling to make capital commitments. Second, his domestic sales techniques did not work in the postwar world where investors would no longer purchase on patriotic grounds.

[16] See Rottenberg (2001: 107–13) for a discussion of Cooke's downfall.

railroad finance, and were unwilling to deal with states, preferring to trade in federal debt. As a result, the war led to a permanent decline in the Rothschild's transatlantic influence.[17]

Notwithstanding the Rothschilds' diminished interest in American finance, the Americans still needed to import capital, and in the ensuing years much of it came from Continental Europe, and in particular from Frankfurt. The German-Jewish bankers came to prominence by facilitating this capital influx. The leading individuals in these banks mostly came to America between the late 1830s and the 1850s.[18] While a few entered the country with sufficient capital and expertise to enter the banking world immediately, most immigrated with limited resources and financial expertise, and started business in peddling or retailing. The most important of the banks to emerge from the German-Jewish community were the New York houses of JW Seligman & Co and Kuhn, Loeb & Co.

Joseph Seligman came to America from Bavaria in 1837, and was later joined by his seven brothers, who made a success out of general merchanting. They were staunch supporters of the Union cause during the Civil War, fulfilling a number of contracts to supply Army uniforms, and entering the finance business by successfully peddling upward of $200 million of US government securities in Europe.[19] In the wake of this experience, the brothers decided to augment their general trading activities by moving into banking. J. & W. Seligman was founded in New York in 1864; in 1864 houses in London (Seligman Brothers & Co.) and Frankfurt (Seligman, Stettheimer a/M.) followed, and New Orleans and Paris offices were opened in 1866 and 1868.[20]

The Seligmans were (and remained) closely associated with Ulysses S. Grant, which eased their rise as investment bankers. They were appointed in 1869 the government's agents for the transmission of funds to foreign countries; their debut as an issuing house occurred in 1872, and the New York firm rapidly developed into an issuing house for corporate securities.[21] After some frantic negotiations, in 1874 the firm collaborated with the Rothschilds on a government issue, and the

---

[17] Ferguson (1998: 628).

[18] Supple (1957) discusses German-Jewish immigration. He traces the evolution from immigration of an elite of German-Jewish investment bankers, and documents the social, as well as business, connections linking the members of this elite. Further discussion of these bankers appears in Carosso (1970: 18–20) and Redlich (1968: 361).

[19] See Muir and White (1964: ch. 2) for a description of the Seligman brothers' activities before the formation of their bank.

[20] Muir and White (1964: 31, 49, 51–2).   [21] Muir and White (1964: 57, 62–4).

two firms frequently worked together on such issues in subsequent years.[22] Through the 1890s the firm was increasingly connected with the financing of urban and industrial growth; it was at the end of the century one of the leading investment banks.

Kuhn, Loeb was founded in 1850 by Abraham Kuhn and Salomon Loeb as a general merchandising and clothing store in Lafayette, Indiana: this business was dissolved in 1865, and the partners opened a private New York bank in 1867. The firm rose to prominence after it was joined in 1875 by Jacob Schiff, who shortly thereafter married Salomon Loeb's daughter. After Loeb's 1885 retirement, Schiff became the head of the firm. Among nineteenth-century investment bankers, he ranked second only to JP Morgan. Like Morgan, he rose to prominence via railroad financing and, like Morgan, he was associated later in his career with the export of American capital. Unlike Morgan, however, he did not sit on the boards of the companies that he floated, and Kuhn, Loeb did not become the depository of the securities that it floated; nor did it open any offices outside New York. And, unlike Morgan, Kuhn, Loeb were unwilling at the turn of the century to participate in industrial issues, which they regarded as 'speculative'.[23]

A number of other leading twentieth-century bankers had similar antecedents. Marcus Goldman came to America from Bavaria in 1848 to peddle and then to run a clothing store, before moving in 1869 to New York City, where he opened a banking and brokerage house, specializing in commercial paper dealing. Goldman Sachs was born in 1872, when Goldman admitted Samuel Sachs as a partner. Henry Lehman entered America from Bavaria in 1844 and ran a clothing store. After his brothers Emanuel and Mayer joined him, Lehman Brothers entered the cotton broking business in 1847, and moved thence into financial markets. Lehman Brothers and Kuhn, Loeb were eventually to merge in 1977.

The German-Jewish bankers formed a close-knit circle, linked by cultural and familial ties. They retained close links with Germany, often educating their children and finding their spouses there. Supple (1957: 145) characterizes their position by the end of the century as follows:

[...] they went to the same clubs, attended the same synagogues, chose their friends and wives from within their own limited circle, were connected with

---

[22] Muir and White (1964: 72–5).   [23] Redlich (1968: 385–7).

the same philanthropic and communal activities, and displayed over their lifetime the same interest in German culture.

Chapter two stressed the importance of close-knit communities in creating private laws, discussing, for example, the importance of reciprocity within the Maghribi trader community. It seems plausible that the close-knit nineteenth century of German-Jewish investment bankers could have fostered the same type of private law making. We argued in chapter three, and throughout the rest of the book, that private laws and close communities are central assets for investment bankers. It is perhaps unsurprising that this community was so successful in tapping German sources of capital in the nineteenth century, and hence that it rose to a position of such importance in the investment banking world.

'Yankee' Investment Banking Networks

If the German-Jewish immigrants formed a close-knit circle, so also did the commercial 'Yankee' elite of New England. Many had been Atlantic merchants, specializing in gold, currency, and foreign exchange, or had been merchant bankers. They had strong international connections, particularly in London. This group spawned a number of leading investment banking houses, and was the progenitor of John Pierpont Morgan, the greatest investment banker of all.

JP Morgan's early career illustrates the importance of transatlantic relationships in nineteenth-century investment banking. As we saw in the previous chapter, his father, Junius Spencer Morgan, was a partner in Peabody & Co., the premier American house operating from London. Peabody had a 'very intimate association' with Duncan, Sherman & Co., a New York house[24] and in 1857, Junius Spencer sent John Pierpont to apprentice with them.

The young Pierpont Morgan proved rather impetuous. For example, in 1859 he (successfully) gambled the company's capital on a ship load of coffee that had arrived in New Orleans without a buyer.[25] As a result of this and similar incidents, Duncan, Sherman & Co. refused in 1860 to admit JP Morgan to their partnership. With the benefit of hindsight, this was a mistake. Its immediate consequence was that JP Morgan left to establish JP Morgan & Co., and that this firm replaced

---

[24] Burk (1989: 13).   [25] Johnson (2000: 35).

Duncan, Sherman as American agent for Peabody & Co.[26] Duncan, Sherman failed during the 1873 panic.

Pierpont did not immediately shed himself of his proclivity for what Carosso (1970: 21) characterizes as 'dubious enterprises'. This may explain the decision in 1864 to form Dabney, Morgan & Co., with the stabilizing influence of Charles H. Dabney, an experienced former partner (and also the accountant) of Duncan, Sherman. In the same year, Peabody's partnership with JS Morgan ended. Peabody had already retired from the business: the London firm continued as JS Morgan & Co.

Pierpont Morgan's subsequent rise to eminence is closely associated with Drexel & Co. of Philadelphia, whom we encountered in chapter five, and above in connection with Jay Cooke's Civil War funding efforts. In 1863 the partnership agreement for the Drexels' New York house, Read, Drexel & Co.[27] expired, and the firm was replaced by Drexel, Winthrop & Co., of which the Drexels had two-thirds, and Robert Winthrop one-third.[28]

The Drexels had a long association with JS Morgan. We saw in the previous chapter that they became in 1854 one of Peabody's American correspondents. Notwithstanding Anthony Drexel's rather short-sighted decision in 1864 to withdraw his account from Peabody and transfer it to Brown, Shipley & co.,[29] the houses remained in contact. The Franco-Prussian war of 1870–1 strengthened their relationship. Morgan had been moving slowly into government finance, leading a Chilean issue in 1867 and a Spanish issue in 1869, and the French turned to him when the war prevented them from using either the Rothschilds or the Barings to market their bonds.[30] Morgan was comfortable with the loan because none of the many French regimes since 1789 had repudiated a financial obligation contracted by an earlier regime. He was not shaken by Bismark's threat to make repudiation of the loan a condition of peace, and profitably bought the bonds after they dipped on this news.[31]

---

[26] Winkler ([1930] 2003: 56) states that the elder Morgan was angered by the decision to deny his son a partnership, and that this is why Duncan, Sherman lost Peabody's business. Certainly, it was by this time in JS Morgan's gift: Peabody had turned control of his business over to Junius in February 1858 (Burk, 1989: 23).

[27] See p 150.   [28] Rottenberg (2001: 69).   [29] Rottenberg (2001: 71).

[30] With houses in Paris and Frankfurt the Rothschilds were unwilling to participate in war finance, while the Barings had already underwritten a Prussian loan. See Burk (1989: 30–1).

[31] Burk (1989: p. 35)

Since 1868, the Drexels had had a five-sixths share of a Paris house, Drexel, Harjes & Co. Junius Morgan used the Paris house to remit the proceeds of their loan to the French government, and as a result had a trusting relationship with the Drexels. This trust was created at an opportune time: the partnership agreement for Dabney, Morgan & Co. expired in 1870 and Pierpont was considering retirement on the grounds of ill health. So when late in 1870 Anthony Drexel called on Junius Morgan in London to ask for advice about strengthening his New York and Paris houses, Junius saw an opportunity for his son. He wrote to Drexel on January 27, 1871 to suggest that Pierpont take a partnership in the New York house.[32]

That Drexel found the prospect of a close relationship with Morgan's London house attractive is evident from the generous partnership terms that he offered Pierpont: he was prepared to grant him the larger of 50 percent of the profits of the New York house, and 15 percent of the combined profits of the combined Philadelphia and New York houses. For this, Pierpont would be asked to contribute only $15,000 of the initial $1 million capitalization of the New York house.[33] In return, the Drexels would benefit from Pierpont's dynamism and business insight as well as a very attractive link to JS Morgan's London house.

This offer appears to have been sufficient to overcome Pierpont's reservations, although Drexel had to sweeten it by agreeing that Pierpont and his family could take a fifteen-month European holiday almost immediately after the creation on July 1, 1871 of Drexel, Morgan & Co.

The three Morgan firms—Drexel, Morgan Co., Drexel & Co., and JS Morgan & Co.—formed a very powerful force in international finance over the succeeding years. They had a first class distribution network, which allowed them to place American securities in Europe, and their experience of railroad securities dated back to the early 1850s.[34] After 1870, neither the Rothschilds nor the Barings proved equal to the Drexel–Morgan partnership in the railroad market.[35] Pierpont Morgan was famously established as the leading railroad financier by his 1873 success in placing 250,000 New York Central shares on behalf of William Vanderbilt, without moving the price.[36]

---

[32] Rottenberg (2001: 95).   [33] Rottenberg (2001: 97).
[34] Carosso (1987: 54–6).   [35] Carosso (1987: 220).
[36] Carosso (1987: 230–2).

Pierpont Morgan's leading position in the organization started to be established in the 1880s. Railroad leaders looked increasingly to New York for the capital they needed to build the interregional rail system, and at the same time, JS Morgan suffered from poor health, and started to shed some of his business responsibilities.[37] Throughout this decade, there was no formal institutional connection between JS Morgan & Co., and Morgan, Drexel & Co. This changed when, after the 1890 death of the elder Morgan, Pierpont Morgan became the senior partner in JS Morgan & Co., although he remained formally subordinate to Anthony Drexel in Drexel, Morgan & Co. After Anthony Drexel died in 1893 and his son resigned his partnership, Pierpont was free to reorganize the Philadelphia and New York houses as he saw fit. He merged their capitals, made himself head of both organizations, renamed the New York firm JP Morgan & Co., and continued to call the Philadelphia house Drexel & Co., although it had no Drexel family representation among the partners. After 1895, Pierpont was the undisputed head of the London, Paris, New York, and Philadelphia houses: 'he was, at fifty-eight, not only the most prominent private international banker in the United States but also a major figure among those of the Old World.'[38]

Although JP Morgan & Co. was the leading investment bank at the end of the century, for the last part of the century it jockeyed for position with, and later continued to compete with, the European houses. We have already discussed Belmont & Co.'s association with the Rothschilds. The Barings also had American representation: their agent was Thomas Wren Ward from 1830 to 1853, after which his sons Samuel and John assumed the agency. The Ward brothers eventually gave way to the Boston firm of Kidder, Peabody & Co.

Kidder, Peabody grew out of the house of JE Thayer, opening for business in April 1865.[39] The firm opened an account with the Barings in 1878, and in 1886 became the Barings' exclusive American agent. Kidder, Peabody participated in the postwar funding of treasury short-term obligations in the 1870s, and was involved in the 1880s in the long-term refinancing of the Civil War debts, selling obligations in Boston and elsewhere. The firm was increasingly involved in the railroad business, financing in excess of sixty carriers in the 1870–93 period, and forming some close financing relationships, for example

[37] Carosso (1987: 246–7).
[38] Carosso (1987: 274–307) describes the changes in the Morgan firms between 1890 and 1894. The quotation is from p 305.
[39] Carosso (1979: 13).

with the Atchison, Topeka & Santa Fe railroad. Although the firm was sometimes frustrated at the Barings' unwillingness to participate fully in the business, Kidder, Peabody also involved itself in the profitable corporate reorganization business.[40] The close relationship with the Barings was broken by the 1891 reorganization of the firm, when it was dissolved and re-formed as two distinct partnerships: Kidder, Peabody & Co. in Boston, and Baring, Magoun & Co. in New York, each an agent of the other.[41]

Kidder, Peabody's major competitor in Boston was the firm of Lee, Higginson & Co., which was founded in 1848 as a broking and foreign exchange business.[42] As the firm moved into investment banking, its strength derived not from its international connections, but from the close relationships it had with the directors of various New England financial institutions that were based in Boston, and which provided the firm with a steady flow of funds.[43] Like Kidder, Peabody & Co., Lee, Higginson were intimately connected with railroad financing. At the end of the nineteenth century they were rather old-fashioned; they experienced an upswing because of the vision of two key individuals: Gardner Martin James and James Jackson Sorrow. The latter is credited with two extremely forward-looking initiatives: he built up an efficient statistical department; and he started to organize the retail distribution of securities.[44]

JP Morgan & Co., Kidder, Peabody & Co., and Lee, Higginson & Co. were all private Yankee banks. One of their major Yankee competitors, the First National Bank of New York, was an incorporated commercial bank. Founded in 1863, the driving force behind its investment banking operations was George Fisher Baker, a major stockholder in the First National and a close friend of Pierpont Morgan, with whom he frequently collaborated. Baker brought three former Cooke partners into the bank after the 1873 failure of Jay Cooke & Co. Two of these men, Harris C. Fahenstock and James A. Garland, were security market experts. Between them, Baker and Fahenstock propelled First National Bank to a leading position among investment banks: Baker was a railroad financier and organizer as early as 1880, and by 1900 First National was one of the most important investment banks in America.[45]

---

[40] Carosso (1979: 17–21).   [41] Carosso (1979: 33).   [42] Carosso (1970: 11).
[43] Carosso (1970: 26).   [44] Redlich (1968: 388).
[45] Redlich (1968: 390) and Carosso (1970: 23).

After 1900, the National City Bank of New York was the second commercial bank with a leadership role in investment banking. It had resources amounting to $275 million and was dominated by James Stillman, who owned almost one-fifth of its capital and had been its president since 1891: the other important shareholders were JP Morgan & Co., William and John D. Rockefeller, Kidder, Peabody & Co., Jacob J. Schiff, and Robert Bacon, formerly a Morgan partner. Redlich (1968: 391) tells us that 'Stillman owed his presidency of the bank to the Rockefellers and was generally considered to be the representative of their banking interests'. The National City Bank became active in investment banking only in the last few years of the nineteenth century.

INVESTMENT BANKING AFTER 1873

We have already noted that the 1873 panic laid the institutional foundations for much of twentieth-century investment banking. The succeeding years also saw the adoption of a number of practices that are fundamental to our theory of investment banking. The period saw the development of the investment banking syndicate, the rise of investment banking activism and, in the railroad reorganizations and the first merger wave, the advent of a clear investment bank advisory business.

Transactions

The transactions against which the end-of-century developments in investment banking practice played themselves out were the refinancing in the 1870s of the long-term Civil War debt, and continuing government calls on the capital markets, the continued financing of the railroads, and the emergence of other forms of corporate finance.

The refunding of the Civil War debt occurred during the 1870s. It involved the sale of almost $1.4 billion of federal bonds between August 1871 and June 1879. Much of the selling occurred in London. The American firms most closely involved in the refinancing therefore had strong European connections. The business came at a time when the Morgan firms had decided to build up their securities market activities (see p. 160) and, with the Rothschilds, they took most of the refinancing business.[46]

Railroads were the largest customers of the investment banks throughout the last quarter of the nineteenth century. From its

[46] See Carosso (1987: 175–90) for a discussion of these loans.

postpanic nadir of 1,606 miles in 1875, new railroad construction increased by 1879 to 5,006 miles, and construction continued to expand until 1893. Between 1873 and 1893, the combined outstanding issues of railroad bonds and stocks increased from $4.8 to $9.9 billion.[47]

Railroad financing was dominated by firms who had the reputation and contacts to raise capital in Europe, either directly, as in the case of the Morgan firms and Kuhn, Loeb, or indirectly, as with Kidder, Peabody, who relied upon their relationship with the Barings. Although these private banks underwrote many of the railroad issues, they never came close to monopolizing the railroad business: outside the major East Coast cities, commercial bankers were the main underwriters and distributors of railroad securities.[48]

Finally, the large railroad networks opened up unprecedented distribution opportunities for industrial firms, and allowed them to service very large capital investments.[49] As a result, very large industrial concerns began to emerge which could not rely upon retained earnings for finance. Beginning in the 1880s, they increasingly used investment banks to access the capital markets. The flotation of stock by industrial partnerships that recapitalized as corporations served to increase stock ownership. While the major investment banks involved themselves in the largest of these transactions,[50] many of them regarded common stock transactions as speculative, and some did not participate in financing industrial corporations until the close of the century.[51]

The Rise of the Syndicate

The modern investment banking syndicate was developed in the postwar capital markets. It was characterized by cooperation in the selling of new issues. Although it was previously used in England, the syndicate was introduced to America by Jay Cooke:[52] see, for example, the discussion above of the American and European selling groups for the $300 million 1872 federal loan.

---

[47] Carosso (1970: 29).   [48] Carosso (1970: 32–3).

[49] Chandler (1990: 53–8).

[50] For example, Lee, Higginson, and JP Morgan arranged the consolidation of the Thomson-Houston Electric Company with the Edison Electric Company to form the General Electric Company, with initial capitalization of $50 million (Carosso, 1978: 43).

[51] Carosso (1970: 44) gives Kuhn, Loeb as an exemplar of this attitude.

[52] Redlich (1968: 360).

Syndication was rendered inevitable by two developments: the increasing expectation that investment bankers would underwrite the issues that they marketed; and the increasing size of issues, in line with the greater capital requirements of railroads and the industrials. Underwriting was the practice by which investment bankers guaranteed the sale of a new issue: ultimately, it evolved to today's practice, whereby the bank purchases the entire issue from its client and then markets it.

Today's investment banks have generally identified a market for their issues before they purchase them, and as a result they bear minimal underwriting risk. In the nineteenth-century, however, underwriting was a hazardous occupation: as we have already seen, Jay Cooke's failure was a consequence of his underwriting of the Northern Pacific Railroad. It was therefore natural that several investment bankers should join together and coordinate their selling effort, for example by agreeing not to undercut one another. Moreover, when investment banks had distinct networks, combining forces increased the reach of their selling operation.

Although investment banks would sometimes sell sovereign debt for low fees in order to build a reputation, syndication was a profitable activity. At the end of the nineteenth century, the usual fees and commissions for syndicate members were between 2.5 and ten percent of the amount of their participation. Spreads on securities were also high, ranging from about three percent for railroad bonds, to as much as 14 percent for public utility companies.[53]

We can see in the nineteenth-century investment bank many of the enforcement norms that we discussed in chapters two and three. During the last quarter of the century, investment banks started to form close relationships with clients, many of which continued into the 1920s. For example, from about 1880 Kuhn, Loeb were the 'principal bankers' of the Pennsylvania railroad, and by 1900 they were the principal bankers of ten major railroads. Kidder, Peabody were closely associated with the Atchison, Topeka and Santa Fe railroad.[54] The Morgan firms were preeminent railroad financiers for much of the period concerned: among others, they were closely associated with the Baltimore & Ohio,[55] the New York Central and the Union Pacific.[56] Close associations of this type facilitated the expensive information gathering that was performed prior to an issue: Carosso (1970: 56)

---

[53] Carosso (1970: 76).   [54] Carosso (1970: 33–4).
[55] Carosso (1987: 77–8).   [56] Carosso (1987: 230–5).

reports that it was not uncommon to spend $10,000 investigating a corporation that was planning a $2 million issue.

Close associations of this type had two significant further consequences. First, the danger of losing a profitable relationship served to keep the investment banker honest in his dealings with a firm, even when his honesty could neither be contracted upon nor proved in court. Second, when an investment bank formed a close and public relationship with an issuer, the bank's reputation was to some extent tied up in the fortunes of the issuer. We argue below that this provided the bank with incentives to monitor the firm on behalf of the dispersed bondholders. As a result, a reputable lead banker sent a strong signal of quality to the capital markets, and issuers were therefore prepared to pay more for such a banker.

Syndication provided for the type of quasi-legal contracting upon which we argue investment banking depends. Syndicate membership was in the lead investment banker's gift, and the corporation had little if any say in the matter.[57] This was efficient, in that the investment banker was in a far better position to gather information about the performance of syndicate members than the issuer and, crucially, because syndicate members had long-term relationships and hence were in a position to punish one another for malfeasance.

Carosso (1970: 59–60) points to these effects. Investment bankers were influenced in their choice of syndicate members by the issuer's previous banking relationships. The originating banker would expect reciprocity in the awarding of syndicate places. While syndicate members had the right to reject participation, it was widely believed that participation was not really optional. The *New York Times* asserted in 1905 that 'firms and individuals who are permitted to participate in syndicates cannot discriminate between promising and unpromising syndicates without being excluded altogether in future.'[58] This is precisely the type of extra-legal contracting that we discussed in chapter two: here, it is being used to maintain the lead banker's liquidity network, as in chapter three.[59]

---

[57] Carosso (1970: 58).   [58] Cited by Carosso (1970: 60).

[59] Carosso (1970: 60) cites additional contemporary sources that support our hypothesis that investment bankers used syndicates to create private law. A 1909 quotation from a corporate executive runs as follows: 'These things are so much a matter of custom and business honor that legal questions rarely arise among the syndicate members or between them and the managers.' A New York attorney gave an explanation in 1910 for syndicate honesty that relied on something a little more prosaic than honor: 'Should one of the participants fail to keep his promise, the

The success of a syndication therefore depended upon the reputation of the lead manager, who managed the combined networks of the syndicate members. Syndicates were also forums within which investment bankers could acquire the reputations upon which their activities depended. Underwriters therefore fought hard to win the lead manager role, and participants (then and now) placed enormous emphasis upon the order in which their names appeared on the 'tombstone ads' that reported deals. If banks were too low on the pecking order, they would turn down syndicate membership.[60]

Investment Banker Activism

As investment bankers formed increasingly close relationships with their clients, their reputations and financial capital became increasingly tied up in the success of their clients. It was natural that they should attempt to protect both by assuming a more active role in overseeing the financial affairs of their corporate clients after they issued securities. This type of investment banker activism became commonplace in the years after the Civil War, and probably reached its apogee at the close of the century. It typically involved investment banker representation on corporate boards.

By the end of the century, all of the leading investment banks were active board participants, but they typically exerted their influence only to prevent negative behavior: in their dealings with corporations, they were otherwise 'hands-off'.[61] Hence, although it subsequently attracted the attention of federal investigators, it appears that investment banker activism was concerned with effective corporate governance. Investment banker board participation reflected enlightened self-interest rather than an attempt to rob corporations blind.

Investment banking is entirely concerned with the resolution of contractual problems between agents with conflicting objectives. Contemporary investment bankers could rely upon their strong reputations to convince investors that they would manage the conflicts of interest to which they were inevitably exposed so as to maximize value. Evidence in support of this hypothesis is provided by Brad De Long

result would probably be not a suit for breach of contract, but banishment from the syndicate list.'

[60] For example, after Barings' reputation was damaged by the Argentinian crisis of 1890, the Morgan firms refused to participate with the firm in Argentinian offerings unless their name was accorded at least equal prominence with the Barings: see Burk (1989: 53–7).

[61] Redlich (1968: 380).

(1991), who examines the effects of JP Morgan's turn-of-the-century activism. For the 1910–12 period, he finds that the presence of a JP Morgan member on the board added about 30 percent to the price of common stock equity value.

Morgan's men added value by representing dispersed investors. De Long quotes a remark by Morgan to railroad executives: 'Your railroad? Your railroad belongs to my clients'. The anticipation that Morgan would represent their interests made investors more willing to buy bonds peddled by his house, and so reduced the corporate cost of capital. It is therefore unsurprising that corporations were in general eager for their bankers to sit on their boards:

'A corporation often was as anxious to have the banker who brought out the issue represented on its board as was the banker himself. The corporation's reputation among investors was improved by such an association, and the vendibility of its securities was enhanced'. (Carosso, 1970: 70)

This remark emphasizes again the importance of the investment banker's reputation in resolving informational problems over which formal legal contracting was impossible. Since by the end of the nineteenth-century investment bankers were largely selling their reputations, entry into the market was difficult. Although a number of authors have failed to find any formal barriers to entry, De Long argues as we do that the difficulty of building a reputation itself created a significant barrier to entry. It is for this reason that firms like Morgan and Kuhn, Loeb were able for such extended periods to generate supernormal profits from their investment banking activities.

Corporate Reorganizations

Many modern investment bank advisory functions, such as M&A, are of relatively recent origin. However, investment banks were engaged in advisory work in the late nineteenth century, through the reorganization of financially distressed businesses, and in particular of railroads.

Although railroads issued a lot of stock in their very early days, increasing capital needs resulted in a rising level of indebtedness. Table 6.1 illustrates the trend in the last quarter of the century.

Railroad borrowings were initially performed via mortgage bonds, which were secured on the physical property of the railroad. This was in contrast to the English system, where railways were financed through debentures, which gave the holder a claim on the income

Table 6.1. *Dollar increase in stocks and bonds issued by US Railroads, 1875–95*

	Stocks ($ million)	Bonds ($ million)	Ratio of Bonds to Stocks(%)
1875–9	405	250	62
1880–4	1,367	1,350	99
1885–9	733	1,159	158
1890–5	687	813	118

Source: Tufano (1997, table 1).

produced by the railway's property, but not on the property itself.[62] A bondholder with a claim on a mile of track might find it hard to realize its value, but in America he was formally entitled to it.

The railroad industry was highly susceptible to the vicissitudes of competition. Saddled as the railroads were with an increasing level of fixed rate railroad debt, it is unsurprising that the century witnessed more and more default on railroad debt. Before 1870, there were only 14 railroad receiverships involving lines of more than 100 miles; by the end of the depression of the 1890s, more than 700 corporations had been in receivership at one time or another, and perhaps a third of all US railroads had been through receivership.[63]

Nineteenth-century corporations could not fall back upon a federal bankruptcy code when they needed to restructure their liabilities. Although Northern capitalists favored the introduction of such a code, they faced opposition from agrarian interests in the South, who feared any law which they believed could deprive them of their farms. Congress passed three bankruptcy laws in the nineteenth century before, in 1898, they created one which survived its childhood.[64] This code was of little use for large businesses, and in any case, it came too late for many railroads. The reorganization methods for the railroads were created by the major investment banks, operating in conjunction with a sympathetic court system.

As we have already seen, the investment banks played an important role in the foundation of the railroads, and both their reputations and their financial capital were closely tied up with the success of their offerings. They therefore had a vested interest in resolving financial

---

[62] A (possibly contrived) analogy to a fruit-bearing tree is frequently drawn: debenture-holders could gather the fruit, but could not capture the tree.

[63] Martin (1974: 688).

[64] Skeel (2001: ch. 1) outlines the political history of the 1898 Bankruptcy Act.

distress when it arose.[65] They did so by innovating, with the cooperation of the courts, a body of reorganization law which was known as
the *equity receivership*.

The equity receivership rested upon two common-law powers: that
of the courts to appoint receivers to preserve the value of a debtor's
property; and the mortgage holder's right to foreclose on mortgaged
property after debtor default. An equity receivership began when a
creditor's bill was filed on a defaulting debtor, as a result of which
the courts appointed a receiver to oversee the defaulting debtor's
property. In over 90 percent of cases between 1867 and 1897, the courts
appointed the managers of defaulting railroads as receivers.[66] The
receiver had the means to stop all collection efforts, thus preventing a
socially costly creditor asset-grab, and hence served a similar purpose
to today's stay on assets. With the receiver in place, the mortgage
holders would file a foreclosure bill, asking the court to schedule a
sale of the property—an 1848 precedent allowed for wholesale, rather
than piecemeal, sale.[67]

The foreclosure sale after an equity reorganization was invariably
to the corporation's combined securityholders. Representatives of
each type of investor formed 'protective committees' which accepted
deposits of securities which gave them proxy voting rights. Ultimately
a single 'reorganization committee' would be formed which (at least
in theory) represented the interests of all securityholders. In general,
the reorganization committee was dominated by investment bankers.
It would agree a formal workout plan, establishing what type of claim
on the reorganized firm would be granted to each class of securityholder.[68] The business would then be sold in its entirety to the
reorganization committee, which would transfer its assets to a new
firm (generally with an extremely similar name), and distribute claims
on the firm in accordance with the workout plan.

As presented here, there are two problems with this type of reorganization, both of which were resolved by judicial innovations. The
first concerns small-scale securityholders. In a situation of collective

---

[65] JP Morgan recognized this when, in the early years of the twentieth century,
he said, 'I feel bound in all honour, when I reorganize a property, and am morally
responsible for its management, to protect it, and I generally do protect it' (cited by
Carosso 1987: 476).
[66] Tufano (1997: 20). Of course, this created obvious managerial incentive problems: we discuss below innovations in corporate governance which were designed to
counter these effects.
[67] Skeel (2001: 57–8)
[68] Tufano (1997: 13) provides a schematic representation of the reorganization.

bargaining of the type described here, there is a danger that large investors will collude to undermine the interests of small investors, by fixing the terms of the reorganization plan to favor certain types of securities, and either outvoting the representatives of the others or ensuring their acquiescence by making side-payments (i.e. bribes) to them. To avoid this danger, the federal courts began in 1885 to set minimum payments, known as 'upset values', which each class of securityholder would receive if they rejected the reorganization plan.

Setting the upset price was very difficult. The courts could not expect to have all of the information they needed to establish a 'fair' price. A reorganization could not succeed, and the social value created by the corporation could not be protected, if sufficient investors did not accept its terms. Setting a high-upset price created a danger that many investors would 'hold out' by refusing the reorganization committee's exchange proposal. In practice the courts avoided this problem by setting very low-upset prices. This gave the reorganization committee, largely composed of investment bankers, a great deal of power. Many contemporary observers believed that, in large corporations, minorities were unlikely actively to be ripped off by the majority, and hence that this was reasonable.[69] The policy certainly reflected both the probusiness attitude of the judiciary, and also the prevailing (and probably correct) belief that the social value of railroads was too high to permit a lone creditor to force their closure.

The second difficulty with the reorganization process was that the negotiations involved were very protracted: for example, after the Cairo & Vincennes railroad failed in April 1873 to make a payment on its mortgage bonds, the Morgan-led reorganization of the firm took eight years from start to finish.[70] In the meantime, the firm needed additional working capital if it was to be maintained as a going concern. But new creditors would rank below the impaired claims of prior lenders, and hence would be unwilling to provide the needed funds: a problem of 'debt overhang', which had the potential to scupper the reorganization.[71]

Nineteenth-century courts overcame the debt overhang problem with the 1872 invention of the *receivers' certificate*, a court-issued certificate which guaranteed its holder first priority of payment after the

---

[69] Spring (1919).   [70] Carosso (1987: 238–42).
[71] The standard modern reference on debt overhang is Myers (1977).

workout.[72] Suppliers and other investors with receivers' certificates could provide the firm with the capital it needed without worrying that their claims would be subordinated to those of preexisting claimants.

The reorganization plan frequently included arrangements for governance in the postreorganization firm. The use of voting trusts became a standard feature of reorganizations in the late 1880s. Their role was to protect the interests of the securityholders by delegating the votes of the equity holders to a group of three to five professional trustees, of which the most notable were JP Morgan and his associates. Although they were initiated by equity holders, voting trusts were in practice more concerned with protecting bondholder interests. Over half of the equity receiverships of the 1890s used voting trusts: by 1908, they were standard practice.[73] A significant side effect of their ubiquity was to increase the power of the investment bankers. Tufano (1997: p. 29) states that 'By control over reorganization committees, bankers like Morgan could come to gain power over the railroads, and by voting trusts they could maintain some modicum of direct control, at least until a distressed railroad's finances were once again on solid ground.'

Other governance innovations for reorganized firms were contractual, designed to sharpen managerial incentives. For example, preferred shareholders might be given a right to veto additional stock issuance, or, as, for example, in the reorganization of the Northern and Western Railroad, they might be given control of the reorganized firm in the wake of a missed dividend.[74]

Reorganizations typically simplified the corporate's capital structure. Fixed charges were always substantially reduced, so as to lower the likelihood that the reorganization would fail. To achieve this, secured mortgage holders would generally exchange all or some of their bonds for income bonds of the type which were common in English railway financing.[75] Junior debtholders' claims were generally dismissed as valueless, while common and preferred stockholders

---

[72] See Tufano (1997: 8) and Skeel (2001: 66).

[73] Tufano (1997: 28–30) discusses the role of voting trusts in equity reorganizations.

[74] Tufano (1997: 28)

[75] In a study of railroad reorganizations between January 1907 and December 1917, Daggett (1918) finds that total-fixed charges for reorganized companies dropped from $73,387,204 to $53,029,704. He documents the reduction in mortgage bonds which accomplished this. For example, the St. Louis and San Francisco line saw mortgage bonds lowered from 83 percent to 57 percent of its total liabilities.

generally had an opportunity to participate in the reorganized company upon making a cash payment, which was known as an 'assessment'. Cash requirements which could not be met through the assessment were generally provided for via a fresh bond issue, sponsored by the reorganizing bank.

Evidence presented by Tufano (1997: 17) suggests that an assessment was on average a positive NPV investment. To the extent that it was, priority was being violated, since junior debtholders should have ranked above the shareholders. Both contemporary and modern observers have argued that both the use of assessments and the issuance of receivers' certificates undermined investor property rights. For example, Martin (1974: 686) contends that the equity receivership 'demonstrate[s] the extent to which "private property" was subordinated in that supposed age of *laissez faire* to a broadly defined public welfare in reorganization proceedings.' Tufano (1997: 34) points to the 'bewilderment' of the readers and editors of the nineteenth-century press that courts could modify preexisting contracts by allowing in some cases payment of unsecured creditors above secured ones, and by issuing receivers' certificates. The Supreme Court ruled on these practices in 1879 and 1886 respectively, pronouncing both legal.[76] Tufano argues that financiers responded with 'weaker' contracts that reduced their exposure to judicial interference.

To be sure, the judicial innovations of the equity receivership constituted *ex post* contract alteration. We argued in chapter two that when they come from legislatures, such alterations generally weaken property rights. The innovations in this instance came however from the large financiers who had property rights in the distressed firm. Aside from their fees, their securities were reorganized on the same basis as those of the smaller investors. Since they acted in their own interests, the larger investors probably maximized the company's surplus. One could argue that many of the protests of the smaller investors reflected frustration at their inability to free ride upon the reorganization committee's efforts by holding out for their mortgage bond security. *Ex ante*, they would certainly have preferred to commit not to do this. Hence, by allowing for meaningful collective decision-making,

---

[76] The respective cases were *Fosdick v. Schall*, 99 US 235 (1879) and *United Trust Co. v. Illinois Midl & Co.*, 117 US 435 (1886) see Tufano (1997: 33).

the equity receivership was arguably an innovation that *strengthened* investor property rights.[77, 78]

The Supreme Court recognized concerns about claimant priority in reorganizations in the 1913 case *Northern Pacific Railway v. Boyd*.[79] The court noted that one could justify the exclusion of unsecured creditors only if the secured creditors owned the road outright, and that whether this was the case depended upon a rather subjective judgment of company value. The Court therefore ruled that if shareholders were offered participation, so should unsecured debt holders be, possibly with an assessment. Notwithstanding the irritation that this ruling caused practitioners, they adopted it without too much pain, and the equity receivership continued to dominate the reorganization of large companies right up to the end of the 1920s.

The equity receivership developed without legislative assistance as a body of law crafted by the investment bankers who typically performed reorganizations, with the assistance of the courts. Initially, very few of the procedures were codified, and the law grew out of repeated interactions between the same group of attorneys, representing the same investment banks, who were better able in discussion with judges to appeal to precedents.[80] It therefore used many of the skills that we have repeatedly argued were incubated within investment banks.

Investment banks earned fees for managing reorganizations, independently of those they received for floating any securities which were issued during the reorganization. This was therefore their first purely advisory business. And it was an extremely profitable one. At the end of June 1894, in the wake of the 1893 panic, the Inter-

---

[77] This statement is not without caveats. In 1884 Jay Gould established a precedent that the managers of a firm could place it into receivership, and hence guarantee that they would be its receivers. It is hard to argue that the capitalists whose property they controlled would have wished *ex ante* to contract for this, and hence it must be regarded as an attenuation of their property rights.

[78] Smith and Strömberg (2005) examine renegotiation in bankruptcy and reach conclusions that are supportive of the hypothesis advanced in this paragraph. They argue that observed negotiating patterns outside the shadow of formal bankruptcy law are likely to minimize *ex ante* distortions. Equity receiverships featured this type of bargaining; so too do today's venture capital-financed corporations, where investors have the right to seize assets in the wake of 'default', but management cannot file for bankruptcy protection. In this case, as in the 19th cent. equity receivership, we see senior creditors voluntarily allowing violations of absolute priority.

[79] 228 US 482 (1913)

[80] Skeel (2001: 68).

state Commerce Commission reported that 192 railroads were in receivership, operating 41,000 miles of track, and with a capitalization of $2.5 billion. There were rich pickings available for firms with extensive experience of railroad financing like JP Morgan & Co. and Kuhn, Loeb & Co. For example, JP Morgan & Co., who were preeminent railroad financiers, charged fees of $500,000 and $600,000 for the 1895 reorganizations of the Lake Erie and Western Railroad, and the Reading railroad, respectively.[81] In addition to its advisory fees, the reorganizing bank could expect to earn significant fees on any associated bond issuance, and would generally capture the reorganized firm's banking business for at least a decade after the reorganization.

The First Merger Wave

We have already discussed the emergence of capital-intensive production in the nineteenth-century America. It was accompanied by very rigorous competition which many contemporary observers, possibly influenced by their involvement in the reorganizations of the preceding subsection, regarded as socially wasteful. The most important voice in this chorus was that of Pierpont Morgan. In his dealings with solvent and insolvent railroads, he consistently attempted to cajole competitors into forming coalitions which would allow for the orderly and stable development of their businesses, and which would protect his bondholders from the harmful effects of competition. He was largely unsuccessful until corporations, weakened by the 1893 panic, decided that horizontal combination was preferable to destabilizing competition.

Naomi R. Lamoreaux (1985) documents the details of the merger movement which ran from 1895 to 1904. Consolidation statistics from her book appear in table 6.2.

Between 1895 and 1904, 1,800 firms disappeared into merged entities. Of the consolidations for which she has market share information, Lamoreaux finds (1985: 2) that 77.4 percent of postconsolidation corporations had a market share in excess of 40 percent, while 45 percent had a market share of over 70 percent. Many of the firms formed at this time remained preeminent for most of the following century: examples are US Steel, DuPont, International Harvester, Pittsburg Plate Glass, American Can, and American Smelting and Refinery. Lamoreaux provides a penetrating analysis of the reasons for, and

[81] Carosso (1987: 373–82).

Table 6.2. *Consolidations per year in the US manufacturing sector*

Year	Number	Year	Number
1895	4	1900	21
1896	3	1901	19
1897	6	1902	17
1898	16	1093	5
1899	63	1904	3

Source: Lamoreaux (1985: 2, table 1.1).

the competitive effect of, the mergers. However, she is silent on their financing.

The merger wave was a source of concern to many contemporary observers, who feared its possibly monopolistic consequences.[82] Carosso (1987: 433) states that the vertical and horizontal combinations of American businesses that occurred at the turn of the century 'were the operations that commanded the press's attention and inspired the public's awe and fear'. The mergers were financed, and to a large extent were brokered, by the largest investment bankers. Hence a side effect of the merger wave was to highlight their central position in the American economy.

Pierpont Morgan and his firm played a leading role in the merger wave. His largest consolidation was the February 1901 organization of US Steel, which was formed by combining eight existing steel companies to create the largest firm in the world, with a capitalization of over $1.4 billion. The impetus for its formation came from Pierpont Morgan himself. Andrew Carnegie had decided to extend Carnegie vertically down into manufacturing, and so to engage existing manufacturers in what he called a struggle for 'survival of the fittest'.[83] Concerned for the future of Federal Steel and National Tube, both of which he had brought to the market, Morgan attempted to seek a solution that would stabilize the entire industry. Negotiations between him and Carnegie were complicated, not least because neither man liked the other. It was hard to decide which firms should join the combined entity, and on what terms. When the terms of the deal were finalized, $200 million of securities were marketed by a syndicate led by JP

---

[82] In fact, Lamoreaux (1985) makes a convincing case that, with few exceptions, the mergers were not anticompetitive.

[83] Carosso (1987: 466–73) provides a detailed discussion of the formation of US Steel.

Morgan & Co., and with 300 participants, of whom 26 accounted for 68.8 percent of the total, and only four were allocated over $1 million of securities.

Creating US Steel was very profitable business for JP Morgan & Co. The fees for the syndicate were $50 million, of which JP Morgan & Co.'s share was $12.5 million. While some commentators regarded these as reasonable returns on the financial and reputational risks taken by Morgan, others deemed them to be entirely unreasonable. Morgan was involved in a number of other consolidations at this time: in 1902 he was responsible for the formation of International Harvester and of International Marine Corp., although the latter was ultimately to prove unsuccessful. His firm remained closely identified with the financing and the policies of early twentieth century consolidations for well over a decade.

JP Morgan & Co. may have been the preeminent investment banking player in the merger wave, but it certainly was not the only one. N. 50 on page 171 discusses the work that Lee, Higginson performed with JP Morgan & Co. to form the General Electric Company. Likewise, Kidder, Peabody & Co. had an active part in sponsoring, planning, and distributing the securities of a number of the industrial giants launched at this time, among them the American Sugar Refining Company, P. Lorillard & Co., and New England Cotton Yarn. It also helped to turn Procter and Gamble (P&G) from a family partnership into a publicly owned corporation and, in 1901, helped to plan the reorganization of Erie Telegraph and Telephone Company, extending American Telephone and Telegraph's facilities and virtually eliminating AT&T's most important rival, the Telephone, Telegraph, and Cable Company.[84]

CONCLUSION

By the first decade of the twentieth century, the investment banker sat at the heart of America's economy. Redlich (1968: 381–2) tells us that at this time, not more than six firms were responsible for managing the organization of the large-scale sector of the economy, and not more than twelve men. The firms were JP Morgan & Co., First National and the National City Bank of New York, Kuhn, Loeb & Co., and to a lesser extent the two Boston houses Kidder, Peabody & Co., and Lee, Higginson & Co. The four most powerful men in these firms

---

[84] See Carosso (1979: 30–1).

were Morgan, Baker, Stillman, and Loeb: note that two of them were commercial bankers.

For most of the period covered in this chapter, these men operated within a political and legal environment that recognized the sanctity of private property and of contract, but which otherwise left them largely alone. The arrival of large business taxed preexisting institutions, and much of the experimentation to find newer and more appropriate organizational and financial forms was performed by investment bankers. With little state support they created institutions that facilitated capital raising. As we have seen, for this they had to build and to maintain reputations among investors who were spread across America and Europe. Their own capital was relatively modest but, with a few exceptions, their reputations were with large-scale investors, and with large corporations and governments.[85]

The public had become increasingly aware of the influence of the investment bankers. They saw their role in the end-of-century merger wave and if they needed further evidence of Morgan's omnipotence, they got it in the autumn of 1907, when for two months Morgan, with capital assistance from Baker and Stillman of the First National and City Banks of New York, served as a lender of last resort for a financial market buffeted by a panic triggered by the October failure of the Knickerbocker Trust Company. His actions saved dozens of stock exchange members, and several larger financial institutions, from failure. He exhibited both an immense mastery of the financial markets and also an incredible degree of influence.[86]

Morgan's 1907 triumph probably represented the high-water mark for financial capitalism. Investment banks sat at the nexus of so many of the formal and informal contracts that drove the American economy that they naturally became a focus of legislative attention. In the argot of chapter two, special interest groups and politicians naturally sought to bring the extra-legal property rights of investment banking under the control of the law, where it would be possible to transfer them noncontractually. They were aided in this endeavor by emerging legal and political philosophies that justified state interference in areas that previously had been regarded as private. In the next chapter we examine the process by which this happened in the first part of the twentieth century.

---

[85] Lee, Higginson had started at the end of the century to build a retail sales network: see p. 169.

[86] Carosso (1987: 535–49) describes the panic and Morgan's response to it.

7

Leviathan and the Investment Banks

The nineteenth-century emergence of the investment bank was largely supported by the law. Legislators and the courts were increasingly sympathetic to the needs of business and, bolstered by the prevailing liberal economic consensus, they developed a framework of property rights and contract law within which trade could occur and economic agents could innovate freely. The nineteenth century thus saw the slow retreat of the state from the private life of its citizens. Against this backdrop, investment banks evolved in response to the technological needs of the economies within which they operated. We have seen that they did so by building networks of investors and by forming close peer relationships which allowed them to place securities as widely as possible. Their private law-making skills seeped into the public arena through the medium of the equity receivership, a body of large company bankruptcy law that was largely designed by the investment banks.

If investment banks evolved in response to technological pressures in the nineteenth century, most of their early twentieth-century development was in response to legal and legislative changes. Nineteenth-century industrialization had rendered some activities redundant. Moreover, while the new middle classes were prosperous, many of them felt economically neutered in the face of the new giant corporations. These two effects caused a series of political and jurisprudential movements which attempted in the first half of the twentieth century to shift the balance of economic power away from the large corporations. The result was the legitimization of a legal philosophy that promoted state involvement in what had hitherto been regarded as the private realm of contract.

This change of emphasis had profound effects upon the investment banking industry. We argued in chapter two that large concentrations of extra-legal power are likely to become a focus of attention from politicians who would like to sequestrate them for the benefit of their constituents. Early twentieth-century political thought both regarded high finance as pernicious, and also provided a justification for undermining it. As a result, investment banks were under fire from legislators almost from the start of the new century. They experienced mounting pressure until, during the Great Depression of the 1930s, legislation was passed that transformed the face of the investment banking industry.

As we will see later in this chapter, political attempts to acquire investment bank power did not end with the New Deal. The first half of the century closed with an antitrust law suit brought by the government against the investment banking industry. The law suit gave the investment bankers a chance for the first time in the century to bring their own evidence and witnesses to defend themselves against the accusations leveled against them. It ended with the total collapse of the government's case, and brought to a conclusion a half century of increasingly open warfare between legislators and investment banks.

We begin this chapter by examining the legal and political changes that underpinned the institutional development of the investment bank in the early twentieth century. We then outline the major political and legislative alterations to the investment banking landscape in this period, before summarizing important nonpolitical developments. We conclude our discussion with a brief analysis of the government's antitrust law suit against the investment banks.

CHANGES TO THE LEGAL AND POLITICAL ENVIRONMENT

Legal thinking at the turn of the nineteenth century reflected the political economy that had underpinned the development of the market economy during that century. The law recognized a clear distinction between public and private domains of action. Within the private domain, it had a purely enabling role: the courts enforced property rights and adjudicated over contractual disputes but, in line with a classical conception of the rule of law, they attempted to do so in accordance with a body of laws which reflected no particular purpose. The law 'aspired to create a system of processes and principles that could be shared even in the absence of agreed-upon ends'.[1]

Toward the end of the nineteenth century, the courts began to behave as activists in maintaining the above system.[2] The most

---

[1] Horwitz (1992: 16).
[2] Friedman (2005: 269–72) gives a number of examples of court activism.

famous example of this was the 1905 Supreme Court decision on *Lochner* v. *New York*,[3] which overturned as unconstitutional a New York labor law that established maximum hours for bakery workers. The Court argued that any such restriction upon labor contracts interfered with the worker's right to dispose of his labor time as he pleased. Hence, the decision underscored the judiciary's conviction that contracting within the private realm should lie outside the sphere of influence of the legislators.

Lochner was the legal affirmation of the classical liberal philosophies that permeated social life in the last decades of the nineteenth century. It elevated to the level of a constitutional right the freedom to contract, and so was a charter against active economic regulation. However, it was out of step with emerging ideas about the relationship between business, the state, and the individual. The ruling came at the end of the merger wave that we discussed in chapter six (pp. 182–4). The mergers were one of a series of economic developments that revolutionized working life in America. They generated a feeling of alienation in many Americans, which was reflected in the Populist movement of the 1890s, and the Progressivism of the 1900–14 years.

Populism was a working-class movement which grew out of the economic hardships experienced by farmers in the South, the North-West, and in the mountain states as a result of commodity price falls in the years after 1870, culminating in the agrarian crisis of the 1890s. Farmers felt that they had been displaced by the economic advances of the nineteenth century, and populist rhetoric appealed to their nostalgia for a (largely mythical) settled, preindustrial rural society. The populist mind-set contrasted this arcadian past with the rootlessness of the modern world, and saw life as a struggle between the small man and monopolies, trusts, and the money power. Indeed, a widespread populist belief held that 'all American history since the Civil War could be understood as a sustained conspiracy of the international money power'.[4]

Unsurprisingly, populists did not see the 1895–1905 merger wave in a particularly positive light. In particular, the investment bankers who controlled the money trust attracted populist opprobrium. They were condemned in nationalistic and frequently anti-Semitic terms.[5]

---

[3] 198 US 45 (1905).   [4] Hofstadter (1962: 70).
[5] Hofstadter (1962: 78) states that populist writers 'expressed that identification of the Jew with the usurer and the "international gold ring" which was the central theme of the American anti-Semitism of the age'.

Although populism had a low electoral impact, and had vanished as a stand-alone political force by the end of the century,[6] it was notable as the first American political movement that argued that the federal government had some responsibility for the living conditions of the common person. Moreover, its distrust of large industrial concerns and of the investment banks was to resurface in the pre-First World War progressive movement.

Like populism, progressivism reflected the angst of Americans whose lives were being changed by industrialization. Many of these people, unlike the natural supporters of the populists, were drawn from the rapidly expanding middle class. The emergence of the large corporation left many feeling economically impotent. Although they were prosperous, they believed that the individuals who ran the corporate economy were making decisions that affected them, and about which they knew nothing. In the words of Woodrow Wilson, they felt that 'somewhere, by somebody, the development of industry is being controlled'.[7]

In the years before the First World War, the progressivist impulse dominated political thinking in both of the main parties. Moreover, it was not antipathetic per se to big business, from which the prosperity of the prewar years clearly flowed. However, progressives believed that wrongdoing was inherent in American life, even among the most outwardly respectable people. This 'realist' conception of business life lay at the root of their dislike of the large industrial combines, and it led them to question the nineteenth-century ideal of a clear distinction between public and private life. If the private actions of 'plutocrats' had an effect upon thousands of other citizens,[8] then, reasoned the progressives, the small people should themselves combine, so as to provide a counterbalance to the monopolies, the trusts, and the money power. They could do so through trade unions, but the most important type of cooperation was through government.

---

[6] The People's Party, which represented the populist movement in national politics, put up a presidential candidate, General James B. Weaver, in the 1892 presidential elections. With 8.5 percent of the total vote, he was a marginal figure, although he carried four states. The Democrats subsequently adopted some Populist policies, and the People's Party self-destructed in 1896 by adopting William Jennings Bryan, the Democratic Party candidate.

[7] Hofstadter (1962: 228).

[8] Hofstadter (1962: 225) states that the progressives had a fear that 'the great business combinations, being the only centers of wealth and power, would be able to lord it over all other interests and thus to put an end to traditional American democracy'.

So in stressing the effect of monopoly capital upon the individual, the progressives arrived at a philosophy that justified state intervention in the private sphere. But their stated reason for doing this was not to establish state control over production and distribution, and nor was it to redistribute wealth per se. Progressives turned to government intervention with reluctance, as a way of rescuing competition from what they saw as the monopolistic stranglehold of the large corporations: the state must be 'neutral': neither for nor against big business, but for the 'public interest'.[9]

Arguments of this nature, however sincerely made, are disingenuous. Any state intervention in the economy involves the redistribution of some property rights. It must therefore be accompanied by judgments as to what constitutes the public interest, and what the appropriate competitive landscape should be. One might applaud the progressive attempt to protect the small entrepreneur and his way of life, but it is dishonest to suggest that their policies did not transfer property rights extracontractually. In their way, the progressives were engaged in central planning just as much as the New Dealers a quarter of a century later would be.

The arguments in the preceding paragraph are entirely consistent with the discussion on pages 59–62 of chapter two. Then as now, investment bank profits derived from their ability to sustain extra-legal contracting. Their profits at the start of the twentieth century were enormous, as was their economic influence. It was natural that both should become the focus of political groups: in the early twentieth century, these were the progressives, whose political legitimacy derived from their appeal to the small town values which many believed were threatened by the large corporations.

The progressives' arguments were soon reflected in jurisprudence. If the decisions of the large corporations affected the small man in ways that he could not control, was the will theory of contracting[10] really valid? And if it was not, what did contractual obligations really reflect? If, as progressive intellectuals argued, the state could legitimately define the competitive parameters of social life, then, at least in theory, it could surely also determine the meaning of a contract.

This argument came at a time when problems in nineteenth-century legal formalism were becoming apparent. Disputed contracts were interpreted in terms of the wishes that a 'reasonable person' would

---

[9] Hofstadter (1962: 232–5).   [10] See page 134.

exhibit at the time of contracting. But there was no a priori reason to believe that either of the parties to a contract were 'reasonable': it appeared, as Oliver Wendell Holmes noted, that in interpreting a contract, the courts *imposed* an obligation, *irrespective* of the intentions of the contracting parties.[11] For progressive thinkers such as Holmes, this was entirely proper: if the state could legitimately interfere in the distribution of property rights, they reasoned, then property rights and contractual obligations clearly existed only to the extent that the state sanctioned them. Indeed, argued Homes, the court imposed obligations 'because of some belief as to the practice of the community or of a class, or because of some opinion as to policy'.[12]

The progressives had started from a vaguely elucidated conception that large corporate actions had effects too wide-ranging to enumerate in a contract. As a result, the cause of events could not necessarily be traced, and hence it could not serve as the basis for the assignment of liability. This breakdown of *objective causation* rendered contract law insufficient to govern the actions of the trusts, the monopolies, and the money power. They concluded that the state should manipulate economic conditions, and their argument led ineluctably to the conclusion that there was no private sphere.[13] Hence the courts did not discover and document a common law created through social interaction: they made it.[14] The post-First World War jurists who developed this line of thinking became known as 'legal realists'.

The progressives had let the genie out of the bottle. If the state had a role in defining contractual obligations, the relationship between a person and his possessions was transformed from a private matter to one involving his relationship with the various social actors who were affected by his use of the possessions. So, argued the legal realists, when the state granted property rights, it also created social relations. Although these relations might serve a useful purpose, they were not sacred: since the state created them, it could also alter them. A massive gestalt shift had occurred: from its nineteenth-century role as a neutral facilitator of private social interaction, the state had acquired legitimacy as the creator and manipulator of social relations. In Morris Cohen's (1927) statement of this perspective, 'the whole business of

---

[11] Horwitz (1992: 38).   [12] Quoted by Horwitz (1992: 49).
[13] See Horwitz (1992: 57) for a discussion of objective causation.
[14] See Horwitz (1992: 190), citing justice Benjamin N. Cardozo: 'the law is not found, it is made.'

the state depends upon its rightful role to take away the property of some (in the form of taxation) and use it to support others'.[15]

Far from viewing the law as a forum within which independent agents could play out economic interactions, legal realists believed that one should recognize the law's role in constructing social reality, and use it for the 'social good'. This was the philosophy that Justice Cardozo was reflecting when he stated that 'there can be no wisdom in the choice of a path unless we know where it will lead'.[16] In a few short years, the views epitomized by the *Lochner* judgment (p. 189) had been entirely reversed. By 1930, legal thinkers increasingly regarded as legitimate a regulatory state that used the law actively to pursue social reform and social engineering.

Between the turn of the century and 1930, reformist thinkers had moved in a few easy steps from the desire to protect the small entrepreneur to Oakshott's conception of the state as an 'enterprise association'.[17] In such a state, the law stresses *ends* rather than *means*. The market ceases to be a neutral forum for the exchange of property rights, but is instead viewed as a social artifact that can be modified in line with the state's requirements. And, if property and markets are social constructs, then there is no natural law, prepolitical, theory of property. In pursuit of its goals, the state can reassign property rights and override private legal arrangements.

It is impossible to provide a noncontestible definition of the 'common good': the phrase is interpreted differently by different people, and at different times. But the intellectual legitimization of the purposive state justified political competition to use state power to enact social programs that extended far beyond anything considered reasonable in the nineteenth century. During the prosperous years before 1914, the received progressive wisdom was in the ascendancy, and the state's power was intended to shift property rights from the owners of large corporations to the small entrepreneur. In later years politicians were actuated by different concerns, largely as a result of the severe depression of the 1930s.

The influence of progressivism declined after the First World War: Hofstadter (1962: 276–9) argues that this was a reaction by those who paid for America's decision to enter the war to Wilson's attempt to ascribe this decision to high moral standards. In any event, the 1920s

---

[15] From his 1927 Cornell Law Review article 'Law and Sovereignty', cited by Horwitz (1992: 165).
[16] In *The Nature of the Judicial Process* (1921), cited by Horwitz (1992: 190).
[17] See p. 43 of chapter two.

saw a partial return to the individualism that underscored prepro-
gressive political thought. The ideas unleashed by the progressives
did not vanish, but for a time many Americans embraced large-scale
capitalism and the prosperity it brought them.

The end of the 1920s was marked by the stock market bubble, and
its subsequent bursting: between September and November 11, 1929
share prices dropped by 45 percent. The subsequent recession became
a depression when the 1931 European crisis crossed the Atlantic. By
1933, a quarter of the workforce was unemployed, and industrial productivity and national income stood at half their 1929 rates.[18] Herbert
Hoover, the republican occupant of the White House, was an adherent
of the laissez-faire policies that had apparently succeeded in the 1920s,
and saw no role for the government in relieving the hardship of the
unemployed. In any case, the machinery of the state was inadequate
for this purpose: when in 1932 he did distribute surplus wheat to the
hungry, it had to be distributed by the Red Cross.[19]

When he accepted the Democratic nomination for the presidency,
Franklin D. Roosevelt famously promised the American people a
'New Deal'. He replaced Hoover with 57 percent of the popular
vote, and he entered the White House with a strong belief in the
power of government to do good. The progressives had never had to
contend with a depression, and the depression influenced the social
application of government power under the New Dealers. They were
not concerned with entrepreneurial activity and competition per se:
with them, the focus of American reformism shifted toward social
security provision, unemployment insurance, wages, and housing.[20]
Their approach to these problems was managerial: while there was
element of Brandeisian progressivism within the New Deal,[21] New
Dealers did not in general attempt to bust the trusts, but tried rather
to 'solve the problems of the business order through a gigantic system
of governmentally underwritten codes that would ratify the trustifi-
cation of society'.[22]

The managerial approach of the New Dealers manifested itself
partly in faith in experts. This had been a feature of progressive

---

[18] Seligman (1982: 11).   [19] Heale (2004: 77).   [20] Hofstadter (1962: 306).
[21] The New Dealers lacked a consistent ideology, but Leuchtenburg (1963: 33)
identifies three components to their thinking, although different members of the
administration emphasized the various components to different extents: 'from the
Populists came a suspicion of Wall Street and a bevy of ideas for regulating agriculture; from the mobilization of the First World War they derived instrumentalities for
central direction of the economy; from urban social reformers of the Jane Addams
tradition arose a concern for the aged and indigent.'
[22] Hofstadter (1962: 310–11).

thinking, which was permeated by a modernist emphasis upon the value of science and scientific method in solving social problems.[23] Relatively ineffective attempts to act upon this faith by setting up regulatory agencies separated from the state were made with the 1887 creation of the Interstate Commerce Commission and the 1914 establishment of the Federal Trade Commission. FDR's reliance upon expertise was manifested early on, when his 'Brains Trust' helped him to his first presidential term:[24] later on it took the form of delegation of power to regulatory agencies.

There was a progressive element within the New Deal, which waned and then waxed.[25] However, unlike the progressives, the New Dealers on the whole accepted as inevitable the growth of big business and, as we have seen, their approach was concerned with the management and regulation of big business in pursuit of their social goals. Their use of expert regulatory agencies was therefore unfettered by concerns about the possible deleterious effects of a significant concentration of regulatory power. They followed their reasoning to the logical conclusion that an agency could be effective only if it acquired some of the powers that had hitherto been vested in the legislative and judicial branches of the state. James Landis, the second chairman of the SEC (see p. 209) and later Dean of the Harvard Law School, was a particularly eloquent exponent of this perspective, stating in 1938 that 'with the rise of regulation, the need for expertness becomes dominant; for the art of regulating an industry requires knowledge of the details of its operation',[26] and urging the agencies' right to a

...near-exclusive jurisdiction over technical regulatory problems, and the agencies' right to combine in a single regulatory body the functions historically embodied by the Constitution's three conceptually separate branches of government.[27]

---

[23] Heale (2004: 12 and 37).

[24] The 'Brains Trust' was a group of college professors who helped FDR to formulate policy: its members were Raymond Moley and Gardiner Means, both of whom were lawyers, and Rexford Guy Tugwell, an agriculture expert. The Trust was disbanded after the election, although its members remained influential in the new administration. See Leuchtenburg (1963: 32).

[25] Leuchtenburg (1963: 147–64) argues that FDR became increasingly frustrated by the difficulties of collaborating with big business, and that in his 'second hundred days' he adopted a more Brandeisian approach to government. Nevertheless, the only wholly Brandeisian legislation of the New Deal was the Holding Company Act (see p. 211).

[26] Horwitz (1992: 216)   [27] Seligman (1982: 125).

In the light of the preceding discussion it is unsurprising that investment banks were under fire for most of the first half of the twentieth
century. As we saw in chapter six, investment banks organized the
most important corporate consolidations at the turn of the century,
they sat on the boards of the largest companies, and they were responsible for financing corporate America, and in an era of low taxation,
for meeting a large part of the government's financial needs. It was
an article of faith for the progressives that any institution with such
enormous power must be using it to damage the American people,
and hence that it should be broken up.

The relationship between the New Dealers and the investment
banks was different, but it was no less corrosive. Much of the coordination of economic activity that the New Dealers believed was the
job of the state was arguably performed by the investment bankers.
Naturally, though, investment bankers had different goals to those of
the New Deal-era state. The observation that the clash of New Deal
values with the undirected power of the investment banks led to conflict is value-neutral; so is the prediction that, in line with the theory
of chapter two, the New Dealers would attempt to annex investment
banker powers for their own goals. The following section traces the
impact that an increasingly powerful and hostile state had upon the
investment banks.

LEGISLATION, REGULATION, AND INVESTMENT BANKING

The twentieth century opened with a legal ruling that was to have
a significant impact upon the securities industry for the succeeding
thirty years. As we saw at the end of chapter six, commercial banks
had in the last decades of the nineteenth century become increasingly
involved in investment banking. A 1902 ruling by the Comptroller of
the Currency that national banks were not authorized by the National
Bank Act to engage in this business threatened to undermine this
involvement. But in 1903 the First National Bank of Chicago found
a response to this ruling, in the guise of the security affiliate.[28]

A securities affiliate was a state bank with its own capital, established so that ownership of the affiliate was given pro rata to the
holders of the national bank's shares. The shares of both banks were
conjoined, so that it was impossible to sell a holding in one without
selling the corresponding shares in the other (the affiliate's share

---

[28] Redlich (1968: 393).

certificates were often printed on the reverse side of the national bank's shares). The Comptroller raised no objection to this idea, ruling that as they were state banks, oversight of securities affiliates was a problem for the states. Since securities affiliates could perform investment business, national banks could use them to act as de facto investment banks. This idea was a popular one: by 1930, eleven large affiliates had combined assets of $535 million, and commercial banks originated 44.6 percent of new issues in that year. A *Harvard Business Review* article of 1934 concluded that there was little to choose between the securities affiliates of national banks and private investment banks.[29]

At least when they were created, securities affiliates seemed like a fairly uncontroversial idea. The first clash between the state and the investment banks came with the Armstrong Committee of 1905. Insurance companies were known to have close relationships with investment banks: investment banking houses had representatives on many insurance company boards, and they frequently called upon insurance companies to participate in new issues. The progressive trust-busters argued that the relationship between the two industries was rather one-sided: at the time, the insurance companies appeared to need the investment banks more than the investment banks needed them.[30]

The relationship between the investment banks and the insurance companies can be explained in terms of the theories of chapter three. Investment bankers who brought their expertise to bear on insurance company boards risked their reputations at the same time; concern for their reputations mitigated the conflicts of interest which arose as a result of their joint roles as representatives of issuing companies, and board members of the insurance companies that bought bond issues. Because their reputation was at stake, investment bankers provided insurance companies with valuable certification when they served on their boards; reputational considerations served further to sharpen effort incentives.

Contemporary observers were however worried that something rotten was gnawing at the heart of big finance: concern about

---

[29] Carosso (1970: 276).
[30] Public concern was aroused by a series of articles by the Boston stockbroker Thomas W. Lawson published in August 1904 under the title 'Frenzied Finance', describing the close relationship between insurance companies and investment banks.

investment banks and other worries[31] led the New York Superintendent of Insurance to recommend the 'elimination of Wall Street control' in June 1905; in July of that year state senator William W. Armstrong was appointed chairman of a joint committee of the Senate and Assembly to investigate insurance company business in New York State. Some of the testimony appeared to prove an imbalance of power between insurance and investment companies: for example, the treasurer of the Mutual stated that investment banks sold more bonds in Europe in a week than the Mutual bought in a month.

Observers then and now questioned the freedom of insurance companies to refuse participation in new issues.[32] Chapters two and three of this book argued that investment banks use the threat of future exclusion to enforce an extra-legal agreement to participate in every one of the investment bank's syndicates: in the light of this theory, it is unclear that insurance companies *should* have been able to refuse to invest. But this was not the contemporary perspective: although the Armstrong Committee uncovered no evidence that investment bankers dominated the financial policies of the companies with which they were associated, it was followed within a year by reform laws in twenty states.[33] The statutes most relevant to investment banks prohibited insurance companies from underwriting security issues, and they barred insurance companies from investing in corporate stock.

By the standards of later interventions, the Armstrong Committee constituted a relatively minor skirmish between the state and the investment banks. Calls for legislation to rein in the investment banks grew more strident. Although nothing came of it, in January 1908 Roosevelt asked in a special message to Congress for legislation regulating speculation and margin trading, while in December of that year the governor of New York established a committee to investigate speculation on the State's securities and commodities markets, whose recommendations were too anodyne to satiate public demands for action.[34]

The clamoring for action led in April 1912 to the creation of a subcommittee of the House Banking and Currency Committee to

---

[31] The battle for control of the Equitable Life Assurance Society between the cofounder's son, James H. Hyde, and the president, James W. Alexander, is documented by Carosso (1970: 114–15): it revealed excesses and abuses that triggered the ensuing investigation.
[32] See North (1954) for a modern discussion of the facts.
[33] Carosso (1970: 122–5).   [34] Carosso (1970: 132–3).

investigate the 'concentration of money and credit': that is, the so-called 'money trust'. The committee was chaired by Arsène P. Pujo, and its counsel was Samuel Untermeyer, a corporate lawyer million-aire who brought to the job a profound skepticism of high finance and a preconception that there was insufficient competition in large-scale finance.

The Pujo Committee set out to prove that a money trust existed that suppressed competition in finance. It argued that the trust was led by JP Morgan & Co., which with the First National Bank of New York and the National City Bank of New York comprised the 'inner group', while Lee Higginson & Co., Kidder, Peabody & Co., and Kuhn, Loeb & Co., along with Chicago's three largest commercial banks, were the inner group's closest allies.

We have already argued that the extra-legal contracts upon which investment banking rests require the banks to form long-term rela-tionships: these allow bankers to learn about their counterparts, and the threat of exclusion from future deals encourages their coun-terparts to participate in every deal, and to remain honest. At the same time, the importance of investment banking reputation in build-ing and maintaining these relationships creates significant barriers to entry. It is therefore unsurprising that a small number of investment bankers dominated the industry in 1912, and that they repeatedly dealt with one another.[35] Our theory suggests that these facts need not indicate collusive and dishonest behavior, but this was not the light in which Untermeyer saw things.

If there was a money trust, then it was using its dominance of the issuance business to award itself lucrative contracts. Untermeyer argued that this problem could be resolved by introducing compul-sory competitive bidding for underwriting business. A letter from Morgan to the committee explained in language which is consonant with our theory why he felt that new issues should not necessarily be subject to competitive bidding: 'while in good times it is possible that [private corporate securities] might be subscribed for at public auction, in bad times there would be no one to bid for them'.[36]

The committee was also profoundly skeptical regarding the pres-ence of investment bankers on the corporate boards of the firms they

---

[35] George F. Baker of the First National Bank could not in questioning recall a transaction over $10 million in the previous decade which had not been financed by one or more members of the inner group or its close associates: see Carosso (1970: p. 144).
[36] Carosso (1970: 147).

had brought to market. JP Morgan & Co. insisted that this practice stemmed from the banker's responsibility as sponsor 'to keep an eye on its policies and to protect the interests of investors in the securities of that corporation',[37] a responsibility which we argue stems from the banker's desire to protect his reputation. But the committee saw JP Morgan & Co.'s influence as evidence of the malign influence of the money trust.

Similarly, Untermeyer saw in the relatively unchanging composition of underwriting syndicates more evidence of the money trust's machinations, while we argue that this is an inevitable consequence of the technological limitations which make investment banking necessary in the first place. Morgan acknowledged in his testimony to the committee that he always offered syndicate participation to the First National Bank, of which he was a director and a member of the executive committee, and that he would expect them to include his firm in their syndicates. The committee's majority report argued that, rather than ensuring long-term participation and honesty, this type of reciprocity eliminated competition for large security issues.[38]

Pierpont Morgan died in Rome on March 31, 1913. His death came precisely one month after the Pujo Committee submitted its final report, and it marked the end of the era of laissez-faire financial capitalism. The Committee had failed to prove the existence of the money trust they set out to find, but this did not stop them claiming that the 'great and rapidly growing concentration of the control of money and credit in the banks of [a] few men' was evidence of a money trust.[39] We have argued that this is a misguided interpretation of the facts of the investment banking industry, and so did the two minority reports from the committee.[40]

When Congress met in special session on April 7, 1913 it failed to enact any of the Pujo Committee's recommendations. Nevertheless, public sentiment demanded action: the Morgan firm responded by announcing that its partners would resign from the boards of 27 corporations; George Baker and other members of the 'inner

---

[37] Carosso (1987: 638).   [38] Carosso (1987: 630–1).   [39] Carosso (1970: 151).
[40] One of these, signed by a Michigan Republican named Henry McMorran, argued that the investigation had cast 'a sinister light . . . over many banking practices which was not justified by the facts, that no effort has been made to show the reasonable and commendable explanation of these practices, and that in many cases an impression has been given to the country as to the character and motives of leading bankers which is altogether unfair'. See Carosso (1970: 151).

group' followed suit.[41] The investment bankers were retreating from the activism that had characterized their late-nineteenth-century operation.

The Pujo Committee's findings were disseminated to a wide audience and had a long-lived impact, in large part because of the efforts of the progressive lawyer Louis D. Brandeis, then one of Woodrow Wilson's closest advisers, and from 1916 a leading progressive member of the Supreme Court. Brandeis was the author of the classic 1914 polemic, *Other People's Money and How the Bankers Use It*, which drew heavily upon the testimony to the Pujo Committee. Its conclusion that investment bankers controlled American business, using 'reservoirs of the people's savings' was widely accepted, and hung over federal investigations of investment banking for the next thirty years.[42] And in the slightly longer run, the money trust investigation had some important legislative consequences. An attempt to empower the ICC to supervise and regulate the issuance of railroad securities failed in 1914, but in 1920 the Transport Act succeeded in doing so.

Fourteen months before the Pujo Committee opened, the Kansas state legislature passed a licensing bill for the securities industry that heralded an era of financial regulation. This occurred in response to the urging of the Kansas bank commissioner, a retired greengrocer and populist politician named J. N. Dolley. The bill was the first of several state laws intended to protect the small investor from crooks who would 'sell building lots in the blue sky', and which were therefore known as 'Blue Sky laws'.[43]

The Kansas legislation went some way beyond the corresponding legislation in the United Kingdom, which simply required honest disclosure. Every security issued in Kansas had to be registered under the Act, and the bank commissioner was able under the Act to veto a new security if he believed its registration to be 'unjust, inequitable or oppressive to any class of contributors'. Moreover, the commissioner was empowered to prevent a corporation from operating in Kansas if he believed that its securities did not 'promise a fair return'.

To modern ears (or at least to our modern ears), this sounds rather repressive. The Kansas laws shifted property rights from investors, who had formerly had the power to deploy their capital where they saw fit, to the bank commissioner, who could now determine on their behalf what was a fit investment. The market's discovery role was

---

[41] Carosso (1970: 179–80).   [42] Carosso (1970: 180–1).

[43] Seligman (1982: 44–5).

certainly undermined. It is impossible to say what the deadweight costs of this law were for Kansas. Dolley, the greengrocer who masterminded its introduction, claimed that the Act had saved 'at least six million dollars' in its first year of operation, and that fewer than a hundred of the fourteen or fifteen hundred companies applying for a permit had been granted one by the Banking Department. The first of these statements is of course a wild hyperbole which is impossible to substantiate; the second was revealed in a 1913 report by the Canadian Undersecretary of State to be a fiction: in fact, only 62 firms had been refused a permit.[44]

The facts were no barrier to the expansion of the Blue Sky laws. Within two years of the adoption of the Kansas Blue Sky laws, 23 states had adopted their own variants, of which 17 were identical to the Kansas law, or were modeled upon it. The Kansas laws survived a 1917 Supreme Court challenge to their constitutionality, and by 1933 every state except Nevada had a securities law. Only eight states had sufficient funds to support full-time securities commissions: in other states, the regulations were enforced by state officials like the railroad commission or the state auditor. They therefore became the focus of rent-seeking politicians, and their main consequence was a distortion of investment business in the states. The laws were easy to evade, were riddled with exceptions, and were poorly policed. Although New York was regarded as having the most effective Blue Sky laws, NYSE officials estimated in 1932 that approximately a half of the billion dollars of fraudulent securities peddled annually in the United States were sold in New York.[45]

While state regulation of the securities markets was ineffective, private regulation fared very well. The NYSE had detailed prelisting disclosure requirements which were far more precise than those of many Blue Sky laws: these provisions were lauded even by the critics of contemporary corporate finance.[46] Again, this is unsurprising in the light of our discussion in chapters two and three. As a private club, the NYSE could not rely upon public funds to perpetuate its existence: it had to maintain its reputation, and to provide a valuable service to its members. Its wish to maintain standards was therefore unadulterated by the temptation to grant favors to political allies. We argued in chapter two that such a body will eventually attract the attention of legislators, who see in its power base a politically valuable

---

[44] Seligman (1982: 45).   [45] Seligman (1982: 45–6).
[46] Seligman (1982: 46–7).

asset. As we shall see below (p. 209), this is precisely what happened to the NYSE during the New Deal.

Investment bankers did not accept the violent opprobrium that they attracted during the first two decades of the twentieth century lying down. Its inevitable consequence was that they diverted some resources from their economic role of facilitating corporate finance, and expended them on protecting their reputations, and the rents which they derived from them. Their response was the Investment Bankers Association of America (IBA), which was founded in August 1912 as a splinter group of the American Bankers Association. Whether as a strategic response to political pressure or because it was their true position, the IBA came out in favor of laws designed to protect investors and to require issuers to furnish the public with more financial information. They argued strenuously though that both the laws and their enforcement should be uniform, and within a year of their formation they started to lobby for the type of disclosure-based legislation that they favored.[47]

As we noted above (p. 193), the boom years of the 1920s saw a retreat of the progressive philosophy. Nevertheless, the growth in the numbers of uninformed small shareholders attracted securities sales people of questionable honesty, and fraudulent practices received a lot of publicity during the decade.[48] The possibility of federal securities regulation never went away. Ironically, the decade saw a sharp increase in competition, as new retail markets and new issuing industries enabled a number of young turks to enter investment banking, and to challenge the hegemony of the old establishment firms. These older firms and the IBA were the only real voices of conservatism during the decade.[49] Neither the competition that the progressives had always demanded nor the caution of the older firms could save the investment banking industry from the consequences of the 1929 crash:

'The reputation of the investment banker, which the elder Morgan once said took years to cultivate, was destroyed by the 1929 stock market debacle and the events that followed it.'[50]

The crash of October 1929 called into question the widely touted financial expertise of the investment banks, who certainly had not seen it coming. (Of course, we argue that investment banks are not

---

[47] See Carosso (1970: ch. 8) for a detailed exposition of the facts of the IBA's formation.
[48] Carosso (1970: 252).   [49] Carosso (1970: 255).   [50] Carosso (1970: 300).

gifted with second sight: they are simply good at coordinating the pro-duction and dissemination of price-sensitive information.) Like most Americans, investment bankers did not feel the full force of the crash until the 1931 failure of Kreditanstalt, Austria's largest bank, which precipitated a worldwide depression that caused severe hardship for millions.[51]

We noted on page 194 that Herbert Hoover favored a hands-off gov-ernmental response to the crash. He was not however a supporter of the financial sector, and he became convinced in 1932 that the market was being undermined by pools of short sellers. In an attempt to prove this, and hence to bring the culprits to book, he established in 1932 an investigation of stock market practices. Although the committee's work got off to a slow start, it began to have a major impact when it was reconvened after Franklin D. Roosevelt's election with Ferdinand Pecora as its counsel.[52]

The Committee was intended to reach a particular conclusion, and in Ferdinand Pecora it had the ideal chairman for its job. He was 'a wholesale subscriber to the Brandeis bigness-is-badness thesis', who 'often treated Wall Street witnesses as if they had something to hide'.[53] He got off to an excellent start in his examination of the dealings of Charles E. Mitchell, the president and board chairman of National City Bank, and 'the representative banker of his gener-ation'.[54] Mitchell's official salary was $25,000, but in a spectacular failure of corporate governance, he had awarded himself bonuses on top of this in excess of $1 million in 1927 and 1928. He had also engaged in questionable tax avoidance practices, although he escaped prosecution for these. Pecora further uncovered evidence that when the National City Bank's securities affiliate, the National City Company, pushed Peruvian government debt, it did so despite its knowledge that it was a very bad investment. The hearings finished Mitchell.[55]

Pecora moved from the National City Bank to JP Morgan & Co. The Morgan name still had enormous mystique, and the hearing

[51] Carosso (1970: 300–6).

[52] See Seligman (1982: 12–20) for the establishment of the committee, and a discus-sion of its almost farcical early proceedings.

[53] Seligman (1982: 21). Leuchtenburg (1963: 59) describes Pecora as 'a tribune of righteousness', and quotes Morgan's description of his experience at the bar of the tribunal: 'Pecora has the manner and the manners of a prosecuting attorney who is trying to convict a horse thief. Some of these senators remind me of sex suppressed old maids who think everybody is trying to seduce them.'

[54] Seligman (1982: 23).   [55] Seligman (1982: 26–9).

was conducted in the full glare of the contemporary media spotlight. The most interesting aspect of the Morgan interrogation was Pecora's acquisition of a partnership agreement: no one outside the firm had ever seen one before. It gave JP Morgan, Jr, as senior partner, full and final authority to decide disputes, to 'compel any partner at once to withdraw and retire from the partnership', to determine the distribution of the firm's undivided profits, and to dissolve it at any time he saw fit.[56] But Pecora was unable to find evidence in the private banks of the sorts of gross abuses that had occurred in the National City Bank. The public was most exercised by the revelation that, although they had paid over $58 million in taxes between 1917 and 1928, the Morgan partners had declared no taxable income in 1931 and 1932. This was not however unreasonable: the net worth of JP Morgan & Co. and Drexel & Co. dropped by 55 percent between 1929 and 1931.[57]

Although the Pecora Committee was far from neutral, it did uncover some evidence of corporate malpractice in (generally publicly owned) investment banks. The post-Pecora consensus among a public battered by the depression was that the investment banks should have their wings clipped. The New Deal legislative program responded to this belief with a legislative program designed to bring the investment banks under the supervisory purview of the new regulatory agencies.

The centerpiece of the blizzard of regulations enacted in FDR's first hundred days was the National Industrial Recovery Act (NIRA), which was signed by FDR on June 16, 1933. The NIRA was passed in order to suppress competition, which the New Dealers believed was driving down prices and causing bankruptcies, job losses, and low wages. The NIRA offered businesses protection from the antitrust laws if they signed up to codes of fair practice governing prices and production quotas. The codes were administered and policed by the National Recovery Association (NRA). The NRA eventually produced 55 codes that affected 2.3 million employers and 16 million workers. Enforcement via the courts was sometimes rather heavy-handed, and its main effect in many parts of the economy was to increase prices and create cartels.[58]

---

[56] Carosso (1970: 339).   [57] Seligman (1982: 31–8).
[58] Powell (2003: 121). The most notorious enforcement example concerns the immigrant who was fined and jailed for three months because he pressed a suit for 35 cents rather than the 40 cents mandated by the NRA dry-cleaning code.

The effect of the NIRA on industries like investment banking which had always in the past policed themselves is not as clear cut. We have already seen that for a number of technical reasons, investment bankers did not compete aggressively on price. Hence the price codes created by the Act were less obviously harmful in this industry. At the same time, as we noted on page 58 of chapter two, an industry that already relies upon self-policing might benefit from the added commitment power that comes with legal enforcement of its codes. There is therefore a case for NRA-style enforcement of investment banker codes of practice.

The NIRA acted as a catalyst for the IBA to come up with a basic code of practice, which was adopted by the NRA and signed into law by FDR on April 23, 1934. The code included the disclosure practices which by then were legally mandated anyway (see p. 207), and supplemented them with detailed rules for issuing new securities. It outlawed price discrimination between small and large investors (of course, we argued on page 85 of chapter three that this was a regressive step), and required investment bankers to publish in the prospectus the price at which they had purchased an issue. The code applied to all investment bankers, although registration was optional. In an echo of the early NYSE rules (see p. 135 of chapter five), registered banks were prohibited from dealing with unregistered banks, which served to strengthen the power of the rules.[59]

Although the Supreme Court struck the NRA down as unconstitutional in a 9-0 decision on the 'sick chicken case' in May 1935,[60] the self-regulatory body it engendered remained in the shape of the Investment Bankers' Conference, Inc. (IBC). The IBC worked with the new SEC (p. 209) to create a national self-regulatory investment banking association. Membership of the association would afford some advantages in dealing with the SEC which were not open to nonmembers, and the association would have the power to expel those who violated these rules. Again, the argument of chapter two suggests that the combination of state power (in the form of the privileges granted by the SEC) with self-regulation would generate the commitment value needed to maintain the private laws that characterize a self-regulatory organization.

The association described in the previous paragraph was actually embedded in law by the Maloney Act of June 1938. This replaced the IBC by the National Association of Securities Dealers (NASD), which

<hr/>

[59] Carosso (1970: 386–7).   [60] See Leuchtenburg (1963: 145).

was an association of OTC brokers and dealers that policed rules for OTC trades.[61,62]

Most of the New Dealers were strong believers in government action, and most were antipathetic toward Wall Street. Their appetite for financial regulation was never going to be satiated by the self-regulation provided for by the NIRA. The first piece of legislation aimed directly at large-scale financiers was the Securities Act of 1933. It sought to ensure that adequate disclosure accompanied public security issues. This was not a new idea, and the industry had pushed for full disclosure federal legislation since the 1880s. The Act required companies to file a detailed statement with the Federal Trade Commission (FTC) and, after July 1934, with the SEC. The registration statement did not become effective until twenty days after filing, and during this 'cooling-off' period no sales could be made.[63]

Ironically in the light of New Deal distaste for Wall Street, the Securities Act may have tempered the positive effects of its disclosure rules with conduct-of-business rules that generated rents for market participants. Mahoney (2001) argues that the Act benefited the wholesale investment banking aristocracy by suppressing competition from retail investment houses in the form of 'beating the gun' by soliciting buy orders ahead of other syndicate members, and discounting the offer price to garner orders. These laws were favored by the major banks, largely because they protected the syndicate system: while we have argued that the commitment value of a new law may have been welfare-enhancing precisely because it supported valuable extra-legal institutions like the syndicate, Mahoney notes that this particular law served to increase industry competition, and he argues that the law may have been a response to rent-seeking efforts by the investment bankers.[64]

While they welcomed the disclosure requirements of the Securities Act, industry players were dismayed by a provision in the law that held company directors personally responsible for any misstatements

---

[61] Carosso (1970: 386–9).

[62] Over-the-counter trades are performed outside the auspices of any exchange. The Maloney Act therefore allowed OTC traders to generate the commitment powers that traders on the NYSE acquired by virtue of the Exchange's laws.

[63] Carosso (1970: 356–7).

[64] A eulogistic defense of the sentiments and procedures that gave rise to the Act appears in de Bedts (1964: ch. 2), who characterizes it as 'the inheritor of centuries of Anglo-Saxon experience' (p. 54). In de Bedt the Pecora hearings find an enthusiastic cheerleader, and JP Morgan is damned for, among other things, 'legal, albeit shocking evasions of income tax payments' (p. 46).

in the registration statement. For example, the corporate attorney Arthur Dean argued that the Act might 'seriously impede recovery' and make it more expensive to raise capital.[65] At the same time, an increasing body of opinion demanded some direct regulation of stock exchanges.

The initial proposals for stock exchange regulation were drafted by Morris Cohen and were introduced to both houses of Congress as the Fletcher-Rayburn Bill. Their content reveals a lack of understanding of the private law that financial institutions provide. First, the Bill called for securities exchanges to register with the FTC, which would be given power to approve or to disapprove exchange rules and regulations. Second, section 10 of the proposed legislation attempted to abolish floor traders, so that specialists would be barred from trading on their own accounts. Broking houses would be prohibited from dealing or underwriting securities. Hence section 10 'would have ended all private transactions on the exchange floor, permanently transforming the Exchange into a clerical agency for the execution of off-floor orders'. Third, the Bill set statutory margin requirements for stock trading.[66]

These measures would have undermined the mechanisms that we described in chapters two and three. The first would dramatically have circumscribed the ability of exchanges to build reputations for enforcing a particular package of listing laws. Since these packages constitute one of the few dimensions along which exchanges can compete, it would have restricted their ability to do so, and so would have undermined their incentive to innovate market design. The second rule was presumably intended to remove conflicts of interest from the trading floors. As with investment banks, though, trading floors would not exist unless there were conflicts of interest: without them there would be no trade. The specialist, like the investment banker, serves a valuable purpose precisely *because* he is trusted to face these conflicts without straying from the straight-and-narrow. His flow of business, and the rents he derives from it, rely upon his maintaining a reputation for honest dealing. Preventing him from dealing would destroy the economic value embedded in his reputation, and hence would diminish the efficiency of the market. Finally, extending margin is credit business. When the legislature assumes responsibility for lending money it throws away the relationships and the accumulated

---

[65] Seligman (1982: 71).   [66] Seligman (1982: 85–6).

expertise of market participants. Once again, something valuable is being destroyed without any obvious return.

Fortunately for American capitalism, a massive media campaign orchestrated by the NYSE president Richard Whitney convinced the legislators that the Bill would stifle fundraising and result in the forced liquidation of many stocks; this killed the first version of the Fletcher-Rayburn Bill.[67] The redrafted Bill was passed in 1934 as the Securities Exchange Act. It relaxed margin laws, delegated enforcement not to the FTC but to a new SEC, and also altered the 1933 Securities Act, so as to reduce the stringency of its civil penalties. The NYSE achieved an almost total victory regarding exchange membership: floor traders continued subject to SEC rules, while the specialist system was very nearly unchanged. Broker–dealer segregation did not occur.[68]

The poor governance in securities affiliates had placed depositors at risk. The Banking Act of June 1933, popularly known as the Glass–Steagall Act, addressed both problems, firstly by establishing the Federal Deposit Insurance Corporation to protect depositors, although this measure was neither requested nor supported by FDR's administration;[69] and secondly, by abolishing security affiliates: the Act required a complete separation of investment and commercial banking. As a result, private banks had to choose between securities and deposit-taking business. Partners and officials of security firms were also prohibited from serving as directors or officers of commercial banks that were members of the Federal Reserve System.[70]

Although long-established specialist investment houses such as Kuhn, Loeb & Co. and Lehman Brothers were scarcely affected by the Glass-Steagall Act, it changed the shape of the investment banking business for the next 66 years.[71] The major commercial banks closed or span off their affiliates, thus reducing significantly the amount of capital available to float new issues. Two-thirds of the private bankers elected to stay in the securities business, although JP Morgan & Co. and Brown Brothers Harriman & Co. remained in deposit banking: both continued to serve only large corporations, and both now had to submit to government regulation. The Banking Act also led to the establishment of new securities firms: First Boston grew out of

---

[67] Perhaps unsurprisingly in the light of n. 64 above, de Bedts (1964: 63) argues that Whitney's statements at this time 'can only be seen as an exercise of incredibly poor judgment or incredible arrogance, or more likely a combination of both'.

[68] Seligman (1982: 89–100).   [69] Golembe (1960).   [70] Carosso (1970: 371).

[71] It was repealed by the Gram–Leach–Bliley Act of 1999.

the security affiliate of the First National Bank of Boston; Morgan Stanley & Co. was founded a year after the demise of JP Morgan & Co.'s investment banking business by three Morgan partners and two from Drexel; Brown Harriman & Co. was constituted of officers and directors of National City Co. and Brown Brothers Harriman & Co.[72]

The Glass–Steagall Act was an immediate source of controversy, and remained so until it was repealed. By the end of the 1920s, bank security affiliates—notably Chase National Bank and National City Co. of New York—were sponsoring over half of all new security issues. The Glass–Steagall Act cleared the way for the private banks to reestablish control of this market. Macey (1984) argues from this observation that the true motive of the Act was the protection of investment bankers at the expense of the commercial bankers. Given the genuine distaste within FDR's administration for Wall Street, this seems a little far-fetched. Langevoort (1987) argues on the contrary that the progressive Carter Glass was motivated to draft his Bill by the belief that it would encourage commercial banks to channel money toward small companies, rather than into the securities markets. If so, Glass was ignoring an endogeneity problem: in other words, the fact that the volume of commercial bank investment funds was likely to alter in response to the Banking Act. Some modern literature examines the Act: Puri (1996) finds that pre-1933 investors welcomed commercial bank underwriters as valuable certifiers of quality, and Kroszner and Rajan (1994) find evidence that concern for their reputation prevented commercial banks from acting on the conflicts of interest they faced.

New Deal antipathy toward investment bankers found expression in two further arenas: holding company regulation, and the bankruptcy courts.

A very large proportion of American utility companies were owned by holding companies, which were either directly controlled by investment bankers, or had been created by deals which were masterminded by investment bankers. In 1932 the three largest holding companies, including the Morgan-controlled United Corporation, were responsible for 45 percent of the electricity generated in the United States, while four holding companies controlled more than 56 percent of the total mileage of the countries natural gas transportation system; gas production was similarly largely controlled by holding companies.

[72] Carosso (1970: 372–4).

This system of production was regarded with extreme suspicion by the New Dealers: the 84 volumes of hearings and evidence produced between 1928 and 1935 by the FTC on the subject began with the statement that 'no large holding-company structure has grown to its present size without the aid of investment bankers'. The upshot was the Public Holding Company Act 1935, which gave the SEC wide-ranging powers to regulate all utility security issuance, to bar new securities if they seemed 'detrimental to the public interest', and to break up holding companies owning unrelated networks. The powers that the SEC thus acquired over an entire industry were the subject of a mass registration boycott by the utilities, and it was only after the Act was upheld in a 1938 Supreme Court decision that it could be properly enforced.[73]

The Supreme Court that upheld the Public Holding Company Act was a very different one to that which Roosevelt inherited when he first became president. His early years in power were bedevilled by concerns that the Supreme Court might rule New Deal legislation unconstitutional, as they did the NIRA. At the start of the New Deal, four members of the Supreme Court bench (McReynolds, Sutherland, Van Deranter, and Butler) were 'conservatives' (i.e. classical rule of law liberals), and three (Brandeis, Cardozo, and Fiske Stone) were reformers. If either of the remaining two members (Evans Hughes and Roberts) voted with the conservatives, they could hole the New Deal below the waterline.[74]

In 1937, at the start of his second term of office, FDR, frustrated by Supreme Court decisions that undermined his programs, and fearing that major social legislation might be ruled unconstitutional, attempted unsuccessfully to resolve his problems via legislation that would allow him to add a new Supreme Court justice to the bench for every member over 70 who had served more than ten years. For many people, this was a step too far in the direction of the activist administration, and the so-called 'court-packing' bill failed. Nevertheless, Justice Van Devanter retired soon afterward and, for reasons apparently unrelated to the bill but otherwise hard to explain, Roberts started to vote with the reformers. Subsequent resignations meant that within two and a half years of the rejection of the measure, FDR had five of his own appointees on the bench (Justices Black,

---

[73] This paragraph and the preceding one draw upon Seligman (1982: 128–38). The quotation from the FTC document appears on p. 128.
[74] Leuchtenburg (1963: 143).

Reed, Frankfurter, O'Douglas and Murphy). The 'Roosevelt Court' 'greatly extended the area of permissible national regulation of the economy'.[75]

One could argue that massive utility holding companies served no useful purpose. However, this is not an accusation that one could level at the equity receivership which we described in chapter six (pp. 176–82). By the late 1920s the equity receivership was an effective body of law, designed by financiers and lawyers and tested in the marketplace. The importance of investment bankers to the receivership made it a natural target of the New Deal, however. Legislative dabbling in this field came early in the New Deal, when FDR's administration was still employing a broadly collaborative approach toward the business community. Although there were broader concerns regarding the legitimacy of equity receiverships in non-railroad restructurings, the 1933 amendments to the 1898 Bankruptcy Act served mostly to codify existing practice. They were welcomed by Wall Street, which foresaw assistance in dealing with holdouts and with cross-State restructurings, which required multiple state-by-state ancillary receiverships.

But this was not the end of the story. The Securities Exchange Act of 1934 (see p. 209 above) instructed the SEC to investigate the protective committees used in restructurings. The resultant report was written by William Douglas, an ambitious attorney who was to be one of the most activist SEC chairmen, and later a Supreme Court Justice. His report was characterized by violently anti-Wall Street rhetoric. He either ignored or failed to appreciate that, precisely because they intermediate between competing agents who struggle to write standard contracts, investment bankers are inevitably exposed to conflicts. Rather, he used the conflicts as evidence of systemic weaknesses, and he ignored the strong reputational incentives for firms such as JP Morgan to resolve conflicts.

Douglas's report led ultimately to the 1938 Chandler Bill, although it jockeyed for position with two rival bills (the Sabath and Lea bills). Rather tellingly, Skeel (2001: 113–19) demonstrates that the SEC was not immune from the conflicts of interest before which it accused investment bankers of bending: to a large extent, it was actuated in its negotiations over the Bill by a desire to protect its turf.

Chapter X of the Chandler Act brought New Deal hostility toward Wall Street to bear upon the design of corporate reorganizations. It

---

[75] Leuchtenburg (1963: 231–8).

required *all* reorganizations to turn management of the ongoing business and of the reorganization over to a trustee, whereas previously
these jobs were undertaken by the preexisting management of the
firm and its bankers, respectively. The trustee took powers to formulate a reorganization plan entirely away from the creditors, and the
firm's bankers were explicitly precluded from advising, or serving
as, the trustee. So the New Dealers got their way, and they moved
the investment bankers out of corporate reorganizations. However
well meant, their legislation had the consequence of removing from
the reorganization expertise born of long association with the firm,
and of excluding the institutions which, by virtue of their ability to
manage networks of investors, were most able to coordinate financial
reorganizations. The unsurprising consequence was a reduction in
filings for bankruptcy, from over 500 in 1938 to an average of about
100 through the 1950s and 1960s.[76]

The year 1938 also saw a renewed slump in the American economy. Concerned that he was creating an underclass of state depen-
dents, Roosevelt cut state spending sharply in June 1937. The consequence in the autumn was a sharp reduction in production and
capacity utilization. By early 1938 many American once again faced
extreme hardship. Coming as it did hard upon the heels of the court-
packing bill and a series of violent strikes during which Roosevelt
sat on the fence between labor and capital, this slump was politically
very damaging. Progressive members of the administration began to
demand action against the big businesses which they believed were
responsible for the current recession. After vacillating for months,
FDR embarked in June upon a fresh bout of spending and at the same
time asked Congress to vote funds for an investigation into the concentration of economic power. The result was the Temporary National
Economic Committee (TNEC), chaired by Senator Joseph O'Mahoney
of Wyoming.[77]

Investment banking was not at the center of the TNEC's enquiry,
but it came in for some criticism. As in preceding enquiries, the
proceedings were politically motivated, and investment bankers were
neither allowed to call their own witnesses, nor to cross-examine the
Committee's. Some of the issues raised by the TNEC were to resurface
later in the *U.S.* v. *Morgan Stanley et al.* antitrust trial (p. 220).

---

[76] Skeel (2001: 126: table 4.1). Further discussion of the consequences of the
Chandler Act appears on p. 251 of chapter eight.

[77] See Leuchtenburg (1963: 244–57) for a discussion of the recession and
Roosevelt's response to it.

The most important of the concerns raised by the committee concerned the separation of investment and commercial banking, as required by the 1933 Banking Act. Evidence heard by the committee appeared to suggest that 'inheritance' determined which of the new investment houses undertook the underwriting business of the broken up commercial banks. For example, Morgan Stanley had a close association with the clients of JP Morgan. Moreover, many issuers retained close links both with their commercial bank, and with the investment house which it span off after the 1933 Act. It appears however that clients were simply following the individuals with whom they had relationships before 1933. In a business characterized by repeated dealing within a close relationship this does not seem surprising.[78] This question would re-surface in the Morgan trial, when the progressive concerns would be conclusively demonstrated to be without foundation.

The final regulatory issue that would resurface in the Morgan antitrust trial concerned competitive bidding for underwriting business. Regulators and legislators had argued for sometime that a system under which issuers were obliged to sell securities to the highest bidder would break up the investment banking monopolies. Investment bankers strenuously resisted legislation to compel compulsory competitive bidding. For example, although competitive bidding was not formally examined in the TNEC hearings, Harold Stanley spoke at length on the subject, arguing that it led to 'casual intermittent connections' between issuer and banker, and that as a result, issuers received no advice from bankers, while bankers had to accept an issue as presented, or to pass it up.[79] Certainly, our theory of chapters two and three suggests that, if competitive bidding prevented an investment bank from earning rents on its relationships, it would also undermine any value that the investment bank added as an enforcer of extra-legal contracts. Indeed, competitive bidding has seldom been used in situations where it was optional.

A movement in the late 1930s to force issuers to open their underwriting business to competitive sealed bidding was spearheaded by

---

[78] See Carosso (1970: 408–20) for an outline of the Brandeisian case against the investment bankers, and of the evidence that, in the contemporary words of Joseph Ripley, of National City Co. and then Brown, Harriman and Co., corporations would do business with 'people whom they had successfully and satisfactorily done business in the past'.

[79] Carosso (1970: 422). See also page 199 for Pierpont Morgan's remarks to the Pujo Committee on this subject.

three people: Robert R. Young, chairman of the Alleghany Corporation and the director of the Chesapeake and Ohio Railroad, Cyrus Eaton, the head of Otis & Co., a Cleveland investment banking house, and Harold Stuart of Halsey, Stuart & Co. (see p. 218). All were motivated either by political or commercial concerns,[80] but their lobbying had some effect: in pursuit of its requirement under the Public Utility Holding Company Act to supervise holding company security issues, the SEC adopted on March 1, 1939 the 'arm's-length bargaining' rule U-12F-2, which prevented utility companies from paying underwriting fees to investment banks with whom they were affiliated unless the issue was awarded competitively, or it was impractical to offer it competitively.[81] The rule was badly worded and hard-to-enforce. The IBA came out strongly against compulsory competitive bidding, but to no avail: in April 1941 rule U-12F-2 was replaced by rule U-50, which required competitive public sealed bidding for all issues of registered utility holding companies and their subsidiaries under the SEC's jurisdiction.[82] The new rule generated howls of protest from industry insiders, who argued that it would result in state control of the capital markets. Their protests were in vain: in 1944 the ICC ruled that all railroad security offerings should be sold competitively.[83]

Competitive bidding changed the organization of securities issues: the issuer had to write its own prospectus, possibly with the help of an investment bank, which would be paid a fee for its assistance; investment bankers used syndicates to bid for the business. It had repercussions for the institutions that most vigorously opposed it, as in 1947 they found themselves on the receiving end of a Justice Department antitrust suit (p. 220).

INDUSTRY EVOLUTION

Although we argue that the most important influence upon investment banking in the first half of the twentieth century was the polity, demographic and technological changes also altered the composition of the industry. This section provides a brief survey of these changes. Much of the material covered here is drawn from Carosso (1970).

---

[80] See Carosso (1970: 423–44). Young was feuding with the Morgan interests, and both Eaton and Stuart were concerned to win business: indeed, Stuart acknowledged in court in 1952 that this was the case.

[81] Carosso (1970: 436–7).

[82] See Carosso (1970: 443). There were some minor exceptions to the rule.

[83] See Carosso (1970: 445). The rules did not apply to stock issues, nor to the types of issues that were exempted from U-50.

Railroad companies remained the most important investment banking clients at the start of the twentieth century, and their issuance business was dominated by the old-established partnerships we discussed in the previous chapter. Their reputations and experience presented would-be entrants to the market with a substantial barrier to entry. A strong reputation may itself be a hindrance in new markets, however. The emergence at the start of the century of new markets in the securities of public utilities, department stores and small family companies presented an opportunity, but a firm that took it exposed its reputation. As a result, the long-established houses were less willing to enter these businesses, and newer players were able to emerge.

An important beneficiary of this effect was Goldman, Sachs & Co., whom we encountered on page 164 of chapter six. At the turn of the century the firm was largely a commercial paper trading house, but it had ambitions to enter the underwriting business. After it was warned off the railroad business by incumbent banks, it got its chance in the retail industry, performing its most important early issue in 1906 when it underwrote a $10 million issue of common and preferred stock for Sears, Roebuck & Co., at a time when the retailer's annual turnover was only $50 million. For the three decades following this deal it shared its underwriting business with Lehman Brothers, bringing the client list it had acquired in the commercial paper business and combining it with Lehman's superior capital resources.[84]

In addition to the new markets which they built, the younger and more aggressive investment banks developed new approaches to sales. While the older houses stayed out of the retail investment markets, the newer firms were the first since the days of Jay Cooke (p. 161) to use newspaper advertisements and to send salespeople to meet putative clients. At the same time as, and to some extent as a result of, the growth of retail business, regional branches and relationships were increasingly seen as important. The small provincial houses of Chicago were able to tap mid-western saving and as a result, they began for the first time to challenge some of the New York houses for business.[85]

The growth of retail investment banking was accelerated by World War I. Up until the American entry into the conflict, US investment banks floated loans for all of the combatant nations. For the first time,

[84] See Endlich (1999: 37–41). The relationship with Lehman was a stormy one, increasingly characterized by resentment and mistrust on both sides until it was formally dissolved in 1936.
[85] Carosso (1970: 101–8).

the US ceased to be a debtor nation, and became a creditor nation. As a noncombatant, America profited from the war and acquired a leading role in international finance.[86]

America's entry into the war on April 6, 1917 resulted in massive demands on the capital markets. The first Liberty Loan Act was passed on April 24, and authorized the Treasury to borrow up to $5 billion. Many believed that a loan of this size simply could not be raised. The first issue was a $2 billion bond. This proved hard to shift, and so the Treasury mounted an intensive nationwide sales effort which saw the government selling smaller denomination bills to individuals rather than large denominations to institutions. The campaign resulted in oversubscription by one-half.[87] The same advertising and sales techniques were employed for subsequent drives, and all were oversubscribed. The 1919 Victory Loan of March 1919 ran to $4.5 billion, and its successful sale was described by the Treasury as 'the greatest financial achievement in history and a wonderful manifestation of the strength and purpose of the American people.'[88]

Bankers had estimated the bond market in 1917 at 350,000 investors. In fact, four million subscribed to the first Victory Loan, and subscriptions in subsequent loans increased to 9.4, 18.4, 22.8, and 11.8 million. This was the first experience of securities market investment for millions of Americans. Their experience created a new and lucrative market for the investment bankers.[89] Indeed, the expanding securities markets led to the establishment of some new retail-oriented houses, such as the Federal Securities Corporation, which was founded in Chicago in 1919, and was soon national in scope.[90]

Small denomination bond sales caused a massive increase in transactions volume, and this gave rise to a problem which continued to trouble investment bankers for the rest of the century. Processing systems within the investment houses were so weak that they found it impossible to handle the increased volume of trades. On some days the processing of orders ground to a halt. 'From a booking view point, very few brokerage firms had any conception of just how they "stood", and it was a fortunate firm whose clerks kept them up-to-date'.[91]

Retail investors remained important through the 1920s. With the exception of blue-blooded houses such as JP Morgan & Co. and Kuhn,

---

[86] Carosso (1970: 222).   [87] Carosso (1970: 221).   [88] Carosso (1970: 226).
[89] Carosso (1970: 226–8).   [90] Carosso (1970: 236–7).
[91] Carosso (1970: 234), citing Robert L. Smitley, 'Wall Street's Red Tape', *The Magazine of Wall Street*, XIX (Feb 3, 1917), p. 592.

Table 7.1. *Corporate issues, by class of security, 1919–29 (millions)*

Year	Bonds and notes	Stocks	Total
1919	1,122	1,546	2,668
1920	1,750	1,038	2,778
1921	1,994	275	2,269
1922	2,329	621	2,950
1923	2,430	736	3,166
1924	2,655	865	3,520
1925	2,975	1,247	4,222
1926	3,354	1,220	4,574
1927	4,769	1,738	6,507
1928	3,439	3,491	6,930
1929	2,620	6,757	9,377

Source: Carosso (1970: 243).

Loeb & Co., most firms expanded their retail sales function to some extent. Competition in the newer retail markets was very lively. One of the young turks was Halsey, Stuart & Co., Inc. of Chicago. The firm built its reputation in the early 1900s by trading utility bonds at a time when they were still considered pretty racy. They only traded in bonds, but they adopted new sales techniques, using newspaper advertising as early as 1904 and in 1928 pioneering the use of radio advertising. The firm installed the first private wire system to connect offices in different cities, and it started a formal training program for its sales people. By 1930 the firm ranked third, and ahead of Morgan, in the total volume of issues managed during the 1927–31 period.[92]

The supply of securities was revolutionized during the 1920s. The securities markets were increasingly used by utilities, smaller industrials, and municipalities, while the relative importance of railroads fell. There was also a massive boom in foreign security issuance. American investment in foreign securities between 1922 and 1929 amounted to $4.6 billion, which surpassed England's capital exports.[93] At the same time, table 7.1 illustrates increased share issuance in a booming market. For the first time ever, share issuance outstripped bond issuance in a single year.

As we have already seen, the stock market crash and the subsequent depression had profound ramifications for the composition of the

---

[92] Carosso (1970: 259–60).   [93] Carosso (1970: 245).

investment banking industry. Of the well-established firms, the crash almost finished off Kidder, Peabody, which was rescued by Morgan, while Lee, Higginson could not survive the revelation, in the wake of his suicide, that their long-established client Ivar Kreuger was a fraudster who had embezzled funds.[94] Some of the newer firms were lucky to survive the crisis, too. The Goldman Sachs Trading Company was an investment trust founded in December 1928 that initially generated huge paper profits for the partners and then collapsed during the Crash. The reputational damage that this caused Goldman, Sachs took at least two decades to repair.[95]

The slow recovery from the depression allowed the reemergence of retail securities sales. The most important participant in this business during the second half of the twentieth century was Merrill Lynch. The firm was the descendant of one started by Charles E. Merrill in January 1914,[96] which became Merrill Lynch & Co. in October of that year, when he was joined by his partner, Eddie Lynch.[97] The firm entered the investment banking world through markets that were ignored by the long-established houses, in particular the market for chain store securities.[98] After Merrill's war service, the firm continued to underwrite chain store security issuance, and it held substantial stakes in many of the companies it brought to market. It also held large investments in the film industry, acquiring a controlling stake of the Pathé Exchange studio: the profits from this deal were invested in Safeway stores.[99]

Merrill was one of the few who saw the crash coming, and who liquidated his holdings in time to survive it.[100] He disengaged himself from investment banking for most of the succeeding decade, moving into the retail industry and managing the Safeway chain.[101] When he returned to Wall Street in the 1940s he called his firm Merrill Lynch & Co., even though Lynch had died in May 1938. His strategy was very different from the one he had followed in the 1920s: he aimed to create a volume securities brokerage offering the same value for money to small investors that the Safeway stores offered to ordinary shoppers. In pursuit of this goal, Merrill trained his staff properly and upheld high ethical standards. The strategy was extremely successful: Merrill Lynch opened branch offices all over America and gave millions of moderate-income Americans the chance to build investment

---

[94] Carosso (1970: 309–18).   [95] See Endlich (1999: 45–6).
[96] Perkins (1999: 66).   [97] Perkins (1999: 72).   [98] Perkins (1999: 73–7).
[99] Perkins (1999: 96–100).   [100] Perkins (1999: 105).
[101] Perkins (1999: ch. 7).

portfolios. Like Goldman Sachs in the early 1900s, Merrill Lynch used its mastery of a new market to build a reputation that would propel it into the first rank of investment bankers, and by the end of the century it had outpaced many of the firms that dominated the industry when it entered it.

UNITED STATES VERSUS MORGAN STANLEY

On October 30, 1947 the Justice Department filed the first suit against the alleged money monopolists under the Sherman Act, charging seventeen investment banks and the IBA with offences similar to those leveled by the Pujo Committee. The resultant trial lasted two and a half years, from November 1950 to May 1953. It drew a line under the political and legal clashes that had characterized the investment banking industry in the first half of the twentieth century, and it set the course of the industry for at least the next two and a half decades.

The seventeen defendant banks[102] were accused of participating in a conspiracy to suppress investment banking competition which had started around the time of Morgan's 1915 syndication of a large Anglo-French war loan. However, it was never completely clear how they were chosen: some had previously been cited by the Pujo Committee or the TNEC, while others, like Goldman and Lehman, had worked together in the past. But the list of defendants was certainly not a roster of the largest and most important of American investment banks. It seemed that possibly the only thing that they had in common might be their concerted opposition to moves toward compulsory competitive sealed bidding. Indeed, the charges against the defendants initially incorporated the accusation that this opposition was illegal. This accusation was dropped during the trial.

Harold Medina was the trial judge. In his corrected case opinion (Medina [1954] 1975, 3–9), he states that the heart of the government's case was 'the triple concept' of 'traditional banker', 'historical position', and 'reciprocity'. The 'traditional banker' phrase was coined during the TNEC hearings. It referred to the idea that the defendant bankers recognized that the first of them to manage an

---

[102] They were Morgan Stanley & Co., Kuhn, Loeb & Co., Smith Barney & Co., Lehman Brothers, Glore Forgan & Co., Kidder, Peabody & Co., Goldman, Sachs & Co., White, Weld & Co., Eastman Dillon & Co., Drexel & Co., the First Boston Corporation, Dillon Read & Co. Inc., Blyth Read & Co, Inc., Harriman, Ripley & Co., Inc., Stone & Webster Securities Corporation, Harris Hall & Co. (Incorporated) and Union Securities Corporation.

offering for a given issuer was entitled to head all subsequent issues. The plaintiff argued that traditional banker relationships survived the Glass–Steagall Act due to inheritance along 'predecessor–successor' lines. The traditional banker arrangement was alleged to have been designed to eliminate competition among the defendants and so to preserve their hold over their clients' businesses.

'Historical position' was the accusation that, once an investment banker had participated in a syndicate for a given issuer, he was entitled to participate in the same terms in all future syndicates for the same issuer. This would clearly lock competitor banks out of the market.

Finally, the Justice Department charged that investment bankers used agreed-upon formulas to assign syndicate participations to one another based upon a detailed 'reciprocity record' which each was alleged to maintain.

Our theory of investment banking stresses the importance of long-term relationships and cross-monitoring. If investment banks are to enforce extra-legal contracts then they must rely upon their reputations. These are created in repeat relationships, in which each of the counterparts knows that the other values the long-term flow of business sufficiently to abide by the private law that governs their dealings. We should therefore expect investment banker clients to form long-term relationships with their underwriters. Clients move from one banker to another only in the wake of bad service, and, if the enforcement mechanisms embodied in a continuing relationship are effective, we should seldom see this occur. In other words, evidence which appears to support a 'historical banker' thesis is likely simply to be evidence of satisfactory banker–client relations.

Chapter three also discussed syndicates. In the context of the Morgan trial, two points are of relevance. First, investment bankers place their reputations on the line when they underwrite new issues. The selection of syndicate members is therefore rather more than a mechanical exercise of sharing out the profits: the lead manager must trust his counterparts. Hence, like the clients in the previous paragraph, they are likely to form long-term syndicate relationships with their peers. Second, we argued in chapter three that it is in the interests of investment banks that their reputations be as exposed as possible. In this way they can convince their clients that reneging on a single transactions will have the greatest possible costs, and so they can attract business. We argue that syndicates serve this purpose by enabling bankers to observe one anothers' behavior, and to report it to the issuing client. If this is the case, then investment bankers will continue to trade with one another for as long as no bank does something to impair its reputation. Since investment bankers will work to maintain their reputations, syndicate memberships should not change rapidly. In short, observations that appear to imply 'historical position' and 'reciprocity' arrangements are susceptible to a far more innocent explanation.

Although the hearing was lengthy and extremely costly, in many ways the investment banking community welcomed it. Unlike the other hearings described in this chapter, the defendants in the Medina case were able to call their own witnesses, to present their own evidence, and to cross-examine the government's witnesses. This had a massive effect upon the trial's outcome: when the investment bankers presented their case, Medina commented that the huge quantities of data marshaled by the government in support of their accusations were misleading and designed to fool. The defense data revealed a 'pattern of no pattern':[103] defendant rankings in underwriting league tables varied enormously from one year to another, while they were about as successful in competitive sealed bidding as they were in negotiated transactions.[104]

The government's case collapsed entirely when their chief witness, Halsey Stuart, took to the witness box. His testimony was inconsistent with the government's case, and he stated that, unless invited to bid for underwriting business, there was no point in doing so, since the issuer 'generally resents the ringing-door-bell type of approach'.[105]

Medina dismissed the government's case with prejudice, so that it could not be retried. In doing so, he outlined the wide-ranging and complex conspiracy which the defendants were accused of sustaining, and continued in scathing terms:

And all this is said to have gone on for almost forty years, in the midst of a plethora of congressional investigations, through two wars of great magnitude, and under the very noses of the Securities and Exchange Commission and the Interstate Commerce Commission, without leaving any direct documentary or testimonial proof of the formation or continuance of the combination and conspiracy. The government case depends entirely upon circumstantial evidence'.[106]

---

[103] Carosso (1970: 478).   [104] Carosso (1970: 484).
[105] Medina ([1954] 1975: 225).   [106] Medina ([1954] 1975: 9).

CONCLUSION

Financial capitalism saw its heyday at the start of the twentieth century. A small number of investment bankers sat at the nexus of the contracts that allocated capital in the American economy. To many contemporary observers, the investment bankers looked like titans who had accreted an excessive degree of power, which they used irresponsibly to feather their own nests at the expense of the ordinary working people whom they had disenfranchised.

Events in the ensuing fifty years gave the lie to this story. While investment bankers relied upon their reputation for facilitating value-enhancing trade to maintain their wealth and their positions, legislators did not. The growth of the regulatory state created a leviathan which was no match for the investment banking community. A series of congressional investigations forced investment bankers onto the back foot, and much of their energy in the first half of the century was expended on responding to increasingly fierce demands for state intervention in their activities. Ultimately, these demands resulted in the 1930s in a total reorganization of the industry, and in its wholesale regulation.

The 1950–3 Medina antitrust trial brought the early-twentieth-century regulatory assault upon investment banks to its crescendo. Although we have argued that the litigation was ill-conceived, if successful it would have had a profound effect upon the operation of the banks. It is hard to see how, in the wake of a judgment in the government's favor, investment banks could have continued to fulfill their main economic purposes, as outlined in chapter three. Such a judgment would surely have resulted in a wholesale reconstruction of American capitalism.

The collapse of the government's case heralded a period of relatively light state involvement in the operation of the capital markets. Changes to the investment banking landscape in the ensuing years were once again largely susceptible to technological explanations. These are the topic of the next chapter.

8

The Modern Industrial Revolution

Judge Medina's 1953 decision on *U.S.* v. *Morgan et al.* marked the end of a protracted period of state interference in the investment banking industry. The succeeding years saw the information technology revolution. A gale of creative destruction blew through the world economy and it was this revolution,[1] rather than a political one, that shaped the investment banking industry in the second half of the twentieth century.

Early computerization opened the door to back-office automation, and retail-oriented banks restructured to take advantage of the resultant economies of scale. At the same time, a revolution in financial economics was occurring, which generated an expanding body of tools and techniques that could be widely applied in investment analysis and other aspects of investment banking. These tools acquired practical significance when desktop computers permeated investment banks in the 1970s. Previously, investment bankers had acquired their skills through lengthy on-the-job apprenticeships. Financial economics reduced some of their skills to a formal body of knowledge that was more science than the art it replaced. To the extent that their skills remained important, the codification of practice and the computerization of their business also increased the scale at which human capitalists could operate.

The displacement of human capitalists from some investment activities caused the most profound upheaval in investment banking practice since the early days of the business. Unlike traditional investment banking skills, 'financial engineering' could be taught at arm's length in a professional school. The consequence was a drop in the relative importance of investment banker reputation in the markets where practice was most codified. As a result, the barriers to entry

---

[1] In his presidential address to the American Economic Association, Michael Jensen (1993) 'modern industrial revolution' to describe these changes. We discuss his work later in the chapter.

into these markets were lowered by the new financial economics,[2] and competition became more intense. Investment banks responded by expanding their operations to take advantage of the economies of scale that distributed processing and codification enabled.

As we note in our opening paragraph, information technology fueled a modern industrial revolution. The commissars of this revolution in the United States were investment bankers: they organized the deals through which the corporate world was reengineered, and they created the securities that financed these deals. Corporate America's return to the financial capitalism that had served her so well at the end of the nineteenth century created new human capital-intensive work for the investment bankers who advised the merging, acquiring and acquired corporations.

The modern industrial revolution had a global reach. Improved communications increased enormously the opportunities for cross-border trade in financial markets. Since this trade was relatively new, it was characterized by contractual incompleteness and enforcement problems. The eighteenth-century Atlantic traders of chapter four had flourished in such an environment by creating private law and writing reputational contracts, and the late twentieth-century investment banker human capitalists did so, too. For example, we will see later in the chapter that they deployed their skills to create a new Eurobond market.

Of course, the early twentieth-century expansion of the state was not reversed in this period, and investment bankers were not isolated from political developments. We discuss two in this chapter, one of which was undoubtedly beneficial for investment bankers and the American economy, and one of which was rather more controversial. The former was the 1978 replacement of the Chandler Act by a new bankruptcy code which unwound many of the most irrational elements of its predecessor, and in particular enabled investment banks to return to the reorganization market. The latter was the prosecution of Michael Milken, one of the main architects of the leveraged takeover boom of the 1980s, a move which could be likened to the progressive backlash of the first decade of the century.

We start our discussion in the next section with a discussion of the technological changes that lie at the heart of our analysis.

---

[2] See p. 92 of chapter three for a discussion of the reptuational barriers to entry into investment banking.

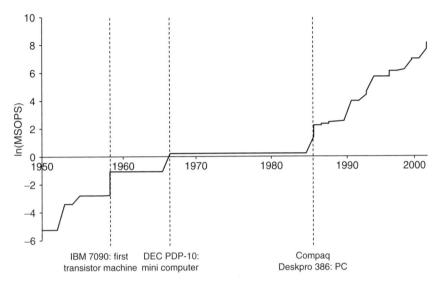

Figure 8.1. *Advances in processing power, 1950–2001 (Nordhaus 2001, appendix 2)*

EARLY COMPUTER ADVANCES

Nordhaus (2001: appendix 2) documents advances in computer power between 1950 and 2001. Changes in the maximum available speed of computation are illustrated in figure 8.1, expressed in a standard information-theoretic measure: millions of standardized instructions per second (MSOPs).[3] The maximum processing speed grew rapidly during the 1950s and 1960s, after which it leveled off until the mid-1980s.

Early computers were well-suited to batch-processing: that is, to preplanned runs of standardized computer tasks, frequently on an overnight basis; real-time responses to user-defined computer queries were still some way in the future. Hence the most natural early commercial applications were in standardized clerical areas.

Insurance companies had to perform large-scale batch processing for their policyholders. At the start of the twentieth century, the largest firms were administering over a million policies, each of which was subject to the vagaries of state-by-state regulation.[4] They were

---

[3] We ignore supercomputers, which were intended for scientific rather than commercial application through the period under consideration.

[4] Yates (2000: 130–1). Railroads, with their large networks and sophisticated accounting procedures, were the other early adopters.

therefore eager consumers of office automation technology, and they were early adopters of the electromechanical punched-card-tabulating technology developed by Herman Hollerith for use in the 1890 US Census. Similarly, they were early adopters of the new electronic computer technology. Univac delivered the first two computers to the insurance industry in 1954.[5]

IBM dominated the market for punched card readers in the first part of the century. Although Thomas J. Watson, Sr, president of the company from 1914 until 1949, could see no commercial applications for computers prior to 1950,[6] the firm responded aggressively when opportunities for commercial computing arose.[7] It took an early lead in insurance computing market by capitalizing on its position in the card-reader market. Insurance companies had been attempting to encourage the development of systems that would more directly dovetail with their existing card-based systems. While Univac's initial plans for commercial computing revolved around machines that used magnetic tape for data storage, IBM responded to insurance company requests by developing a card-operated system (IBM 650), as well as tape-based systems offering high-speed conversion between cards and tape. IBM thus smoothed the transition from card readers to computers with technology that complemented existing systems, and with a distribution and support network with which users were already comfortable.[8] In doing so, they captured the insurance market: by 1955 over twenty computers had been installed in the industry, but Univac had still sold only two of them.[9]

Investment banks were slow adopters of both punched card and computer technology. The most important reason for this was the fragmented nature of the investment banking business. We argued on page 93 of chapter three that investment banks face a trade-off between economies of scale and reputation preservation. Rapid

---

[5] Univac's early success in this market was due in large part to collaboration with the insurance industry. See Yates (1999: 7–11) for further details of the insurance industry's influence on the development of commercial computing systems.

[6] See Freeman and Soete (1997: 172). Also see Cortada (1993: 154) for a discussion of the widespread perception that Watson was an exceptionally astute businessman and a visionary.

[7] Cortada (2000: 199–201).

[8] Yates (1999: 18–21). IBM's sales policy was based upon leasing, while Univac planned to sell its machines. The IBM 650 was shipped at the end of 1954 at a monthly rental rate between $3,250 and $3,750. By comparison, the first Univac sold for $1.25 million.

[9] See Cortada (1993) for a detailed account of the evolution of commercial data processing from its inception to the mid-twentieth-century rise of electronic computers.

expansion into new markets may generate high profits, but it also places the investment bank's reputation at risk. When information is difficult to find and to interpret the investment bank's reputation is particularly valuable, and hence it is generally unwilling to chance it by entering markets with which it is unfamiliar. This was the situation in turn-of-the-century America, and as a result, investment banking was extremely fragmented.[10] This situation continued to obtain in the middle of the century: most investment banks could not then justify investment in card-reading technology, because its minimum economic scale was around 1500 transactions per day.[11] Although trading volume was expanding fast and the members of the NYSE would have benefitted from a *collective* deal settlement system,[12] *individually* they maintained their own records and systems, and it was not rational for most of them to invest in computer systems.[13]

The trade-off between reputation risk and computer technology adoption was most favorable for the retail investment banks. These firms could generate sufficient deal flow to justify technology adoption without entering new markets in which their reputations would be at stake. Furthermore, they could use the new technology to *enhance* their existing reputations, by providing customers with rapid and accurate deal settlement and funds transfer.

Nevertheless, even Merrill Lynch, easily the largest, most geographically diffuse and most attentive to modern management practices of the retail investment banks, was slow to adopt the new technology. For example, the firm's first public report, covering the period from April 1, 1940 to January 3, 1941, provides a revealing snapshot of how the firm allocated its 'expense dollar'.[14] Salaries alone accounted for

---

[10] Medina ([1954] 1975: 22) states that 'in or around the year 1905 or 1906', only five investment banks maintained national securities networks. The most prominent banks, JP Morgan & Co. and Kuhn, Loeb & Co., did not, concentrating instead upon the New York area.

[11] Cortada (1993: 108).

[12] In 1920, the Exchange opened The Stock Clearing Corporation to serve as a centralized system for delivering and clearing securities among members, banks, and trust companies.

[13] Chandler (1990) makes a similar argument regarding the appearance of large corporations and their adoption of large-scale, capital-intensive production technologies in the wake of the second industrial revolution. These technologies were employed, and the modern corporation was born, only when improved communications networks enabled the large markets that sustained the throughput necessary for efficient use of the technology.

[14] Although NYSE members were required to make financial reports available to customers, Merrill's report, similar to modern corporate annual reports, was the first

58 percent of the firm's expenses. The next largest expense categories were insurance and taxes (nine percent) and stationery and supplies (eight percent). Wire costs and office rental followed closely at seven percent and six percent of total expenses, respectively. The remainder of expenses were allocated to telephone and telegraph (four percent), ticker and time service (three percent), advertising (three percent), and statistical service (two percent).[15] In sum, although Merrill Lynch was a consumer of the latest communications technology, the expense report provides no evidence of significant investment in data-processing technology.

The impetus for the retail banks to invest in computers came in the late 1950s. They had cut their overheads during a market downturn in 1957, and when trading volume increased sharply in 1958 they invested in IBM data processing systems to help them to cope with the heightened demand.[16] The following year saw the arrival of computers built using transistor, rather than valve, technology, and was something of a watershed year for the adoption of modern computer technology. RCA and IBM both announced plans to open computer service centers targeted at the Wall Street financial district that would enable time sharing of data-processing capacity as an alternative to exclusive use leased (or purchased) equipment. This move appears substantially to have lowered the minimum scale of computerized securities transaction processing, and it certainly lowered the risk of experimenting with the new technology.[17]

E. F. Hutton was the first to experiment with the RCA service center. Ronello Lewis, a Hutton partner, announced that the firm would shift 'about 1/5 of its clerical load to RCA' including 'trade confirmations, stock records, margin records, and monthly statements'.[18] The announcement was noteworthy both for the apparently experimental

of its kind among NYSE members. The report was issued shortly after Charles Merrill rejoined the firm having agreed with Win Smith that substantial cost reductions in office space, equipment rentals, and communications were feasible and sufficiently large to offset the firm's recent losses. See Perkins (1999: 152, 167).

[15] *New York Times*, March 25, 1941, p. 4.

[16] *Wall Street Journal*, November 21, 1958, p. 1.

[17] At the low end of data processing needs, RCA offered systems for lease beginning at about $7,000 per month. Lease rates for larger capacity systems began at $25,000 per month. Both small and large capacity systems could be purchased for about 50 times the monthly lease rate (for entry, level prices of $350,000 and $1.25 million). In contrast, IBM's service center, for example, offered a minimum scale of 15 hours computing time at less than $300 per hour for users in the financial district. See *Wall Street Journal* October 9, 1959 and *New York Times*, August 4, 1959.

[18] See *New York Times*, July 26, 1959.

nature of the plan and because Lewis had worked both for RCA and Olin Mathieson before recently joining Hutton. Upon joining the firm, Lewis observed that he viewed Wall Street office procedures as 'thirty years behind the times', and he commented derisively on fears associated with adopting new technology, including a concern that outsourcing data processing would expose customer lists or trade secrets to competitors.

Lewis estimated that Hutton would pay RCA $300,000 to handle 20 percent of its clerical load (about what he estimated it would cost to perform the work internally). This was not a trivial sum: he estimated that back-office operations absorbed about 25 percent of commission dollars. Assuming that the hourly rates on offer from the service centers corresponded even approximately the with per-hour rates reflected in lease or purchase prices, Hutton was clearly at the high end of capacity requirements for existing systems. Adopting the new technology wholesale would have been costly, and would presumably have engendered substantial in-house resistance, as well as presenting logistical challenges as old business methods were replaced with new ones. Thus, by allowing for small-scale adoption and experimentation, the service centers opened by IBM and RCA should have dramatically lowered both financial and psychological barriers to the adoption of the new technology.

At the start of the 1960s, the largest of the retail investment banks had adopted the new computer technology. However, many had not, of which Hayden, Stone, Glore Forgan, and Goodbody & Co., the fifth-largest brokerage firm, were the most prominent. The arrival of computer technology and its partial adoption within the investment banking community was to alter the operation of the financial markets. The following section describes the changes that occurred in the 1960s.

EARLY CHANGES TO MARKET STRUCTURE

Trading Patterns

Figure 8.2 illustrates ownership patterns for US equities in the second half of the twentieth century. In 1945 over 90 percent of outstanding US equities were held by households, so that institutional traders (pension funds, unit trusts, insurance companies, and other collective investment vehicles) were relatively unimportant. This pattern changed during the following half century. One of the catalysts for this

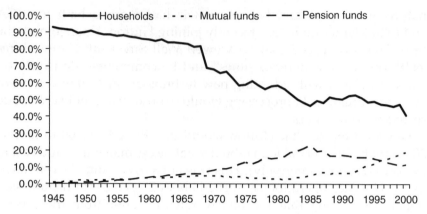

Figure 8.2. *Holdings of outstanding US equities, 1945–2000*
Sources: Federal Reserve Board and Flow of Funds Accounts.

was the development of information technology.[19] Computer systems facilitated the automation of routine administrative tasks. As a result, it became economic for fund managers to accept small investments, so that collective investment vehicles that allowed for market participation and risk-sharing could be sold to people who in the past were not regarded as sufficiently affluent to play the stock markets. The rise of institutional trading coincided with the adoption of computers by retail investment banks in the 1960s: total institutional trading volume did not exceed 28 percent of total NYSE volume in the postwar period until 1963,[20] but by 1969, 52 percent of NYSE trading volume was generated by institutional investors.

Institutional investors trade with greater frequency and in larger quantity than do households, and after a relatively slow postwar period, the 1960s witnessed an enormous increase in US capital market activity.[21] The NYSE's daily trading volume averaged slightly over 2.2 million shares per day (on a total open interest of 5.6 billion shares) during the 1950s. As figure 1.3 illustrated, trading

[19] Another was a postwar increase in pensions saving, in part because pensions provision provided a means for firms to compete in tight labor markets when the price mechanism was undermined by wage controls in the Second World War, the Korean War, and during the oil shocks of the 1970s. See Kohn (2004: 274).
[20] Seligman (1982: 351).
[21] Further evidence of increased institutional trading activity is the growth from 2 percent to 12 percent of NYSE volume transacted through block trades of 10,000 shares or more between the last quarter of 1964 and the first quarter of 1969. See Seligman (1982: 352).

volume then entered a sustained period of explosive growth. Average daily trading volume in 1960 was about three million shares; the figure then nearly quadrupled by 1970, and then quadrupled again by 1980. The growth in trading volume was even more rapid from 1980 onward.

Retail Investment Bank Business

When a retail firm like Merrill embraced computer technology it could use its computers to provide settlement and information systems to new branch offices at minimal marginal cost. It was therefore easy for these firms to exploit the growth in trading volumes by rapidly expanding their retail networks. By 1970, Merrill had 275 retail brokerage offices dispersed throughout the United States. Their nearest competitor in this regard was FI DuPont, with 101 retail offices.

At a time when brokerage fees were still fixed, firms like Merrill earned large profits from their retail brokerage networks. They were also able to leverage their ability to place securities through their networks into a position in underwriting syndicates. Hence, as trading volumes increased and Merrill developed new ways to place new securities, it expanded its business from its retail base into more traditional investment banking functions.

Figure 8.3 illustrates this point. It shows the share of Merrill's total revenue accounted for by commissions, principal transactions, and investment banking between 1961 and 1970. Commissions accounted

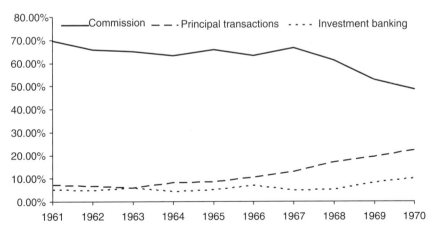

Figure 8.3. *Merrill Lynch revenue sources, 1961–70*

Source: IPO prospectus.

for about 70 percent of the firm's $192 million revenue in 1960, with principal transactions and investment banking representing about seven and five percent of the total, respectively. Over the ensuing decade, the revenue share from principal transactions tripled, while investment banking's revenue share nearly doubled. Although commissions grew from $134 million in 1961 to $230 million in 1970, the latter figure represented only 49 percent of revenues.[22]

The advent of computers and the subsequent expansion of its retail network transformed Merrill's operations. Although the firm underwrote a larger dollar share of negotiated securities offerings in the 1935–49 period than four of the defendant firms in the *U.S.* v. *Morgan et al.* trial (see p. 200), it was viewed by the government as sufficiently benign to be safely excluded from the list of defendants.[23] During the 1961–3 period the firm rose to sixth in the rankings,[24] and by the early 1970s Merrill topped the equity tables and was challenging prominent wholesale banks like Morgan Stanley and First Boston for the overall lead.

Technological change altered the composition of the investment banking industry. Although Merrill Lynch was the most successful retail investment banker to enter the underwriting business in the 1960s, Dean Witter, Eastman Dillon, and Paine Webber followed a similar strategy. The resultant high levels of competition made the market relatively less attractive for the traditional wholesale incumbents, and this was one of the reasons that they began aggressively to pursue pure advisory business for which retail firms were less able to compete.

Servicing Institutional Investors

The emerging institutional investor base represented a new market. We argued on page 93 that new markets represent an entry opportunity for investment banks, because incumbents may be unwilling to risk their reputations by entering them. The new institutional investor class created an opportunity for two 'wholesale'

---

[22] Merrill's experience is representative of the broader NYSE membership, of which the dominant wholesale firms like Morgan Stanley were a relatively small fraction. See Hayes (1979).

[23] For the period in question, Morgan Stanley led the way, managing 20.69 percent of the dollar value of negotiated issues. Merrill Lynch ranked 17th with a share of 0.41 percent, which exceeded that of defendant firms Union, Harris Hall, Eastman Dillon, and Drexel ('Defendants' Tables', M-2, 1).

[24] See Miller (1967: 159, table 2.29).

banks, Goldman Sachs and Salomon Brothers, neither of whom was among the top ten in securities underwriting during the 1961–3 period.[25]

Both firms worked aggressively to build an institutional investor client base. As a result, Goldman rose over the course of a 'few' years from 33rd to third position in brokerage commissions by July 1971, behind only Merrill and Bache, and was especially gaining market share in both block trading and arbitrage, where Salomon was a primary competitor.[26] Similarly to Merrill's use of its retail network, both Goldman and Salomon were able to use their ability to place securities with institutional investors to gain entry to the security underwriting business. By 1970 both were in the top ten security underwriting investment banks.

The Back-Office Crisis

Merrill Lynch's investment in computer technology placed it in a strong competitive position relative to those of its counterparts in the retail market who had not computerized their back-office operations. It was able to handle larger volumes of trades than nonadopters, and it could do so more cheaply. In a completely free market, Merrill would have been able to capitalize upon this difference by undercutting firms that had not installed computer systems. However, commission rates were still fixed in the 1960s and this was not an option.

The technological divide between firms like Merrill that had computerized their settlement systems and those that had not became apparent not through price competition, but as a result of the problems created by the rapidly increasing volume of trade in the late 1960s. New York Stock Exchange member firms relying upon manual back-office procedures were unable to cope with the transaction volume that faced them and as a result member firms faced a back-office crisis in the 1967–70 period, which Seligman (1982: 450) characterizes as 'the most serious failure of securities industry self-regulation in the [Securities and Exchange] Commission's history'. Losses associated with 'too much business' led approximately 160 NYSE member firms

---

[25] By 'wholesale' we typically refer to old-line banks like Morgan Stanley and Kuhn, Loeb devoted primarily to serving the needs of a select corporate clientele. In contrast to 'retail'-oriented firms, they tended to maintain few, if any, branch offices, but could count a large number of prominent corporations among their underwriting and advisory clients. See Hayes (1971, 1979) for a classification of the prominent banks, along with the branch and client statistics.

[26] *New York Times*, July 17, 1971.

either to merge with competitors or to dissolve their operations. Contemporary press descriptions of back-office operations at these firms paint a picture of mass confusion.[27]

In 1968, the standard measure of operational inefficiency became the frequency with which a firm failed to complete a transaction through the delivery of stock certificates. Among the major retail firms, Goodbody suffered 'fails' in excess of 30 days equal to about 52 percent of its capitalization, while Hayden, Stone, and Glore Forgan suffered fails equal to about 28 and 49 percent of their respective capitalizations. In contrast, failures reported by Merrill Lynch (2.3 percent) and Bache (4.2 percent) were modest. Among wholesale firms, those suffering the highest fail rates were those, like Goldman Sachs (60 percent of capital) and Bear, Stearns (77 percent), with large institutional trading operations. In contrast, Morgan Stanley, Lehman Brothers, and Kuhn, Loeb all suffered fail rates of the order three percent of capitalization or less.[28]

The NYSE initially attempted to contain the crisis by shortening the trading day, and then began to close on Wednesdays to allow member firms to process backlogged transactions. Trading volume and fails began to decline when the markets slowed in 1969, but subordinated lenders responded to the change in market conditions by withdrawing capital from the troubled firms. This created fears of a run on brokerage houses, to which NYSE member firms responded in 1970 by coordinating the acquisition of Goodbody by Merrill Lynch, the merging of Hayden, Stone with CBWL Inc., and the rescue of FI DuPont, Glore Forgan by a group led by H. Ross Perot.[29] Donald Regan, the chief executive officer of Merrill Lynch, reported in 1972 that Goodbody's demise was assured by last-minute efforts to automate their back-office operations. A number of other firms, including Lehman Brothers, suffered from their pursuit of a similar strategy.

The back-office crisis persuaded the securities trading industry of the virtues of computerization, and the exchanges subsequently upgraded their operations. In 1972, the NYSE and the American Stock

---

[27] See, for example, *New York Times*, December 23, 1970, p. 35.

[28] See Morrison and Wilhelm (2005*b*) for further details of a sample of 23 prominent wholesale and retail investment banks.

[29] Interestingly, Perot admitted at the time that his motive for backing DuPont was not to enter the brokerage business but to build an EDS data center on the back of operational shortcomings still prevalent on Wall Street. See *Institutional Investor*, March 3, 1971, p. 155.

Exchange introduced the Securities Industry Automation Corporation to provide automation and data processing services. This was followed in 1976 by the introduction of the NYSE's DOT system, which provided for computerized delivery of orders to the floor and for automatic execution if the floor member handling a stock (the specialist) chose not to improve upon current market quotes. In 1978 the Intermarket Trading System (ITS) was introduced as the first electronic system aimed at integrating, and thus promote competition between, the various securities exchanges.[30]

Finally, the crisis was the catalyst for changes to Exchange membership rules, and hence to the organization of the retail part of the investment banking sector. Many retail banks had avoided computerization because they believed that their operations were too small to justify the necessary capital expenditure. We have already argued (p. 228) that investment bank size is optimally selected by trading off the reputational dangers associated with a move into new markets against the benefits that come from larger-scale operations. The settlement problems of the late 1960s demonstrated conclusively that computerization had shifted the balance in favor of economies of scale. Hence retail banks had realized at the start of the 1970s that they needed to increase their capitalization and their operating scales sufficiently to justify investment in back-office computerization.

Attempts by retail investment banks to increase their capitalization were however stymied by an NYSE rule that prohibited public ownership of its members. Pressure to repeal this rule had started to build in the 1960s, but the Exchange had been unwilling to do so for fear that a consequence would be an antitrust suit challenging another Exchange rule, which prevented institutional investors from joining the Exchange on the grounds that their primary purpose was not the transaction of business as a broker or dealer in securities.[31] In the wake of the back-office crisis the Exchange relaxed its rules, and triggered a wave of IPOs by retail-oriented investment banks. Donaldson, Lufkin, Jenrette, a rising institutional broker, stated that it had been forced to decline institutional business for want of the capital necessary to computerize and fund the expansion of its block-trading business, and it was the first firm to go public. Fifteen more

---

[30] See Seligman (1982: ch. 12) for a detailed account of the early debate surrounding the development of a 'national market system'.
[31] Seligman (1982: 467).

NYSE member firms shortly followed suit, including Merrill Lynch, EF Hutton, Bache, Paine Webber, and Dean Witter.[32]

When the NYSE relaxed its membership rules, it was forced to face the question of institutional investor membership. The institutions had been attracted to Exchange membership in the 1960s because existing NYSE rules required members to charge a fixed commission rate on trades by nonmembers. As the effort required to perform a stock trade is invariant to the number of shares traded this rule was illogical and undermined price competition among both brokers and investment management firms. The change in membership rules that occurred in the wake of the back-office crises resulted inevitably in a relaxation of the commission-fixing rules. By 1972, the SEC had enabled competitive commission rates for transactions exceeding $500,000, which accounted for about five percent of commission income. This ceiling was reduced steadily, and fixed commissions were finally abolished on May 1, 1975. By year end 1980, commissions as a percentage of transaction value had declined by 57 percent for institutional investors and by 20 percent for individual investors.[33]

REAL-TIME COMPUTATION

As we saw on page 227, computing speed increased rapidly after the Second World War through to the 1967 introduction of the first minicomputer, after which it leveled out until the middle of the 1980s. Developments in this period reduced the cost of computing. Figure 8.4 illustrates the trend, showing the cost per million instructions. To provide a concrete illustration, the speed to price ratio of the IBM 4341 in 1979 was 1,143,000 times the ratio for the comparable IBM machine in 1953 (the 650).[34]

Task Management in the Front Office

The collapse in the 1980s of per-unit computation costs facilitated the introduction of distributed, desktop microcomputers. For the first time it was possible for workers to interrogate their own computers in real time, rather than running large batch processes of the type we discussed on page 227. Almost immediately, investment banks started

---

[32] See Seligman (1982: 467) and, for additional detail, Morrison and Wilhelm (2005*b*). We discuss the rationale for investment bank flotations in greater detail in the following chapter.

[33] Seligman (1982: 484).   [34] Cortada (1993: 193).

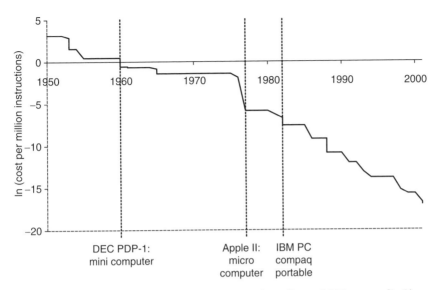

Figure 8.4. *Cost of computing, 1950–2001 (Nordhaus, 2001: appendix 2)*

to use real time computer applications to assist their front office staff. For example, account managers at major institutional trading houses such as Salomon, Merrill, and Goldman began to use computers to track the positions and preferences of their institutional investors.[35] One obvious consequence of this was that one person could manage many more accounts: in other words, front-office computerization extended the reach of the human capitalist.

Front-office staff could only interrogate computers in real time if they knew how to speak to them. The most important tool in facilitating this was the electronic spreadsheet. Spreadsheets allow people without a computer programming background to manipulate large tables of data, and to calculate statistics concerning their contents with ease. This was a massive boon to financial analysts, whose job involves the projection of corporate cash flows into the future so that they can be discounted back to today for valuation purposes. Before the advent of the spreadsheet analysts had been forced either to work with pencil, paper, and a hand calculator, or to operate within an inflexible analytic environment designed by a technology expert. They could now easily design and modify models for themselves, and could easily recalculate their figures so as to understand the sensitivity of their results to the assumptions that they made. Hence, like account

[35] *New York Times*, October 19, 1986, p. 150.

management software, the spreadsheet extended the reach and increased the effectiveness of the front-office human capitalist. It was the basis of the so-called 'deal factories' that First Boston pioneered in the early 1980s.[36]

Moves toward front-office automation have continued to gather pace in recent years, and human capitalists are increasingly displaced by new technologies. Hedge funds increasingly rely upon computers to perform real-time price analysis and to suggest arbitrage trades. Today's institutional investors can submit orders to electronic intermediaries, and have them instantly routed without human intervention to whichever worldwide exchange can offer the most competitive price. This type of trade has created increasingly international competition between exchanges. And this competition has forced the exchanges to bypass the human agency even of their member brokers: large investors can now obtain direct access to the London Stock Exchange's electronic trading platform.[37]

Underwriting Practice

Throughout this chapter, we have stressed the importance of the trade-off identified on page 93 of chapter three between realizing economies of scale and the associated reputational risk of moving into unfamiliar markets. Batch-processing technology tilted the balance in favor of expansion for retail investment banks, for whom the technology was useful and the reputational dangers inherent in expansion were low; because they found the technology less applicable and expansion would have exposed their reputations, wholesale banks did not adopt it.

Distributed processing created a similar trade-off in securities underwriting. While new technologies open the door to the automation of many underwriting activities, adopting them diminishes the extent to which the investment bank risks its reputation in underwriting, and so diminishes the value of reputation to the process. Using the technology does not *risk* the underwriter's reputation; it merely removes it, and its beneficial effects, from the issuance activity. Nevertheless, the central trade-off is a familiar one: new technologies will be

---

[36] See *Fortune* January 20, 1986 and Baker and Smith (1998: 55) for Jerome Kohlberg's observations on the spreadsheet's impact on the leveraged buyout (LBO) business. In chapter ten we discuss the importance of spreadsheets in the recent move toward the outsourcing of investment analysis.

[37] 'Supercomputers Speed Up Game', Edward Taylor, Aaron Lucchetti, and Alistair MacDonald, p. C1, *Wall Street Journal* April 14, 2004.

introduced into the underwriting process to the extent that they generate efficiency gains that outweigh the cost of removing the investment banker's reputational capital from it. Our central argument is that investment bankers use their reputations to generate socially valuable information about new security issues. Hence a new technology will be introduced into the underwriting process when either information discovery is less relevant, or when the technology substitutes for the investment banker's information discovery role.

Information discovery is less important when securities are easily valued. For example, fixed-income securities yield a well-defined cash flow stream. Because they are senior to equity securities, they are more likely to realize their promised cash flows. In many instances, close or perfect substitutes for new bond issues already trade in liquid markets. Each of these features diminishes the marginal value of the information accessible through an investment bank's investor network.

Equity cash flows are less easily valued. Furthermore, information about specific equity issues is closely held by a few insiders, particularly in industries like pharmaceuticals, where only a limited number of people really understand the value of an innovation. Investors in this market are subject to a winner's curse problem (see p. 85 of chapter three), and as a result rely more upon the certification that a reputable underwriter brings to an issue. Hence, investment banker networks and investment banker reputation are both particularly valuable in equity underwriting.

Our argument suggests that, because bond offerings are easier to price and rely less upon investment bank reputation than equity offerings, they should be the first to experience disintermediation. This prediction is borne out by the evidence regarding 'off-the-shelf' securities offerings. These stem from the March 1982 adoption of SEC Rule 415,[38] which provides for prospective issuers to file 'shelf registration' documents for the sale of a maximum amount of a specific class of securities at one or more points within two years of the registration.

In line with our argument, shelf-registered offerings were most common among debt securities for which intermediation demand was weaker. In 1982, 38 percent of the dollar value of negotiated debt offerings was sold off-the-shelf, and by 1984 this figure had risen to 52 percent of debt offerings. In contrast, only 1.6 percent of equity was sold off the shelf in 1982, rising to 20 percent the

---

[38] See Auerbach and Hayes (1986).

following year and then dropping back to nine percent in 1984.[39] The immediate consequence of the introduction of shelf registration was to place downward pressure on margins in the more commodity-like transactions. Because they were under greater competitive pressure, a secondary consequence was to force banks to seek more efficient ways of providing their intermediary services.

While we argued on pages 76 and 85 of chapter two that underpricing of IPOs and investment banker discrimination over share allocations are a feature of efficient stock offerings, both have been the source of recent criticism of traditional underwriting methods. Many critics of the traditional relational approach to underwriting suggest that a better system would be to offer securities for sale at auction, using an explicit set of rules for pricing and allocation which neither the investment bank nor the issuer would be able to override. Their protagonists argue that the case for such auctions is greatly strengthened by the development of the Internet, which dramatically reduces the cost of appealing to, and obtaining feedback from, a large cross section of the investor community. Hence, arguably, the need for investment banker reputation is greatly diminished, while the efficiency gains from computerization are greater than ever before. Experiments in this type of disintermediated sale of complex securities have been under way since the 1998 founding of W.R. Hambrecht.[40]

THE REVOLUTION IN FINANCIAL ECONOMICS

New Theory

Advances in financial economic theory altered investment banking practice and transformed the financial marketplace in the second half of the twentieth century. In this section we briefly outline these developments, as a precursor to a discussion of their effect upon trading and underwriting practice.[41] The major developments came in two stages: first, work on portfolio theory allowed for the accurate measurement of investment characteristics and performance; and

[39] Auerbach and Hayes (1986: figures 7.2 and 7.3).

[40] See Wilhelm (2005) for a detailed discussion of the debate as well as of the expanding body of academic literature that bears on the economic function of investment banks in securities offerings. As of January 31, 2006, Hambrecht had completed 16 electronic IPO auctions. The largest was for $141 million; only two others exceeded $50 million.

[41] For an accessible lengthier account of the theoretical developments, see Bernstein (1996b).

second, work on relative pricing allowed for the creation and valuation of new and complex derivatives instruments.

The first major step in the creation of financial economic theory came from work in the 1950s that provided methodologies and formulae for quantifying the *riskiness* of portfolios of securities.[42] Building on this work, a number of authors developed theories to predict the relationship between the riskiness of a security and its expected return.[43] These models are based upon relatively simple statistical measures of risk and return, but they need a large number of price observations if they are to be accurately estimated. Increased computer power and rising trading volumes ensured that this was possible.

The second conceptual step forward concerned *relative valuation*. Security and firm valuation both rest upon estimates of future cash flow streams, which are discounted to the present. The rate at which cash flows are discounted depends upon both the time value of money and the riskiness of the cash flow stream. Armed with the risk measures from the previous paragraph, analysts can draw comparisons on a risk-adjusted basis between alternative securities providing similar cash flow streams. In the extreme, securities with identical cash flows and the same risk should have the same price in a well-functioning market. If they do not then traders have an incentive to 'arbitrage' the difference, by selling the expensive security and buying the cheap one to lock in a riskless profit.

If markets function well, arbitrage opportunities of this type should be few and far between. Exploiting them tends to push up low prices and to drive down high prices until all profit potential is exhausted. Hence the implications for market equilibrium that flow from such 'no arbitrage' arguments provide a foundation for analyzing the *relative* risk and prices of a wide range of financial instruments.

This argument was the basis of the financial economic research that had perhaps the greatest impact upon financial practice. Work by Black and Scholes (1973) and Merton (1973) showed how, by creating a portfolio of shares and bonds, a trader could create precisely the cash flows that come from a complex derivative security.[44] It follows from

---

[42] See Markowitz (1952).

[43] The most important of these were the Capital Asset Pricing Model of Sharpe (1964), Litner (1965) and Mossin (1966), and the Arbitrage Pricing Theory of Ross (1976).

[44] In their original work, the derivative was an option: see page 9 for a definition of these instruments. The method that Black, Scholes, and Merton created can be applied to any derivative contract.

the no arbitrage discussion of the previous paragraph that the value of the portfolio must be the same as the value of the derivative. Their work in this field won the 1997 Nobel Prize in economics for Merton and Scholes. Sadly, Black died before his contribution was recognized by the Nobel committee.[45]

Trading Room and Investment Management Practice

The revolution in financial economics had clear implications for the extent to which human judgment can be replaced by standardized practices. If one can write an equation that accurately describes the linkage between two or more securities, then *human judgment* regarding the relationship between the security prices is redundant, and there is nothing to prevent it from being codified for repetitive electronic execution. The second wave of computing advances enabled this shift toward large-scale codified trading. Pricing, trading, and risk-management practices that previously had relied upon judgment exercised by individual traders were increasingly computerized. Advances of this nature did not displace human agency completely, but they did increase dramatically the reach of human capitalists capable of exercising the best judgment. In extremis, codification reduced some trading strategies to complex but codified computer algorithms. By the end of 2004, an estimated 25 percent of equities trading volume was driven by algorithmic trading strategies. The dominant platforms for algorithmic trading are now maintained by the bulge bracket banks like Goldman Sachs: they are used both for proprietary trading and as a prime brokerage service to institutional investors, chiefly hedge funds. In 2004, about $200 million dollars was spent on information technology components for algorithmic trading.[46]

---

[45] Merton's and Scholes's Nobel lectures, both of which were published in the June 1998 issue of the *American Economic Review*, provide an accessible discussion of the technology and its applications over the quarter century following its discovery. For a comprehensive technical treatment, see Merton (1990). For earlier Nobel Prize–winning work that also rested upon no arbitrage arguments, this time in the field of corporate finance, see Modigliani and Miller (1958).

[46] This included $123 million on order management systems, $50 million on routing systems, and $30 million on databases. For a detailed discussion of the major platforms, activity levels and IT spending levels, see Aite Group, LLC. (2005), 'Algorithmic Trading' and 'Bulge Bracket Firms and Algorithmic Trading'. Aite also estimate that in the United States alone, the securities industry spent over $26 billion on IT in 2005, with JP Morgan and Morgan Stanley each spending over $2 billion. See *The Economist*, February 2, 2006.

The effect upon investment banking practices of the revolution in finance is revealed by a simple comparison of modern university finance textbooks with those of the past. Earlier texts tended toward description, and hence depended heavily upon accounting presentations of particular examples. In contrast, modern treatments employ the analytical tools of the economist, and they emphasize general principles. The modern emphasis upon the application of general principles to multiple financial topics is redolent of the engineer's application of physical principles. The frequent modern allusions to 'financial engineering' refer to a series of techniques that create and value complex financial securities using theoretical building blocks that can be acquired in the classroom. Modern financial innovations are frequently created by combining these blocks to create tailored deal structures to fit the client's requirements, or to perform 'regulatory arbitrage' of the gaps between economic logic and accounting and regulatory practice.[47]

Through the 1980s an understanding of the new financial economics was increasingly regarded as essential for trading room personnel and portfolio managers. As we have seen, this knowledge can be codified in textbooks and acquired in the classroom. Hence, business schools were increasingly regarded as an important tool for disseminating essential practical knowledge. The trend manifested itself in the hiring practices of the 1980s, when there was a sharp increase in the recruitment of entry-level bankers from top MBA programs.[48]

The Value of Dealing Room Reputational Capital

The financial economics revolution has led to a sharp rise in competition. Skills that previously could be acquired only through a long apprenticeship within a financial institution can now be learned in the classroom, and are therefore in unrestricted supply. To some extent,

---

[47] See Miller (1986) for an interesting early discussion of the link between financial innovation and these advances in financial economic theory.

[48] In the years 1970–1 degree-granting institutions conferred about 26,000 masters degrees in business. In 1985–6, the number rose to about 67,000 degrees (US Dept. of Education, Digest of Education Statistics, 2001). In 1965, only eight percent of Harvard's MBA class accepted jobs in investment banking. 21 percent of the graduating class of 1969 entered investment banking and this remained the record until 1986 when 29 percent went into investment banking (*Wall Street Journal*, June 16, 1987). Similarly, 18.8 percent of NYU's graduating class went into investment banking in 1986. In addition to technological forces, the trend was influenced in the 1960s by pressure to replace a generation of retiring partners for whom relatively few successors were groomed during the post-Second World War era (Hayes, 1971).

the human element in investment banking has been commoditized. Moreover, investment banks are less reliant upon reputation to certify the skills of their people. The consequential reduction in barriers to entry has narrowed the profit margins for many investment banker human capitalists, and competitive pressures have led market participants to seek scale economies. The pursuit of economies of scale has, in turn, increased the relative demand for financial over human capital, to fund investments in technology and to provide a cushion against greater risk-taking.

A consequence of this change is that investment banks that operate primarily in the securities markets have found that the value of their reputation is greatly diminished. Bankers who saw this coming had an incentive to liquidate their reputation while it lasted, by selling inappropriate and expensive products to customers who were still prepared to trust them. This is one interpretation of the precipitous ascent and subsequent decline of Bankers Trust in the mid-1990s.[49]

Bankers Trust rose to prominence on the back of the advances in information technology and financial economics. In the mid-1970s it was a moderately sized commercial bank, with a respectable presence in the New York retail banking market.[50] Like the rest of the American economy, the retail banking sector was transformed by information technology. A particularly significant development was the advent of the automated teller machine, which lowered the marginal cost of performing many routine transactions to zero. Retail banks that adopted this technology on a sufficient scale to cover its fixed costs therefore achieved significant economies; the cotemporaneous deregulation of interest rates enabled them to beat non-adopters in price competition. Bankers Trust was not well positioned to achieve the necessary economies of scale, and by 1984 it had withdrawn from retail banking.

As information technology closed one business line for Bankers Trust, it opened another. Desktop computing and financial economics were combined from the late 1970s to codify a good deal of security market practice. As we noted on page 225, this lowered the barriers to entry for security-related businesses. Under the leadership of Charles

---

[49] Background information for this section is drawn from *Bankers Trust New York Corporation*, Harvard Business School, case no. 9-286-005, 1985 (revised 7/19/91), *Fortune*, September 7, 1992, *The Economist*, March 12, 1994 and April 8, 1995 and *Wall Street Journal*, April 22, 1994, March 17, 1995, and April 18, 1995.

[50] Bankers Trust was the seventh largest commercial bank in the United States, and the fifth largest in New York, where it maintained a network of over 100 branch offices.

Sanford, who would become the bank's chairman in 1987, Bankers Trust took advantage of this change by moving aggressively into trading businesses that relied upon the new financial economics. By the end of the 1980s, Bankers Trust was recognized as the leading innovator in the OTC derivatives market. The firm's spectacular ascent was due partly to its wholesale adoption of the new financial theory, and partly to its privileged status as a commercial bank.

In contrast to a traditional investment bank like JP Morgan & Co., Bankers built its new business upon financial engineering techniques that its employees learned in the major professional schools.[51] It did not maintain the strong client relationships that were associated with traditional investment banking, and it relied upon its reputation for financial sophistication to capture what business it received in traditional investment banking activities.[52] In 1991, financing transactions accounted for only six percent of the firm's profits, and client advisory services for another 17 percent.[53] The firm's real profits were made in the trading businesses where it could most effectively deploy its technical skills. In both 1992 and 1993, Bankers made profits in excess of $1 billion and in 1993, 31 percent of these were derived from the sale of risk-management products, and 56 percent from proprietary trading.[54]

Bankers Trust's reliance upon traded financial instruments allowed it to subject its risk position to sophisticated computer analysis. The firm was a pioneer in adopting the VaR analysis that we discussed on page 27, using its systems to compute a formal measure of risk-adjusted return on capital (RAROC) for its portfolio. This type of analysis is commonplace today, but its early implementation by Bankers Trust gave the firm an advantage in identifying the most attractive business lines, and in deploying its capital accordingly. For example, Bankers Trust used its RAROC systems to identify commercial loans as a poor use of capital, and it adopted a 'zero hold' policy, under which all loans carried terms that made them strong candidates for resale or participation.

[51] The *Wall Street Journal* noted on April 22, 1994 that Bankers Trust attracted the 'best and brightest among the mathematics wizards coming out of the top schools like MIT and the Wharton School at the University of Pennsylvania.'

[52] As we note below, Bankers Trust had a policy of not holding positions. This allowed them to make the most of their capital base, but it undermined the firm's attempts to enter the underwriting business. Its greatest successes in underwriting were in junk bonds, where it helped to fill the void left by Drexel (see p. 260 below).

[53] K. Singh and A. Perold, 1994, *Bankers Trust: Global Investment Bank*, Harvard Business School case no. 9-295-010.

[54] *Wall Street Journal*, April 22, 1994.

Bankers Trust combined its technical expertise with a higher credit rating than most of its competitors. This was partly a consequence of the firm's extensive use of RAROC systems, but it also derived from its commercial banking license, which allowed it to accept deposits. Unlike other creditors, depositors are relatively unconcerned with the riskiness of the banks to which they lend, because they are protected by a deposit insurance fund, which will bail them out if the bank fails. Moreover, there is a widespread perception that the consequences of a very large commercial bank failure would be so catastrophic that no regulator would allow it to happen. As it grew, Bankers Trust was increasingly perceived as 'too big to fail', which gave its nondepositor creditors an additional degree of comfort in their lending. Hence, Bankers could carry out its risky business with a lower cost of capital than its competitors, and it attracted a correspondingly higher credit rating. In the early stages of the OTC derivatives market this gave the firm a substantial competitive advantage, particularly in the growing market for cross-border transactions whose enforcement remained uncertain.[55]

But it was inevitable that the forces that enabled Bankers Trust to rise so rapidly to the top of the derivatives business would eventually start to undermine its position. Bankers entered the derivatives markets by building a team of very talented employees who were well-versed in new financial and information technologies. As we noted above, many of their skills were learned not through a lengthy on-the-job apprenticeship, but were instead absorbed in mathematical university classes. If Bankers could attract these people as they left the professional schools then so too could their competitors. And as financial engineering skills permeated the broad investment banking market, competition would intensify, and trading spreads would narrow. Bankers Trust's reputation as a uniquely able financial engineer therefore had a strictly limited shelf-life. At the same time, the bank's commercial banking license was increasingly in jeopardy, as its

[55] In principle, investment banks competing in the derivatives markets could have raised their credit ratings by increasing their capitalization. As we note in the following chapter, this was in fact occurring at the time, but some important investment banking functions remained relatively less dependent on financial capital. While Bankers Trust had a relatively small presence in these areas, its competitors did not and as a result, it would have been highly inefficient for them to post sufficient capital to maintain a AAA credit rating. In the early 1990s, a number of investment banks, led by Merrill Lynch and Salomon Brothers, addressed this problem by establishing AAA-rated subsidiaries that enabled them to focus their capital on the businesses for which it was necessary. Similar technology is widely employed today by commercial banks in their asset securitization business.

risk-taking activities came under increasing scrutiny by regulators who had come to view it as similar to a hedge fund.[56]

Bankers was an extremely and increasingly aggressive trader. Whether its strategy was a deliberate attempt to maximize profits without regard for its reputation while it still had a competitive edge and a commercial banking license, or whether it was a response to the increasingly competitive environment, is hard to say. But it seems clear that the aggressive pursuit of profits, and the high-powered incentive schemes that accompanied it, created an environment in which employees showed little concern for the long-term reputation of the firm. As we have argued, their attitudes were a rational response to the challenges that faced Bankers as its formerly unique talents became ubiquitous, but they resulted in a rather more rapid decline than was necessary. In 1993 three clients, Procter & Gamble, Gibson Greetings, and Mead, suffered substantial losses on contracts that ultimately were judged to more nearly have served Bankers Trust's interests than to have addressed risk-management problems.[57] Arguably, the rogue traders whom Bankers blamed for these trades were responding to incentives that reflected the firm's rapidly shrinking franchise in the OTC derivatives market. Certainly, the reputational damage that Bankers Trust sustained in the wake of these cases was far more profound than the direct costs that they experienced,[58] and it became impossible for it to continue as an independent force. The firm was acquired in 1999 by Deutsche Bank.

NEW HUMAN CAPITAL BUSINESSES

We have analyzed many businesses in which the value of human capital has been eroded by the technological advances of the last 50 years. But new technology has also created fresh opportunities for investment bank human capitalists. Investment bankers coordinated corporate America's response to the emergence of computer technology. Starting in the 1980s, this involved an explosion in levels of security issuance relative to the economy (see figure 8.5). It also generated an increasing requirement for advice both from reorganizing bankrupt companies, and from companies who were merging.

---

[56] *Fortune*, September 7, 1992.   [57] *Wall Street Journal*, April 22, 1994.
[58] In December 1994 and without admitting guilt, Bankers paid a $10 million fine in relation to the Gibson Greetings losses; in May 1996 Bankers and P&G reached an out-of-court settlement in which P&G paid Bankers $30 million, less than a third of what Bankers claimed they were owed on derivatives trades.

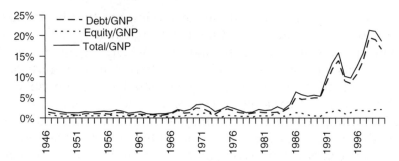

Figure 8.5. *Underwritten debt and equity (common and preferred) as a percentage of GNP*

> *Sources*: US Department of Commerce, Federal Reserve Board, and SIA Factbook.

Before we examine the development of the new advisory businesses, we touch briefly upon the opportunities that expanding global securities markets created for investment bankers to deploy their ability to create and to enforce private law.

Private Law Making

Private law was important in the development of the Eurobond markets. A July 1963 decision by the US government to tax foreign issuers of dollar bonds in America sent these borrowers to Europe, where they issued dollar-denominated debt outside the jurisdiction of the US authorities. The first such bond was brought to market by S.G. Warburg, a British merchant bank, although US investment banks were quick to follow them to the market. A significant market rapidly developed for debt offerings sold outside the borrower's domestic market and denominated in an international currency (usually not the borrower's home currency). Although many of these bonds were not issued in Europe, they were known collectively as Eurobonds.

Competition in the Eurobond market was intense, and the competition led to innovation, evidenced, for example, by the early development of rival systems for clearing transactions, each of which was regarded as 'more modern and less costly than most of the national clearing systems'. All of this took place outside of a state-sponsored political or regulatory infrastructure, but it could not have occurred without simultaneous advances in communications and computing technology.[59]

---

[59] See Hayes and Hubbard (1990: ch. 2 and 3) for a detailed account of the market's early evolution.

In the early years of the derivatives market, valuation and trading technologies developed faster than the laws that supported them. The global OTC markets for derivatives therefore generated substantial interjurisdictional conflicts in their early days, arising in this case from enforcement uncertainty in cross-border transactions. Initially, the market depended heavily on reputation and the ability of counterparties to postfinancial capital as a performance bond. Ultimately, the International Swap Dealers Association (ISDA) emerged to support the standardization of contracts and their enforcement.[60]

Reorganization Advisory Work

The equity receivership, which we described on pages 176–182 of chapter six, was a common law mechanism for dealing with the reorganization of financially distressed firms which was largely created by investment bankers. It allowed the banker to bring his familiarity and relationship with the debtor to bear upon debt renegotiations, and it relied upon the enlightened self-interest of the investment banker to balance the many competing interests in the reorganization process. As we discussed on page 212 of chapter seven, the 1938 Chandler Act swept all of this away, and replaced it with a statute-based approach. Chapter X of the Act, which was intended to govern the reorganization of publicly held companies, made no use of the special skills and relationships of the investment banker. It is hardly surprising that, as we noted in chapter seven, it resulted in a significant drop in bankruptcy filings.

Although the intention was that public firms would reorganize under chapter X of the Chandler Act, an alternative procedure, chapter XI, was available for smaller, closely held firms with less secured debt. Chapter XI did not require the firm's management to step down, it did not impose absolute priority, and it involved little SEC oversight. Moreover, any firm could petition for chapter XI reorganization, whereas chapter X reorganizations required a demonstration of the

---

[60] On a similar note, Ljungqvist, Jenkinson, and Wilhelm (2003) provide evidence that US banks, specifically, promoted global integration in primary equity markets through the diffusion of bookbuilding practices. In a close parallel with the chapter six discussion of early investment banks enabling capital flows from European investors into the United States, they demonstrate that the success of US banks rested, in no small part, on their ability to bring their networks of sophisticated investors to bear in non-domestic markets. Frankel (1998) provides a detailed account of the interplay between public and private lawmaking bodies in cross-border asset securitizations, and also draws an analogy between law in this market and the capacity for trusts formed under Anglo-American legal systems to divide control and property rights among different parties.

need for greater structure and oversight provided therein.[61] For most large firms, the choice was simple and a new generation of reorganization law boutiques rose to prominence by guiding public firms into the friendlier confines of chapter XI.[62] Their would-be regulators found it difficult to cast this geographically diffuse group as a powerful elite that was threatening to the economy at large.

The boutiques had considerable success in helping firms to avoid the burdens of chapter X, but Charles Seligson observed that the 'SEC's authority to insist that cases be transferred to chapter X hung "like the sword of Damocles" over the proceedings.'[63] The SEC did not have the resources to challenge each of the increasingly large number of chapter XI filings by public companies during the late 1950s and early 1960s, but when it did challenge them it was frequently successful.[64] Thus, in spite of the loophole that enabled public firms to pursue chapter XI reorganization, the danger that they would be denied the option gave managers a strong incentive to take actions that would strengthen their case for chapter XI reorganization in the event of financial distress.

The loose guidelines followed by the SEC in challenging chapter XI filings reflected the Commission's mandate to protect the interests of *public* securities holders. A firm that wanted to leave open the option of a chapter XI filing would therefore issue public securities only to those investors who were likely to favor chapter XI. Chapter X reorganizations involved strict adherence to absolute priority, and hence were favored by debtholders, whereas equityholders would favor a chapter XI filing, whose more flexible rules left open the possibility of negotiations that would violate absolute priority in their favor. Hence, if they favored chapter XI over chapter X filings, managers who weighed the threat of financial distress when raising new debt had a clear incentive to issue private rather than public debt.

---

[61] See Skeel (2001: 162) for a fascinating account of how this unintended loophole generated regulatory arbitrage and litigation, and led to calls for bankruptcy reform that culminated with the passage of the Bankruptcy Code of 1978.

[62] Skeel (2001: 162) identifies Benjamin Weintraub, Harris Levin, Charles Seligson, and George Triester as key figures within this group, whose practices provided the basis for the chapter 11 guidelines set forth in the 1978 Code.

[63] Skeel (2001: 160–1).

[64] Skeel (2001: 164) notes that although several Supreme Court decisions favored SEC challenges to chapter XI filings, Justice Douglas' opinion in the 1956 *General Stores Corp.* v. *Shlensky* case substantially undermined the Commission's influence by explicitly calling for case-by-case consideration of the appropriate reorganization chapter.

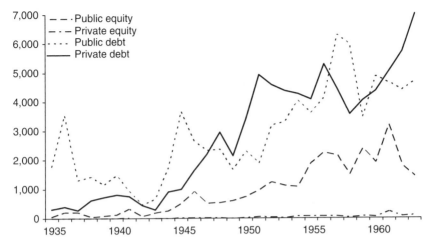

Figure 8.6. *Public and private securities issuance, 1935–63*
Source: Longstreet and Hess (1967: 338, table 6.1).

This discussion suggests an explanation for figure 8.6, which illustrates a sharp rise in private securities placements coincidentally with the decline in chapter X filings. Historians and financial economists have in the past explained this trend as reflecting the costs and uncertainties in the registration process introduced by the 1933 Securities Act.[65] However, the above argument suggests that, at least in part, the change may have reflected the introduction of, and the market's adaptation to, the Chandler Act. As the figure shows, private debt offerings accounted for almost the entire value of privately placed securities between 1938 and 1963.

As we will see in the next subsection, takeover activity expanded in the 1970s, and much of it was financed using debt securities. As a result, instances of financial distress in America increased. This made the problems in the Chandler Act more apparent, and resulted in the 1978 Bankruptcy Code. The new code eliminated the uncertainty and conflict that surrounded the filing venue under the Chandler Act by

[65] See Carosso (1970: 425) for a discussion in the context of the TNEC hearings of 1939–40. Abramovitz (1942) reviews the TNEC reports on savings and investment and draws attention to the substantial (although not dominant) role of large insurance companies in directing capital for corporate investment. By providing an easily identified market of large scale, sophisticated investors, the continued growth of institutional investment diminished the importance of the investment bank's distribution function. Longstreet and Hess (1967) provide a detailed account of the market's evolution and the changing role of the investment banker.

combining chapters X and XI of that Act to form the new chapter 11. At a stroke, chapter 11 reversed most of the provisions in the Chandler Act that had prevented investment banks from taking an active role in corporate reorganization. It also allowed managers to continue to control bankrupt companies as they had under the old equity receivership, and it sharply diminished the threat of financial distress faced by the managers of distressed firms. The SEC's involvement in corporate restructurings was ended, and the new code shifted supervision to an entity called the US Trustee, which played a part that Skeel (2001: 181) characterizes as a 'pale echo of the SEC's former role'.

The 1978 Code also addressed the incentives faced by professional advisers. The Bankruptcy Act of 1898 prescribed an 'economy of administration standard', which, in an attempt to preserve the value of the corporate estate, effectively limited the fees paid to professionals involved in a reorganization to below-market levels. The consequence was that it was hard for distressed companies to find good professional advice. Despite the fact that large firms routinely made their way into the safe harbor of chapter XI, only a few boutiques specialized in providing advice to distressed firms, and banks typically did not maintain specialized restructuring groups.[66] When they did provide professional advice, banks did not expect to receive adequate compensation for their work.

Two prominent reorganizations from the 1970s illustrate this point. The valuation services provided by First Boston during the long and complicated reorganization of Equity Funding Corporation yielded a 'relatively modest fee' given the scale of the project. Similarly, Kuhn, Loeb advised the trustees in the reorganization of the Penn Central Railroad in the hope that its efforts would be rewarded with the opportunity to manage a divestiture of assets.[67]

Section 328 of the 1978 Code rejects the economy standard by authorizing the trustee to employ a 'professional person on any reasonable terms', so long as that person is disinterested.[68] This immediately

---

[66] See Baker and Smith (1998: 52).

[67] Personal correspondence with James W. Harris, March 8, 2006. Mr Harris headed Lehman's restructuring group before founding the restructuring advisory boutique, Seneca Financial (Kuhn, Loeb merged with Lehman in 1977). See the *Wall Street Journal* for summaries of the Equity Funding Asset transfer (October 3, 1977: 18) and the naming of Kuhn, Loeb as adviser to the Penn Central trustees (November 20, 1970).

[68] See 11 U.S.C. 328(a) and (c). But the adoption of Section 330(a)(2) under the 1994 Code gave courts and trustees a clear assurance of their authority to review and challenge professional fees. Section 101(14) defines disinterested status for an

resulted in the creation of new reorganization advisory profit centers in investment banks. The first banks to establish restructuring groups were Lehman (in 1981) and First Boston.

M&A Advisory Work

Advisory work encompassing mergers and acquisitions and restructuring services is a highly visible and well-compensated activity, but it is a relatively recent addition to the investment banking landscape. Throughout the first half of the twentieth century the major investment banks typically did not identify pure advisory functions as a specific line of business and advice was generally not rewarded directly with fees.[69] Instead,

> Investment bankers would counsel CFOs on the appropriate mix of debt and equity and would undertake due diligence investigation of corporate affairs required in conventional public issues of new securities. Investment banks undertook financial structure and strategy studies typically without charge, in the confident expectation of attractive management and distribution fees on future offerings in which they would be lead underwriters.[70]

This loose linkage between advice and compensation was sustained by relational contracts that rested on repeat dealing and reputational concerns.[71] Table 8.1 demonstrates the strength of underwriting relationships for twelve major banks during the 1950s and

investment banker: banks that have worked for a filing firm within the three years prior to the filing date do not meet the standard.

[69] According to Carosso (1970: 45–6), in the early part of the century banks typically received stock in the firms that they advised. An electronic search of the *New York Times* and The *Wall Street Journal* for simultaneous mentions of 'merger' and 'fees' in articles published between 1900 and 1960 yielded little evidence of direct fee payments for advisory services except for those paid to attorneys. A noteworthy example was the payment of $581,000 in cash and securities with estimated value of nearly $180,000 that Samuel Untermeyer received for work in connection with the consolidation of Utah Copper and Boston Consolidated Copper. The *Wall Street Journal* (January 21, 1910: 6) identified the fee as one of the largest on record. Untermeyer went on to fame as counsel for the Pujo Committee (see p. 198 of chapter seven).

[70] Hayes and Hubbard (1990: 130).

[71] Eccles and Crane (1988) coined the term 'loose linkage' in the context of an industry study founded on over 300 interviews conducted in seventeen US investments banks in 1986 and 1987. Given the dearth of public information available for many of these banks, the study is an exceptionally valuable contribution to knowledge of management practice within the industry.

Table 8.1. *Client underwriting relationships in the 1950s and 1960s*

Bank	1950–9			1960–9		
	Number of clients	Exclusive relationships (%)	Fraction of clients deals managed (%)	Number of clients	Exclusive relationships (%)	Fraction of clients deals Managed (%)
Blyth	308	26	63	152	32	64
Kidder, Peabody	185	32	64	252	40	70
First Boston	191	35	69	167	32	68
Lehman	129	37	65	193	33	65
White, Weld	129	26	58	174	28	61
Merrill Lynch	129	26	57	127	18	54
Goldman Sachs	80	24	61	141	34	64
Halsey Stuart	102	8	45	73	15	54
Morgan Stanley	82	26	58	65	57	81
Smith Barney	67	27	60	87	38	69
Salomon	52	15	53	117	6	50
Harriman	37	38	67	45	42	67
Average		**27**	**60**		**31**	**64**

Note: See n. 72 below for details of the data.

1960s.[72] On average, 27 percent of bank relationships during the 1950s were exclusive relationships. The fraction of clients with whom relationships were exclusive rose slightly during the 1960s. Similarly, during both decades, these banks managed a bit more than 60 percent of the transactions carried out by firms for which they were the dominant manager. In sum, through the 1960s underwriting relationships remained exclusive in the extreme and hence banks could provide advisory services with a reasonable expectation of compensation through subsequent securities transactions.

By 1971, however, industry observers were lamenting a new 'account-switching' trend.[73] As technological change led to an increasing degree of codification and commoditization of investment banking practice, it became increasingly possible to separate the advisory role of investment banks from the transaction execution function. As a result, investment banks found it harder to bundle their advisory work with their transaction execution business: if they wanted to be

[72] The data were collected from *Corporate Financing Directories* published by the *Investment Dealers' Digest*. They include public offerings, both underwritten and nonunderwritten, and private placements made with the services of underwriters. Issuers are defined as a bank's client if they carried out more than one offering during the decade and the bank for which they are identified as a client managed more of the firm's transactions than any other bank. In cases where two or more banks managed the same number of deals for a single firm, each was credited with having the firm as a client. A client relationship is classified as exclusive when the bank managed every transaction carried out by a client firm during the decade. Firms that issued only once during the decade are excluded because their banking relationship is exclusive by definition. Thus the results reported in table 8.1 understate the number of a bank's clients and the number of exclusive relationships. The percentage of client's deals managed is the average fraction of a client's deals managed by the bank in question. For example, during the 1950s, there were 308 issuing firms that carried out more than one transaction and for whom Blyth was the bank most frequently engaged to manage the firms' transactions. For 26 percent (80) of these issuing firms, Blyth managed every transaction during the decade. On average, Blyth managed 63 percent of the transactions carried out by its 308 client firms.

[73] 'Why Account-Switching is Accelerating', *Corporate Finance*, May/June 1971. Although concern within the industry remained high, Asker and Ljungqvist (2005) show (using a different measure of exclusivity for the 1970–2003 period) that relationship exclusivity did not diminish sharply until the mid-1990s. Similarly, although the propensity of firms to switch banks varied considerably during the 1970–2003 period, the trend in account-switching was relatively modest. Although we do not have sufficient data from the 1950–70 period to draw direct comparisons with these findings, we suspect that the industry's response to the relatively mild change in the landscape early on simply reflected a deeply embedded assumption that clients would remain captive indefinitely.

compensated for the advice which they gave, they had to demand a fee for it.

Banks, investment banks, and accounting firms therefore started to build merger departments in the mid-1960s: in a page-one article, the September 3, 1965 *Wall Street Journal*, reported that 'merger-makers' were starting to become 'a major factor in the corporate world.' The magnitude of the business was still relatively small at this stage. For example, Morgan Guaranty had opened a one-man merger department as recently as 1963. Lehman Brothers arranged about 20 mergers in 1964, or about double their average in previous years, earning 'payments' of $733 million.[74]

Possibly the preeminent advisory house at this time was Lazard Freres.[75] The advisory business in this bank was the creation of Andre Meyer, who was arguably the person most instrumental in the creation of a specialized investment bank advisory role. Meyer and his family came to New York in 1940 to escape the Vichy government in Paris. At this time, the New York Lazard office operated in much the same way as other investment banks did: they advised companies on financing strategy and they earned fees when their advice led to a securities underwriting mandate.[76] However, Meyer 'detested securities underwriting, dismissing it [as] mindless business'.[77] His early success in Europe had derived from a modern version of 'merchant banking' involving principal investment in, and oversight of, underperforming firms. As client demands became more complex and the conglomerate merger wave of the 1960s began to gather force, Meyer carved out a fee-generating role for Lazard in New York as an adviser and deal-maker. As Felix Rohatyn began to emerge from Meyer's considerable shadow in the middle of the decade, Lazard was in a

[74] It is not clear what form the 'payments' referred to in the article took, but bank fees at the height of the merger wave of the 1980s averaged between 50 and 60 basis points on the value of transactions involving targets of more than $10 million (*Corporate Finance*, February 1990: 17). Thus, it is implausible that this figure reflects direct fees for advisory services.

[75] The firm had 20 partners in 1965 and nominal capital per partner of $875,000. Lazard reported a constant capitalization of $17.5 million through 1980. The *New York Times* (May 28, 1972) reports a limited partner of the firm claiming this low figure was used to avoid a capital contest with other firms and suggested $60 million as a more accurate estimate. Given the enormous private wealth of the firm's senior partners as well as that of their close contacts, even this number probably understates the resources that the firm could have marshaled on short notice.

[76] Reich (1983: 45).   [77] Reich (1983: 48).

position to earn $2.1 million in advisory fees between 1966 and 1969 from ITT alone.[78]

Seligman (1982: 418) reports that between 1962 and 1969, 22 percent of the *Fortune* 500 manufacturing firms were acquired, and that over 80 percent of the acquisitions during this period were conglomerate mergers. Nevertheless, M&A advisory work still accounted for a relatively small part of investment banker revenue at the start of the 1970s.[79] In that decade, the US economy entered what Jensen (1993) characterizes as a 'modern industrial revolution', rivaling that of the late nineteenth and early twentieth century. It was necessary to reorder productive activity in response to the rapidly changing technological environment. In America, this involved an unprecedented level of corporate restructuring activity, as New Deal laws and regulations that constrained capital markets as a vehicle for exercising corporate control were eroded.[80] Between 1976 and 1990, 35,000 mergers and acquisitions were completed in the United States with a total value of $2.6 trillion (1992 dollars), of which 172 involved successful hostile takeovers.[81] Investment banks responded by moving aggressively into the market for M&A advice.

Over this period new specialized practices emerged for buyouts. The first of these was the 'bootstrap' acquisition, which began to appear with increasing frequency among small businesses after the Second World War.[82] The typical targets for bootstraps and for what later became known as LBOs were mature firms which were perceived as inefficiently managed but which had a capacity for throwing off a steady stream of cash. Investors seeking to gain control of the firm's assets would buy out existing owners with a small infusion of their own equity and a large amount of debt, which would be

---

[78] This amount does not include fees arising from the firm having leveraged its role as adviser to capture ITT's underwriting business, traditionally controlled by Kuhn, Loeb. See Reich (1983: 224–35).

[79] For example, Merrill Lynch's IPO prospectus gave no indication of a distinct M&A department, and nor did it identify any revenues between 1961 and 1970 as having arisen directly from advisory services. Morgan Stanley's M&A department was founded in 1972 by the firm's future president, Robert Greenhill (*The Deal* February 17, 2006). Greenhill, along with Felix Rohatyn, was the early prototype for the modern 'dealmaker'. They and others, like Joseph Parella and Bruce Wasserstein at First Boston, Geoffrey Boisi at Goldman Sachs, and Eric Gleacher at Morgan Stanley rose to prominence in their firms as advisory revenues skyrocketed in the 1980s. See *Investment Dealers' Digest*, April 28, 1986, pp. 26–9.

[80] See Roe (1991) and Jensen (1989).   [81] Jensen (1993: 837)

[82] The following discussion draws upon Baker and Smith (1998: ch. 2).

serviced by the firm's cash flows. If all went well, the acquirer would later sell the leveraged equity stake at a substantial premium.

The LBO grew out of the market for bootstraps. Jerome Kohlberg, then at Bear, Stearns, began experimenting with bootstraps in the early 1960s and by the end of the decade he had begun a specialized Bear, Stearns buyout practice along with George Roberts. They received little support within Bear, Stearns for their efforts and in 1976 they and Henry Kravis resigned Bear, Stearns partnerships to start a boutique firm, Kohlberg, Kravis, and Roberts (KKR). KKR would develop the LBO as one of the most important financial innovations of the last quarter of the century.

We have argued that technological changes rendered industrial restructuring inevitable. The LBO was an important tool by which this was accomplished in America. Leveraged buyouts allowed takeovers to be financed with little equity by small entrepreneurs who relied to a significant extent upon large-scale borrowing. Any size constraint to takeover activity was therefore removed.

Because LBOs relied to such a great extent upon debt finance, they typically involved bond issues that were subinvestment grade at the time of issuance. Prior to 1977 the market for this type of 'junk' bond was composed primarily of 'fallen angels': that is, of bonds issued at investment grade which were subsequently downgraded.[83] Drexel Burnham Lambert was a distant descendant of the firm in which J. Pierpont Morgan got his start in business (see p. 167) and in the 1970s had an established trading presence in the market for subinvestment grade debt, where the head of operations was Michael Milken. Acting on a conviction that the default rates on these bonds did not justify the high yields at which they traded, Milken almost single-handedly developed the market for the original-issue junk bonds upon which the LBO movement rested. The market grew from barely $10 billion at the beginning of the 1980s to over $200 billion outstanding, or over 20 percent of the total public corporate bond market, at the close of the decade.[84]

---

[83] Investment grade bonds comprise those rated Baa and above by Moody's or BBB and above by Standard & Poors, Duff & Phelps, and Fitch. Some regulated institutions, such as insurance companies, are prohibited from holding subinvestment grade bonds in their portfolios.

[84] Taggart (1990). The period witnessed a general shift from bank lending to debt raised through public debt markets. Between 1977 and 1983, commercial bank loans accounted for 36.6 percent of the total credit market debt raised, but only 18.2 percent of the total raised between 1984 and 1989. Over the same time intervals, borrowing

Drexel was not a prominent player in securities underwriting at the start of the 1980s, but it rapidly became the dominant force in both the primary and the secondary markets for junk bonds.[85] The firm underwrote 287 (46 percent) of the 618 subinvestment grade debt issues brought to market between 1978 and 1985, and in dollar terms accounted for 57 percent of the $46 billion of new issues brought to market.[86] Drexel's market power was such that, even in the face of increasing uncertainty regarding its survival, during its last full year of operations in 1989 the firm held 38.6 percent of the market for junk bond underwriting, or more than four times its nearest competitor (Shearson Lehman).

Michael Milken almost single-handedly built the market through a systematic application of the principles outlined in chapter three. He maintained an extensive network of repeat investors, over whom he ultimately gained considerable influence. Some investors became sufficiently confident in Milken's ability to place their funds in blind trusts under his control.[87] Investors placed their trust in Milken because he invested heavily in credit analysis and postissuance monitoring of the firms whose issues he backed. It was not unusual for Milken to buy back bonds at the issue price from dissatisfied investors and, until he was ousted under pressure from the US Department of Justice, Drexel was the primary source of secondary market liquidity for the entire market, including bonds which they did not underwrite. From the issuer's perspective, Milken's reputation for raising funds from his investor network on short notice was equally strong. More than a few LBOs were undertaken with a nonbinding verbal commitment or 'highly confident' letter from Milken guaranteeing the financing necessary for the transaction's success. By most accounts,

through public debt markets increased from 30.5 percent to 54.2 percent of total debt raised.

[85] The discussion here draws upon Benveniste, Singh, and Wilhelm (1993), who provide details of Drexel's rise to prominence.

[86] Altman and Nammacher (1987).

[87] This was one factor behind Milken's ability to raise the large sums of money on very short notice that made junk bonds a particularly attractive form of financing for hostile takeover bidders. As Michael Jensen (1989) observed, Milken's fund-raising capacity effectively eliminated the size of the acquirer as a consideration in a takeover attempt. Having said this, it is worth noting that, although junk bond financing played an important role, it was not the dominant form of financing during the 1980s mergers and acquisitions boom. *Mergers & Acquisitions* (May/June 1987, May/June 1990) reported that acquisition-related junk bond financing grew from 4.3 percent of the value of completed deals in 1985 to 9.1 percent at its height in 1988. Of the 4,001 deals completed in 1988, only four percent involved junk bond financing.

Milken was maniacal in his efforts to build and sustain confidence within his investor and client networks.[88]

The merger boom of the 1980s and the creation of the LBO were a partial return to the financial capitalism of the 1890s. Like Pierpont Morgan, investment bankers like Milken were extremely activist in their dealings with borrowers. Like the originators of the equity receivership, they created new techniques in corporate governance: the high levels of indebtedness of firms formed by LBOs acted as a valuable disciplining device on managers, who were forced to concentrate upon value maximization if they were to avoid bankruptcy.[89] In short, LBOs ushered in a 'dual revolution in the American economy—one in corporate finance, another in corporate governance—that profoundly altered patterns of managerial power and behavior.'[90]

Political Backlash

We argued on page 60 of chapter two that a successful private law institution is likely to become the focus of attention from politicians and bureaucrats seeking to control the economic rents that it generates. We saw an example on pages 197–203 of chapter seven, when we discussed the populist behavior toward the 'money trusts'. And, just as the financial capitalism of the 1890s resulted in the 1900s in a political backlash, the financial capitalists of the 1980s experienced a backlash in the 1990s. The most obvious consequence of this was Michael Milken's fall from grace.

A large fraction of trade in the junk bond market rested on Milken's personal reputation. The market attracted little interest from regulators before it became quite large. As it became important, the market came under intense scrutiny, in no small part because of its connection with both the increasingly aggressive tactics employed in the market for corporate control and, later, with the savings and loan crisis.[91] Rudolph Giuliani's use of the draconian powers of the Racketeer Influenced and Corrupt Organizations (RICO) Act to extract guilty pleas on six felony counts from Drexel was virtually unprecedented,

---

[88] As one Drexel employee noted 'If a company is in trouble, you're on the phone every week to them, finding out things like what the receivables are. Milken's conception is this is a franchise, and he is not willing to besmirch the name with anything going bad.' *Institutional Investor*, August 1986, p. 86.

[89] Jensen (1986).

[90] Baker and Smith (1998: ch. 3). Jensen's (1993) address to the American Finance Association provides a broader perspective on the takeover boom.

[91] It is perhaps noteworthy that the thrift crisis was widely regarded as a consequence of bureaucratic bungling. See, for example Kane (1989).

but it was extremely effective. The plea agreement forced Milken out of the market and temporarily placed Drexel under the control of former SEC chairman John Shad, who presided over the initial regulatory investigation of the firm.[92] Although the market subsequently went through a brief period of significant decline, it ultimately continued to flourish as Milken's competitors stepped in to fill the gap he left. The market's survival in the face of such upheaval suggests that it serves a real economic function.

Whether the civil and criminal penalties imposed upon Milken and Drexel were in proportion to their alleged misdeeds, it is unlikely that they had a major long-term effect upon the development of the original issue junk bond market. Even if he had not been prosecuted, it is unlikely that Milken would have retained control of the market indefinitely, or that his doing so would have served economic efficiency. Milken's commitment to building and preserving confidence in the market was important in its early days, when original issue junk bonds were relatively novel and had few close substitutes in the market against which they could be easily valued. As both investors and issuers gained experience with the new financial instrument, the value of Milken's willingness to buy back bonds at their issue price or to provide issuers with verbal guarantees regarding his ability to raise new capital would have diminished rapidly. As the market matured and Milken's reputation became less central to its operation, it seems likely that the quasi-rents he extracted from it would have been battered by competition from new entrants. Thus we can agree with the first half of Roger Lowenstein's statement in the *Wall Street Journal* that 'Mr. Milken's arrival was the greatest boon that the junk bond market ever received. His forced departure was the second greatest.'[93] When the market no longer needed his reputation, Milken's departure would have occurred anyway. In the language of chapter two, the state's intervention in this case destroyed Drexel's property rights over its information network. Fear of similar future interventions undermined the property rights of later property right innovators, and so diminished their incentive to create new financial markets in the future.

CONCLUSION

Investment banking in the second half of the twentieth century was shaped by dual revolutions in computer technology and in financial

---

[92] See Fischel (1995).   [93] *Wall Street Journal*, September 5, 1996, C1.

economics. These had two major effects. First, they resulted in the codification and standardization of a number of activities that had in the past been the exclusive preserve of the human capitalist. Many investment banker skills could now be acquired in professional schools, and competition levels in the associated businesses increased to unprecedented levels. At the same time, technological change in the real economy created a need for investment bankers who could help to perform the necessary reorganization of the corporate landscape. These bankers relied upon the type of tacit skills that had traditionally been the preserve of the investment bank.

Investment banking at the end of the twentieth century was therefore a rather bipolar activity. At one extreme, investment banks continued to provide the type of relationship-intensive services that they had always sold, in both advisory work and in complex security underwriting. At the other, they were engaged in capital-intensive business that was high-volume, low-margin, and largely commoditized. Arguably, these two business lines do not sit happily together. We have argued that investment banks are concerned with reputationally based relationship businesses. On this basis, although the second business line involves activities that were traditionally performed by investment banks, it is hard to argue that it is currently an investment bank activity. We return to this line of reasoning in the final chapter of the book. The next chapter discusses the internal organization of the investment bank.

9

Inside the Investment Bank

> The only trades which it seems possible for a joint-stock company
> to carry on successfully without an exclusive privilege are those of
> which all the operations are capable of being reduced to what is called
> a routine, or to such a uniformity of method as admits of little or no
> variation. Of this kind is, first, the banking trade; ... (Smith, 1776: vol.
> V, ch. 1)

At least in the context of investment banking, Adam Smith's above
intuition was entirely correct. From their origins in the eighteenth-
century Atlantic trade, investment banks were concerned mostly with
complex business where human judgment was indispensable. This
type of business could not be reduced to a routine and, just as Smith
predicts, it was not performed by joint-stock companies. It was only
after the joint revolutions in information technology and financial economics allowed for the codification of some security market activity
that, in line with Smith's statement, investment banks started to float.
This chapter provides a precise explanation for these facts.

We argued in chapter three that the central investment bank activity
is the creation of private law in situations where the precise quantification of the parameters of trade is impossible, either as a consequence
of their extreme complexity, or because it would involve the disclosure
of facts that would undermine the value of the exchange. The skills
needed to fulfill this role are hard to pass on at arm's length: they are
best learned through day-to-day contact with an expert mentor and
once learned, they cannot easily be codified and widely disseminated
at arm's length. This type of skill was characterized by Polanyi (1966)
as *tacit*.

Investment banking is not the only professional service industry
in which tacit human capital is central. Many elements of law, management consulting, and even accounting remain arts in spite of the
best efforts of professional schools to codify practice. In such firms
the most important assets are embedded in the employees and are

highly mobile. These firms therefore face two key problems. First, how can senior staff be incentivized to provide the mentoring that junior employees need if they are one day to fill senior positions themselves? And second, how can the firm prevent its skilled employees from leaving the firm to work for the highest bidder?

These problems would be easy to resolve if it was possible to establish clear property rights over an investment banker's human capital. It could then form the basis of a contract between junior agents who required mentoring, and the senior agent capable of providing it; similarly, an employee who acquired human capital at one employer could be contractually committed to pay for it if he left. But the nature of tacit human capital precludes its measurement and documentation. Hence, like the price-relevant information that is central to the investment bank's operation, it is impossible to establish property rights over tacit human capital.

We know from our analysis in chapter three of the investment bank's information network that an appropriately designed private institution can substitute for formal property rights. The structure and operation of the information network generate the right incentives for the production and alienation of price-relevant information, even though this information cannot be the subject of a court-enforceable legal contract. The creation and sale of tacit human capital is likewise intermediated by an appropriate organizational structure:[1] in this case, the partnership. We argue that partnerships depend upon their reputations to attract business. The members of a partnership therefore have a financial interest in its reputation: we argue that this is sufficient to incentivize them to mentor the next generation of partners.

We stressed throughout chapter eight the trade-off that investment banks face between economies of scale and reputational exposure when they contemplate expansion into new markets: see, for example, the discussion on page 228. The discussion of the previous paragraph highlights an additional cost to expansion: if, either because it impairs the bank's reputation or for some other reason, it reduces mentoring incentives then some valuable tacit human capital may be lost. Hence technological advances that replace tacit skills with codified

---

[1] Romer (2002) makes a similar point in a discussion of nonrival goods: that is, those which can be employed simultaneously by many people without degradation of quality. Like the knowledge, skills and reputations upon which investment bankers rely, most forms of intellectual property are nonrival goods.

knowledge tilt the trade-off further in favor of expansion.[2] This is precisely what we observed in chapter eight. Batch processing codified many of the activities of retail banks, and had little effect upon the wholesale banks. It was therefore the retail banks that were the first to go public, immediately after the NYSE permitted this in 1971.[3] Only later, when distributed processing allowed the use of advances in financial economics to codify front-office practice,[4] did the balance shift in favor of public ownership for the wholesale firms, who went public in a second wave during the 1980s.[5]

We continue our discussion in the next section with an analysis of the most important features of partnership firms in investment banking. We then present in some detail our theory of partnership firms and their going-public decision, and we discuss the evidence that supports our theory. After public firms had resolved the trade-off of the previous paragraph in favor of size, they still had a clear incentive as public companies to reconstruct as many of the contractual features of the partnership as possible, in order to incentivize the creation and the retention of tacit human capital. We conclude the chapter by describing two attempts to achieve this through formal contracts.

INVESTMENT BANK PARTNERSHIPS

Partnership Features

What is the defining characteristic of a partnership? The question is not a trivial one. Historically, it certainly could not be answered with reference to the liability of its members. Through most of the nineteenth century, differences in the liability faced by the shareholders of a corporation and the members of a partnership were a matter of degree rather than of kind.[6] Lamoreaux (1998: 67) provides

---

[2] Daniel Bell (1973) also identifies scientific advances that increase the capacity for codifying theoretical knowledge as a driving force in industrial development.

[3] See page 237.   [4] See pages 238–49.

[5] The technological argument developed here can also shed light on the reorganization of securities exchanges that has played out over the last few decades. As we write, the NYSE itself has just gone public via merger with Archipelago (completed March 7, 2006), a publicly traded electronic commerce network. See also the discussion on page 240 of chapter eight. In the spirit of our analysis of chapter three, Benveniste, Marcus, and Wilhelm (1992) discuss the trade-offs facing exchanges choosing between electronic platforms and human intermediation. Mulherin, Netter, and Overdahl (1991) provide a fascinating account of the historical efforts of exchanges to maintain property rights over the prices they produce.

[6] Horwitz (1992: n. 165, 92 and 96–8). Shareholders in public corporations were held liable for more than the value of their shares under a variety of constitutional

ample evidence that the many small and large firms that jettisoned the partnership form in favor of incorporation in the latter part of the nineteenth century did not do so in order to shed liability.

Similarly, although modern Internal Revenue Service rules require that a partnership's tax returns report each partner's fractional income share, any argument that partnerships are characterized by an equal division of profits is on shaky ground.[7] From its inception in 1865 through to 1913 equal profit sharing was decidedly not a feature of the JS Morgan (and after 1910, Morgan, Grenfell) partnerships: see Carosso (1987: tables 2 and 15). Nor was it true at the founding of Morgan, Dabney, when Morgan and Dabney shared equally at 40 percent with James Goodwin holding the remaining 20 percent share (Carosso, 1987: 107). Pierpont Morgan's share in the profits of JP Morgan & Co. from 1900 to 1913 ranged from 35 to 42 percent, about three times that of any other partner (Carosso, 1987: 614).

A better definition of the partnership concerns its members' power to commit one another. Anglo-American common law in the first part of the nineteenth century held that a willingness among business associates to share the profits from a business venture evidenced a willingness to accept liability for contracts that any of their number made on behalf of the partnership.[8] This willingness defines the partnership's relations with its trading partners, all of whom should be able to rely upon this shared liability. The US Supreme Court Justice John Marshall made this clear in his widely cited opinion in *Winship* v. *The Bank of the United States*[9] that 'the trading world ... must trust to the general powers contained in all partnerships'.

Marshall's opinion provides a characterization of the partnership, but it creates some complexities. First, it may not be clear whether a partner is trading on his own behalf, or whether he is trading on behalf of the partnership. Creditors in the first half of the nineteenth century attempted to profit from this confusion by suing the business partners of their counterparties in personal trades for unpaid debts.[10]

---

and statutory enactments, and the 'trust fund doctrine' promulgated by the courts (identifying a corporation's capital as a trust fund for creditors) only began to erode during the 1890s.

[7] Levin and Tadelis (2005: n. 16) claim that as late as the 1950s, a firm that deviated radically from equal profit sharing risked its legal partnership status, presumably in the United States. This claim appears to be undermined, at least in the context of early investment banks, by the remarks in the following sentence.

[8] Lamoreaux (1995, 1998) and Lamoreaux and Rosenthal (2005).

[9] 30 US 529 (1831).   [10] Lamoreaux (1995: 46).

After considerable litigation and debate, Justice Story's (1859) treatise on the law of partnership sought to resolve the confusion by focusing on the 'intentionality' of parties, as expressed in their power relationships. Lamoreaux (1995: 59) describes Story's conception of the partnership as an agreement that 'conferred an equality of power on the contractees'. Hence, even if their contract called for power-sharing, a ship's owner could not contractually commit the members of its crew.

The second consequence of Marshall's ruling was a restriction on the partnership's ability to qualify a member's general ability to commit his partners. If, as Story argued, partnerships are defined by their obligations to honor their members' trades, then they cannot override this obligation contractually. We argue that this sharing of power is the distinguishing economic feature of partnership firms. Hence, a partnership firm is one that is entirely controlled by its managers, each of whom is bound by the decisions of the others. This type of corporate control is often referred to as 'ownership'. Hence, because they cannot vote out the managing partners, outside partners do not have ownership rights in the sense that the outside shareholders of a corporation do.[11]

A consequence of this definition is that senior partners take significant risks when they admit new junior members to the partnership. Placing one's reputational capital at the disposal of a junior associate risks its dissipation, and hence strengthens the junior's bargaining position relative to his mentor. In effect, some of the surplus created by the senior agent's human capital is transferred to the junior without the benefit of a detailed intermediating contract: while the terms of this trade may be well understood by both counterparties, they are not enforceable in a court. We have already seen two clear instances of this in the history of the Morgan firms. When Peabody admitted the elder Morgan to his partnership (p. 149), he gave a highly regarded American businessman access to his major clients, and some of this contact occurred before the partnership agreement was signed.[12] In the early years of the partnership, Peabody was therefore exposing

---

[11] Note though that a corporation that was closely held by its managers would qualify under our definition as a 'partnership'. Both before and after the 1971 change of NYSE rules, many investment banking firms were privately incorporated in this way for tax reasons: for example, John Loeb stated that tax considerations were the only reason for Loeb, Rhodes's private incorporation in 1977 (*New York Times* July 10, 1977: 85).

[12] Carosso (1987: 36–8).

his business to a potential competitive threat. Similarly, the extraordinarily generous terms on which Pierpont Morgan entered the Drexel partnership (p. 167) clearly represented a transfer of reputational capital that was not formally compensated.

Story's insistence that a partnership's counterparties should be able to rely upon its members' ability to commit their partners may have reflected the contemporary technological difficulties of publicizing the precise details of a partnership agreement.[13] But it seems more likely that it reflected a general unwillingness among partnership firms to publicize details about their agreements, or of other aspects of their internal operation. For example, no one outside the JP Morgan & Co. partnership had ever seen the partnership agreement until the firm was forced during the Pecora hearings to divulge its contents (see p. 204). In general, partnerships appear to design into their operation features intended to render their activities *opaque* to the outside world. For example, partnerships frequently exhibit relatively flat pay scales, an 'up-or-out' employment policy, and an emphasis upon teamwork, all of which make it harder for outsiders to learn the quality of individual employees before it is revealed through a firing decision.[14] We argue below that the strong tendency among partnerships toward opacity reflects an interest in protecting their investments in tacit human capital.

Any member of a so-called partnership 'at will' can dissolve the partnership at any time, and for any reason, and in practice, the power-sharing feature of *any* partnership gives its members considerable power to force dissolution, irrespective of whether it is

---

[13] While the French Code de Commerce required partnerships to draft formal agreements for registration with the government, and publication in a newspaper of record, and hence allowed partnerships to impose limits on the abilities of partners to commit the firm with the confidence that these would be enforced in the courts (Lamoreaux and Rosenthal, 2005), we are not aware of any similar mechanism in the United States or Great Britain, either now or in the past.

[14] Endlich (1999: 21) provides a striking example of the cultural tendency within the Goldman Sachs investment banking partnership toward downplaying individual accomplishment. Gilson and Mnookin (1985: 365, n. 89) observe that the holdup threat presented by marketing the firm through the writing and lecturing of individual lawyers '...may account for the recent development of seminars for existing and potential clients put on by a single law firm. These seminars are designed to provide direct information concerning quality to potential clients, but unlike writing and lecturing by individual lawyers, this approach features a number of the firm's lawyers as opposed to a single star...'

at will.[15] Nevertheless, the ability of any individual to force dissolution in professional service partnerships is greatly circumscribed by their reliance upon human capital rather than upon financial capital or physical assets. While the latter are generally easily valued and liquidated, human capital cannot be sold. There is nothing to prevent a partnership being reformed after a forced dissolution without the parties that forced the dissolution. Moreover, even to the extent that aspects of a partnership such as its brand can be liquidated, the difficulty of valuing individual contributions to a pool of tacit assets leaves each partner at the mercy of his peers.[16] In short, partnership stakes in professional service firms such as investment banks are in practice *illiquid*: a member who wishes to cash out does so at the convenience of his partners, and at their price. Investment bank liquidity is frequently contractually limited, too. For example, cash-constrained new partners are seldom expected to make a substantial capital contribution upon entry; instead, a new partnership share is subject to strict withdrawal limits on the share's associated capital amount.[17]

In short, partnerships appear deliberately to court opacity and illiquidity. The consequence of this is that partners cannot rely upon capital market discipline to help them to iron out governance problems. In a perfect world, they would trust one another. In the real world, where this ideal is only partially achievable, they must monitor one another.

These governance problems were a feature of the eighteenth- and nineteenth-century partnerships that we studied in chapters four to

---

[15] Lamoreaux (1995, 1998) discusses the relative ease of forcing partnership dissolution. She argues that the threat of costly dissolution may help to mitigate holdup problems among partners. However, she notes that it is manifested in the typically short contractual lives of partnerships and the absence of 'firmness' which Blair (2003) suggests prevents partnerships from 'locking up' the capital necessary for large-scale, continuous production.

[16] For several decades following James McKinsey's death in 1939, new partners bought out old partners at the book value of their shares to make cashing out less attractive (*The Economist*, March 22, 1997, Management Consultancy Survey, p. 19). Similarly, until 1996 Goldman Sachs forced retiring partners to cash out over several years, and the management committee could if it wished to extend the payout schedule (Wilhelm and Downing, 2001: ch. 7). Leslie D. Corwin, a specialist in partnership law, suggested in 1997 that 'If a firm is unwilling to cash out a partner, which often happens when a partner is moving to a competitor, the only recourse may be to sue.' (*New York Times*, June 8, 1997: F9.).

[17] Carosso (1987: 169) provides particulars of these arrangements in the Morgan firms. They were extremely pervasive throughout the industry, and they remain a common feature of today's banking partnerships.

six. New partners were well-known to their seniors, and the most important selection criterion was invariably their trustworthiness. For this reason, throughout the history of the investment bank family members were an important source of partners. We noted this tendency in the eighteenth-century Atlantic trade on page 113 of chapter four. The Rothschilds took it to its extremes: we discussed the interlocking family partnership agreements that governed the operation of their five houses on page 143 of chapter five. Although the trust that the Rothschilds were able to vest in their network of family partners enabled them to prosper in a world with minimal provision for formal cross-border contracts, ultimately it restricted their success: we noted on page 151 that the family's inability to find a member willing to take an American partnership prevented them from succeeding in this market, and was probably their greatest strategic oversight.

In contrast, the House of Brown, which also had its origins as a family firm, adopted a far more flexible approach. As we noted on page 115, they rapidly extended the partnership beyond the family. This enabled the Baltimore-based firm to establish a strong operation in Liverpool when that city was at the peak of its economic importance during the early nineteenth-century cotton boom. Perkins (1975: 68–74) notes however that there were numerous points of conflict between family and nonfamily partners. The Browns were technological innovators, as evidenced by their early adoption of the telegraph to maintain uniform exchange rates throughout their branch system, and their pioneering use of credit analysis, formal risk management techniques, and new administrative methods. Many of these contributions were partly responses to the tensions in the partnership.

In chapter six we identify two leading groups of investment banking networks as central to late nineteenth-century investment banking: the New England 'Yankees', and the German-Jewish community. We noted on page 164 that the German-Jewish banking crowd in the late nineteenth century often looked to itself for business partners as well social contacts and marital partners. Similarly, Carosso (1987: 169–72) identifies two sources for Morgan partners: in many cases they were drawn from a small circle of well-established businessmen with family or social ties who shared a set of common business and nonbusiness values; in others, partners were developed from within the firm. In every case, the investment bankers attempted to guarantee the trustworthiness of new partners by drawing them from a relatively narrow social circle with which they were closely acquainted.[18] This approach persisted at least into the 1960s, at which time associates began for the first time to be hired in meaningful numbers from MBA programs, although even then it is not clear that recruitment was entirely meritocratic.[19]

In summary, organizational control is shared within partnership firms. As a result, senior agents place their reputational capital at the disposal of the junior agents. Partnerships are *opaque*: it is hard for outsiders to understand how they operate, and to identify before promotion decisions occur which agents are the most talented. Partnership stakes are *illiquid*: the value of an agent's stake in the firm depends upon the value it places upon tacit assets, and so when he withdraws his stake, he is at the mercy of his partners. Moreover, in exchange for the loan that they receive to buy into the partnership, junior partners in investment banking firms generally accept contractual limitations on their access to capital. The opacity and illiquidity of partnership stakes result in governance problems: the members of a partnership have to monitor one another. It was for this reason that early investment banking partnerships tended to recruit from social milieu with which they were familiar.

Partnership Firms, Reputation and Human Capital[20]

We have stressed the importance of tacit human capital in investment banking, and in other professional service businesses. This section explains why these businesses are typically constituted as partnerships.

Tacit skill enables investment bankers to perform a number of key activities. The knowledge required to manage the information networks employed in securities issuance was historically largely tacit; so too was the ability to manage client relationships, or to provide advisory services to merging or restructuring firms. We argued in chapters two and three that information networks substitute for formal property rights over price-relevant information, and so facilitate the efficient allocation of capital to innovative ideas. Similarly, the M&A advice provided by investment banks has in the last 30 years

---

[18] Carosso (1987: 169) states that the Morgans were mainly concerned to find partners who were 'able to command the confidence of the firm's clients and add strength to one or more of their operations'.

[19] See Chapter 8, n. 48 for details of the change in hiring practices.

[20] For a more formal exposition of the material in this subsection, see our 2004 paper with the same title (Morrison and Wilhelm, 2004).

contributed to the efficient restructuring of corporate America. Hence tacit knowledge is not only profitable for investment bankers: it has considerable social value. It is therefore desirable that it should be incubated, and passed from one generation to the next.

But tacit skills can only be acquired through close on-the-job contact with an expert, who passes his knowledge on through a close mentoring relationship. Mentoring of this type is costly for the expert: if he avoided it, then he could spend more time with his clients, and so generate a higher return on his own human capital. Hence, it is reasonable to expect junior agents to pay for the mentoring that they receive at the start of their careers. But formal contracting to accomplish this is impeded by the impossibility of establishing formal property rights over tacit knowledge. A senior agent with tacit skills could accept payment for training from a junior agent without mentoring her; similarly, a junior agent could withhold payment, claiming that mentoring had not occurred. In both cases the nonverifiability of tacit knowledge transfer would preclude court adjudication.

The contracting problem of the previous paragraph is fundamental. The absence of formal property rights over tacit human capital undermines its transfer from one generation to the next, and hence it has the potential to reduce social welfare. We argued in chapter three that the information networks that investment banks create are an organizational response to the technological problems of establishing property rights over price-relevant information. Similarly, the partnership is an organizational response to the impossibility of contracting formally over tacit knowledge transfer.

If senior agents are to have an incentive to pass their tacit knowledge on to the next generation, they must either be paid for mentoring, or they must experience a sufficiently large loss from a failure to mentor. The former approach is the standard one when property rights are well-defined and formal contracts are enforceable: we have argued that these conditions do not obtain in the context of tacit knowledge. Partnerships embody the second approach to incentivization. They achieve this by tying an agent's fortune to the success of the junior partners whom he has mentored.

Recall that partnerships are opaque: pay scales at a particular promotion level are flat and employees tend to work in teams. Outsiders therefore find it difficult to identify the talented junior agents. The most important indicator to outsiders of ability is the promotion decision. Partnerships in general practice an 'up-or-out' approach to career development: those employees who are deemed worthy of promotion are revealed to be the best in their cohort; conversely, nonpromotion sends a weaker signal to the labor market where the departing employee must seek work.

Transparency is a choice variable. The fact that partnerships choose to be so opaque indicates that opacity serves a purpose. One reason this is so is that it gives the partners considerable bargaining power in their dealings with junior staff. Because tacit knowledge is hard to measure, an employee's income if he leaves the firm will be determined by his reputation, and his reputation is in turn determined by the promotion decision. An employee who turns down promotion is indistinguishable from one who was turned down for promotion, and will therefore suffer in the labor market. Hence the partners are able to attach stringent conditions to promotions. In particular, they are able to persuade new partners to accept highly illiquid stakes in the firm.

Illiquid partnership stakes tie the new partner to the firm. Although, as a consequence of opacity, the outside labor market has no direct evidence of it, promotion to partner signals an agent's quality. The illiquidity of his partnership stake prevents the agent from immediately taking this signal to the labor market, and selling his skills to the highest bidder. Instead, he is forced to remain in the firm and to deal with its clients. Although they have insufficient evidence to judge his quality for themselves, the clients will pay a high fee for his services, because they trust the firm's promotion decision. The clients will however learn the new partner's skill for themselves through their experience of dealing with him. If their experience does not accord with the expectations they formed from the promotion decision then they will lower their opinion of the partnership firm.

When partners use the bargaining power that derives from firm opacity to force new partners to accept illiquid partnership stakes, they therefore make a commitment to expose the firm's reputation to the new partner. We commented upon precisely this type of exposure on page 269, when we noted the risks that George Peabody and Anthony Drexel took when they admitted Junius and Pierpont Morgan to their respective partnerships. This exposure serves a purpose: if the junior partner is revealed to be of low quality, then the firm's reputational capital will be damaged, and every partner will experience a pecuniary loss.[21] Hence senior partners will be less willing to promote low-quality partners and, crucially, low-quality

---

[21] Bar-Isaac (2003) shows that a senior agent with an established reputation can commit to work hard by forming a partnership with an agent of unproven quality.

partners will be less willing to accept a partnership that they know will inevitably lose much of its value when their lack of ability is revealed. But the value to the senior partners of their stake in the business is determined by the price that the junior partners are willing to pay them for it. We have argued that skilled employees will pay more for a partnership than unskilled employees. Partners therefore mentor junior employees in order to protect the firm's reputation and hence to guarantee that they will be able to sell out at a satisfactory price when they retire.

The argument of this section is rather involved, but it can be easily summarized. The impossibility of formal property rights over tacit knowledge preclude its transfer from one generation to the next via a formal contract. Partnerships provide an organizational solution to this problem. They rely upon their reputation to extract high fees from their clients. Because partnerships are by design opaque, new partners can be forced to accept an illiquid stake in the business. The illiquidity of the new partners' stake exposes the firm's reputation and hence ensures that skilled agents will pay significantly more for a partnership stake. The reason that partners mentor junior employees is therefore to maximize the value of their partnership stake.

The Demise of Investment Banking Partnerships[22]

The crux of the argument in the preceding section is that, because partnerships rely upon their reputations to generate superior returns, the need to protect the firm's reputation is sufficient motivation for partners with tacit knowledge to mentor junior employees.[23] A partner who shirks his mentoring responsibilities does not incur the costs of training junior employees, but in reducing the quality of the talent pool from which new partners are drawn he lowers the price at which he can sell his partnership. The trade-off between the benefits and costs of shirking is however affected by the size of the partnership. While each partner receives all of the benefits of shirking, by virtue of the partnership's profit-sharing arrangements he shares the costs

[22] Morrison and Wilhelm (2005*b*) make most of the arguments in this subsection in a more formal way.

[23] Corporate reputation plays a related role in some other papers. Tadelis (1999) shows in a model of pure adverse selection how the reputation associated with a traded name may convey information about its owner. He extends this work to show that the value of a traded name can provide incentives (Tadelis, 2002). See also Kreps (1990), who argues that firms that deal repeatedly in the labor markets have an incentive to acquire a reputation for not economizing on wage bills in each period.

with his partners. Hence, increasing the size of the partnership makes shirking relatively more attractive than mentoring. To be sure, cross-monitoring within the partnership can serve to mitigate this effect, and this is one reason that investment bankers tended in the past to select their partners from among their social circle. But, like the incentive effect of reputation loss, cross-monitoring is less effective in a large partnership. At some stage, large-scale operations are incompatible with tacit knowledge transfer within a partnership.

So free-rider problems place an upper bound upon the maximum partnership size that can support mentoring.[24] This adds an additional nuance to the reasoning we employed in chapter eight, where we argued that investment banks face a trade-off between economies of scale and possible reputational damage when they expand into new markets. Reputational damage for an investment banking partnership may arise not simply because it exposes itself to markets in which it is less expert, but also because in expanding its scale, the bank undermines its senior partners' mentoring incentives and so lowers the average level of tacit knowledge in the upcoming partners.

An investment bank will therefore expand its operations in response to technological changes of the type that we studied in chapter eight if the technology generates sufficient economies of scale to compensate it for the reputational capital loss that it will experience when it becomes so large that its partners no longer have an incentive to mentor. When this happens, there is no particular reason why the bank should continue to operate as a partnership. As soon as expansion is optimal, the bank should attempt to capture as many economies of scale as possible. This requires capital, and so we would expect it to respond to the changed technological environment by floating itself as a publicly owned corporation.

This is precisely what happened in the 1970s and 1980s. Investment banks in the middle of the twentieth century were still heavily dependent upon human capital, and their clients relied upon banks' reputations to certify the quality of their staff. In line with our theory,

---

[24] That profit-sharing results in free-rider problems when effort is not observable is well understood: see, for example, Holmstrom (1982). Some authors have also pointed to positive consequences of profit-sharing in partnerships. For example, Levin and Tadelis (2005) argue that profit-sharing raises the quality threshold for new partners above the level that would obtain in public firms, and hence provides a valuable signal in situations where customers are unsure of partner ability. Garicano and Santos (2004) argue that profit-sharing provides incentives for partners to direct work to the person who can handle it most effectively.

the market was fragmented: banks were small (see page 228), and their operations were opaque.[25] We documented in chapter eight the adoption in the 1960s of batch-processing technology. This created massive economies of scale in retail investment banks. As they were concerned more with the distribution of stocks to small investors than with the management of networks of large institutional investors, the retail banks were arguably less dependent upon tacit knowledge than were their wholesale counterparts.

Since the costs to retail banks of undermining tacit knowledge production were small, and the operational and reputational benefits of technology adoption were potentially substantial, they were natural candidates for expansion. The back-office crisis of 1967–70 (pp. 235–238 of chapter eight) indicated that it would be increasingly difficult for retail firms to survive if they did not expand. By the end of the 1960s there was therefore a great deal of pent-up demand for capital to finance expansion among retail-oriented investment banks. The NYSE changed its rules to admit joint-stock corporate members in 1970, and a wave of sixteen retail investment banks floated in short order (see p. 237).

At this stage there was still little impetus for flotation by wholesale-oriented investment banks. Their underwriting and trading businesses were still largely dependent upon relational contracting and tacit human capital, and mainframe computation did not bring sufficient economies of scale to these activities to justify a flotation and the consequential reduction of tacit knowledge.

---

[25] Merrill Lynch provides a noteworthy counterexample. In 1940, the firm began publishing an annual report for public dissemination and, initially, was the only NYSE member to do so (Perkins, 1999: 164). At the time Merrill Lynch maintained the largest network of retail branch offices and was setting the stage for trading access to its distribution network for securities underwriting participations. The firm's annual reports gained considerable attention from the financial press and appealed to a prospective retail clientele questioning the trustworthiness of Wall Street firms in the aftermath of the market crash. Some competitors eventually followed suit. This early example of promoting transparency is not particularly challenging to our theory in the sense that key features of the firm's human capital were well codified by this time. In fact, Merrill was among the first companies in the United States to institute (in 1945) a formal training program for its employees (Perkins, 1999: 195). Competitors benefited from the firm's efforts as evidenced by the defection of about 25 percent of the graduates of its training programs during its first two decades. The firm tempered at the margin the incentive to defect among nonpartners by refusing to rehire employees who left the firm for other brokerages and with a delayed-withdrawal, profit-sharing program (Perkins, 1999: 198–200).

As we documented in chapter eight, wholesale bank businesses were transformed by the arrival of desktop computers that could be interrogated in real time by front-office staff. These computers facilitated the introduction of the formal modeling techniques of financial economics into corporate finance, and in particular into securities valuation and trading. They had two implications for human capitalists in these businesses. First, the adoption of formal economic tools reduced many of the formerly tacit skills of the investment banker to routines that could be codified and taught in the classroom. Second, because much of their activities were automated, their skills could be applied on a far greater scale. Hitherto unheard-of economies of scale could therefore be achieved in wholesale investment banking.

In short, microcomputers served both to reduce the value of human capital to investment bankers and to increase the scale at which they could operate. Moreover, there was a competitive exigency for their adoption: as we noted on page 245, the lower reputational barrier to entry resulted in competition in trading businesses that drove down spreads, and raised the minimum scale at which participation was profitable. Wholesale banks that did not expand sufficiently would be unable to compete in securities trading businesses, and they needed capital to support their expansion.

The consequence of these trends was a second wave of investment bank flotations, this time by wholesale-oriented houses. The onset of this wave can be identified with the 1978 and 1979 acquisitions of White, Weld, and Loeb Rhoades by Merrill Lynch and Shearson. By 1987, only Goldman Sachs and Lazard Freres among the major wholesale houses remained as private partnerships: they eventually floated in 1999 and 2005, respectively.

The order in which the wholesale firms went public is significant. The early movers were particularly active in the securities markets, where, in response to the factors identified above, spreads were narrowing and economies of scale were increasing. As expertise in financial economics dispersed and computers became increasingly powerful, the specialized partnerships that dominated the derivatives markets well into the 1980s were absorbed by commercial banks that could provide the capital required to operate at a commercial scale.[26] The holdouts were those firms that, like Goldman and Lazard,

---

[26] Perhaps the most prominent of the derivatives-trading partnerships were O'Connor & Associates, CRT, and Cooper Neff. They were acquired by Swiss Bank, Nations Bank, and BNP, respectively.

generated a greater proportion of their income from advisory work. As we argued in chapter eight (pp. 249–62), these firms continued to rely upon tacit knowledge, and hence faced a higher opportunity cost of going public. At the same time, the new technologies generated fewer economies of scale in advisory businesses, and so they had less to gain from expansion. It is therefore unsurprising the advisory firms delayed flotation for as long as they did.

The trends that we have outlined in this section are illustrated by graphs that appear elsewhere in the book. As formerly tacit knowledge was increasingly codified after 1970, individual invest-ment bankers could achieve greater economies of scale from their human capital. This is apparent in figure 1.5, which shows a sharp rise in the amount of financial capital per employee in the largest five investment banks by capitalization. At the same time, financial capital was increasingly central to a business that relied upon codifi-able risk-taking ventures. This is witnessed by the steady rise of total investment bank capitalization in figure 1.4. The increasing economies of scale among investment banks led inevitably to a consolidation of business among the largest firms. This trend is also illustrated in figure 1.4, which shows a steady drop throughout the second half of the twentieth century in the capitalization of the top 11–25 investment banks as a percentage of the top ten.

THE JOINT-STOCK INVESTMENT BANK

As investment banks in their quest for economies of scale abandoned the formerly ubiquitous partnership form in favor of public own-ership, they were forced at the same time to jettison the attributes that made the partnership so conducive to tacit knowledge formation and transmission. Unlike partnerships, public companies separate ownership from managerial control. Hence, the opacity which in a partnership allows the senior partners to write efficient contracts with junior partners would in a public company generate severe gover-nance problems. At the same time, public companies could not attract investors if their shares were designed to be illiquid, as a partnership firm's are. Furthermore, direct shareholder monitoring of managerial actions is impossible in a joint-stock company, and free-rider problems in mentoring are exacerbated by the presence of a substantial body of outside investors to share the capital losses caused by an abnegation of mentoring responsibilities.

In short, as we noted in the previous section, it is harder in a joint-stock investment bank to incentivize mentoring than it is in a partnership, and it is also harder to prevent skilled staff from putting their abilities up for auction after they have acquired them at the expense of an employer. The immediate consequence of these observations has been a dramatic increase in investment banker mobility in the last thirty years. Investment banks have adopted a number of approaches to stem this trend. First, they have leaned where possible upon the investment banker's need for firm-specific skills to make the most of her abilities. Second, they have relied upon formal black-letter law, both by writing Covenants Not to Compete into employment contracts and by seeking patent protection for financial innovations. None of these approaches has proved as effective as the extra-legal property rights created and enforced through the partnership form: in general, increased codification and greater scale of operation have conspired to diminish the tacit dimension to much investment banking.

Partnership Tenure Patterns and Banker Mobility

The increasing codification of many investment banking skills made it increasingly easy in the second half of the twentieth century for clients to measure the quality of their investment bankers. Not only were transcripts from professional schools available for the first time: clients could use new techniques developed by financial economists to compare both the performance of fund managers and also the pricing of complex deal structures. At the same time, the rising scale of principal trading and the increasing precision with which investment banks could measure the performance of their traders made it extremely difficult to avoid the dissemination of performance information outside the firm, not least because this dissemination was in the interests of the traders. The opacity of investment banker operations was therefore breaking down even before they started to go public: subsequently, it vanished entirely.

The consequence of increased transparency, coupled after flotation with an increase in share liquidity, was a steady increase in investment banker mobility, as the tradition that experienced bankers would spend their entire career with one firm was overturned. This trend is hard to document, because of difficulties in the systematic identification and tracking of the career paths of prominent bankers, but several data sources provide evidence that is consonant with the predictions of our theory. First, the NYSE maintains annual Directories of Member

Table 9.1. *Average partner tenure in 17 prominent investment banks*

	1952		1960	
	Number of partners	**Avg. partner tenure**	**Avg. partner tenure**	**% Change from 1952**
Paine Webber	36	16	16	0.00
Hayden Stone	14	16	12	−25.00
Shearson Ham	13	19	16	−15.79
Merrill	64	19	14	−26.32
White, Weld	21	20	19	−5.00
Smith Barney	20	22	21	−4.55
Hutton	16	23	18	−21.74
Morgan Stanley	14	23	24	4.35
Goodbody	18	24	17	−29.17
Cowen	9	24	24	0.00
Goldman	13	24	22	−8.33
Hornblower	27	24	20	−16.67
Dean Witter	26	26	19	−26.92
Lehman	19	26	23	−11.54
Kidder	17	27	25	−7.41
Wm Blair	8	27	28	3.70
A. Brown	8	28	27	−3.57

Firms that record partnership rolls for member firms. These records enable consistent tracking of the admission to and departure from banking partnerships. Most prominent investment banks fall into this category. There was almost a one-to-one mapping from partnership rolls into rolls reporting the holders of voting stock as banks began in the late 1950s to incorporate privately.

Table 9.1 uses these reports to measure the average life tenure of the 1952 and 1960 partner (or voting shareholder) cohorts reported by 17 prominent banks. Banks are reported in order (from shortest to longest) of the average tenure for their 1952 cohort. The averages range from 16 years as partner (or voting shareholder) for the 36 members of Paine Webber's 1952 cohort to 28 years for the eight members of Alex. Brown's cohort. Retail houses relied less upon tacit skill and it is perhaps unsurprising that they have the lowest partner tenure.

Investment bank computerization began in 1958 (see p. 230) and, as we argued above, it became harder to maintain the opacity upon which staff immobility had hitherto rested. Hence, we see falls in average partner tenure between 1952 and 1960, and these are most pronounced among the retail firms for which batch-processing technology was most important. Goodbody, Dean Witter, and Hornblower, all of which were retail brokerage firms, saw sharp declines in their partner tenure that brought them into line with their peers within the retail segment of the industry.[27] In contrast, there is little change in partnership tenure for the wholesale banks (Brown, William Blair, Kidder, Goldman, Cowen, Morgan Stanley, and White, Weld) from the 1952 to the 1960 cohort.

As the investment banks started to go public barriers to staff movement fell more rapidly. However, at this time identification of key individuals in the NYSE's annual directory became less systematic as banks began to go public, and as a result we are less able to draw meaningful comparisons with the 1952 and 1960 cohorts reported in table 9.1. However, there was widespread recognition within the industry that times were changing. For example, John Whitehead, Goldman's senior partner, observed in the *Institutional Investor* in 1973 that 'until the last two or three years, it was very unusual for top people to move'. A related article in *Corporate Financing* describes at length the sudden tendency for investment bankers to switch firms.[28]

We can provide a bit more texture by using electronic searches of the *New York Times* and the *Investment Dealers' Digest* to track Goldman partners identified in the NYSE member firm rolls.[29] We find no indication that any partner left the firm to join a competitor between 1955 and 1973. Moreover, we can document only a few instances during this period in which bankers from competing firms joined Goldman as partners. This pattern persisted at Goldman through to at least the

[27] The decline in partner tenure for the 1960 cohort at Goodbody was attributable in large part to the problems that led to its failure later in the decade (see p. 236). But as we explained in chapter eight, these problems stemmed from a failure to adopt the computer technology that was in any case transforming this industry.

[28] See 'Why are all these investment bankers changing jobs?' *Institutional Investor* January, 1973 and 'Why your investment banker is switching firms', *Corporate Financing*, November/December 1972. These articles, written by John Thackrey, received wide attention within the industry. Given our emphasis in chapter eight upon the increased codification of investment banking practice, it is noteworthy that on p. 25 of his 1972 article, Thackrey identifies this trend with the replacement of 'presumed spontaneity, imaginativeness and inventive capitalism with routine, with procedures, with systematic group work...'

[29] The information that follows was gathered through electronic searches of the historical *New York Times* files from 1955 through 1964 and the *Investment Dealers' Digest* from 1965 forward.

early 1990s.[30] Goldman's experience is representative of the industry until the early 1970s but is less so thereafter. In general, deviations from this pattern correspond with the relative timing of the bank's public offering: banks that went public earlier generally faced or participated in poaching efforts earlier than their peers.

Cultural Barriers to Employee Mobility[31]

An investment banker who is able to trade options at one bank will be able to deploy his skills in the service of another. Many other investment banking skills could in theory be shifted from one bank to another: technically, they are 'general' rather than 'specific'. A worker with general skills can auction his time on the labor market, and hence can extract all of the return from them. Naturally, this is a desirable state of affairs for a skilled worker, but it may harm unskilled agents, since employers will not expect to derive a return from investments they make training their workers. When skills are codifiable this is not a major problem, since workers can finance their human capital acquisition through a program of formal education.[32] When skills can only be acquired through instruction on the employer's premises, it may result in underinvestment in training.[33] We have already argued that a technologically driven shift from on-the-job acquisition of tacit knowledge to formal teaching of codifiable skill was a consequence of increased labor mobility that arose in the wake of the going-public wave for investment banks.

But the shift to the formal acquisition by investment bankers of codified knowledge was not total. One reason for this was the role of firm-specific skills in tying agents to their employers. When an employee requires a detailed understanding of a firm's informal procedures to perform his task, he will find it harder to be effective in a different organization. Alternative employers will anticipate this and will pay him less to move. This restricts the employee's mobility, and

---

[30] See Wilhelm and Downing (2001) for a summary of events that led to growing retention problems beginning in the early 1990s.

[31] See Morrison and Wilhelm (2005a) for a formal model of the idea underlying this discussion.

[32] The first person to make this observation formally was Becker (1964).

[33] In the context of a different professional services industry, Hillman (2001) documents sharp reduction in training activities coincidentally with a sharp rise in lawyer mobility in the United States: 'Mentoring is haphazard, if it exists at all. Firms point to the new economics of law practice and ask law schools to do more' (Hillman, 2001: 1078).

so makes it cost-effective for his current employers to finance some of his training in general skills.[34]

The types of firm-specific skills that were historically important in investment banks related to modes of in-house communication. It is not enough for an investment banker to have a good idea for, say, trading or laying off underwriting risk: he must also communicate it to his superiors, and convince them that it is worth risking the firm's capital on. This requires an understanding of the firm's lines of communication, many of which will be tacit: it may, for example, require a knowledge of the position of the coffee machine, or an understanding of a private company language. This type of knowledge is hard to acquire, and it is notoriously hard to write down. We refer to it as the firm's 'culture'.[35]

Employees who move from one company to another frequently experience a degree of cultural dissonance as they struggle to come to terms with changed modes of communication.[36] Hence, cultural skills represent the type of firm-specific knowledge that ties an employee to a firm and so provides it with an incentive to provide general training. Cultural differences between investment banks continued to serve as something of a barrier to employee mobility after they started to float.

One way for investment bankers to overcome cultural communication problems at the level of the work unit was to move between firms as a team. Team transfers have certainly emerged in the last two decades as an important phenomenon in investment banks. A prominent early example was that of Bruce Wasserstein and Joseph

[34] Similarly, Acemoglu and Pischke (1998, 1999) show that firms may pay for general training in the presence of labor market frictions that compress wage differentials for skilled workers. They suggest that wage differentials may be compressed because of labor market matching costs of one type or another, or because of labor market intervention which raises minimum wages.

[35] Culture has been studied by social scientists since the word was introduced to the English language by the anthropologist Edward B. Tylor (1871). Sociologists and anthropologists have devoted a great deal of effort to explaining why an adequate definition of culture is hard to come by. Our approach is close to Bower's (1966) early characterization of it as 'the way we do things around here'.

[36] The difficulties of moving from one organizational culture to another are illustrated by experimental work performed by Weber and Camerer (2003). They gave one subject eight from 16 pictures and they recorded the time he took to give another subject sufficient information to enable her to select the same pictures in the same order. Over 20 rounds of the same game, the time taken to perform this task dropped an average of 249 seconds to 48, as the subjects found verbal shortcuts for describing the pictures. Merging teams so that one member was unfamiliar with the private language developed by the other two raised task completion times to 130 seconds, after which convergence to premerger competence levels was extremely slow.

Parella who, as we noted in chapter eight, pioneered the 'deal making factories' of the 1980s. When they left First Boston in 1988 to start their own M&A advisory firm, they were followed in short order by over 21 First Boston bankers (and by a number of major clients). More recently, Frank Quattrone led a team of Morgan Stanley technology bankers to Deutsche Bank in 1996 only to leave two years later for Credit Suisse First Boston, taking with him a good part of his original team. In chapter ten we examine the more recent trend toward teams of bankers leaving the large, full-service, publicly traded banks to establish specialized operations in the spirit of the traditional banking partnerships.[37]

For as long as internal communications systems remained tacit, they required specific skills. It was however inevitable that, like the functional front-office activities, internal communications would in time be codified. The increasing ubiquity of computer systems eventually resulted in applications that supported formal modes of communication within companies. The most notable of these relate to risk management. As computer power has increased, it has become easier for investment banks to capture huge amounts of price and deal data in real time, and to employ the statistical tools of the financial economist to quantify both the risks to which they are subject, and also the performance of their employees. The wide adoption of risk management systems like the VaR approach of page 27 in chapter one has replaced informal cultural ways of communicating within dealing rooms with a technical skill that can be learned in a classroom, and which is highly transferable. The cultural ties that in the past bound investment bankers to their employers are therefore being steadily weakened, and labor mobility in affected businesses has increased accordingly.[38]

---

[37] Deutsche Bank suffered another large-scale defection to CSFB in 1999 when a group of Alex. Brown health care bankers (who joined Deutsche Bank via its acquisition of BT Alex. Brown) left, taking about two dozen members of their team with them. See *Investment Dealers' Digest* July 5, 1999. The firm filed a lawsuit attempting to prevent the bankers working for CSFB and bringing along fellow bankers and clients. Ironically, Deutsche Bank was itself the subject of a 1996 lawsuit, which was filed by ING Barings during the period in which Deutsche Bank was actively poaching bankers from other firms.

[38] Murphy and Zábonjník (2004a, 2004b) also argue that advances in management and computer science have caused an increased emphasis upon general, as opposed to firm-specific, skills. They use this to explain increased CEO mobility and wages, and they provide evidence in support of their theory that CEOs are more likely than ever before to have an MBA.

Of course, cultural factors remain important in investment banking. Cultural differences are particularly pronounced between retail brokerage firms and wholesale investment banks. Cultural clashes between such firms can have a pronounced effect upon their effectiveness when they merge. At the time of the merge between Salomon and Smith Barney the ratings agencies commented upon this risk, and noted that it was an important ratings consideration.[39] More recently, as we noted on page 7 of chapter one, the recent combination of the wholesale investment bank Morgan Stanley with the retail broking firm Dean Witter caused massive ructions, which ultimately forced out the CEO, Phillip Purcell, in favor of a more traditional human capitalist, John Mack.

Covenants Not to Compete

In the absence of formal property rights over tacit knowledge, partnerships created an extra-legal environment within which senior agents could commit themselves to mentor the upcoming generation. For as long as they operated at a relatively small scale, partnerships achieved what a formal contract could not. But the information technology revolution expanded the efficient scale for investment banking so far that the partnership form had to be abandoned, to be replaced by joint-stock ownership. Further advances in computing and financial economics broke down the remaining cultural barriers to interfirm banker mobility, until today extra-legal attempts to tie investment bankers to a single firm seem highly ineffective. Investment banks have responded in two ways. First, they have attempted to use formal black-letter law contracts to restrict employee freedom of movement; and second, they have experimented with legislative protections for their intellectual property. We discuss the former in this subsection and the latter in the next.

As we noted on page 274, formal contracting can never be the basis of a perfectly efficient level of human capital acquisition because it is impossible to establish formal property rights over the central asset, tacit knowledge. But, to the extent that tacit knowledge remains socially useful, it is desirable that firms should have an incentive to invest in it. Covenants Not to Compete, or CNCs, are an attempt to provide this incentive. Employment contracts with a CNC restrict the employee's ability to work for a competitor within a specific period

---

[39] See the *Investment Dealers' Digest, Inc.* Mergers & Acquisitions Report of September 29, 1997 (p. 4).

after leaving the firm, typically a few months. Covenants Not to Compete have been recognized by the law for sometime, but they have become commonplace in employment contracts only over the past decade.[40]

Employees sign CNCs because they believe that in doing so, they are giving their employers an incentive to invest in their general training. Because it is impossible to contract directly over mentoring, the CNC is not however a perfect substitute for the partnership. There is a danger that the employee will leave and take his skills with him in circumstances not covered by the contract. It may also be hard to renegotiate the contract after training has occurred, so that the newly minted human capitalist may not be employed in the most efficient manner.[41]

The above difficulties explain why investment banks, who could rely upon the incentives inherent in their partnership form, did not emphasize formal CNC contracts until employee mobility became a problem.[42] By the late 1980s the employment contracts of senior Wall Street bankers commonly featured CNCs. As team transfers became increasingly popular in the 1990s (see p. 285), CNCs became increasingly common even in the employment contracts of less senior bankers.[43]

As a commitment device, CNCs are undermined by enforcement problems. In some states, notably Massachusetts, the courts have looked favorably upon them. Other states, particularly New York and California, have been less willing to enforce CNCs.[44] This problem

---

[40] See Blake (1960), Stone (2004: 130), and Whitmore (1990).

[41] Posner, Triantis, and Triantis (2004) argue that when renegotiation is difficult, an appropriate choice of contractual scope can give the employee bargaining power to counterbalance the power of the employer, thus achieving first best.

[42] For example, the IPO registration statements filed by such early movers as Merrill Lynch, EF Hutton, and Dean Witter, make no mention of contractual mechanisms for retention of key people. By the mid-1980s, the registration statements filed by Bear, Stearns, and Morgan Stanley, refer to such methods but they are not central themes in the prospectus. By contrast, retention plans are at the center of the discussion in the recent IPO prospectuses filed by Goldman Sachs, Lazard Freres, and Greenhill.

[43] See *Investment News*, April 24, 2000, *Investment Dealers' Digest*, July 6, 1998 and *Investment Dealers' Digest*, March 19, 2001.

[44] See Malsberger (1996) for a state-by-state summary of the statutory and common-law limits of covenant enforceability. For comments on this by attorneys and bankers, see *Investment News*, April 24, 2000 and *Investment Dealers' Digest*, March 19, 2001. Both articles suggest that recent court decisions have been more favorable toward employers. Gilson (1999) suggests that California's relatively weak enforcement of CNCs contributed to the interregional knowledge transfers that Saxenian (1994) believes explain why Silicon Valley continues to succeed while Route 128 in Massachusetts declines. Gilson's argument suggests that CNCs create socially

has led investment bankers to explore alternative contractual means of tying their key workers to the firm. They have become more creative in using deferred stock and option compensation payouts to discourage staff from leaving the firm, and have even traded business with competitors in exchange for agreements not to poach employees.[45]

Financial Patenting

Covenants Not to Compete are a crude attempt to create through black-letter law the incentive which used to be supplied by the partnership form to create tacit human capital. The shift toward codification of investment banking practice rendered this approach inevitable although, as we have seen, it was only partially successful. A related problem arises when the product of human capital is not protected by formal property rights: if an innovating investment bank's competitors can follow it straight into a market, the returns from innovation become correspondingly smaller and, despite its social utility, innovation levels decline.

Historically, the lack of property rights was not a major concern. Tufano's study (1989) of 58 financial innovations introduced between 1974 and 1986 suggested that first movers, most of whom were large banks, enjoyed sufficient cost advantages and reputational gains from innovation to obviate the need for formal protection from plagiarism, despite the fact that innovators rarely performed more than one deal before they were copied by their competitors.[46]

---

excessively strong property rights: this may be a result of the restrictions on alienability that come from poor renegotiability. Although no 'natural experiment' of the type analyzed by Gilson exists in investment banking, it is notable that financial innovation flourished alongside increasing banker mobility within the weak enforcement environment maintained in New York during the last quarter of the twentieth century. If there is merit in Gilson's argument, stronger enforcement coupled with increased patenting should undermine financial innovation.

[45] See the *Daily Deal*, July 12, 2004 where a headhunter is quoted claiming that 'Anyone who has been at Lehman since at least 1998 is basically unhireable by another firm, because they have something like $20 million in stock [that remains unvested]'. Such restricted stock units commonly vest in tranches or 'cliff-vest' between two and five years from the date of grant. On the latter point, the six major banks who underwrote Lazard's 2005 IPO agreed 'to specified limitations on their ability to hire [Lazard's] managing directors or employees and such underwriters have agreed to abide by such commitments for a specified time period'. See *The Business*, June 12, 2005, p. 10.

[46] See Tufano (2003) for a recent survey of the literature on financial innovation, much of which was influenced by his 1989 paper.

However, codification and computerization helped investment bankers more easily to reverse-engineer their competitors' innovations. This reduced the returns from innovation, and by extension, lowered the incentives to create the human capital from which innovation flows. The natural response was to use intellectual property law to seek formal legal protection for financial innovations. The earliest attempts to do so tied the innovations to the computer systems upon which they relied: the complex trading rules embedded in computer software were protected by trade secret laws and by nondisclosure agreements.[47]

Thus interest in financial patenting arose in parallel with attempts to patent computer software. The courts were at first unwilling to enforce patents on software and, to the extent that many financial innovations were embedded in software, they were therefore also unwilling to extend patent protection to them. Successful attempts to patent software until the middle of the 1990s tied it to the computer hardware upon which it ran. For example, the US District Court of Delaware upheld in 1983 a patent claim by Merrill Lynch for its Cash Management Account, on the grounds that the firm had successfully tied the implementation of the business method to a computer system. However, as software became increasingly distinct from the hardware on which it ran, software patenting in general, and financial patenting in particular, became increasingly hard.[48]

Merges (2003: 1) describes the 1998 Federal Circuit Court of Appeals decision on *State Street Bank* v. *Signature Financial*[49] as a 'major inflexion point in U.S. law'. The State Street case established definitively that 'methods of doing business' were patentable. As a result both financial patenting and business method patenting in general rose sharply.[50] But the quality of the patent applications was not uniformly high. Patent applicants failed in many instances to give proper attribution

---

[47] See Heaton (2000) and Merges (2003). One prominent example of litigation stemming from these protections is *Investors Guaranty Fund, Ltd.* v. *Morgan Stanley & Co., Inc.*, 50 US P.Q.2d [BNA] 1523 [S.D.N.Y. 1998].

[48] For a simple and highly illuminating discussion of this topic, see Merges (2003). For example, early attempts to patent such software as a spreadsheet application required patent attorneys to make the convoluted argument that, in switching from one application to another, users were reconfiguring the hardware upon which the software ran.

[49] 47 US P.Q.2d (BNA) 1596 (Fed. Cir. 1998).

[50] Lerner (2002) analyzes the rise of finance patents. For a critical survey of business method patenting, commenting in particular on the low quality of patents in this area, see Merges (1999).

to 'prior art', and a number of successful patent applications made general claims that rested upon well-known theoretical principles.[51] In the face of these problems, the industry successfully lobbied for a 'prior user right' that protected firms that had developed secret business methods from patent infringement actions.[52]

Investment bankers traditionally relied upon the private law embedded in their client relationships and in particular in their partnership agreements to protect the fruits of their intellectual effort from appropriation by their competitors. The late twentieth-century revolutions in information technology and financial economics both undermined these institutional forms, and also provided industry participants with tools that helped them more rapidly to recreate their clients innovations. It is for this reason that the industry has turned to formal patent protection. While it is too early to judge the impact that patent protection will have upon the industry, it is clear that it is an imprecise way of protecting the property rights that previously were maintained outside the formal law. Financial patents are hard to document, and patent applications are still of rather variable quality. A good deal of residual uncertainty remains concerning their enforceability. Firms that, like hedge funds, can rely upon less formal methods, such as straightforward opacity, to protect their ideas are likely to continue to do so. And, to the extent that opacity in one part of the business is inconsistent with opacity in another, we might expect organizations for which intellectual property is extremely important to break up their constituent operations. We return to this theme in chapter ten.

CONCLUSION

Since the inception of their business, investment bankers have relied upon tacit knowledge. Historically, it underpinned their management of client relationships, the placement of new securities, the selection and management of trading strategies, and a host of advisory activities. Like the price-sensitive information that lies at the heart of investment banking, it is impossible to establish formal property rights over tacit knowledge. Hence investment bankers had to find extra-legal mechanisms that would allow them to maintain this knowledge, and to pass it on through mentoring relationships. We have argued in this chapter that the partnership form provided these mechanisms.

---

[51] See Lerner (2002), Heaton (2000), and Wilhelm (2005).
[52] The right is embodied in section 273 of the Patent Act: see Merges (2003: 6).

The parallel late twentieth-century revolutions in information processing and financial economics led to a fundamental restructuring of investment banks. Increased codification of knowledge, coupled with new economies of scale, caused the banks to abandon the partnership form in favor of joint-stock ownership, which allowed them to raise the capital they needed to expand their operations. The consequence was a massive increase in labor mobility within the investment banking world, and a reduction in the strength of the investment bank's property rights over both tacit knowledge and financial innovations.

As extra-legal modes of intellectual property protection eroded, investment banks turned increasingly to black-letter law for protection against appropriation. Innovations in employment contracts such as CNCs were intended to protect investment bank investments in the general human capital of their employees, while the recent explosion in financial patenting is an attempt to prevent appropriation of innovative ideas.

But it is precisely because formal property rights over general human capital and financial innovations are so difficult to establish that investment banks turned in the first place to organizational and extra-legal ways of protecting their investments. In short, none of the formal legal mechanisms for intellectual property protection is a perfect substitute for the informal mechanisms that they replace. And in some parts of the industry, most notably in advisory work, tacit and general human capital continue to sit at the heart of the business, while economies of scale remain negligible. The case for public ownership in these businesses is therefore tenuous: to the extent that they can be separated from large-scale codifiable activities like trading and investment management, it would seem sensible to do so. The recent rise of the investment bank advisory boutique is therefore perhaps unsurprising. Indeed, one could argue that these boutiques are the only firms that today embody the relational and tacit activities that historically were associated with investment banking. This is the topic of the final chapter of the book.

10

What Next?

Financial markets lie at the heart of capitalist economies. They provide a forum within which the rights to control productive enterprise and to receive the cash flows that it generates can be bought and sold. When financial markets function well, an entrepreneur endowed only with a good idea will be able to raise the finance needed to develop it. Trading in financial markets generates information that helps investors to allocate capital to its most efficient uses, and it helps to ensure that productive assets, whether intellectual or physical, end up under the most effective ownership.

Some of the trade in financial markets relies upon information that is not in the public domain, and over which it is impossible to contract legally. In this book we have advanced the thesis that investment banks evolved to facilitate the creation and exchange of this information in marketplaces that are governed by home-made law. We argue that skills upon which they relied can be traced back to mediaeval trade within closed communities like the Maghribi. The trans-Atlantic information networks upon which investment banking was built were developed by eighteenth-century commodity traders, some of whose descendants later came to dominate the nineteenth-century financial world.

The eighteenth-century Atlantic trade, the nineteenth-century market for government and railroad bonds, and the twentieth-century development of industrial stock markets all rested upon tacit skill. Investment bankers and their antecedents relied upon personal relationships and knowledge born of long experience. Even to the extent that they were written down, their activities were virtually unenforceable in court, and most of their actions were in any case entirely hidden from the public gaze. Investment banking relied upon trust and long-lived reputation, and investment bankers drew their colleagues and many of their business contacts from their immediate social circle.

The information technology revolution has changed all of this. Investment bankers used to do much of their risk management during the hiring process;[1] risk positions at today's firms are captured and analyzed using computer systems. Computer systems in modern investment banks increase the scale at which the experts who use them operate. And, while the individuals who design and operate these systems are as smart and as essential to the banks in which they work as their predecessors, their skill is increasingly of a different type. Securities trading and valuation is an increasingly codifiable activity that can be learned in professional schools. Even the management of security market business is being systematized, as the processes through which risk models are accepted and trades are booked are increasingly tracked using computer systems.

Is this activity really investment banking as we described it in chapters four to seven of this book? Security market participants rely more and more upon black-letter law to regulate their activities. Advances in financial economics allow for the immediate quantification of performance, and hence in some markets have lowered the importance of reputation as an intermediating device: we saw a graphic illustration of this effect on page 246 of chapter eight. For sure, relationships still matter, but in securities markets characterized by increasing product commoditization and aggressive price competition they are of diminishing importance. If securities market trade no longer rests upon private law, is it really an investment banking activity?

Of course, investment banking is whatever the investment banks do. But we believe that the gulf between the tacit skills of the traditional human capitalist and the codifiable skills of the modern securities market player is widening, that it is central to an understanding of the current tensions in the industry, and that it is likely to inform future developments. This chapter is devoted to an analysis of these issues.

LARGE, COMPLEX BANKING ORGANIZATIONS

Chapter nine emphasizes the impact that systematization and computerization had upon investment banking in the late twentieth century. These effects were also at work in the commercial banking world, although they had a longer provenance there: Adam Smith observed the potential for codification of retail banking activity as early as 1776 (see page 265 above). When computer analysis of commercial loan default statistics became possible, codification spread beyond straightforward customer service and into small loans: the advent of

---

[1] We are indebted to Dr Joseph Langsam of Morgan Stanley for this observation.

Altman's (1968) Z-Scores heralded the widespread use of credit scoring to assess commercial loan applications and consumer credit requests. As we noted on page 246 of chapter eight, further computerization in the 1980s reduced still further the importance of human agency in retail banking, so that smaller firms like Bankers Trust could not attain the scale necessary to participate.

As commercial banks built formal risk models and embraced computer technology their profit margins shrank. At the same time, the emergence of the junk bond market represented an encroachment by the investment banks upon businesses that traditionally had been the preserve of the commercial banks: 35 per cent of the $38 billion of new junk bond issuance in 1992 was used to refinance bank debt.[2] It was therefore natural that commercial banks should wish to use their new technical skills in the security markets. Although the Glass–Steagall Act was not formally repealed until 1999, commercial banks were given increasing freedom through the 1990s to compete for corporate security underwriting mandates.

The erosion of the division between commercial and investment banking began with the Fed's approval in December 1986 of an application by Bankers Trust to underwrite commercial paper. Their successful application was soon followed by applications from a small group of major money center commercial banks. In January 1989 the Fed approved applications to underwrite corporate debt issues by Citibank, Bankers Trust, Chase Manhattan, J.P. Morgan and Security Pacific; approval for these firms to underwrite corporate equity issues followed a year later. Securities activities within commercial banks were initially confined to so-called Section 20 subsidiaries, named for the section of the Glass–Steagall Act under which they were established; within the subsidiaries, risky underwriting activities could account for no more than five per cent of gross revenue.[3]

Commercial banks also competed in traditional investment bank activities by developing loan sales markets and by lending in support of the highly leveraged buyouts, acquisitions, and recapitalizations

---

[2] *Wall Street Journal*, May 18, 1993. For a more detailed account of the emergence of competition between commercial and investment banks, see Benveniste, Singh, and Wilhelm (1993).

[3] The gross revenue restriction was raised to 10 per cent in September, 1989 and continued to be ratcheted up throughout the 1990s. Commercial banks nevertheless had an incentive to expand their low-risk underwriting business in federal, state, and local government issues so as to relax the dollar constraint on their corporate issuance business.

of the late 1980s. The market for loan sales grew very rapidly: by 1988 outstanding loans in this market stood at $53 billion.[4] As we note on page 248 of chapter eight, commercial banks had a cost advantage over their investment bank competitors both because they had a deposit insurance subsidy, and as a result of the widely-held perception that the largest banks were too big to fail. Moreover, they were able to bundle lending and underwriting business in a way that the investment houses could not: by the early 1990s investment banks were complaining that commercial banks were winning underwriting mandates by "tying" them to commercial loans. This pricing strategy was so successful that by the late 1990s even the most reputable investment banks were forced to increase their lending capacity in order to compete.[5]

In moving into debt underwriting, commercial banks were playing to their strengths: debt securities had much in common with commercial loans, bond valuation was susceptible to the technical approaches they had created for their lending business, and there were clear complementarities between the businesses. Similarly, we saw in footnote 26 on page 279 that the commercial banks brought their capital to the derivatives trading partnerships in the late 1980s. Once again, they were building on their core competencies: derivatives trading at this time was a largely codified activity which commercial banks could manage, and they were able to operate at a scale that was essential as these businesses became increasingly competitive.

The tendency towards consolidation in the more codified aspects of investment banking is illustrated in figure 10.1, which provides a summary of the ten largest investment banks by capitalization as of 2001, and their organizational form from 1954 onward.[6] Two waves of consolidations are illustrated. The first, which runs from 1970 to 1988, is the series of investment bank mergers and flotations that occurred when the NYSE responded to technological pressures by relaxing its rules to permit its members to incorporate: we discuss these mergers in chapters eight and nine. The second wave of mergers runs from

---

[4] Benveniste, Singh, and Wilhelm (1993: p. 113)

[5] See "Morgan Stanley injects about $2 billion into bank unit, aiming to boost lending," *Wall Street Journal*, August 16, 2001, B7. Ljungqvist et al. (2006) and Drucker and Puri (2005) provide evidence of the influence of lending relationships on the issuer's choice among banks to underwrite securities issues. Drucker and Puri also provide further background on tying practices and their scope.

[6] Figure 10.1 is intended to be illustrative rather than comprehensive.

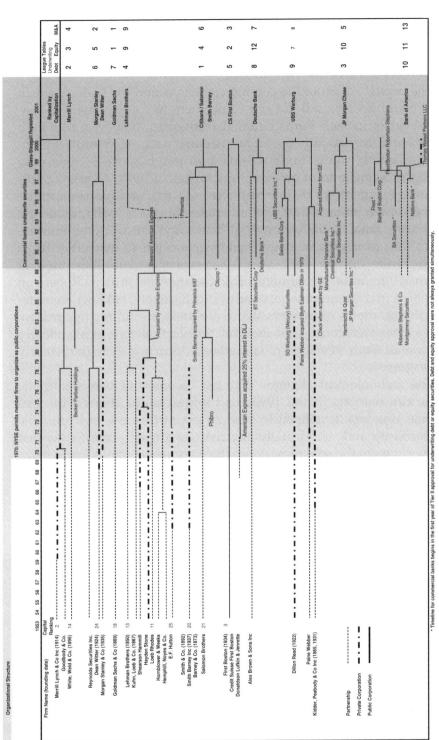

Figure 10.1. *Origins and precursors of leading investment banks*

* Timeline for commercial banks begins in the first year of Tier II approval for underwriting debt or equity securities. Debt and equity approval were not always granted simultaneously.

1989 to the end of the century and reflects the effects of the gradual relaxation of the Glass–Steagall Act.

The capitalization of the commercial banks and the scale at which they could operate still did not equip them to compete with investment banks in tacit human capital businesses, however. Although their early forays into the debt markets were successful, significant access to equity underwriting business frequently came only with the acquisition of an existing investment bank. Moreover, this type of acquisition was a risky strategy: the key human capitalists upon whom tacit investment banking business relied frequently found the scale of the commercial banks and the working environment that they presented uncongenial, and left to join other firms or to strike out on their own. Of the acquisitions illustrated in figure 10.1, those of Hambrecht & Quist, Alex Brown, Robertson Stephens and Montgomery Securities (collectively, HARM) are noteworthy examples of mergers that were unsuccessful for this reason: these firms were small, and their relationships were typically closely associated with key individuals whose departure was particularly damaging.

The technological changes that led commercial banks into the securities markets in the 1990s had wider ramifications. Financial engineering has developed to such an extent that it is now possible to parcel up and sell virtually any risk. As a result, credit risks that formerly were the sole preserve of the commercial banks are increasingly transferred, via either securitizations or the credit derivatives market, to other financial institutions. Similarly, insurance company investment portfolios are increasingly susceptible to the type of risk management that has taken hold in the investment banking world. It is perhaps unsurprising that, in parallel with their move into investment banking, the commercial banks started to experiment with mergers that involved other types of financial institution.

This process of financial consolidation was particularly in evidence in Europe, where it was unconstrained by regulation. Between 1985 and 1999 the value of European merger and acquisition deals involving a commercial bank and an insurance company was $89.6 billion, or 11.6% of all acquisitions by European financial institutions.[7]

---

[7] For a detailed discussion of the rationale behind conglomeration, see Berger et al. (2000), Milbourn, Boot, and Thakor (1999) and Dierick (2004). Santos (1998) discusses mergers between banks and insurance firms. See Lown et al. (2000) for detailed discussion about, and statistics concerning, the development of the European bancassurance market. A detailed discussion of conglomeration experience in the Benelux countries is provided by the National Bank of Belgium (2002).

The forces that resulted in European conglomeration were also at work in the United States: the Federal Reserve was responding to them in 1998 when it approved the merger of Citicorp and Travelers. Finally, the November 1999 passage of the Gramm–Leach–Bliley Act dismantled the legal barriers to the integration of financial services firms that had been erected by the 1933 passage of the Glass–Steagall Act.[8]

When the Glass–Steagall Act finally faded away, American investment bankers could have been forgiven for anticipating a period of relatively light regulatory intervention. Had they done so, they would have been mistaken. A recurrent theme throughout this book has been the natural tendency of regulators to bring as much of any business as they can under their purview. They are able to do so firstly when it is technologically possible, and secondly when regulatory intervention is perceived as legitimate. More and more of the technological barriers to regulation are being toppled by advances in computing; the expansion of the regulatory state was to be legitimized by public concern about corporate governance.

A series of crashes and frauds at the turn of the century involving Enron, WorldCom, Waste Management, Global Crossing, and others generated a climate in which corporations and their managers were seen as uncontrollable and which strongly favored the interventionist approaches that characterized the New Deal's approach to financial regulation. At the same time, auditing firms were widely perceived as using their auditing operations as "loss-leaders" to sell non-auditing services. Enron's collapse from the seventh largest firm by market capitalization to an empty and fraudulent shell, and the evidence that WorldCom created billions of false earnings by capitalizing expenses, provided the basis for arguments that strong medicine was needed to restore public confidence in the financial markets. The Sarbanes–Oxley Act, which entered the statute books 29 days after the disclosure of accounting irregularities at WorldCom in the summer of 2002,[9] was the response.

The Sarbanes–Oxley Act was the first substantive change to corporate governance law since the 1933 Securities Act. The 1933 Act was concerned mostly with complete and accurate disclosure about securities and, while some changes to the legislation in favor of the Federal regulation of behavior occurred in the ensuing

---

[8] The regulation of financial conglomerates is analyzed in some detail by Freixas, Lóránth, and Morrison (2005).

[9] Perino (2003).

70 years,[10] the Sarbanes–Oxley Act was the first attempt to shift the law in favor of the substantive regulation of corporate procedures and practices. The Act imposes rules for company audits, imposes restrictions upon corporate compensation policy, forces firms to create formal and verifiable systems to track and to check internal controls, and imposes significant penalties upon those who transgress the new laws.

While Sarbanes–Oxley is not specifically aimed at investment banks, it has affected their activities. Engle, Hayes, and Wang (2004) demonstrate that the costs it imposes upon public companies have enhanced their incentive to go private. More significantly, compliance with the Act has imposed substantial direct costs upon investment banks. Particularly in the famous sections 404 and 409, which require companies to codify their practices and to report in real time material changes to the company's financial situation, Sarbanes–Oxley undermines the emphasis within the traditional investment bank upon tacit knowledge.[11]

In summary, in the final decade of the twentieth century commercial banks were pushed into the security markets by a combination of advances in financial economics, innovations in information technology, and legal changes. Their greatest successes were in the debt markets, where practice was most codifiable, and where their capital, their scale, and their deposit insurance subsidy gave them a comparative advantage. They experienced problems in markets where tacit human capital remained important, such as equity underwriting, and advisory work. Attempts to purchase the tacit skills upon which operations in these markets rest met with mixed success, because many human capitalists preferred not to work for commercial banks. The passage of the Sarbanes–Oxley Act requires large incorporated firms to quantify their operations, and so makes it harder still for human capitalists to flourish in large institutions.

The shift towards scale in the investment banking mainstream has therefore undermined some of the tacit activities upon which investment banking rests, and attempts to regulate this shift have made matters worse. The following sections discuss the industry's response to this trend.

---

[10] See Ribstein (2002) for examples.
[11] See Altinkiliç, Hansen, and Hrnjić (2006) for an extensive discussion of governance within modern investment banks.

TRADING OFF REPUTATION AND
FINANCIAL CAPITAL

The model outlined in chapter nine suggests that incentives to pre-serve reputation capital are undermined by technological forces that drive investment banks to achieve larger scale.[12] This trend introduces tensions into investment banking firms. On the one hand, as bank-ing functions become more commodity-like, they lend themselves more nearly to arm's-length contracts that depend less on reputation-intensive, extra-legal enforcement than on formal law. On the other hand, many functions remain heavily dependent on tacit skills and reputation. The consolidation movement described in the preced-ing section has created considerable tension, as full-service banks have attempted to operate both tacit and codified functions under one roof. Recent developments at Goldman Sachs shed light on this tension.

Table 10.1 shows Goldman Sachs's sources of net revenue for the three years preceding its 1999 public offering and for the year ending November 30, 2007. Between 1996 and 1998, Goldman's net revenue from investment banking ranged from 34 per cent to 40 per cent of total net revenue. In 2007, investment banking accounted for less than 16 per cent of total net revenue. In contrast, net revenue from trading and principal investment accounted for 68 per cent of net revenue in 2007 after ranging from 28 per cent to 44 per cent between 1996 and 1998. Moreover, in 2007 the firm's asset management division closed a $20 billion private equity fund, operated the world's second-largest hedge fund group, and the largest mezzanine fund.

In spite of the relative decline in its investment-banking revenue, in 2006 Goldman was still the top advisor for mergers and acquisitions. However, it shared revenue and credit on about 50 per cent of the transactions on which it advised as opposed to 33 per cent in 2001.

---

[12] For further evidence of the extreme measures towards which technological advances are driving security industry players, consider recent competition among trading firms to "co-locate" with the central computers of electronic exchanges. In a December 15, 2006, front page article, the *Wall Street Journal* noted that, over the past three years, about 40 firms moved computers used in trade submission into the same building, or at least into the same neighborhood, as that occupied by exchange mainframe computers. In addition to smaller trading firms, the group includes Mer-rill, Goldman, Deutsche Bank, and J.P. Morgan. In one instance, Tradebot, a Kansas City-based trading firm, improved its speed of execution through Archipelago from 20/1000 of a second to 1/1000 of a second by moving its computers from Kansas City to Archipelago's New York building. The firm's CEO, Dave Cummings, contended that "we'd be out of business" had his firm not moved its computers.

Table 10.1. *Sources of net revenue for Goldman Sachs. Levels of net revenue (millions of US dollars) and percentages of the total are reported for major business lines for the three years prior to the IPO, and the year ending November 30, 2007*

	Year Ending in November			
	1996	1997	1998	2007
Net Revenue From Business Lines				
Investment Banking	2,113	2,587	3,368	7,555
Trading & Principal Investments	2,693	2,926	2,379	31,226
Asset Management & Securities Services	1,323	1,934	2,773	7,206
Total Net Revenue	6,129	7,447	8,520	45,987
Percentage of Net Revenue from Business Lines				
Investment Banking	34	35	40	16
Trading & Principal Investments	44	39	28	68
Asset Management & Securities Services	22	26	33	16

Fees for the 12 months ending August 14, 2006 were 0.31 per cent of $802 billion in transactions as opposed to 0.37 per cent for the preceding year.[13] In summary, although it remains the premier investment bank, even Goldman is facing an erosion of margins and a substantial relative decline in the importance of its traditional investment banking functions.

Goldman's CEO, Lloyd Blankfein, recently argued that "We couldn't have had the client business we have today if we hadn't developed our skills and expertise as principals[...]" to facilitate transactions on which the firm advised. An anonymous senior executive in the firm noted that "We used to agonize about how having a failed private equity fund or an aggressive one would affect our reputation. Today they don't worry about it. It's about generating earnings."[14] The theory developed in this book provides an explanation for the rise of capital-intensive functions in general, and for the competitive pressure to commit capital in support of traditional investment banking functions. With respect to the latter, although advisory functions remain a largely tacit activity, even they are not immune

[13] "Goldman loses cachet in M&A as companies seek multiple advisers," Bloomberg.com, August 14, 2006. In the same article, David Baum, former head of U.S. mergers and acquisitions for Goldman is quoted as saying that "The commercial banks have used their ability to provide loans to either be an actual adviser or at a minimum to get M&A credit for deals."

[14] Both quotations are from the New York Times, June 11, 2007.

to current developments in information technology. For example, some investment analysis activities are being codified, particularly as the bundling of investment analysis and investment banking is legislatively circumscribed. As the non-tacit dimension of analysis is separated from the tacit dimension, it can increasingly be performed virtually anywhere. J.P. Morgan has been outsourcing operational jobs to India for some time: it now performs a wide range of processing, risk management, research, and analysis on the subcontinent. Goldman Sachs and Morgan Stanley both have a significant presence in India.[15] One analyst recently suggested to us that the junior analyst's role is increasingly that of a project coordinator.[16] As a consequence, the ability to commit financial capital in support of advisory services becomes relatively more important in distinguishing a firm from its competitors.

As the relative importance of financial capital rises, incentives to build and preserve reputation capital are undermined. Because reputation remains the lifeblood of advisory functions, Goldman's strong standing within this industry segment should serve as a relatively strong counterbalance to the firm's incentives to engage in proprietary activities, such as private equity investment or proprietary trading, that might place client relationships at risk. The same is less likely to be true of firms with weaker advisory franchises. For this reason, we believe that it is no coincidence, for example, that with the exception of Morgan Stanley, the banks that have suffered most during the recent subprime mortgage crisis are also those that maintain relatively weak advisory functions. Other things being equal, one would expect there to be less effective pressure from the advisory function to reign in risk-taking behavior that places the firm's reputation at risk.

One apparent consequence of the crisis is a rising premium on executive expertise and leadership in risk management as incentives to preserve reputation capital diminish. Lloyd Blankfein, Goldman's CEO, has become the poster child, along with James Dimon (J.P. Morgan) and Richard Fuld (Lehman), for a new breed of CEO who "can't be fooled too easily by bond traders."[17] Commentary on the NYSE's CEO (and Goldman alum) John Thain stepping in to replace Stan O'Neal as Merrill's CEO emphasized his background in risk

---

[15] See "Wall Street jumps on the offshoring bandwagon," Khozem Merchant and David Wighton, *Financial Times*, 5 December, 2005 and "Investment banks now take passage to India," *Financial Times*, 6 December, 2005.

[16] Personal conversation with Logan Moncrief, January 11, 2006.

[17] See "Merrill Taps NYSE's Thain as CEO," *Wall Street Journal*, Nov 15, 2007, p. A1.

management and operational background as well as his experience running Goldman's mortgage desk during the late 1980s. Vikram Pandit's appointment to head Citigroup can be similarly interpreted. But even in the best-managed of circumstances, one would expect tension between financial capital and reputation capital-intensive functions. In the next section we examine one response to this tension.

SMALL, FOCUSED INVESTMENT BANKS

We argue in chapter nine that the partnership form favored by the traditional investment bank reflected its reliance upon tacit skills (see page 273). The importance of peer-group monitoring within partnerships and the risk of free-riding placed limits upon the size of the old investment bank partnerships, and hence upon their capitalization. For most of the period that we examine in this book, these limits were not an important concern, but they became relevant in the last decades of the twentieth century when the development of commercial computers created substantial economies of scale. The immediate consequence, as we argued in chapter nine, was a wave of investment banker flotations. This was followed in the 1990s by the blurring of the boundaries between commercial and investment banking that we outlined in the previous section, and the emergence of enormous banking supermarkets that combined commercial, retail, and investment banking.

The well-capitalized full-service banks of today are able to realize economies of scale and scope, but their size has a cost. As we saw in chapter nine, it is hard to incubate tacit human capital in publicly-quoted corporations. There are several reasons for this: the most important is that it is very difficult to tie the human capitalist's fortunes to the reputation of a corporation in the way that the old investment bank partnerships could. As a result, key individuals are less motivated to work hard to secure the future success of their firms. Moreover, a move to public ownership alters governance arrangements: when the firm is no longer owned by its managers, peer-group monitoring will be less effective and, when the firm is very large, codified performance metrics are likely to take the place of the informal evaluations that a smaller partnership can use. In some parts of the business the new metrics may simply be less accurate; in others, they may have a more subtle cultural effect upon efficiency: formal performance measurement undermines the cooperative and collegiate ethos that historically characterized many of the investment bank partnerships. As Morgan Stanley discovered in the wake of their recent acquisition of Dean Witter (page 7 of chapter one), the cultural dissonance that this causes can create significant management problems.[18]

In short, large scale operation, codified management practice, and public ownership all present significant challenges to businesses that rely upon tacit human capital. In some circumstances the ability to offer clients many banking services as part of a single package may generate benefits that compensate for these challenges, but there are many situations where this will not be the case. Many tacit human capitalists have little need for financial capital, and hence can work without the backing of an enormous financial institution. Hence, precisely as the trend for financial consolidation started to gather pace, the market for small investment banking boutiques that sell tacit knowledge also began a rapid expansion. Boutique operations are often private partnerships: if they are not, they tend to be small and focussed, and hence able to foster the collegiality and peer-group monitoring that characterized the older Wall Street investment houses.[19]

The traditional investment bank tacit knowledge activities concern advisory work in both M&A and corporate restructuring, principal investment in corporations, and complex trading. In each of these areas independent human capitalists have started to compete with the large banking houses. We discuss some of the salient features of each market below.

M&A Advisory Work

One of the earliest, and possibly the most important, of the boutique investment banks was Wasserstein Perella, which was founded in 1988 by two CSFB employees, Bruce Wasserstein and Joseph Perella, who between them were arguably responsible for creating the modern M&A market. Perella left the firm in 1993, and it was eventually

[18] The boutique investment bank Fox-Pitt Kelton was founded in 1971 to specialize in research and corporate finance in financial institutions. It was bought in 1999 by Swiss Re, but the marriage was unsuccessful in large part because of cultural differences between the boutique and the parent company ("Swiss Re puts boutique banking unit up for sale," Peter Thal Larsen and Lina Saigol, *Financial Times*, December 14, 2005). Fox-Pitt Kelton was eventually bought out by its management.

[19] Scott Bok, the US co-president of Greenhill & Co., stated in a recent interview that "We're trying to re-create what existed at the bigger Wall Street firms 20 years ago." ("Real Simple", Heidi Moore, *The Deal*, 17 February 2006).

sold to Dresdner Kleinwort bank in 2001 for $1.4 billion.[20] Wasserstein is now the chief executive of Lazard, while Perella left Morgan Stanley in 2005, and at the time of writing is forming a new boutique operation.

As we discuss above, the years since Wasserstein Perella's foundation have seen increasing consolidation amongst the major investment banks. The increasing emphasis within these firms upon capital-intensive business and the codification of practice has reduced the relative importance of advisory work to them: we argue above that it may also have diminished the effectiveness of their human capital-intensive businesses. It is certainly true that tacit human capitalists are increasingly attracted to boutique investment banks. Roger Altman, who founded the successful boutique Evercore Partners upon his 1996 return from a stint in the Clinton Administration with his partner Austin Beutner, notes that "at the big banks, investment banking is being downgraded – the proprietary trading desks are driving these firms now."[21] Robert F. Greenhill, who founded Greenhill & Co. in 1996, made a similar observation in a recent interview.[22]

These trends have made boutique investment banking more appealing and more remunerative for human capitalists. The 1990s saw a steady growth in the number and the influence of boutiques. The corporate governance scandals at the turn of the century (page 299 above) strengthened the business case for boutique firms: precisely because they are so focussed, boutique firms are not exposed to the potential conflicts of interest that may affect a full-service bank, and hence they are particularly attractive to boards that wish to guarantee the impartiality of their advice; among the most common boutique services are fairness opinions for the boards of companies that are about to be sold.[23] Some boutiques have capitalized upon this concern by creating structures designed to minimize potential

---

[20] "Emerging in a different role," Peter Thal Larsen, *Financial Times*, 20 February, 2001.

[21] "When a boutique bank is big business," James Politi, *Financial Times*, 5 February, 2006.

[22] In the interview cited in footnote 19 above, Greenhill said that "I think that if you're in the advisory business, being in a big conglomerate, where your relative contribution is tiny, is not appealing. I think the big conglomerate structure is very questionable if you're really interested in the advisory business."

[23] "When a boutique bank is big business," James Politi, *Financial Times*, 5 February, 2006.

conflicts.[24] In addition, the Sarbanes–Oxley Act has increased the potential costs to a corporate of relying on trust in cases where conflicts are possible, and the heavy administrative burden that the Act imposes upon investment bankers has rendered boutique work more attractive.[25] Investment banking in general, and boutique banking in particular, is built upon specific relationships and the movement of key people has had an effect upon the business: while the large investment houses continue to dominate the M&A market, the boutiques are attracting an increasing amount of large deal advisory work.[26]

Boutiques are currently riding high on a boom in merger activity. The related restructuring advisory business has a longer pedigree, and the boutiques have also successfully operated in this field. This business was particularly important when the dot com bubble deflated at the end of the 1990s, when restructuring was dominated by a small number of bankruptcy specialists: namely, DKW, the Blackstone Group, and Houlihan Lokey.[27] The reasons for boutique dominance in this market at the end of the twentieth century were close to those that obtained at the start of the century: restructuring advisory work is not particularly financial capital-intensive, but it requires careful negotiations that lean upon trust born of long relationships and strong reputations.

Boutique advisory firms provide services built upon tacit knowledge that arguably sits less comfortably within the full-service investment bank than it did two decades ago. We suspect that their role will grow in importance as computerization and codification continue to alter the operations of the large banks. However, as we noted earlier, predicting the scale and scope of their future operations is

---

[24] For example, Simon Robertson Associates will act for only one company in each sector, and will be paid for advice through an annual retainer, rather than on a per-transaction basis: see "Boutiques: Activity surge may test the smaller firms," Lina Saigol, *Financial Times*, 4 October, 2005. Robertson was the president of Goldman Sachs Europe: his August 2005 departure from the firm to create a boutique was perceived as evidence of a generational shift in Goldman, as trading and private equity operations eclipsed its advisory businesses: see "Robertson steps down at Goldman Sachs," Peter Thal Larsen, *Financial Times*, 2 August, 2005.

[25] See "Independence is honourable but big banks are profitable," *Financial Times*, 23 January, 2006, "Corporate financier joins boutique bank," Lina Saigol, *Financial Times*, 29 July, 2003, and "Diversity in banking," *Financial Times*, 27 January, 2006.

[26] See "Boutiques: still not quite the obvious choice for loans," James Politi, *Financial Times*, 27 January, 2005, and "Boutique banks move forward and shake off their 'Elephant's Graveyard' image," Lina Saigol, *Financial Times*, 17 January, 2006.

[27] See "Bankruptcy advisers get fat on restructuring," Robert Clow and Andrew Hill, *Financial Times*, July 11, 2001.

complicated by the fact that even they are susceptible to some degree of codification. Further evidence of increasing commoditization of advisory skills is reflected in the following quotation from a recent article by Wall Street Journal writer, Dennis Berman:

"During the great deal boom of the 1980s, the 'technology' of M&A was husbanded by a few dozen wonks inside New York investment banks and law firms. Over time, this knowledge spread far and wide. The ambitious wanted in on the action, and are now part of the legions trundling down from Connecticut each morning to work on the Street, in private-equity or in-house at a corporation. A company like Johnson & Johnson, for instance, might have some 200 people doing such work internally."[28]

The apparent democratization of advisory functions is likely to change the day-to-day activities of the boutique firms, but we do not think that it will make boutique banking redundant in the near future.

Private Equity Investment

Codification, and the competition that it has intensified, have lowered margins in equity underwriting, while the costs of compliance have risen. The large banks have turned more and more to capital-intensive businesses where they can use their large balance sheets to good effect, both by acting as principal in their trading operations, and by making private-equity investments: that is, by making control investments in unlisted equity.[29] Goldman Sachs, for example, has more capital invested in private equity investments than any of the specialist private equity partnerships[30] and Merrill Lynch has recently made an aggressive move into private equity investments.[31]

The move into private equity is not without its problems, however. The full-service investment banks aim to profit from advising and financing private equity firms: profits from this business have recently reached record levels.[32] Direct competition with the private equity

---

[28] Wall Street Journal, March 1, 2007, p. C1.

[29] See "Investment banks," LEX column, *Financial Times*, 16 December, 2005, for an analysis of these trends.

[30] See "Goldman/private equity," LEX column, *Financial Times*, 28 March, 2006.

[31] "Merrill takes a new turn with buy-out role," James Politi and David Whigton, *Financial Times*, 27 September, 2005.

[32] See "Private equity advice commands a premium," Lina Saigol and Peter Smith, *Financial Times*, 17 October, 2005, stating that "The world's biggest buy-out houses, including Apax, Texas Pacific Group and Blackstone, generated $8.2 billion of investment banking revenues in the first nine months of [2005] – the highest ever on record," and pointing to the "increasingly important link between buy-out groups and investment banks."

specialists has the potential to undermine this business, and to protect against this eventuality, some investment banks have reduced their private equity investments.[33]

If private equity does not sit altogether comfortably within a large diversified investment house, it may be a natural bedfellow for an advisory boutique. The tacit relationship and analytical skills that are important for advisory business are also essential for the type of activist investment management that is essential for a private equity house: indeed, we saw in chapter six how J.P. Morgan & Co. became pre-eminent in the nineteenth century by using its relationships and industry knowledge as an activist investor. Moreover, to the extent that teamwork, cross-monitoring, and tacit lines of communication are important within private equity houses, it seems clear that they will be better organized as focussed boutique operations. Indeed, some of the boutiques that we discussed in the previous section have private equity divisions: for example, investment is an important activity for Greenhill, while Blackstone, which was founded in 1985 as an advisory boutique, is dominated by its private equity activities, and Joseph Perella aims to raise $1 billion in order to combine investment with advice in his new boutique.[34] Of course, combining operations in this way creates potential conflicts: some private equity firms deal with this by avoiding hostile investments, while other boutique operations elect not to invest at all.[35]

Hence, as with the advisory work of the previous subsection, the increased emphasis upon codifiable activities and formal workflow management that has arisen within investment banks in response to both technological and regulatory factors has shifted tacit investment skills into smaller and more focussed organizations. These organizations are a major source of revenue for the full-service investment banks and, when the investment banks retain a presence in the private equity market, they are also a source of competition. As a result, full-service investment banks like Goldman Sachs that have a significant presence in the private equity market have to tread carefully if they are to avoid jeopardizing their reputations or their client relationships. Of course, there is no *a priori* reason to think that they will not succeed:

---

[33] "Goldman/private equity," LEX column, *Financial Times*, 28 March, 2006: Credit Suisse have pulled back from private equity, while UBS have completely exited the market.

[34] "Independence is honourable but big banks are profitable," *Financial Times*, 23 January, 2006.

[35] See footnote 24 on page 307.

investment banks have been dealing with conflicts of interest since their creation.[36]

Hedge Funds

Chapters eight and nine stress the increasing reliance upon technical knowledge in securities trading, and the increasing emphasis within investment banks upon financial rather than human capital. For example, the 2005 Goldman Sachs annual report states on page four of the letter to the shareholders that "The advent of electronic execution and price display systems [...] has permitted us to substitute technology for human capital in markets where price discovery has become commoditized."

As human capital becomes relatively less important than ever before in dealing rooms, investment banks are expanding their trading operations to take advantage of technological economies of scale. It is hard to combine the large-scale closely managed operations of a large modern customer dealing room with the complex and still hard-to-explain activities of the most skilled and advanced traders. These individuals are increasingly electing to work without the organizational and regulatory constraints of the investment bank in specialist trading firms known as "hedge funds." Banks that want to retain these people are increasingly attempting to create in-house hedge funds that will persuade them to stay.[37]

Hedge funds are increasingly important clients for the investment banks, which supply a full range of services to them, providing them with research, executing and settling trades, and even bringing them clients.[38] In other words, they supply most of the codifiable services upon which the hedge fund relies, leaving only the trade selection and management tasks to the fund managers. Although investment banks

---

[36] "Goldman/private equity," LEX column, *Financial Times*, 28 March, 2006, states in line with our arguments throughout the book that "Managing potential conflicts of interests is arguably a core competence of the modern investment bank," and argues that Goldman Sach's move out of hostile principal investments is reputationally motivated.

[37] See "Banking is boring," *Financial Times*, 1 July, 2005, recording a series of moves by key staff from investment banks into hedge funds, and noting that, in order to retain a talented junk bond trader, UBS established an in-house trading portfolio that would be opened to external investors.

[38] See "Hedge funds boost bank income," *Financial Times*, 28 November, 2005, noting that prime brokerage revenues from hedge funds were at record levels, and "The short view," Philip Coggan, *Financial Times*, 12 May, 2005, discussing the range of services that investment banks provide for hedge funds.

continue to assume principal risk on their own account, their hedge fund business could be usefully characterized as separating the most complex investment management part of the trading operation from the bank, while leaving its other activities intact. In short, investment banks are outsourcing their most complex risk-taking business to the hedge funds.

If investment banks are outsourcing the management and compensation of tacit human capitalists to the hedge funds, they are not withdrawing from the risk-bearing function. Some, like UBS, are establishing in-house hedge funds (see footnote 37 above); others are buying stakes in established hedge funds. A recent *Financial Times* article points to this trend, noting that the investment banks are paying "dizzying prices" for direct stakes in hedge funds, "buying big customers, in order to get skills they might have in house."[39] To us this seems entirely plausible: it is precisely because the skills of hedge fund traders are best incubated outside the large full-service investment houses that these houses are standing at arm's length from the funds, taking capital stakes in them, and providing them with the codifiable services that are best maintained within the bank.

Floating Small, Focussed Investment Banks

The focussed firms that we discuss in the preceding subsections were almost all established as private partnerships. As we note in chapter eight this had the advantage of binding the partner's personal wealth to the firm's reputation, and it guaranteed the small scale team interactions upon which tacit businesses rely. It is perhaps surprising that these firms have started to experiment, successfully to date, with public ownership: Greenhill & Co. was floated in May 2004 and the largely advisory investment bank Lazard was sold off a year later. More recently, private equity and hedge funds have explored and, in some noteworthy cases, even experimented with alternatives to the traditional partnership structure. In every such case there is clear evidence of a desire to preserve elements of partnership that our theory identifies as beneficial to developing and preserving tacit assets.[40]

Flotation ensures that the firm (potentially) has a long life, greater access to financial capital, greater visibility, and it enables the partners

---

[39] See "Buying hedge funds," LEX column, *Financial Times*, 22 February, 2006.
[40] On this point, see the discussion below and offering documents filed by Blackstone, Fortress Investment Group, and KKR.

to realize some of their wealth. We contend that the two waves of investment bank public offerings described in chapter nine primarily were driven by capital considerations. These firms enjoyed sufficiently smooth growth that it was feasible for rising generations of prospective partners to "buy out" their predecessors at fair value so that liquidity considerations would have been second order. Although Greenhill cited raising capital for private equity investment as an important motivation, the firm subsequently has identified the visibility gained through public ownership as a significant benefit.[41] Lazard's public offering clearly was not motivated by a need for additional capital (see the discussion chapter one) but rather provided a means for resolving an ongoing dispute between the firm's long-standing partners and more recently added, but equally influential, partners.

By contrast, we believe that Blackstone's June 2007 public offering, the first by a prominent private equity firm, reflected, in large part, the partnership's inability to provide for an orderly transition from the firm's founding partners, Stephen Schwarzman and Peter G. Peterson. Blackstone, founded in 1985 (as well as several others among the largest private equity firms) was very closely held and underwent enormous growth over a short time period.[42] In recent years, the firm enjoyed unusually favorable market conditions characterized by historically low interest rates and lax debt covenants. The value of Mr. Peterson's stake in the firm benefitted substantially from these conditions and few of the firm's 60 managing directors could have expected them to persist indefinitely. From the perspective of the partnership model developed in chapter nine, Mr. Peterson's announced intention to retire no later than year-end 2008 (at age 82) should have triggered a transfer of his ownership stake to rising partners from among this group. But in this case, "buying out" Mr. Peterson's stake was likely beyond the reach of the firm's junior members, even had Peterson been willing to withdraw the value of his claim over a longer time frame (he was scheduled to receive a payment of approximately $1.88 billion from the $4 billion proceeds raised at the IPO). Again, from the model's perspective, Peterson's (and perhaps Schwarzman's) efforts

---

[41] See "Real Simple," The Deal.com, February 17, 2006.

[42] At the firm's public offering, assets under management stood at about $79 billion having grown from $14.1 billion as recently as 2001 (and $3.1 billion in 1995). The firm's IPO price of $31 per share valued the firm at $33.6 billion. This and other information pertaining to the firm was reported in the firm's June 21, 2007 S1-A filing with the SEC.

to build a market for his ownership stake by way of mentoring junior members of the firm simply could not keep pace with the rapid and unprecedented growth in the value of their ownership stakes.

By generating a liquid market for ownership stakes, an IPO enables partners to more readily take their human capital away from the firm. Naturally, this is a concern for investors: Greenhill & Co. pointed to it in their S-1 filing, tying their directors to the firm for some time after flotation, and explicitly laying out the penalty payments for which they would be liable in the event of a breach of the noncompete clauses of their employment contracts within five years of the float.[43] Concerns over staff mobility were also an issue at the time of the Lazard flotation.[44] They were resolved in part through the contracts that the underwriting firms signed: see footnote 45 on page 289.

Staff mobility is not the only danger faced by a publicly owned boutique investment bank: another is size. Boutiques foster and sell tacit knowledge: Lazard's offer document stated that the firm would profit "on the basis of our intellectual (rather than our financial) capital." We have argued that tacit human capital is harder to maintain in large firms with a presence in many markets and highly codified reporting structures: such firms foster a culture that is inimical to the teamwork and peer-group monitoring upon which tacit human capital businesses rely. To date, boutiques that have successfully floated have resisted the temptation to spread their wings and to move into new markets.

The final risk factor for boutiques that go public is regulation. We noted above that the Sarbanes–Oxley Act has had the unanticipated consequence of driving many investment professionals from the investment banking houses into the boutiques. Flotation re-exposes boutiques to the danger that intrusive legislation will undermine their business models. For example, a private equity house that floats in the United States becomes subject to the provisions of the Investment Company Act of 1940, which lays down rules for the composition of the board of directors, their portfolio composition, and their fee arrangements. The likely incompatibility of these rules with its idiosyncratic requirements led Kohlberg Kravis Roberts & Co. to seek a listing for its $5 billion buyout vehicle on the Amsterdam Euronext

---

[43] For example, Robert Greenhill would have been liable for $56.6 million, and liability for the other managing directors ranged from $2 million to $18.8 million.

[44] See for example "Lazard," LEX column, *Financial Times*, 5 October, 2004, noting that "potential investors in Lazard will not invest unless they can be sure the dealmakers are in for the long run."

exchange. Similarly, Ripplewood Holdings, a US buyout firm, avoided the Investment Company Act when in 2005 it took one of its private equity funds public in Belgium.[45]

It is too early to say whether as publicly quoted companies the boutiques can continue successfully to supply the services that make them valuable. For sure, the permanence and the capitalization that come with a public quotation reassure investors. But public quotation increases staff mobility, brings formal reporting requirements that may undermine the bank's culture, creates a potential overexpansion problem, and raises the specter of regulation.

Private equity and hedge funds recently have experimented with two broad strategies that might be interpreted as attempts to respond to one or more of these concerns. Oaktree Capital Management and Apollo Management, for example, placed substantial private equity stakes with sophisticated investors (144a offerings) that would only trade on the Goldman Sachs Unregistered Equity (GSTrUE) OTC Market.[46] This approach avoids most of the regulatory requirements (reporting and otherwise) associated with a public offering while providing a measure of liquidity. In both cases, the deals were structured such that the firm sacrificed little in the way of transparency, illiquidity (for insiders), and control. Although forced to abide by the reporting requirements of publicly listed firms, Blackstone and Fortress accomplished much the same while gaining even greater liquidity through complex holding company structures that also provided substantial (and controversial) tax benefits to the firms.[47]

It remains to be seen which if any of the organizational innovations described in this section will succeed but the continued success of boutiques depends upon their ability to cope with pressures that ultimately derive from the tension between financial and human capital.

---

[45] See "A planned IPO follows Ripplewood's publicly traded buyout fund in Brussels," *Daily Deal*, 20 April, 2006, "KKR beats target with $5 bn for investment vehicle," Peter Smith, *Financial Times*, 1 May, 2006, and "Private to Public," Janet Lewis, *Investment Dealers' Digest*, 13 March, 2006.

[46] GSTrUE was an interesting innovation in its own right. The immediate interest in the concept generated imitation by a number of Goldman's competitors. Simultaneously, Goldman began the process of gaining patent protection (see the discussion chapter nine). By early November, the competitors reached an agreement to cooperate on a single platform to be operated by the Nasdaq Stock Market. See The *Wall Street Journal*, Nov 12, 2007, page C3.

[47] See each firm's, as well as KKR's S-1 filings for descriptions of the organizational structure and "The Transformers," *The American Lawyer*, November 1, 2007 for a nontechnical discussion.

CONCLUSION

Investment banking became necessary because the informational demands of the capital markets were too complex to be met through the type of arm's-length contracting that the courts can enforce. From their origins in the eighteenth-century Atlantic trade, through their nineteenth century rise as the architects of corporate America, to their role in the modern capital markets, investment bankers have helped to resolve the most complex resource allocation problems. Along the way they have changed in line with the needs of their clients, and in response to technological advances that have changed the nature and the distribution of the information that is their stock-in-trade.

We are either too smart, or not smart enough, to attempt to predict the future. But we suspect that in the investment banking industry, it will emerge from the dialectic between highly capitalized full-service investment banks and relationship-based boutique firms. Investment banking will always rely upon human agency and tacit skill. The challenge for investment banks in the future will be to create within very large companies the smallness that these qualities require.

Bibliography

Abramovitz, M. (June 1942). 'Savings and Investment: Profits vs. Prosperity?', *American Economic Review*, 32(2, Part 2: Papers relating to the Temporary National Economic Committee): 53–88.

Acemoglu, D. and Johnson, S. (Oct. 2005). 'Unbundling Institutions', *Journal of Political Economy*, 113(5): 949–95.

____ and Pischke, J.-S. (Feb. 1998). 'Why Do Firms Train? Theory and Evidence', *Quarterly Journal of Economics*, 113(1): 79–119.

____ ____ (June 1999). 'The Structure of Wages and Investment in General Training', *Journal of Political Economy*, 107(3): 539–72.

____ and Robinson, J. A. (May 2000). 'Political Losers as a Barrier to Economic Development', *American Economic Review*, 90(2): 126–30.

____ Johnson, S., and Robinson, J. (Dec. 2001). 'The Colonial Origins of Comparative Development: An Empirical Investigation', *American Economic Review*, 91(5): 1369–401.

____ ____ and Robinson, J. A. (Nov. 2002). 'Reversal of Fortune: Geography and Institutions in the Making of the Modern World Income Distribution', *Quarterly Journal of Economics*, 117(4): 1231–94.

____ Robinson, J. A., and Thierry, V. (Apr.–May 2004). 'Kleptocracy and Divide-and-Rule: A Model of Personal Rule', *Journal of the European Economic Association*, 2(2–3): 162–92.

____ Johnson, S., and Robinson, J. (June 2005). 'The Rise of Europe: Atlantic Trade, Institutional Change and Economic Growth', *American Economic Review*, 95(3): 546–79.

Aggarwal, R., Prabhala, N. R., and Puri, M. (June 2002). 'Institutional Allocation in Initial Public Offerings: Empirical evidence', *Journal of Finance*, 57(3): 1421–42.

Aghion, P. and Tirole, J. (Nov. 1994). 'The Management of Innovation', *Quarterly Journal of Economics*, 109(4): 1185–209.

Alchian, A. A. and Demsetz, H. (Dec. 1972). 'Production, Information Costs, and Economic Organization', *American Economic Review*, 62(5): 777–95.

____ ____ (Mar. 1973). 'The Property Right Paradigm', *Journal of Economic History*, 33(1): 16–27.

Allen, F. and Gale, D. (2000). *Comparing Financial Systems*. Cambridge, MA: MIT Press.

Altinkiliç, O., Hansen, R. S., and Hrnjić, E. (Mar. 2006). 'Investment Bank Governance', Mimeo, Freeman School of Business, Tulane University, New Orleans, LA.

Altman, E. I. (Sept. 1968). 'Financial Ratios, Discriminant Analysis and the Prediction of Corporate Bankruptcy', *Journal of Finance*, 23(4): 589–609.

——and Nammacher, S. A. (1987). *Investing in Junk Bonds: Inside the High Yield Debt Market*. New York: John Wiley & Sons.

Anand, B. N. and Galetovic, A. (July 2000*a*). 'Information, Nonexcludability, and Financial Market Structure', *Journal of Business*, 73(3): 357–402.

———— (Winter 2000*b*). 'Weak Property Rights and Holdup in R&D', *Journal of Economics and Management Strategy*, 9(4): 615–42.

Anderson, T. L. and Hill, P. J. (Apr. 1975). 'The Evolution of Property Rights: A Study of the American West', *Journal of Law and Economics*, 18(1): 163–79.

———— (Apr. 1990). 'The Race for Property Rights', *Journal of Law and Economics*, 33(1): 177–97.

Aruğaslan, O., Cook, D. O., and Kieschnick, R. (Oct. 2004). 'Monitoring as a Motivation for IPO Underpricing', *Journal of Finance*, 59(5): 2403–20.

Asker, J. and Ljungqvist, A. (Dec. 2005). 'Sharing Underwriters with Rivals: Implications for Competition in Investment Banking', Mimeo, New York University, New York.

Asquith, D. and Jones, J. D. (Oct. 1998). 'Evidence on Price Stabilization and Underpricing in Early IPO Returns', *Journal of Finance*, 53(5): 1759–73.

Atiyah, P. S. (1979). *The Rise and Fall of Freedom of Contract*. Oxford, UK: Oxford University Press.

Auerbach, J. and Hayes, S. L. (1986). *Investment Banking and Diligence: What Price Deregulation?* Cambridge, MA: Harvard Business School Press.

Austin, J. (1995 [1832]). *The Province of Jurisprudence Determined*. Cambridge, UK: Cambridge University Press.

Baker, G., Gibbons, R., and Murphy, K. J. (Nov. 1994). 'Subjective Performance Measures in Optimal Incentive Contracts', *Quarterly Journal of Economics*, 109(4): 1125–56.

———————— (Feb. 2002). 'Relational Contracts and the Theory of the Firm', *Quarterly Journal of Economics*, 117(1): 39–84.

Baker, G. P. and Smith, G. D. (1998). *The New Financial Capitalists: Kohlberg Kravis Roberts and the Creation of Corporate Value*. Cambridge, UK: Cambridge University Press.

Baker, N. (1973). 'Changing Attitudes Towards Government in Eighteenth-century Britain', in A. Whiteman, J. S. Bromley, and P. G. M. Dickson (eds.), *Statesmen, Scholars and Merchants: Essays in Eighteenth-Century History Presented to Dame Lucy Sutherland*. Oxford, UK: Clarendon Press, Ch. 10, pp. 202–19.

Baker, W. E. (Nov. 1990). 'Market Networks and Corporate Behaviour', *American Journal of Sociology*, 96(3): 589–623.

Banner, S. (1998). *Anglo-American Securities Regulation: Cultural and Political Roots, 1690–1860*. Cambridge, UK: Cambridge University Press.

Bar-Isaac, H. (Jan. 2003). 'Something to Prove: Reputational Incentives in Teams and Promotion to Partnership', Mimeo, London School of Economics, London.

Baron, D. P. (Sept. 1982). A Model of the Demand for Investment Banking Advising and Distribution Services for New Issues', *Journal of Finance*, 37(4): 955–76.

_____ and Holmström, B. (Dec. 1980). 'The Investment Banking Contract for New Issues Under Asymmetric Information: Delegation and the Incentive Problem', *Journal of Finance*, 35(5): 1115–38.

Barzel, Y. (1997). *Economic Analysis of Property Rights*. Cambridge, UK: Cambridge University Press.

_____ (Mar. 2000). Property Rights and the Evolution of the State', *Economics of Governance*, 1(1): 25–51.

Baskin, J. B. and Miranti, Jr, P. J. (1997). *A History of Corporate Finance*. New York: Cambridge University Press.

Beatson, J. (2002). *Anson's Law of Contract*, 28th edn. Oxford, UK: Oxford University Press.

Beatty, R. P. and Ritter, J. R. (Jan.–Feb. 1986). 'Investment Banking, Reputation and the Underpricing of Initial Public Offerings', *Journal of Financial Economics*, 15(1–2): 213–32.

_____ and Welch, I. (Oct. 1996). 'Issuer Expenses and Legal Liability in Initial Public Offerings', *Journal of Law and Economics*, 39(2): 545–602.

Bebchuk, L. A. (June 1988). 'Suing Solely to Extract a Settlement Offer', *Journal of Legal Studies*, 17(2): 437–50.

Becker, G. (1964). *Human Capital*. Chicago, IL: University of Chicago Press.

Bell, D. (1973). *The Coming of Post-Industrial Society*. New York: Basic Books.

Benson, B. L. (Jan. 1989). 'The Spontaneous Evolution of Commercial Law', *Southern Economic Journal*, 55(3): 644–61.

Benveniste, L. M. and Spindt, P. A. (Oct. 1989). 'How Investment Bankers Determine the Offer Price and Allocation of New Issues', *Journal of Financial Economics*, 24(2): 343–61.

_____ and Wilhelm, Jr, W. J. (Nov.–Dec. 1990). 'A Comparative Analysis of IPO Proceeds Under Alternative Regulatory Regimes', *Journal of Financial Economics*, 28(1–2): 173–207.

_____ Marcus, A. J., and Wilhelm, Jr, W. J. (Aug. 1992). 'What's Special About the Specialist?', *Journal of Financial Economics*, 32(1): 61–86.

_____ Singh, M., and Wilhelm, Jr, W. J. (Oct. 1993). 'The Failure of Drexel Burnham Lambert: Evidence on the Implications for Commercial Banks', *Journal of Financial Intermediation*, 3(1): 104–37.

_____ Busaba, W. Y., and Wilhelm, Jr, W. J. (Oct. 1996). 'Price Stabilisation as a Bonding Mechanism in New Equity Issues', *Journal of Financial Economics*, 42(2): 223–55.

Benveniste, L. M., Erdal, S. M., and Wilhelm, Jr, W. J. (Aug. 1998). 'Who Benefits from Secondary Market Price Stabilization of IPOs?', *Journal of Banking and Finance*, 22(6–8): 741–67.

―――Busaba, W. Y., and Wilhelm, Jr, W. J. (Jan. 2002). 'Information Externalities and the Role of Underwriters in Primary Equity Markets', *Journal of Financial Intermediation*, 11(1): 66–86.

―――Ljungqvist, A., Yu, X., and Wilhelm, Jr, W. J. (Apr. 2003). 'Evidence of Information Spillovers in the Production of Investment Banking Services', *Journal of Finance*, 58(2): 577–608.

Berger, A. N., DeYoung, R., Genay, H., and Udell, G. F. (2000). 'Globalization of Financial Institutions: Evidence from Cross-Border Banking Performance', *Brookings-Wharton Papers on Financial Services*, 3.

Bernhardt, D., Hollifield, B., and Hughson, E. (Summer 1995). 'Investment and Insider Trading', *Review of Financial Studies*, 8(2): 501–43.

Bernstein, L. (Jan. 1992). 'Opting Out of the Legal System: Extralegal Contractual Relations in the Diamond Industry', *Journal of Legal Studies*, 21(1): 115–57.

―――(May 1996*a*). 'Merchant Law in a Merchant Court: Rethinking the Code's Search for Immanent Business Norms', *Unversity of Pennsylvania Law Review*, 144(5): 1765–821.

―――(Aug. 2001). 'Private Commerical Law in the Cotton Industry: Creating Cooperation Through Rule, Norms, and Institutions, John M. Olin Law & Economics Working Paper 133, Chicago Law School, University of Chicago.

Bernstein, P. L. (1996*b*). *Against the Gods: The Remarkable Story of Risk*. New York: John Wiley & Sons.

Besley, T. (Oct. 1995). 'Property Rights and Investment Incentives: Evidence from Ghana', *Journal of Political Economy*, 103(5): 903–37.

Bias, B., Bossaerts, P., and Rochet, J.-C. (Jan. 2002). 'An Optimal IPO Mechanism', *Review of Economic Studies*, 69(1): 117–46.

Black, F. and Scholes, M. (May–June 1973). 'The Pricing of Options and Corporate Liabilities', *Journal of Political Economy*, 81(3): 637–54.

Blair, M. M. (Dec. 2003). 'Locking in Capital: What Corporate Law Achieved for Business Organizers in the Nineteenth Century', *UCLA Law Review*, 51(2): 387–456.

Blake, H. M. (Feb. 1960). 'Employee Contracts Not to Compete', *Harvard Law Review*, 74(4): 625–91.

Bodenhorn, H. (2000). *A History of Banking in Antebellum America*. Cambridge, UK: Cambridge University Press.

Bolton, P. and Scharfstein, D. S. (Mar. 1990). 'A Theory of Predation Based on Agency Problems in Financial Contracting', *American Economic Review*, 80(1): 93–106.

Booth, J. R. and Chua, L. (June 1996). 'Ownership Dispersion, Costly Information and the Certification Hypothesis', *Journal of Financial Economics*, 15(2): 261–310.

_____ and Smith, II, R. L. (Jan.–Feb. 1986). 'Capital Raising, Underwriting and the Certification Hypothesis', *Journal of Financial Economics*, 15(1–2): 261–81.

Bowen, H. V. (1995). 'The Bank of England During the Long Eighteenth Century, 1694–1820', in R. Roberts and D. Kynaston (eds.), *The Bank of England: Money, Power and Influence, 1694–1994*. Oxford, UK: Clarendon Press, Ch. 1, pp. 1–18.

Bower, M. (1966). *The Will to Manage*. New York: McGraw-Hill.

Brennan, M. J. and Franks, J. R. (Sept. 1997). 'Underpricing, Ownership and Control in Initial Public Offerings of Equity Securities in the UK', *Journal of Financial Economics*, 45(3): 391–413.

Bruchey, S. (1958). 'Success and Failure Factors: American Merchants in Foreign Trade in the Eighteenth and Early Nineteenth Centuries', *Business History Review*, 32: 272–92.

Buck, N. S. (1925/1969). *The Development of the Organisation of Anglo-American Trade, 1800–1850*. Devon, UK: David and Charles.

Burk, K. (1989). *Morgan Grenfell, 1838–1988: The Biography of a Merchant Bank*. Oxford, UK: Oxford University Press.

Calomiris, C. W. and Raff, D. M. G. (1995). 'The Evolution of Market Structure, Information, and Spreads in American Investment Banking', in M. D. Bordo and R. Sylla (eds.), *Anglo-American Financial Systems: Institutions and Markets in the Twentieth Century*. New York: Irwin, pp. 103–60.

Cantor, R. and Packer, F. (Summer 1994). 'The Credit Rating Industry', *Federal Reserve Bank of New York Quarterly Review*, 19(2): 1–26.

Carlton, D. W. and Fischel, D. R. (May 1983). 'The Regulation of Insider Trading', *Stanford Law Review*, 35(5): 857–95

Carosso, V. P. (1970). *Investment Banking in America: A History*. Cambridge, MA: Harvard University Press.

_____ (1979). *More Than a Century of Investment Banking: The Kidder, Peabody & Co. Story*. New York: McGraw-Hill.

_____ (1987). *The Morgans: Private International Bankers, 1854–1913*. Cambridge, MA: Harvard University Press.

Carow, K. A. (Feb. 1999). 'Evidence of Early-Mover Advantages in Underwriting Spreads', *Journal of Financial Services Research*, 15(1): 37–55.

Carruthers, B. G. (1996). *City of Capital: Politics and Markets in the English Financial Revolution*. Princeton, NJ: Princeton University Press.

Carter, R. B. and Manaster, S. (Sept. 1990). 'Initial Public Offerings and Underwriter Reputation', *Journal of Finance*, 45(4): 1045–67.

_____ Dark, F. H., and Singh, A. K. (Feb. 1998). 'Underwriter Reputation, Initial Returns, and the Long-Run Performance of IPO Stocks', *Journal of Finance*, 53(1): 285–311.

Casares Field, L. and Karapoff, J. M. (Oct. 2002). 'Takeover Defenses of IPO Firms', *Journal of Finance*, 57(5): 1857–89.

_____ and Sheehan, D. P. (Mar. 2004). 'IPO Underpricing and Outside Blockholdings', *Journal of Finance*, 10(2): 263–80.

Chandler, A. D. (1990). *Scale and Scope: The Dynamics of Industrial Capitalism.* Cambridge, MA: Harvard University Press.

Chandler, Jr, A. D. (Sept. 1954). 'Patterns of American Railroad Finance, 1830–50', *Business History Review*, 28(3): 248–63.

——— (1977). *The Visible Hand: The Managerial Revolution in American Business.* Cambridge, MA: Harvard Belknap.

Chapman, S. (1984). *The Rise of Merchant Banking.* London: George Allen & Unwin.

——— (1992). *Merchant Enterprise in Britain.* Cambridge, UK: Cambridge University Press.

Chemmanur, T. J. (Mar. 1993). 'The Pricing of Initial Public Offerings: A Dynamic Model with Information Production', *Journal of Finance*, 48(1): 285–304.

——— and Fulghieri, P. (Mar. 1994). 'Investment Bank Reputation, Information Production, and Financial Intermediation', *Journal of Finance*, 49(1): 57–79.

Chen, H.-C. and Ritter, J. R. (June 2000). 'The Seven Percent Solution', *Journal of Finance*, 55(3): 1105–31.

Chen, Z. and Wilhelm, Jr, W. J. (Sept. 2005*a*). 'The Industrial Organization of Financial Market Information Production', Mimeo, McIntire School of Commerce, University of Virginia, Charlottesville, VA.

——— ——— (May 2005*b*). 'A Theory of the Transition of Secondary Market Trading of IPOs.' Mimeo, McIntire School of Commerce, University of Virginia, Charlottesville, VA.

Cheung, S. N. S. (Apr. 1983). 'The Contractual Nature of the Firm', *Journal of Law and Economics*, 26(1): 1–21.

Chowdhry, B. and Nanda, V. (Mar. 1996). 'Stabilization, Syndication, and Pricing of IPOs', *Journal of Financial and Quantitative Analysis*, 31(1): 25–42.

Clark, G. (Spring 1996). 'The Political Foundations of Modern Economic Growth: England, 1540–1800', *Journal of Interdisciplinary History*, 26(4): 563–88.

Cliff, M. T. and Denis, D. J. (Dec. 2004). 'Do Initial Public Offering Firms Purchase Analyst Coverage with Underpricing?', *Journal of Finance*, 59(6): 2871–901.

Coase, R. H. (Nov. 1937). 'The Nature of the Firm', *Economica*, NS 4(16): 386–405.

——— (Oct. 1960). 'The Problem of Social Cost', *Journal of Law and Economics*, 3(1): 1–44.

——— (1988). *The Firm, the Market and the Law.* Chicago, IL: University of Chicago Press.

Cohen, H. (1971). *Business and Politics in America from the Age of Jackson to the Civil War: The Career Biography of W. W. Corcoran.* Westport, CT: Greenwood Press.

Cope, S. R. (May 1942). 'The Goldsmids and the Development of the London Money Market During the Napoleonic Wars', *Economica*, 9(34): 180–206.

Cornelli, F. and Goldreich, D. (Aug. 2003). 'Bookbuilding: How Informative Is the Order Book?', *Journal of Finance*, 58(4): 1415–44.

Cortada, J. W. (1993). *Before the Computer*. Princeton, NJ: Princeton University Press.

—— (2000). Progenitors of the Information Age: The Development of Chips and Computers', in A. D. Chandler, Jr and J. W. Cortada (eds.), *A Nation Transformed By Information: How Information Has Shaped the United States From Colonial Times to the Present*. Oxford, UK: Oxford University Press, ch. 6, pp. 177–216.

Corwin, S. A. and Schultz, P. (Feb. 2005). 'The Role of IPO Underwriting Syndicates: Pricing, Information Production, and Underwriter Competition', *Journal of Finance*, 60(1): 443–86.

Daggett, S. (May 1918). 'Recent Railroad Failures and Reorganizations', *Quarterly Journal of Economics*, 32(3): 446–86.

Davis, L. E. and Cull, R. J. (2000). 'Capital Movements, Markets, and Growth, 1820–1914', in S. E. Engerman and R. E. Gallman (eds.), *The Cambridge History of the United States, Volume II: The Long Nineteenth Century*. Cambridge, UK: Cambridge University Press, pp. 733–812.

—— and North, D. C. (1971). *Institutional Change and American Economic Growth*. Cambridge, UK: Cambridge University Press.

de Bedts, R. F. (1964). *The New Deal's SEC: The Formative Years*. New York: Columbia University Press.

De Long, J. B. (1991). 'Did J. P. Morgan's Men Add Value? An Economist's Perspective on Financial Capitalism', in P. Temin (ed.), *Inside the Business Enterprise: Historical Perspectives on the Use of Information*. Chicago, IL: University of Chicago Press, pp. 205–36.

De Soto, H. (2000). *The Mystery of Capital*. London: Bantam Press.

Demsetz, H. (May 1967). 'Toward a Theory of Property Rights', *American Economic Review*, 57(2): 347–59.

—— (2003). 'Ownership and the Externality Problem', in T. L. Anderson and F. S. McChesney (eds.), *Property Rights: Cooperation, Conflict, and Law*. Princeton, NJ: Princeton University Press, ch. 11, pp. 282–300.

Diamond, D. W. (July 1984). 'Financial Intermediation and Delegated Monitoring', *Review of Economic Studies*, 51(3): 393–414.

—— and Dybvig, P. H. (June 1983). 'Bank Runs, Deposit Insurance and Liquidity', *Journal of Political Economy*, 91(3): 401–19.

Dickson, P. G. M. (1967). *The Financial Revolution in England*. New York: St Martin's Press.

Dierick, F. (Aug. 2004). 'The Supervision of Mixed Financial Services Groups in Europe', Occasional Paper 20, European Central Bank, Frankfurt.

Dixit, A. K. (2004). *Lawlessness and Economics*. Princeton, NJ: Princeton University Press.

Djankov, S., La Porta, R., Lopez-de-Silanes, F., and Shleifer, A. (May 2003). 'Courts', *Quarterly Journal of Economics*, 118(2): 453–517.

Drake, P. D. and Vetsuypens, M. R. (Spring 1993). 'IPO Underpricing and Insurance Against Legal Liability', *Financial Management*, 22(1): 64–73.

Drucker, S. and Puri, M. (Dec. 2005). 'On the Benefits of Concurrent Lending and Underpricing', *Journal of Finance*, 60(6): 2763–99.

Du Bois, A. B. (1971). *The English Business Company After the Bubble Act*. New York: Octagon Books.

Easterbrook, F. H. (1981). 'Insider Trading, Secret Agents, Evidentiary Privileges, and the Production of Information', *Supreme Court Review*, 1981: 309–65.

Eccles, R. G. and Crane, D. B. (1988). *Doing Deals: Investment Banks at Work*. Cambridge, MA: Harvard Business School Press.

Ellis, K., Michaely, R., and O'Hara, M. (June 2000). 'When the Underwriter Is the Market Maker: An Examination of Trading in the IPO Aftermarket', *Journal of Finance*, 55(3): 1039–74.

Endlich, L. J. (1999). *Goldman Sachs: The Culture of Success*. New York: Alfred A. Knopf.

Engle, E., Hayes, R. M., and Wang, X. (May 2004). 'The Sarbanes–Oxley Act and Firms' Going-Private Decisions', Mimeo, Graduate School of Business, University of Chicago.

Fang, L. H. (Dec. 2005). 'Investment Bank Reputation and the Price and Quality of Underwriting Services', *Journal of Finance*, 60(6): 2729–61.

Ferguson, N. (1998). *The World's Banker: The History of the House of Rothschild*. London: Weidenfeld & Nicolson.

Field, A. J. (Jan. 1991). 'Do Legal Systems Matter?', *Explorations in Economic History*, 28(1): 1–35.

Fischel, D. R. (1995). *Payback: The Conspiracy to Destroy Michael Milken and His Financial Revolution*. New York: Harperbusiness.

Frankel, T. (Spring 1998). 'Cross-Border Securitization: Without Law, But Not Lawless', *Duke Journal of Comparative and International Law*, 8(2): 255–83.

Franks, J. and O. Sussman (July 2005). 'Financial Innovations and Corporate Bankruptcy', *Journal of Financial Intermediation*, 14(3): 283–317.

Freeman, C. and Soete, L. (1997). *The Economics of Industrial Innovation*, 3rd edn. Cambridge, MA: MIT Press.

Freixas, X., Lóránth, G., and Morrison, A. D. (Apr. 2005). 'Regulating Financial Conglomerates', Discussion Paper 5036, Centre for Economic Policy Research, London.

Fried, C. (1981). *Contract as Promise*. Cambridge, MA: Harvard University Press.

Friedman, D. D. (1974). *Machinery of Freedom: Guide to Radical Capitalism*. New York: Harper & Row.

Friedman, L. M. (2005). *A History of American Law*, 3rd edn. New York: Simon & Schuster.

Gale, D. and Hellwig, M. (Oct. 1985). 'Incentive-Compatible Debt Contracts: The One Period Problem', *Review of Economic Studies*, 52(4): 647–63.

Galenson, D. W. (Mar. 1984). 'The Rise and Fall of Indentured Servitude in the Americas: An Economic Analysis', *Journal of Economic History*, 44(1): 1–26.

Garicano, L. and Santos, T. (June 2004). 'Referrals', *American Economic Review*, 94(3): 499–525.

Geertz, C. (May 1978). 'The Bazaar Economy: Information and Search in Peasant Marketing', *American Economic Review*, 68(2): 28–32.

Gilson, R. J. (June 1999). 'Legal Infrastructure of High Technology Industrial Districts: Silicon Valley, Route 128 and Covenants not to Compete', *New York University Law Review*, 74(3): 575–629.

_____ and Mnookin, R. H. (Jan. 1985). 'Sharing Among the Human Capitalists: An Economic Inquiry into the Corporate Law Firm and How Partners Split Profits', *Stanford Law Review*, 37(2): 313–92.

Golembe, C. H. (June 1960). 'The Deposit Insurance Legislation of 1933: An Examination of Its Antecedents and Its Purposes', *Political Science Quarterly*, 75(2): 181–200.

Gordon, S. (1999). *Controlling the State: Constitutionalism from Ancient Athens to Today*. Cambridge, MA: Harvard University Press.

Green, J. R. and Stokey, N. L. (June 1983). 'A Comparison of Tournaments and Contracts', *Journal of Political Economy*, 91(3): 349–64.

Greif, A. (Dec. 1989). 'Reputation and Coalitions in Medieval Trade: Evidence on the Maghribi Traders', *Journal of Economic History*, 49(4): 857–82.

_____ (June 1993). 'Contract Enforceability and Economic Institutions in Early Trade: The Maghribi Traders' Coalition', *American Economic Review*, 83(3): 525–48.

_____ (Oct. 1994). 'Cultural Beliefs and the Organization of Society: A Historical and Theoretical Reflection on Collectivist and Individualist Societies', *Journal of Political Economy*, 102(5): 912–50.

_____ Milgrom, P., and Weingast, B. R. (Aug. 1994). 'Coordination, Commitment, and Enforcement: The Case of the Merchant Guild', *Journal of Political Economy*, 102(4): 745–76.

Grossman, S. J. and Hart, O. D. (1986). 'The Costs and Benefits of Ownership: A Theory of Vertical and Lateral Integration', *Journal of Political Economy*, 94: 691–719.

_____ and Stiglitz, J. E. (June 1980). 'On the Impossibility of Informationally Efficient Markets', *American Economic Review*, 70(3): 393–403.

Habib, M. A. and Ljungqvist, A. P. (Summer 2001). 'Underpricing and Entrepreneurial Wealth Losses in IPOs: Theory and Evidence', *Review of Financial Studies*, 14(2): 433–58.

Hammond, B. ([1957] 1967). *Banks and Politics in America from the Revolution to the Civil War*. Princeton, NJ: Princeton University Press.

Hancock, D. (1995). *Citizens of the World: London Merchants and the Integration of the British Atlantic Community, 1735–1785.* Cambridge, UK: Cambridge University Press.

Hansen, R. S. (Mar. 2001). 'Do Investment Banks Compete in IPOs? The Advent of the "7% Plus Contract"', *Journal of Financial Economics*, 59(3): 313–46.

Hart, H. L. A. (1961/1997). *The Concept of Law.* Oxford, UK: Clarendon Press.

Hart, O. (1995). *Firms, Contracts, and Financial Structure.* Oxford, UK: Clarendon Press.

—— and Moore, J. (1995). 'Debt and Seniority: An Analysis of the Role of Hard Claims in Constraining Management', *American Economic Review*, 85(3): 567–85.

Hart, O. D. and Moore, J. (1988). 'Incomplete Contracts and Renegotiation', *Econometrica*, 56: 755–86.

———— (Feb. 1989). 'Default and Renegotiation: A Dynamic Model of Debt', *Quarterly Journal of Economics*, 113(1): 1–41.

———— (1990). 'Property Rights and the Nature of the Firm', *Journal of Political Economy*, 98: 1119–58.

———— (1994). 'A Theory of Debt Based upon the Inalienability of Human Capital', *Quarterly Journal of Economics*, 109: 841–79.

Hartwell, R. M. (1971). *The Industrial Revolution and Economic Growth.* London: Methuen.

Hayek, F. A. (Sept. 1945). 'The Use of Knowledge in Society', *American Economic Review*, 35(4): 519–30.

—— (1973). *Law, Legislation and Liberty, Volume 1: Rules and Order.* London: Routledge & Kegan Paul.

—— (1978). *The Constitution of Liberty.* Chicago, IL: University of Chicago Press.

Hayes, S. L. (Mar.–Apr. 1971). 'Investment Banking: Power Structure in Flux', *Harvard Business Review*, 49(2): 136–52.

—— (Jan.–Feb. 1979). 'The Transformation of Investment Banking', *Harvard Business Review*, 57(1): 153–70.

—— and Hubbard, P. M. (1990). *Investment Banking: A Tale of Three Cities.* Cambridge, MA: Harvard Business School Press.

Heale, M. J. (2004). *Twentieth-Century America: Politics and Power in the United States, 1900–2000.* London: Hodder Arnold.

Heaton, J. B. (Winter 2000). 'Patent Law and Financial Engineering', *Derivatives Quarterly*, 7(2): 7–15.

Hensler, D. A. (Mar.–Apr. 1995). 'Litigation Losses and the Underpricing of Initial Public Offerings', *Managerial and Decision Economics*, 16(2): 111–28.

Hidy, R. W. (1949). *The House of Baring in American Trade and Finance: English Mercant Bankers at Work, 1763–1861.* Cambridge, MA: Harvard University Press.

Hillman, R. W. (Summer 2001). 'Professional Partnerships, Competition, and the Evolution of Firm Culture: The Case of Law Firms', *Journal of Corporation Law*, 26(4): 1061–85.

Hofstadter, R. (1962). *The Age of Reform, from Bryan to F.D.R.* London: Jonathan Cape.

Holmstrom, B. (1982). 'Moral Hazard in Teams', *Bell Journal of Economics*, 12: 324–40.

____ and Tirole, J. (Aug. 1997). 'Financial Intermediation, Loanable Funds and the Real Sector', *Quarterly Journal of Economics*, 112(3): 663–91.

Horwitz, M. J. (1977). *The Transformation of American Law, 1780–1860.* Cambridge, MA: Harvard University Press.

____ (1992). *The Transformation of American Law, 1870–1960.* Oxford, UK: Oxford University Press.

Hughes, P. J. and Thakor, A. V. (1992). 'Litigation Risk, Intermediation and the Underpricing of Intitial Public Offerings', *Review of Financial Studies*, 5(4: RFS/WFA Symposium of Institutional Design): 709–42.

Hume, D. (1777). *Essays, Moral, Political, and Literary*, April (1985) edn. Indianapolis, IN: Liberty Fund.

Ibbotson, R. G. and Jaffe, J. F. (Sept. 1975). '"Hot Issue" Markets', *Journal of Finance*, 30(4): 1027–42.

James, C. (1987). 'Some Evidence on the Uniqueness of Bank Loans', *Journal of Financial Economics*, 19(2): 217–35.

Jenkinson, T. and Ljungqvist, A. (2001). *Going Public: The Theory and Evidence on How Companies Raise Equity Finance*, 2nd edn. Oxford, UK: Oxford University Press.

____ Morrison, A. D., and Wilhelm, Jr, W. J. (2005). 'Why Are European IPOs So Rarely Priced Outside the Indicative Price Range?', *Journal of Financial Economics*, forthcoming.

Jenks, L. H. (1927). *The Migration of British Capital, to 1875.* New York: Alfred Knopf.

Jensen, M. C. (May 1986). 'Agency Costs of Free Cash Flow, Corporate Finance and Takeovers', *American Econmic Review*, 76(2): 323–9.

____ (Sept.–Oct. 1989). 'Eclipse of the Public Corporation', *Harvard Business Review*, 67(5): 61–74.

____ (July 1993). The Modern Industrial Revolution, Exit and the Failure of Internal Control Systems', *Journal of Finance*, 48(3): 831–80.

____ and Meckling, W. H. (Oct. 1976). 'Theory of the Firm: Managerial Behaviour, Agency Costs and Capital Structure', *Journal of Financial Economics*, 3(4): 305–60.

Johnson, H. J. (2000). *Banking Alliances.* River Edge, NJ: World Scientific Publishing.

Johnson, S., McMillan, J., and Woodruff, C. (Apr. 2002*a*). 'Courts and Relational Contracts', *Journal of Law, Economics and Organization*, 18(1): 221–77.

Johnson, S., McMillan, J., and Woodruff, C. (Dec. 2002*b*). 'Property Rights and Finance', *American Economic Review*, 92(5): 1335–56.

Kane, E. J. (1989). *The S&L Insurance Mess: How Did It Happen?* Washington, DC: Urban Institute Press.

Kindleberger, C. P. (1993). *A Financial History of Western Europe*, 2nd edn. Oxford, UK: Oxford University Press.

Klein, B. and Leffler, K. B. (Aug. 1981). 'The Role of Market Forces in Assuring Contractual Performance', *Journal of Political Economy*, 89(4): 615–41.

Knack, S. and Keefer, P. (Nov. 1995). 'Institutions and Economic Performance: Cross-Country Tests Using Alternative Institutional Measures', *Economics and Politics*, 7(3): 207–28.

Kohn, M. (2004). *Financial Institutions and Markets*, 2nd edn. Oxford, UK: Oxford University Press.

Kreps, D. M. (1990). 'Corporate Culture and Economic Theory', in J. E. Alt and K. A. Shepsle (eds.), *Perspectives on Positive Political Economy*. Cambridge, MA: Cambridge University Press, pp. 90–143.

Krigman, L., Shaw, W. H., and Womack, K. L. (May 2001). 'Why Do Firms Switch Underwriters?', *Journal of Financial Economics*, 60(2–3): 245–84.

Kroszner, R. S. and Rajan, R. G. (Sept. 1994). 'Is the Glass–Steagall Act Justified? A Study of the U.S. Experience with Universal Banking Before 1933', *American Economic Review*, 84(4): 810–32.

Krueger, A. O. (June 1974). 'The Political Economy of the Rent-Seeking Society', *American Economic Review*, 64(3): 291–303.

Kyle, A. S. (Nov. 1985). 'Continuous Auctions and Insider Trading', *Econometrica*, 53(6): 1315–35.

Lamoreaux, N. R. (1985). *The Great Merger Movement in American Buisness, 1895–904*. Cambridge, UK: Cambridge University Press.

——(Winter 1995). 'Constructing Firms: Partnerships and Alternative Contractual Arrangements in Early Nineteenth-Century American Business', *Business and Economic History*, 24(2): 43–71.

——(May 1998). 'Partnerships, Corporations, and the Theory of the Firm', *American Economic Review*, 88(2): 66–71.

——and Rosenthal, J-L. (Spring 2005). 'Legal Regime and Contractual Flexibility: A Comparison of Business's Organizational Choices in France and the United States During the Era of Industrialization', *American Law and Economics Review*, 7(1): 28–61.

Landa, J. T. (June 1981). 'A Theory of the Ethnically Homogeneous Middleman Group: An Institutional Alternative to Contract Law', *Journal of Legal Studies*, 10(2): 349–62.

Langevoort, D. C. (Feb. 1987). 'Statutory Obsolescence and the Judicial Process: The Revisionist Role of the Courts in Federal Banking Regulation', *Michigan Law Review*, 85(4): 672–733.

Larson, H. M. (1936). *Jay Cooke, Private Banker*. Cambridge, MA: Harvard University Press.

Lazear, E. P. and Rosen, S. (Oct. 1981). 'Rank-Order Tournaments as Optimum Labor Contracts', *Journal of Political Economy*, 89(5): 841–64.

Leland, H. E. (Aug. 1992). 'Insider Trading: Should It Be Prohibited?', *Journal of Political Economy*, 100(4): 859–87.

Lerner, J. (Apr. 2002). Where Does *State Street* Lead? A First Look at Finance Patents, 1971 to 2000', *Journal of Finance*, 57(2): 901–30.

Leuchtenburg, W. E. (1963). *Franklin D. Roosevelt and the New Deal, 1932–1940*. New York: Harper and Row.

Levi, M. (1988). *Of Rule and Revenue*. Berkeley, CA: University of California Press.

Levin, J. and Tadelis, S. (Jan. 2005). 'Profit Sharing and the Role of Professional Partnerships', *Quarterly Journal of Economics*, 120(1): 131–71.

Litner, J. (Feb. 1965). The Valuation of Risk Assets and the Selection of Risky Investments in Stock Portfolios and Capital Budgets', *Review of Economics and Statistics*, 47(1): 13–37.

Ljungqvist, A. (2007). 'IPO Underpricing', in B. E. Eckbo (ed.), *Handbook of Empirical Corporate Finance*. New York: Elsevier and North-Holland.

—— and Wilhelm, Jr, W. J. (Apr. 2003). 'IPO Pricing in the Dot-Com Bubble', *Journal of Finance*, 58(2): 723–52.

———— (Aug. 2005). 'Does Prospect Theory Explain IPO Market Behavior?', *Journal of Finance*, 60(4): 1759–90.

—— Marston, F. C., and Wilhelm, Jr, W. J. (Dec. 2005). 'Scaling the Hierarchy: How and Why Investment Banks Compete for Syndicate Co-Management Appointments', Mimeo, McIntire School of Commerce, University of Virginia, Charlottesville, VA.

Ljungqvist, A. P., Jenkinson, T., and Wilhelm, Jr, W. J. (Spring 2003). 'Global Integration in Primary Equity Markets: The Role of U.S. Banks and U.S. Investors', *Review of Financial Studies*, 16(1): 63–99.

—— Marston, F., and Wilhelm, Jr, W. J. (Feb. 2006). 'Competing for Securities Underwriting Mandates: Banking Relationships and Analyst Recommendations', *Journal of Finance*, 61(1): 301–40.

Longstreet, J. R. and Hess, Jr, A. P. (1967). 'Characteristics of Corporate Issues in the Post-SEC Period', in I. Friend, J. R. Longstreet, M. Mendelson, E. Miller, and A. P. Hess, Jr. (eds.), *Investment Banking and the New Issues Market*, Cleveland, OH: World Publishing Company, ch. 6, pp. 332–93.

Loughran, T. and Ritter, J. R. (Autumn 2004). 'Why Has IPO Underpricing Changed Over Time?', *Financial Management*, 33(3): 5–37.

Lown, C. S., Osler, C. L., Strahan, P. E., and Sufi, A. (Oct. 2000). 'The Changing Landscape of the Financial Services Industry: What Lies Ahead?', *Federal Reserve Bank of New York Economic Policy Review*, 6(4): 39–55.

Lowry, M. and Shu, S. (Sept. 2002). 'Litigation Risk and IPO Underpricing', *Journal of Financial Economics*, 65(3): 309–35.

Macaulay, S. (Feb. 1963). 'Non-Contractual Relations in Business: A Preliminary Study', *American Sociological Review*, 28(1): 55–67.

Macaulay, S. (1985). 'An Empirical View of Contract', *Wisconsin Law Review*, 1985(3): 465–82.

Macey, J. R. (Winter 1984). 'Special Interest Groups Legislation and the Judicial Function: The Dilemma of Glass-Steagall', *Emory Law Journal*, 33(1): 1–40.

McChesney, F. S. (Jan. 1987). 'Rent Extraction and Rent Creation in the Economic Theory of Regulation', *Journal of Legal Studies*, 16(1): 101–18.

McGrane, R. C. (1935). *Foreign Bondholders and American State Debts*. London: Macmillan.

MacLeod, W. B. (Feb. 2006). 'Reputations, Relationships and the Enforcement of Incomplete Contracts', Discussion Paper 1978, IZA, Bonn, Germany.

Macneil, I. R. (May 1974). 'The Many Futures of Contracts', *Southern California Law Review*, 47(3): 691–816.

—— (Jan.–Feb. 1978). 'Contacts: Adjustment of Long-Term Economic Relations Under Classical, Neoclassical, and Relational Contract Law', *Northwestern University Law Review*, 72(6): 854–906.

Mahoney, P. G. (Jan. 2001). 'The Political Economy of the Securities Act of 1933', *Journal of Legal Studies*, 30(1): 1–31.

Malsberger, B. M. (1996). *Covenants Not to Compete: A State-by-State Survey*, 2nd edn. Washington, DC: BNA Books.

Manne, H. G. (1966). *Insider Trading and the Stock Market*. New York: Free Press.

Markowitz, H. M. (Mar. 1952). 'Portfolio Selection', *Journal of Finance*, 7(1): 77–91.

Martimort, D. (Oct. 1999). 'The Life Cycle of Regulatory Agencies: Dynamic Capture and Transaction Costs', *Review of Economic Studies*, 66(4): 929–47.

Martin, A. (Sept. 1974). 'Railroads and the Equity Receivership: An Essay on Institutional Change', *Journal of Economic History*, 34(3): 685–709.

Mauer, D. C. and Senbet, L. W. (Mar. 1992). 'The Effect of the Secondary Market on the Pricing of Initial Public Offerings: Theory and Evidence', *Journal of Financial and Quantitative Analysis*, 27(1): 55–79.

Mauro, P. (Aug. 1995). 'Corruption and Growth', *Quarterly Journal of Economics*, 110(3): 681–712.

Medina, H. R. ([1954] 1975). *Corrected Opinion of Harold R. Medina*. New York: Arno Press.

Merges, R. P. (1999). 'As Many as Six Impossible Patents Before Breakfast: Property Rights for Business Concepts and Patent System Reform', *Berkeley Technology Law Journal*, 14(2): 577–616.

—— (Fourth Quarter 2003). 'The Uninvited Guest: Patents on Wall Street', *Federal Reserve Bank of Atlanta Economic Review*, 88(4): 1–14.

Merton, R. C. (Spring 1973). 'Theory of Rational Option Pricing', *Bell Journal of Economics and Management Science*, 4(1): 141–83.

—— (1990). *Continuous-Time Finance*. Oxford, UK: Basil Blackwell.

_____ (June 1998). 'Applications of Option-Pricing Theory: Twenty-Five Years Later', *American Economic Review*, 88(3): 323–49.

Michaely, R. and Shaw, W. H. (Summer 1994). 'The Pricing of Initial Public Offerings: Tests of Adverse-Selection and Signalling Theories', *Review of Financial Studies*, 7(2): 279–319.

_____ and Womack, K. L. (Special 1999). 'Conflict of Interest and the Credibility of Underwriter Alanyst Recommendations', *Review of Financial Studies*, 12(4): 653–86.

Milbourn, T. T., Boot, A. W. A., and Thakor, A. V. (Feb. 1999). 'Megamergers and Expanded Scope: Theories of Bank Size and Activity Diversity', *Journal of Banking and Finance*, 23(2–4): 195–214.

Milgrom, P. R., North, D. C., and Weingast, B. R. (Mar. 1990). 'The Role of Institutions in the Revival of Trade: The Law Merchant, Private Judges, and the Champagne Fairs', *Economics and Politics*, 2(1): 1–23.

Miller, E. (1967). 'Background and Structure of the Industry', in I. Friend, J. R. Longstreet, M. Mendelson, E. Miller, and A. P. H. Hess, Jr. (eds.), *Investment Banking and the New Issues Market*. Cleveland, OH: World Publishing Company, ch. 2, pp. 80–175.

Miller, M. H. (Dec. 1986). 'Financial Innovation: The Last Twenty Years and the Next', *Journal of Financial and Quantitative Analysis*, 21(4): 459–71.

Mnookin, R. H. and Kornhauser, L. (Apr. 1979). 'Bargaining in the Shadow of the Law: The Case of Divorce', *Yale Law Journal*, 88(5): 950–97.

Modigliani, F. and Miller, M. H. (June 1958). 'The Cost of Capital, Corporation Finance and the Theory of Investment', *American Economic Review*, 48(3): 261–97.

Morrison, A. D. and Wilhelm, Jr, W. J. (Dec. 2004). 'Partnership Firms, Reputation and Human Capital', *American Economic Review*, 94(5): 1682–92.

_____ _____ (Feb. 2005a). 'Culture, Competence, and the Corporation', Mimeo, Saïd Business School, University of Oxford.

_____ _____ (Feb. 2005b). 'The Demise of Investment Banking Partnerships: Theory and Evidence', Discussion Paper 4904, Centre for Economic Policy Research, London.

Mossin, J. (Oct. 1966). 'Equilibrium in Capital Asset Markets', *Econometrica*, 34(4): 768–83.

Muir, R. J. and White, C. J. (1964). *Over the Long Term . . . the Story of J. & W. Seligman & Co.* New York: J. & W. Seligman & Co.

Mulherin, J. H., Netter, J. M., and Overdahl, J. A. (Oct. 1991). 'Prices Are Property: The Organization of Financial Exchanges from a Transaction Cost Perspective', *Journal of Law and Economics*, 34(2, Part 2): 591–644.

Murphy, K. J. and Zábonjník, J. (May 2004). 'CEO Pay and Appointments: A Market-Based Explanation for Recent Trends', *American Economic Review (Papers and Proceedings)*, 92(2): 192–207.

Murphy, K. J. and Zábonkník, J. (Sept. 2004). 'Managerial Capital and the Market for CEOs', Working Paper, Marshall School of Business, University of Southern California.

Murphy, K. M., Shleifer, A., and Vishny, R. W. (May 1991). 'The Allocation of Talent: Implications for Growth', *Quarterly Journal of Economics*, 106(2): 503–30.

Muscarella, C. J. and Vetsuypens, M. R. (Sept. 1989). 'A Simple Test of Baron's Model of IPO Underpricing', *Journal of Financial Economics*, 24(1): 125–35.

Myers, C. (1977). 'Determinants of Corporate Borrowing', *Journal of Financial Economics*, 5: 147–75.

Myers, M. G. (1931). *The New York Money Market. Volume 1: Origins and Development*. New York: Columbia University Press.

Nanda, V. and Warther, V. A. (Mar. 1998). 'The Price of Loyalty: An Empirical Analysis of Underwriting Relationships and Fees', Working Paper, Graduate School of Business, University of Chicago.

_____ and Yun, Y. (Jan. 1997). 'Reputation and Financial Intermediation: An Empirical Investigation of the Impact of IPO Mispricing on Underwriter Market Value', *Journal of Financial Intermediation*, 6(1): 39–63.

National Bank of Belgium (2002). 'Financial Conglomerates', *Financial Stability Review*, 1: 61–80.

Neal, L. (1990). *The Rise of Financial Capitalism: International Capital Markets in the Age of Reason*. Cambridge, UK: Cambridge University Press.

Nordhaus, W. D. (Aug. 2001). 'The Progress of Computing', Working Paper, Yale University, Department of Economics, Yale University.

North, D. C. (Summer 1954). 'Life Insurance and Investment Banking at the Time of the Armstrong Investigation of 1905–1906', *Journal of Economic History*, 14(3): 209–28.

_____ (1977). *Institutional Change and Economic Growth*. Cambridge, UK: Cambridge University Press.

_____ (1983). *Structure and Change in Economic History*. New York: W. W. Norton.

_____ (1990). *Institutions, Institutional Change and Economic Performance*. Cambridge, UK: Cambridge University Press.

_____ (Mar. 1993). 'Institutions and Credible Commitment', *Journal of Institutional and Theoretical Economics*, 149(1): 11–23.

_____ (June 1994). Economic Performance Through Time', *American Economic Review*, 84(3): 359–68.

_____ and Thomas, R. P. (1973). *The Rise of the Western World: A New Economic History*. Cambridge, UK: Cambridge University Press.

_____ and Weingast, B. R. (Dec. 1989). 'Constitutions and Commitment: The Evolution of Institutions Governing Public Choice in Seventeenth-Century England', *Journal of Economic History*, 49(4): 803–32.

Nozick, R. ([1974] 2002). *Anarchy, State, and Utopia*. Oxford, UK: Blackwell.

Oakshott, M. (1975). *On Human Conduct*. Oxford, UK: Clarendon Press.

Olson, M. (Sept. 1993). 'Dictatorship, Democracy, and Development', *American Political Science Review*, 87(3): 567–76.

Penner, J. E. (1997). *The Idea of Property in Law*. Oxford, UK: Clarendon Press.

Perino, M. A. (Oct. 2003). 'American Corporate Reform Abroad: Sarbanes-Oxley and the Foreign Orivate Issuer', *European Business Organization Law Review*, 3(2): 213–44.

Perkins, E. J. (1975). *Financing Anglo-American Trade: The House of Brown, 1800–1880*. Cambridge, MA: Harvard University Press.

———(1999). *Wall Street to Main Street: Charles Merrill and Middle Class Investors*. Cambridge, UK: Cambridge University Press.

Persons, J. C. and Warther, V. A. (Winter 1997). 'Boom and Bust in the Adoption of Financial Innovations', *Review of Financial Studies*, 10(4): 939–67.

Pichler, P. and Wilhelm, Jr, W. J. (Dec. 2001). 'A Theory of the Syndicate: Form Follows Function', *Journal of Finance*, 56(6): 2237–64.

Polanyi, M. (1966). *The Tacit Dimension*. Garden City, NY: Doubleday.

Posner, E., Triantis, A., and Triantis, G. G. (Oct. 2004). 'Investing in Human Capital: The Efficiency of Covenants not to Compete', John M. Olin Program in Law and Eonomics Working Paper 11, University of Virginia Law School, Charlottesville, VA.

Posner, R. A. (Apr. 1980). 'A Theory of Primitive Society, with Special Reference to Law', *Journal of Law and Economics*, 2(1): 1–53.

Powell, J. (2003). *FDR's Folly: How Roosevelt and His New Deal Prolonged the Great Depression*. New York: Three Rivers Press.

Price, J. M. (1973). 'Joshua Johnson in London, 1771–1775: Credit and Commercial Organization in the British Chesapeake Trade', in A. Whiteman, J. S. Bromley, and P. G. M. Dickson, (eds.), *Statesmen, Scholars and Merchants: Essays in Eighteenth-Century History Presented to Dame Lucy Sutherland*. Oxford, UK: Clarendon Press, ch. 8, pp. 153–81.

Puri, M. (Mar. 1996). 'Commercial Banks in Investment Banking. Conflict of Interest or Certification Role?', *Journal of Financial Economics*, 40(3): 373–401.

Redlich, F. (1968). *The Molding of American Banking: Men and Ideas*. New York: Johnson Reprint Corporation.

Reich, C. (1983). *Financier: The Biography of André Meyer*. New York: William Morrow & Co.

Ribstein, L. E. (Fall 2002). 'Market vs. Regulatory Responses to Corporate Fraud: A Critique of the Sarbanes–Oxley Act of 2002', *Journal of Corporation Law*, 28: 1–67.

Rock, K. (Jan.–Feb. 1986). 'Why New Issues are Underpriced', *Journal of Financial Economics*, 15(1–2): 187–212.

Rodrick, D., Subramanian, A., and Trebbi, F. (Oct. 2002). 'Institutions Rule: The Primacy of Institutions Over Geography and Integration in Economic Development', Working Paper 9305, National Bureau of Economic Research, Cambridge, MA.

Roe, M. J. (Jan. 1991). 'A Political Theory of American Corporate Finance', *Columbia Law Review*, 91(1): 10–67.

Romer, P. (May 2002). 'When Should We Use Intellectual Property Rights?', *American Economic Review*, 92(2): 213–16.

Ross, S. (1976). 'Arbitrage Theory of Capital Asset Pricing', *Journal of Economic Theory*, 13: 341–60.

Rottenberg, D. (2001). *The Man Who Made Wall Street: Anthony J. Drexel and the Rise of Modern Finance*. Philadelphia, PA: University of Pennsylvania Press.

Ruud, J. (1990). 'Underpricing of Initial Public Offerings: Goodwill, Price Shaving or Price Support', Ph.D. thesis, Harvard University.

Santos, J. A. C. (June 1998). 'Commerical Banks in the Securities Business: A Review', Working Paper 56, Bank for International Settlements, Basle.

Saxenian, A. (1994). *Regional Advantage: Culture and Competition in Silicon Valley and Route 128*. Cambridge, MA: Harvard University Press.

Schenone, C. (Dec. 2004). 'The Effect of Banking Relationships on the Firm's IPO Underpricing', *Journal of Finance*, 59(6): 2903–58.

Scholes, M. S. (June 1998). 'Derivatives in a Dynamic Environment', *American Economic Review*, 88(3): 350–70.

Schultz, P. H. and Zaman, M. A. (Apr. 1994). 'After-Market Support and Underpricing of Intitial Public Offerings', *Journal of Financial Economics*, 35(2): 199–219.

Schwartz, A. (June 1992). 'Relational Contracts in the Courts: An Analysis of Incomplete Agreements and Judicial Strategies', *Journal of Legal Studies*, 21(2): 271–318.

Seligman, J. (1982). *The Transformation of Wall Street: A History of the Securities and Exchange Commission and Modern Corporate Finance*. Boston, MA: Houghton Mifflin Company.

Sen, A. (1999). *Development as Freedom*. Oxford, UK: Oxford University Press.

Sexton, J. (2005). *Debtor Diplomacy: Finance and American Foreign Relations in the Civil War Era, 1837–1873*. Oxford, UK: Oxford University Press.

Shapiro, C. and Stiglitz, J. E. (June 1984). 'Equilibrium Unemployment as a Worker Discipline Device', *American Economic Review*, 74(3): 433–44.

Sharpe, W. (Sept. 1964). 'Capital Asset Prices: A Theory of Market Equilibrium Under Conditions of Risk', *Journal of Finance*, 19(3): 425–42.

Sherman, A. E. (June 1992). 'The Pricing of Best Efforts New Issues', *Journal of Finance*, 47(2): 781–90.

—— (Autumn 2000). 'IPOs and Long-Term Relationships: An Advantage of Book Building', *Review of Financial Studies*, 13(3): 697–714.

—— (forthcoming 2005). 'Global Trends in IPO Markets: Book Building vs. Auctions with Endogenous Entry', *Journal of Financial Economics*.

—— and Titman, S. (July 2002). 'Building the IPO Order Book: Underpricing and Participation Limits with Costly Information', *Journal of Financial Economics*, 65(1): 3–29.

Skeel, Jr, D. A. (2001). *Debt's Dominion*. Princeton, NJ: Princeton University Press.

Smart, S. B. and Zutter, C. J. (July 2003). 'Control as a Motivation for Under-pricing: A Comparison of Dual and Single-Class IPOs', *Journal of Financial Economics*, 69(1): 85–110.

Smith, A. (1776/1904). *An Inquiry Into the Nature and Causes of the Wealth of Nations*, 5th edn. London: Methuen.

Smith, Jr, C. W. (Jan.–Feb. 1986). 'Investment Banking and the Capital Acqui-sition Process', *Journal of Financial Economics*, 15(1–2): 3–29.

Smith, D. and Strömberg, P. (2005). 'Maximizing the Value of Distressed Assets: Bankruptcy Law and the Efficient Reorganization of Firms', in P. Honohan, and L. Laeven (eds.), *Systemic Financial Crises: Containment and Resolution*. Cambridge, UK: Cambridge University Press, ch. 8, pp. 232–75.

Smith, W. D. (Dec. 1984). 'The Function of Commercial Centers in the Modernization of European Capitalism: Amsterdam as an Infomation Exchange in the Seventeenth Century', *Journal of Economic History*, 44(4): 985–97.

Spring, S. (Mar. 1919). 'Upset Prices in Corporate Reorganization', *Harvard Law Review*, 32(5): 489–515.

Stigler, G. J. (1966). *The Theory of Price*. New York: Macmillan.

—— (Spring 1971). 'The Theory of Economic Regulation', *Bell Journal of Eco-nomics and Management Science*, 2(1): 3–21.

Stiglitz, J. E. (Mar. 1987). 'The Causes and Consequences of the Dependence of Quality on Price', *Journal of Economic Literature*, 25(1): 1–48.

Stone, K. V. W. (2004). *From Widgets to Digits: Employment Regulation for the Changing Workplace*. Cambridge, UK: Cambridge University Press.

Story, J. (1859). *Commentaries on the Law of Partnership, as a Branch of Commer-cial and Maritime Jurisprudence with Occasional Illustrations from the Civil and Foreign Law*. Boston, MA: Little, Brown & Co.

Stoughton, N. M., Wong, K. P., and Zechner, J. (July 2001). 'IPOs and Product Quality', *Journal of Business*, 74(3): 375–408.

—— and Zechner, J. (July 1998). 'IPO-Mechanisms, Monitoring and Owner-ship Structure', *Journal of Financial Economics*, 49(1): 45–77.

Sufi, A. (Apr. 2006). 'The Real Effects of Debt Certification: Evidence From the Introduction of Bank Loan Ratings', Mimeo, Graduate School of Business, University of Chicago, Chicago, IL.

Supple, B. E. (June 1957). 'A Business Elite: German-Jewish Financiers in Nineteenth-Century New York', *Business History Review*, 31(2): 143–78.

Sussman, N. and Yafeh, Y. (June 2004). 'Constitutions and Commitment: Evidence on the Relation Between Institutions and the Cost of Capital', Discussion Paper 4404, Centre for Economic Policy, London.

Sutherland, L. S. (1946). 'Samson Gideon and the reduction of interest, 1749–50', *Economic History Review*, 16(1): 15–29.

Sylla, R. (Mar. 1976). 'Forgotten Men of Money: Private Bankers in Early U.S. History', *Journal of Economic History*, 36(1): 173–88.

Tadelis, S. (June 1999). 'What's in a Name? Reputation as a Tradeable Asset', *American Economic Review*, 89(3): 548–63.

—— (Aug. 2002). 'The Market for Reputations as an Incentive Mechanism', *Journal of Political Economy*, 110(4): 854–82.

Taggart, Jr, R. A. (Apr. 1990). 'Corporate Leverage and the Restructuring Movement of the 1980s', *Business Economics*, 25(2): 12–18.

Tinic, S. M. (Sept. 1988). 'Anatomy of Initial Public Offerings of Common Stock', *Journal of Finance*, 43(4): 789–822.

Tollison, R. D. (Nov. 1982). 'Rent Seeking: A Survey', *Kyklos*, 35(4): 575–602.

Townsend, R. M. (Oct. 1978). 'Optimal Contracts and Competitive Markets with Costly State Verification', *Journal of Economic Theory*, 21(2): 265–93.

Trevelyan, G. M. ([1938] 1950). *The English Revolution, 1688–1689*. Oxford, UK: Oxford University Press.

Tufano, P. (Dec. 1989). 'Financial Innovation and First-Mover Advantages', *Journal of Financial Economics*, 25(2): 213–40.

—— (Spring 1997). 'Business Failure, Judicial Intervention, and Financial Innovation: Restructuring U.S. Railroads in the Nineteenth Century', *Business History Review*, 71(1): 1–40.

—— (Sept. 2003). 'Financial Innovation', in G. M. Constantinides, M. Harris, and R. M. Stulz (eds.), *Handbook of the Economics of Finance*. North Holland.

Tullock, G. (June 1967). 'The Welfare Costs of Tariffs, Monopolies, and Theft', *Western Economic Journal*, 5(3): 224–32.

Tylor, E. B. (1871). *Primitive Culture*. New York: Gordon Press.

van Bommel, J. (Mar. 2002). 'Messages from Market to Management: The Case of IPOs', *Journal of Corporate Finance*, 8(2): 123–38.

Weber, R. A. and Camerer, C. F. (Apr. 2003). 'Cultural Conflict and Merger Failure: An Experimental Approach', *Management Science*, 49(4): 400–15.

Weingast, B. R. (Apr. 1995). 'The Economic Role of Political Institutions: Market-Preserving Federalism and Economic Development', *Journal of Law, Economics and Organization*, 11(1): 1–31.

—— (June 1997). 'The Political Foundations of Democracy and the Rule of Law', *American Political Science Review*, 91(2): 245–63.

Weiss Hanley, K., Kumar, A. A., and Seguin, P. J. (Oct. 1993). 'Price Stabilization in the Market for New Issues', *Journal of Financial Economics*, 32(2): 177–97.

—— and Wilhelm, Jr, W. J. (Feb. 1995). 'Evidence on the Strategic Allocation of Initial Public Offerings', *Journal of Financial Economics*, 37(2): 239–57.

Whitmore, P. J. (Spring 1990). 'A Statistical Analysis of Noncompetition Clauses in Employment Contracts', *Journal of Corporation Law*, 15(3): 483–534.

Wilhelm, Jr, W. J. (Winter 2005). 'Bookbuilding, Auctions, and the Future of the IPO Process', *Journal of Applied Corporate Finance*, 17(1): 2–13.

——and Downing, J. D. (2001). *Information Markets*. Boston, MA: Harvard Business School Press.

Williamson, O. E. (1985). *The Economic Institutions of Capitalism*. New York: Free Press.

Winkler, J. K. ([1930] 2003). *Morgan the Magnificent, or the Life of J. Pierpoint Morgan*. USA: Kessinger Publishing.

Yates, J. (1999). 'The Structuring of Early Computer Use in Life Insurance', *Journal of Design History*, 12(1): 5–24.

——(2000). 'Business Use of Information and Technology During the Industrial Age', in A. D. Chandler, Jr, and J. W. Cortada (eds.), *A Nation Transformed by Information: How Information Has Shaped the United States from Colonial Times to the Present*. Oxford, UK: Oxford University Press, ch. 4, pp. 107–36.

Index

'Accepting Houses' 126, 158
account-switching 257
Acemoglu, D. 45, 46
activism 47 n21, 170, 174–5, 201
advertising 161, 216, 217, 218, 230
advisory boutiques, *see* boutiques
advisory services 7, 13, 19, 21–2, 30, 34–5, 154, 234, 247, 257–9, 280, 292, 301, 302–3, 305–8
  see also mergers and acquisitions; restructuring advisory services
Alexander Brown and Sons 142
algorithmic trading 244
Altman, Roger 306
Altman's z-scores 294–5
American Civil War 152, 153, 160–3, 168, 170
Amsterdam 98–100, 120, 124–5, 133, 313–14
Anglo-American trade 109, 124 n5, 142, 149
Apollo Management 314
apprenticeships 113, 225, 245, 248
arbitrage 243–4
Armstrong Committee (1905) 197, 198
asset management 6, 22, 29–35, 90, 301
asset securitization 248 n55, 251 n60
assets 15, 27, 37–46, 62, 67–70, 154, 177, 293
  see also human capital
assignment of entitlements 39, 50
Atlantic trade 101, 109–20, 121–6, 142, 153–4, 155, 157–9
  see also merchants
August Belmont & Co. 151, 168

Bache 235, 236, 238
back-office crisis 235–8, 278
Baker, George Fisher 169, 185, 199 n35, 200
Bank of England 104, 105, 106, 119, 125, 146, 148, 150
Bank of the United States of Pennsylvania 145–6

Bankers Trust 246–9, 295
Banking Act (1933), *see* Glass–Steagall Act
Bankruptcy Act (1898) 176 n64, 212, 254
Bankruptcy Code (1978) 226, 252 n61, 253–5
bankruptcy laws 176, 187, 210
  see also Bankruptcy Act; Bankruptcy Code
Barings 115–16, 129, 142–5, 147–9, 152, 160, 166, 167, 168–9, 174 n60
Barnard, Sir John 140
batch-processing technology 227–8, 238, 240, 267, 278, 283
Baum, David 302 n13
Bear Stearns 30, 236, 260, 288 n42
Belmont, August 151, 161, 162
Berman, Dennis 308
Bernstein, L. 54–5, 58
Beutner, Austin 306
Bills of Exchange 124–6, 129, 130, 131, 142, 153
Black, F. 243–4
black-letter law 281, 287, 289, 292, 294
Blackstone Group 19, 309, 312–13, 314
Blankfein, Lloyd 302, 303
Blue Sky laws 201–2
board membership 135, 174–5, 196, 197, 199–200
Bok, Scott 305 n19
bond issues 24, 121, 122, 123, 145, 147–8, 218, 243
  see also government bonds; junk bonds; mortgage bonds; war loans
bookbuilding 84, 251 n60
'bootstrap' acquisition 259–60
boutiques 19, 34–5, 252, 254, 292, 305, 306–8, 309, 313–14, 315
Boyd, Walter 141
Brandeis, Louis D. 201, 204, 211
British industrial revolution 100, 106

brokerage 117–18, 119–20, 150, 164, 217, 244
  see also prime brokerage; retail brokerage
Brown, Shipley & Co. 116, 143, 149, 153, 166
Brown Brothers Harriman & Co. 209, 210
Bubble Act (1720) 114, 117
business schools, *see* professional schools
buyouts 240 n36, 253, 259–60, 295
  see also LBOs

capital accumulation 121, 144
capital markets 1, 101–2, 104 n24, 117–20, 148, 152, 223, 315
  see also securities markets
capital-intensive business 7, 22–4, 34, 91–2, 115, 226, 264, 302, 304, 306, 308
capitalism, *see* financial capitalism
capitalist economies 37, 38, 41, 67
capitalists 38, 67, 72–3, 176, 181 n77
  see also human capitalists
capitalization 1–2, 13–14, 116, 121, 143, 153, 236–7, 280, 296–7, 304
Cardozo, Justice 192 n14, 193, 211
career development 274–5
Carnegie, Andrew 183–4
cash flow 39, 239, 241, 243, 293
CBWL Inc. 236
Chandler Act (1938) 212–13, 251–4
Charles River Bridge Case 127–8
chartered banks 144–6, 148, 153, 169, 170
Chase, Salmon P. 160–1
Chase Manhattan 295
Chase National Bank 210
Citibank 295
Citigroup 304
civil war, *see* American Civil War; English civil wars
clearing 41, 118, 229 n12, 250
CNC, *see* Covenants Not to Compete
Coase, R. H. 49–50, 51, 111
Coase Theorem 49–50
codes of fair practice 205–6
codification 225–6, 244–6, 264–7, 281, 286, 289–90, 294–6, 303, 304, 305, 306, 307–8
coffee houses 117, 119
collateralized loans 29, 39
commercial banks 65–6, 153–4, 169–71, 209–10, 246–9, 279, 294–300

commercial bills 122
commercial information exchange 98–101, 112–14
commercial law 106–7, 129–32, 154
commission-fixing rules 238
commitment 41–2, 48, 76, 82, 87, 94–6, 288–9
commodities trading 133, 142, 153, 155, 160, 293
commoditization 28, 257, 294, 308, 310
common good 193
common law 49, 110, 157, 177, 192, 268
  see also English common law
communication 63, 79–81, 87, 98–101, 112–14, 155, 157–9, 226, 285–6, 309
Communist Manifesto 152
compensation 14–15, 28, 84–5, 96, 289
competition 40, 182, 199–200, 220–1, 234–5, 240, 250, 279, 308–9
competitive bidding 199, 214–15
computerization 90–1, 225–40, 249, 264, 278–9, 282–3, 286, 294–5, 301 n12, 304, 307
consolidations 16–19, 182–4, 196, 296–8, 301, 306
  see also merger waves; mergers and acquisitions
contract law 122, 132–4, 156, 187
contracts 38–40, 46–50, 82–9, 91, 148, 153, 156, 199
  see also enforcement; extra-legal contracts; formal contracts; informal contracts; relational contracts; reputational contracts
Cooke, Jay 160–2, 166, 171, 172
corporate charters 127–8
Corporate Financing 257, 283
corporate governance 156, 174, 177 n66, 262, 299, 306
corporate law 51 n29, 122
corporate reorganization 169, 175–84, 212–13, 251–5, 264, 304
  see also mergers and acquisitions
cotton trade 113–14, 123–4, 142, 143, 159, 272
courts 45–50, 58, 61–3, 70–1, 102–3, 130–5, 154–7, 177, 188–9, 192
Covenants Not to Compete (CNC) 281, 287–9, 292
Cowen 283
credit analysis 261, 272
credit instruments 123, 130
credit risk 297

credit scoring 295
credit services 32, 101, 114, 122–6, 129, 136, 142, 146, 148
Credit Suisse 26 n18, 286
creditors 99, 103, 154, 177, 178, 180–1, 213, 248, 268
cross-monitoring 94–5, 108, 221, 277, 309
cultural factors 44, 49 n26, 91, 270 n14, 285–7, 304, 305, 314
Cummings, Dave 301 n12

Dabney, Morgan & Co. 166, 167, 268
Dartmouth College v Woodward 127, 151
data-processing technology 228, 230–1, 237
'deal making factories' 240, 286
dealing room 26, 28, 244–6, 286, 310
Dean Witter 7, 31, 234, 238, 283, 287, 305
debt contracts 122
debt securities 1, 3, 241, 253, 296
debt underwriting 24, 25, 296
decentralized decision-making 37, 38, 41, 59–62, 101
demand information 5, 68, 72, 74
demographic change 8, 9, 215
Demsetz, Harold 42 n11, 50
derivatives markets 9–10, 26–7, 30, 207, 247, 248, 249, 251
designated order turnaround, *see* DOT system
Deutsche Bank 249, 286, 286 n37
Dimon, James 303
'Discount Houses' 125
discounting, *see* underpricing
disputed contracts 191–2
dissemination of information 66, 70, 95, 99–101, 204, 278 n25, 281
Dolley, J. N. 201, 202
Donaldson, Lufkin, Jenrette 237
DOT system 9, 237
Douglas, William 212, 252 n64
Dresdner Kleinwort 306
Drexel 93, 150–1, 160–1, 168, 205, 220 n102, 260–3
Drexel, Anthony 150, 160, 166, 168, 275
Drexel, Francis 149, 150, 151
Drexel, Morgan & Co. 160, 167–8, 270
Duncan, Sherman & Co. 165–6
DuPont 182, 233, 236

E. F. Hutton 230–1, 238
East India Company 99, 116, 117, 138 n45

Eastman Dillon 234
economic decision-making 37, 41, 62
economic power 60, 187, 213
economic self-determination 37–8
economies of scale 78, 98, 121, 228–9, 237, 246, 255, 277–80, 304, 310
economies of scope 304
1837 panic 123, 146–9, 151
1857 panic 150
1873 panic 162, 166, 170
1893 panic 181–2
electronic auctions 25
employees 13–15, 51–2, 54, 88–92, 265–6, 275, 287–9
  see also mobility
enforcement 46–9, 51–2, 55–8, 62–3, 110, 132–3, 156, 226, 251, 301
England 102–6, 109–10, 117–21, 123–4, 137–41, 146
  see also United Kingdom
English civil wars 103
English common law 103–4, 106, 129, 130–1
entitlements 39, 40, 41–3, 44, 46, 62
entrepreneurs 1, 3, 35, 50–1, 66–7, 81, 121, 152, 260
equitable theories of contract 134
equity investment 3, 22, 26, 72, 253
equity markets 1–2, 24–6, 251 n60
equity receivership 157, 176–82, 187, 212, 251
equity underwriting 24, 25, 241, 295, 297, 300, 308
Eurobonds 226, 250
European banks 148, 151, 168, 297 n7
European capital markets 87, 142 n51, 148, 149, 162 n15, 170, 297
Evercore Partners 306
evolution of investment banking 35, 38, 65, 97, 123, 136–53, 215–20
  see also history of investment banking
exchange of rights 40–1, 48, 63, 193
expectation damages 46 n15, 48 n23, 132–4, 153, 156
extra-legal contracts 51, 52–3, 57–62, 82–7, 121, 173, 214, 221
extra-legal institutions 50–9, 67–8, 71, 111, 126–9, 207, 264
extra-legal property rights 57–62, 83, 91, 96, 157, 185, 281

fair pricing 72, 75, 78–9, 84, 85, 86 n26, 190
family partnerships 143, 184, 272
FDR, *see* Roosevelt, Franklin D.
Federal Deposit Insurance Corporation 209
Federal Securities Corporation 217
Federal Trade Commission (FTC) 195, 207, 208, 211
financial capital 303, 304, 310
financial capitalism 155–6, 185, 200, 223, 226, 262
financial economics 39, 140, 225–6, 242–9, 263–4, 267, 279, 287, 291–4
financial engineering 6, 8, 26–7, 225, 245, 247–8, 297
financial innovation 245, 260, 281, 289–90, 292, 314
financial markets 66, 99–100, 103, 226, 231, 242, 293
financial patenting 29, 281, 289–91, 292
First Boston 209–10, 234, 240, 254, 255, 286
First National Bank of Chicago 196
First National Bank of New York 169, 184, 185, 199, 200
fixed-income securities 241
Fletcher–Rayburn Bill (1934) 208, 209
floor trading 208, 209, 237
flotation 117, 171, 237, 278, 279–80, 296, 311–14
foreign security issuance 218
foreign trade, *see* Atlantic trade
formal contracts 45, 51, 53, 57–9, 63, 267–92
forward contracts 133
Fox-Pitt Kelton 305 n18
franchise 127, 262 n88
free markets 121, 147
free-rider problems 108, 277, 280, 304
frequent traders 72, 73, 76
front-office automation 238–40
FTC, *see* Federal Trade Commission
Fuld, Richard 303
full-service banks 31–2, 34–5, 301, 304, 305, 306, 309, 315
future of investment banking 97, 293–310

GDP 1–2
German-Jewish investment banking 162–5, 272–3
Glass, Carter 210

Glass–Steagall Act (1933) 31, 209–10, 214, 221, 295, 296, 299
global markets 10, 250–1
global networks 121
Glore Forgan & Co. 220 n102, 231, 236
GNP 250
Goldman, Marcus 164
Goldman Sachs 20, 28, 29, 30, 164, 216, 235, 236, 244, 279–80, 283–4, 301–4, 308, 309, 310
Goldman Sachs Trading Company 219
Goldman Sachs Unregistered Equity (GSTuUE) OTC Market 314
Goldsmid 120, 141–2
Goodbody & Co. 231, 236, 283
government bonds 136–41, 147, 152, 160–1, 170, 293
Gramm–Leach–Bliley Act (1999) 299
Grant, Ulysses S. 163
Great Depression 188, 193, 194, 205
Greenhill, Robert F. 259 n79, 306, 313 n43
Greenhill & Co. 19, 34, 288 n42, 306, 309, 311, 312, 313
Greenwich Associates 79 n14, 82
Greif, A. 55, 56–7
gross domestic product, *see* GDP
gross national product, *see* GNP
Gurney & Co. 152

Halsey, Stuart & Co. 215, 218, 222
Hayden, Stone 231, 236
hedge funds 6, 26, 30, 240, 244, 310–11, 314
hedging risk 133
'historical banker' thesis 220, 221, 222
history of investment banking 315
    17th century 98–100, 117–18
    18th century 100, 105–6, 109–20, 127, 134–41
    19th century 101, 107, 129–32, 141–74, 176–8, 187–93
    20th century 1, 175, 181–90, 193–223, 225–64, 265–92, 293–310
holding company regulations 210–12, 215
Holmes, Oliver Wendell 192
Hoover, Herbert 194, 204
Hope and Co. 147
Hornblower 283
House of Brown 113–15, 142–4, 148–9, 159–60, 209–10, 272, 283
human capital 13–15, 40, 88–92, 96, 249–66, 270–80, 304, 305, 310, 313

human capitalists 225–6, 239–40, 244, 246, 249–62, 279, 297, 300, 304, 305, 306, 311

IBA, *see* Investment Bankers Association of America
IBC, *see* Investment Bankers' Conference, Inc
IBM 228, 230, 231, 238
illiquidity 271, 273, 275, 276, 280
incentivization 69–70, 84–5, 114–15, 139, 173, 266–7, 274, 289
incomplete contracts 47–9, 50, 51, 53
incorporation 128, 268, 296
India 303
industrial organization 7, 15–20, 92–5
industrialization 106, 121, 155–6, 172, 187, 190, 225–64
industry surveys 82
informal contracts 53, 58, 73, 75, 77, 81, 88, 92
information leakage 93–5, 96
information marketplace 21, 71–6, 82, 83, 87, 92–6
information networks 72–9, 83–96, 136, 154, 172, 266, 273–4
information producers 69–70, 71–4, 76–9, 83–6, 88, 93–6
information technology 94, 225–64, 265, 287, 291–4, 300, 303
informational assets 27, 38, 68, 70, 154
infrequent traders 72, 74, 78, 139 n46
initial public offerings, *see* IPOs
innovation 68–71, 91, 95, 106, 145, 179, 180–1, 241, 314
   see also financial innovation
innovators 66, 68, 71, 78, 95, 263, 272, 289
Institutional Investor 82, 283
institutional theory 37–96
intellectual assets 68
intellectual property law 91, 287, 290, 292
Intermarket Trading System (ITS) 237
internal organization of investment banks 88–92, 265–92
Internet 242
Interstate Commerce Commission 195
Investment Bankers Association of America 81, 203, 206, 215, 220
Investment Bankers' Conference, Inc. 206–7

Investment Company Act (1940) 313, 314
Investment Dealers' Digest 82, 283
investment management 238, 292
IPOs 76, 79, 83, 85, 87, 237, 242, 312, 313
issuance, *see* securities issuance
issuers 75, 76, 77, 78–83, 93, 96, 203, 214
ITS, *see* Intermarket Trading System

JP Morgan & Co. 16, 27, 31, 92, 165–70, 175, 182–4, 199–200, 204–5, 209–10, 214, 217, 247, 268, 270, 295, 303, 309
JS Morgan & Co. 160, 165–6, 167, 168, 169, 268
J. T. Van Vleck, Read & Co. 150
JW Seligman & Co. 163–4
Jay Cooke & Co. 160–1, 169
Jay Cooke McCulloch & Co. 161
jobbers 117–19, 135, 140, 141
Johnson, S. 45, 46
joint-stock investment banks 265, 278, 280–92
judges 102–3, 129–30
junk bonds 4 n1, 93, 247 n52, 260–3, 295
juries 106–7, 129, 130
jurisprudence, *see* legislation

Kidder, Peabody & Co. 168–72, 184, 199, 219, 220 n102, 283
Kohlberg, Jerome 240 n36, 260
Kohlberg Kravis Roberts & Co. 260, 313–14
Kuhn, Loeb & Co. 163–4, 171, 172, 175, 182, 184, 199, 209, 217–18, 220 n102, 229 n10, 235 n25, 236, 254, 259 n78

laissez-faire systems 86, 155–85, 194, 200
Landis, James 195
law merchant 55, 104 n24, 106–7
law of negotiable instruments 107, 129–32
Lazard Freres 7, 19, 31, 32–4, 258–9, 279–80, 311, 312, 313
LBOs 240 n36, 259–62, 295
lead managers 20 n6, 80, 174, 221
Lee Higginson & Co. 169, 171 n50, 184, 185 n85, 199, 219
legal factors 121–2, 126–36, 153, 156–7, 185, 187–96
legal institutions 45–50, 57–9, 70–1, 97, 101–2
'legal realists' 192–3

legislation 46–7, 60–3, 82, 85–7, 135, 187–8, 196–214
see also individual Acts
Lehman Brothers 20, 26 n28, 164, 209, 216, 220, 236, 255, 258
letters of credit 122, 126, 143–4
leveraged buyouts, *see* LBOs
Lewis, Ronello 230–1
liability 21, 86, 114, 267–8
Liberty Loan Act (1917) 217
liquidation 75–6
liquidity 4, 65–6, 72–6, 83, 85, 86 n26, 99, 314
litigation 22, 46–8, 53, 60, 63, 129–30, 223, 269
loan contracting 137–46
loan sales markets 295–6
loan-making institutions, *see* commercial banks
Lochner v New York 189, 193
Loeb, Salomon 164, 185
Loeb Rhoades 279
London Stock Exchange 116, 119, 120, 240
Lynch, Eddie 219

M&A, *see* mergers and acquisitions
Macaulay, Stewart 52–3
McCulloch, Hugh 161
Maghribi 56–7, 165, 293
malfeasance 54, 63
Maloney Act (1938) 206–7
market structure 4, 92, 141–6, 231–8
Marshall, John 131, 268–9
maturity transformation 65
MBAs 245, 273, 286 n38
Medina, Harold 7, 220–1, 222, 225
Medina antitrust trial 188, 213, 214, 220–2, 223, 225
mentoring 266, 274, 276–7, 280–1, 284 n33, 287, 291, 313
mercantile networks 98, 107–16
see also transatlantic networks
merchant banking 101, 107, 123–6, 129–30, 142–3, 146, 149, 153–4, 158
merchant guilds 56
merchants 98–101, 105, 106–7, 119–20, 126
see also Atlantic trade
merger waves 1, 170, 182–5, 189, 236, 258
see also consolidations

mergers and acquisitions 5, 18–20, 90, 175, 255–62, 273–4, 286, 297, 301, 305–8
see also consolidations
Merrill, Charles E. 219, 230 n14
Merrill Lynch 9, 30, 32 n28, 82, 219–20, 229–30, 233–6, 238, 239, 248 n55, 259 n79, 278 n25, 279, 290, 303, 308
Merton, R. C. 243–4
Mexican War Loan 150, 152
Meyer, Andre 32, 258–9
Milken, Michael 93, 226, 260–3
Mitchell, Charles E. 204
mobility 28–9, 91, 281–7, 288, 292, 313, 314
money trusts 189, 199–201, 262
monitoring 66, 94–5, 108, 115, 138, 304, 305, 313
see also cross-monitoring
monopolies 102, 189–92, 214
Morgan, John Pierpoint 123, 149–50, 164–8, 169, 175, 179, 182, 183–5, 199, 200, 205, 209, 260, 268, 270, 275, 295
Morgan, Junius Spencer 149, 150, 151, 165–8, 269, 275
Morgan antitrust trial, *see* Medina antitrust trial
Morgan Grenfell 268
Morgan Stanley 7, 27–34, 210, 214, 234, 236, 283, 286–7, 303, 305
see also Medina antitrust trial
mortgage bonds 175, 178, 179 n75

NASD, *see* National Association of Securities Dealers
National Association of Securities Dealers (NASD) 206–7
National Bank Act (1864) 196
National City Bank of New York 170, 184, 185, 199, 204–5
National Industrial Recovery Act (1933) 61 n50, 205–6, 207
National Recovery Association 205–6
negotiability 102, 125, 131–2, 136
networks 56–9, 72–9, 98, 107–16, 121, 143, 162–70, 272–3
see also information networks
New Deal 194–6, 205, 207, 210–13, 299
New York Stock Exchange 4, 8–9, 81, 202–3, 209, 232–3, 235–8, 281–3, 296
New York Stock Exchange Board 57 n40, 135–6

New York Times 173, 255 n69, 283
newspapers 99–100, 161
NIRA, *see* National Industrial Recovery
  Act
non-state institutions 38, 45–9, 60–3,
  71–2, 116, 266
  see also courts; extra-legal institutions
North, Douglass C. 44
Northern Pacific Railway v Boyd 181
NRA, *see* National Recovery Association
NYSE, *see* New York Stock Exchange

Oaktree Capital Management 314
objective causation 192
O'Neal, Stan 303
opacity 28–9, 270–1, 273–6, 278, 280, 281,
  282, 291
organizational structure of investment
  banks 88–92
OTC derivatives 9–10, 26–7, 30, 207, 247,
  248, 249, 251
*Other People's Money and How the Bankers
  Use It* (Brandeis) 201
outsourcing 303, 311
Overend 152
overseas trade, *see* Atlantic trade
oversubscription 87, 139–40, 161, 217
over-the-counter derivatives, *see* OTC
  derivatives
ownership 120, 132, 196, 231–2, 269
  see also public ownership

Paine Webber 234, 238, 282
Pandit, Vikram 304
partnerships 89–91, 96, 114–15, 143–4,
  153, 266–92, 304–5, 311
patenting 38, 91, 290–1
  see also financial patenting
Peabody, George 147, 149–50, 151, 166,
  269–70, 275
Peabody & Co. 149–50, 151, 152, 160,
  165–6
Pecora, Ferdinand 204–5
Pecora Committee 204–5, 207 n64, 270
Perella, Joseph 259 n79, 285–6, 305,
  309
Peterson, Peter G. 312–13
political factors 35, 126–9, 155–7, 185,
  187–96, 220, 226
political movements 189–97, 203, 214,
  262
Populism 189–90, 194 n21, 262
portfolio theory 242–4

postal system 99–100
price discovery 76–8, 83, 93, 310
price-relevant information 5, 21, 23, 38,
  66–72, 75, 92–3, 95, 266
primary markets 3–4, 67, 74, 90, 154
prime brokerage 6, 30, 244
private banks 145–51, 153, 161, 171, 205,
  209–10
private equity investment 22, 26, 72,
  253, 301, 302, 303, 308–10, 314
private institutions, *see* non-state
  institutions
private law 135–6, 156, 165, 173 n59,
  187, 226, 250–1, 265, 291
private law institutions 51, 60, 251,
  262
private partnerships 7, 279, 305, 311
private securities issuance 253
professional bodies 54–7, 63, 81
professional schools 26, 27, 28, 225, 245,
  247, 264, 281, 294
profit sharing 268, 276–7
Progressivism 189, 190–2, 193–6, 197,
  201, 203, 214
proprietary trading 20, 21, 34, 73, 244,
  247, 303, 306
prospectus 22–3, 206, 215, 259 n78, 288
  n42
public equity investment 3, 253
public ownership 7, 237–8, 267, 280,
  292–3, 304, 311–14
public securities issuance 1, 207, 252–3
public subscription 137–41
Public Utility Holding Company Act
  (1935) 195 n25, 211, 215
Pujo, Arsène P. 199
Pujo Committee (1912) 198–201, 220

quasi-legal contracting 173
quasi-rents 84, 108, 139, 263
Quattrone, Frank 286

Racketeer Influenced and Corrupt
  Organizations (RICO) Act (1970)
  262
railroads 144–7, 150, 161–3, 167–72,
  175–9, 182, 201–2, 215–16
railways 175–6, 191
RCA 230–1
real-time analysis 238–40, 286
receivers' certificate 178–9, 180
reciprocity arrangements 173, 200, 220,
  221, 222

regulatory intervention 8, 20, 135, 205, 299–300, 313
  see also legislation; self-regulatory bodies; state intervention
relational contracts 5, 38, 52–4, 58, 77 n 8, 90, 255, 278
rent-seeking 60, 61, 62, 63, 82, 128
reorganization of investment banks 212–13, 223, 225, 251–5
  see also consolidations; merger waves
reputation 52–9, 75–88, 92–6, 108, 126, 137–9, 170–5, 208, 221–2, 228–9, 301, 302, 303, 304, 311
reputational capital 15–16, 73–6, 83, 88, 93, 136, 245–9, 269–70, 273–7, 301, 303
reputational contracts 47, 59, 73, 75, 83–8, 90, 226
reputational risk 197, 219, 229, 234, 237, 240, 266, 277, 303
research and development 23, 28–9, 73, 91
restructuring advisory services 32, 175, 181–2, 251–5, 273, 307
retail brokerage 7, 30, 231, 233, 283, 287
retail investment banking 79–82, 216–19, 232–7, 246, 294–5
revenues 1, 6, 13–15, 23, 29–34, 59, 233–4, 259, 295, 301–2
Ripplewood Holdings 314
risk management 9, 10, 22, 243, 244, 272, 286, 293–4, 297, 303–4
risk-adjusted return on capital (RAROC) 247–8
rogue traders 249
Roosevelt, Franklin D. 194–5, 198, 204, 205, 210, 211–12, 213
'Roosevelt Court' 211
Rothschilds 115, 116, 129, 142–4, 147, 151–2, 161, 162–4, 170, 272
rule of law 49, 59, 156, 188, 211

Sachs, Samuel 164
Saloman Brothers 235, 239, 248 n55, 287
Sarbanes–Oxley Act (2002) 299–300, 307, 313
Scholes, M. 243–4
Schwarzman, Stephen 312
Seasoned Equity Offerings, *see* SEOs
SEC, *see* Securities and Exchange Commission
Second Bank of the United States 145

secondary markets 4–6, 8–9, 23, 69–70, 72, 74, 76–7, 90, 261
Securities Act (1933) 86, 87, 207–8, 209, 253, 299
securities affiliates 196–7, 209–10
Securities and Exchange Commission 22–3, 82, 206–7, 209, 211, 212, 235, 238, 252
Securities Exchange Act (1934) 209, 212
Securities Industry Association (SIA) 30, 81
Securities Industry Automation Corporation 237
securities issuance 1, 3–5, 20–2, 89–90, 136–41, 218–19, 249, 252–3
securities legislation 201–2, 207, 209–10, 211, 215
securities markets 6, 21, 35, 104, 134, 217–18, 279, 294
Security Pacific 295
self-regulatory bodies 54, 81, 92, 206
Self-Regulatory Organizations (SROs) 81, 82
Seligman, Joseph 163
SEOs 24, 83 n19
settlement 41, 90, 229, 233, 235, 249
share issuance 218
Shearson 279
shelf-registration 241–2
Sherman Act (1890) 220
shipping 100, 101, 112, 124, 147, 158–9
SIA, *see* Securities Industry Association
Simon Robertson Associates 307 n24
skills 10, 21, 26, 77–8, 112, 120, 124, 225, 248, 294, 301, 302, 311
  see also tacit skills; technical skills
Smith Barney 220 n102, 287
social factors 41, 43–5, 55, 57 n41, 59–61, 126, 178, 189–95, 274
social legislation 211
software patenting 290
spread 23, 24–5, 248, 279
spreadsheets 239–40
SROs, *see* Self-Regulatory Organizations
state intervention 41–5, 59–63, 82, 103, 126–8, 157, 185–223, 225
State Street Bank v Signature Financial 29, 290
Stillman, James 170, 185
stock exchanges 116, 119, 120, 135, 143, 208
  see also London Stock Exchange; New York Stock Exchange

stock market crashes 9, 134–5, 194, 203–4, 218–19
stockjobbers 117–19, 135, 140, 141
Story, Joseph 132, 269–70
Story, William 134
'struck' juries 106–7
subprime mortgage crisis 303
subscriber lists 137–41
Swift v Tyson 131–2
Swiss Re 305 n18
syndicates 20, 80, 94–6, 170–4, 183–4, 200, 207, 220–2

tacit skills 15, 88–90, 113, 264–92; 293–4, 301, 304, 309, 311, 313, 315
takeovers, *see* buyouts; LBOs
taxation 42–3, 193, 268
team transfers 285–6, 288
teamwork 270, 274, 309, 313
technical skills 27, 89–91, 113, 284, 286, 294, 295
technological advances 6–7, 9, 59, 63, 91, 99–100, 157–60, 225–66, 301 n12, 310, 315
    see also computerization; information technology
Temporary National Economic Committee 213–14, 220, 253 n65
Thain, John 303
theory of investment banking 65–96, 170, 221
Thomas Biddle & Co. 145–6, 147
TNEC, *see* Temporary National Economic Committee
'tombstone' advertisements 16 n3, 20 n6, 174
Tradebot 301 n12
traders 55–7, 72, 73, 74, 76, 78, 139 n46, 249
    see also Atlantic trade; merchants
trading floor 208, 209, 237
trading room 26, 28, 244–6, 286
trading volume 8–9, 118, 217, 231–3, 236, 243, 244
training 88–9, 108, 113–14, 274–5, 278 n25, 284–5, 286, 288
    see also professional schools
transactions costs 50, 108, 110–11, 112
transatlantic networks 100–1, 122, 158–9, 165, 293
    see also Atlantic trade; mercantile networks

transfer of entitlements 44, 46, 61
transparency 275, 278 n25, 281
Treatise on the Law of Contracts (Story) 134
trust 15, 55, 107–10, 162, 271–3, 293, 307
trustees 179, 213, 254
turnover 118–19

UBS 16, 17, 26 n18, 310 n37, 311
underpricing 76, 77, 79, 84, 85–7, 242
underwriting 20–1, 136–9, 172, 214–16, 240–2, 255–8, 261, 264, 295
    see also debt underwriting; equity underwriting
Uniform Commercial Code 58
United Kingdom 1, 43, 49, 101–6, 109–10, 123
    see also England
Univac 228
Untermeyer, Samuel 199–200, 255 n69
'upset' prices 178
US Steel 183–4
US v Morgan Stanley et al 188, 213, 214, 220–2, 223, 225, 234

value theories 133–4, 153
Value-at-Risk, *see* VaR
VaR 27–8, 247, 286
voting trusts 179

W. R. Hambrecht 242
Wall Street 194 n21, 198, 207, 210, 212–13, 231, 236 n29, 305
war loans 105–6, 140, 150, 152, 160–2, 170, 216–18
Wasserstein, Bruce 32, 34, 259 n79, 285–6, 305, 306
Wasserstein Perella 305–6
White, Weld 279, 283
wholesale investment banks 207, 234–5, 236, 240, 267, 278–80, 283
will theory of contract 134, 153, 156, 191
William Blair 283
Wilson, Woodrow 190, 193, 201
'winner's curse' 79, 85, 86 n24, 140, 241
Winship v The Bank of the United States 268

'Yankee' investment banking networks 162, 165–70, 272–3

z-scores 295